The President   Page 2   May 13, 1958

ing with Gove
it be known tl
near future
titled to und(

JR:cc

Letters of Note

私密信件博物館

Letters of Note: Correspondence Deserving of a Wider Audience

125封跨越時空的不朽書信

————Author

Shaun Usher

前言

親愛的讀者，

　　你手中的這本好書是我四年心血的結晶。誤打誤撞踏上這條路，收集名人、惡煞、老百姓的書信、字條、電報，帶給我無窮的趣味，更帶給我無盡的成就感。這道旅程的起始點是網站，獲得如潮的佳評後，如今經過悉心策劃，化身為一本實體書，儼然是一座書信博物館，勢必能擄捕你的心，激盪百感，即使學養最豐富的讀者也能借此增長一些知識。隨著世界步入電郵時代，書信寫作藝術日漸式微，而傳統郵件有其重要性，魅力無從匹敵，我希望藉本書徹底彰顯紙筆信的定位。

　　《私密信件博物館》走到今天，始終如一的是宗旨：凸顯一些值得更多人展閱的書信。讀者不久將愛上這部玲琅滿目的精選集，「滿意」兩字不足以形容本書給我的心情。本書的亮眼點處處可見，且讓我隨手抽出幾一把，開開讀者的眼界。書中有一則是「滾石」主唱米克・傑格（Mick Jagger）致藝文名人安迪・沃荷（Andy Warhol）的信，內容以輕鬆的語調傳達專輯封套設計理念。其中一封親筆信出自英國女王伊麗莎白二世，收件人是美國總統艾森豪，信中附有女王的私房煎餅食譜。一封來自解放黑奴的信寫得深刻而精闢，痛斥舊奴主，許多讀者肯定會拍案叫絕。有一封令人痛徹心扉的信是維吉尼亞・吳爾芙（Virginia Woolf）的與夫訣別書，她寫完不久後走上絕路。年輕女歌迷接到伊吉・帕普回信時，適逢人生低潮，溫馨細膩的這封信能暖和最冷的人心。科學家法蘭西斯・克里克（Francis Crick）發現DNA的結構後，寫信向兒子宣佈，文字讓人永難忘懷。六十歲婦人在無麻醉的情況下接受乳房切除手術，寫信告知女兒，內容椎心刺骨。最受人稱道的古人之一達文西的應徵信也收錄於本書。讀者踏上此路時，會讀到情書、回絕書、粉絲信、道歉函，會為之感傷、憤慨、雀躍、震驚。有一封信印在

黏土石板上，年代久遠至紀元前十四世紀。年代最近的信才短短幾年。儘管各信的風格意境互異，每一則都能打動我的心，我也希望讀者全有同感，遠比讀一般歷史書更能穿越時光隧道。書信的言辭通常率真，能顯示當事人的心境，我認為這才是洞悉歷史的不二法門。

同等重要的是精美包裝這些無價的時空膠囊，讓本書賞心悅目。為達成此目標，我與版面設計圈的頂尖高手合作，秉持誠意呈現每一則，以利文字發揮極致潛能。我們儘可能尋找真跡，徵求許可，以複製原版書信，讓讀者有機會見證原文的出處，有些是打字文，甚至也有雕刻文，連污漬、皺褶等特色獨具的缺陷也據實印刷。若找不到真跡，我們退而求其次，以精緻的相片伴隨，為原文增色，其中幾幅相片從未公開過。集結成書後，成果讓我自豪得難以言喻。我唯一的希望是本書能佔據貴書架的一席之地，並且轉贈親朋好友傳閱，只盼能起碼啟發少數幾人，重拾紙筆，甚至取出塵封的打字機，撰寫一封自己的雋永書信。

真情信友，

Shaun

史恩·亞緒爾
《私密信件博物館》

編按：為了完整呈現原文書信的風味，若原文書信中出現錯別字，譯文也酌情保留。

女王食譜

白金漢宮

伊麗莎白二世致美國總統艾森豪
一九六〇年元月二十四日

一九五七年，英國女王伊麗莎白二世登基五年後，接受美國總統艾森豪邀請，首度以女王身份訪問美國。兩年後，在一九五九年八月，女王為回報艾森豪的款待，邀請總統與第一夫人梅咪（Mamie）至蘇格蘭巴爾莫拉爾（Balmoral）城堡。自一八五二年起，該城堡一直為英國皇室御用，佔地遼闊，風格氣派。兩國元首在城堡內討論什麼，外人不得而知，能確定的唯有一事：艾森豪迷戀上女王的小厚煎餅，女王甚至在招待國賓五個月後寄出此信，附帶私房食譜。

親愛的總統先生，

今日閱報見你站在烤肉爐前烤鵪鶉，令我想起我在巴爾莫拉爾城堡承諾寄小厚煎餅的食譜給你卻食言，容我在此趕緊附上，祝你烹飪成功。

此食譜的份量可供十六人食用，若人數較少時，我通常少加一點麵粉和牛奶，但其他食材照食譜使用。

我也試過以轉化糖漿或未結晶糖漿替代白砂糖，效果也非常可口。

我認為，麵粉加牛奶之後應多加攪拌，而且不宜閒置太久才開始煎。

你勤奔走許多國家，我們不僅密切關注，更對你的賣力敬佩有加，進而感嘆，今後被安排太多出訪行程時，萬萬不可自怨！

憶起你前來巴爾莫拉爾，我喜悅在心中，謹以此相片紀念你我共處的歡樂時光。

祝你與夫人萬事順心。

特此，

伊麗莎白・R

食譜

小厚煎餅

<u>食材</u>

四茶匙麵粉

四湯匙細砂糖

兩茶匙牛奶

兩顆完整雞蛋

兩茶匙小蘇打

三茶匙塔塔粉

兩湯匙融化牛油

先打蛋，然後加砂糖，混進大約一半的牛奶，攪拌後加入麵粉，充份攪和之後澆入剩下的牛奶，也把小蘇打和塔塔粉倒進去，輕輕攪進融化的牛油。

<u>足供十六人食用</u>

BUCKINGHAM PALACE

Dear Mr. President,

Seeing a picture
of you in today's newspaper
standing in front of a
barbecue grilling quail,
reminded me that I had
never sent you the recipe
of the drop scones which I
promised you at Balmoral.
I now hasten to do so,

and I do hope you will
find them successful.

Though the quantities are for
16 people, when there are
fewer, I generally put in
less flour and milk, but
use the other ingredients as
stated.

I have also tried using
golden syrup or treacle instead
of only sugar and that can
be very good, too.

BUCKINGHAM PALACE

I think the mixture needs
a great deal of beating
while making, and shouldn't
stand about too long before
cooking.

We have followed with
intense interest and much
admiration your tremendous
journey to so many countries,
but feel we shall never
again be able to claim
that <u>we</u> are being

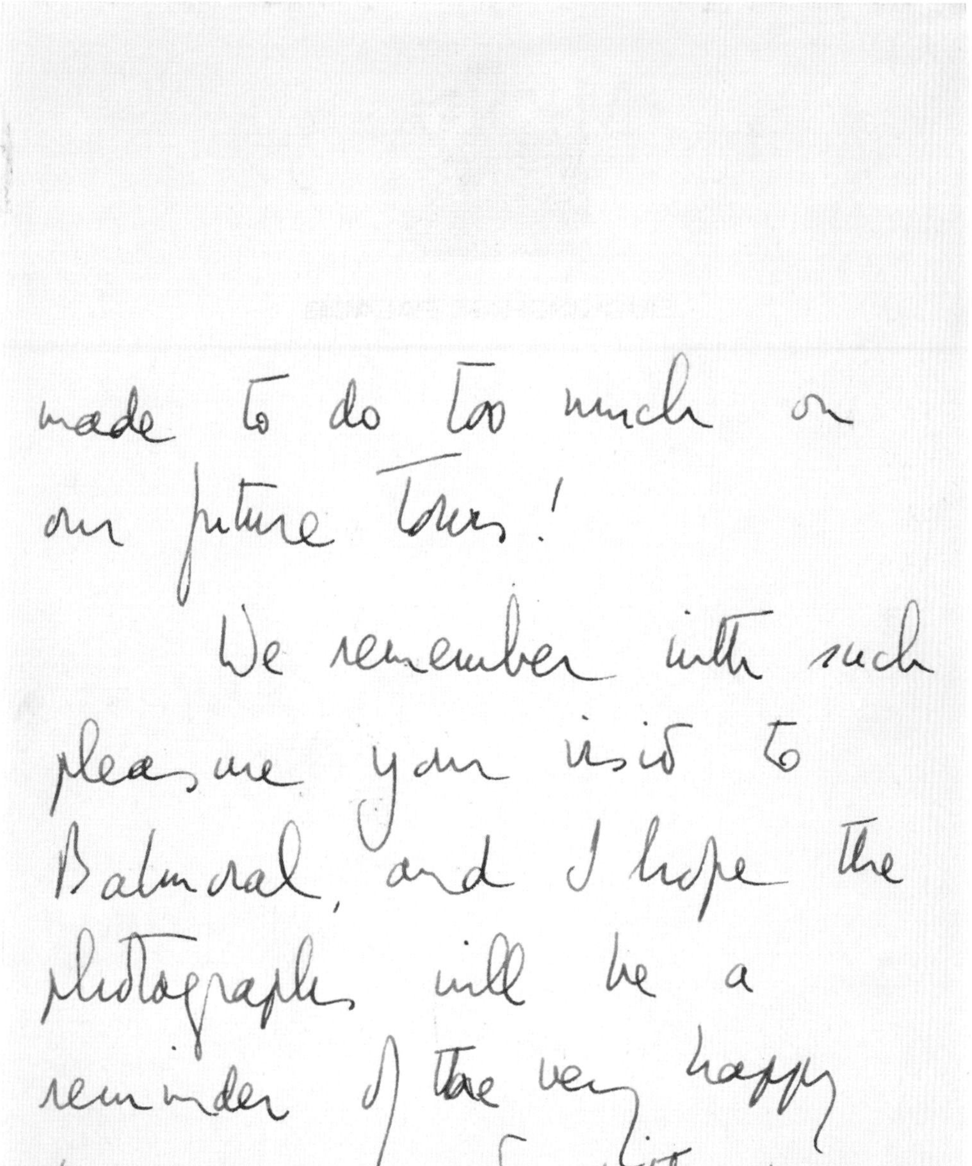

made to do too much on
our future tours!

We remember with such
pleasure your visit to
Balmoral, and I hope the
photographs will be a
reminder of the very happy
day you spend with us.

With all good wishes to you
and Mrs. Eisenhower.

Yours sincerely

Elizabeth R

MENU

Date..................................

DROP SCONES

....

Ingredients

    4 teacups flour

    4 tablespoons caster sugar

    2 teacups milk

    2 whole eggs

    2 teaspoons bi-carbonate soda

    3 teaspoons cream of tartar

    2 tablespoons melted butter

Beat eggs, sugar and about half the milk together, add flour, and mix well together adding remainder of milk as required, also bi-carbonate and cream of tartar, fold in the melted butter.

Enough for 16 people

7632 G.87 2M 2/55 H & S Gp. 902

地獄來信

開膛手傑克致守望會長
喬治・勒斯克（George Lusk）
一八八八年十月

倫敦白教堂區出現連續殺人案，一群民眾憂心之餘組成守望委員會，積極追查凶手。一八八八年十月十五日，守望會長喬治・勒斯克收到這封寒徹人心的信，寄件人自稱是各界聲討的連續殺人魔開膛手傑克，隨信附上一小盒東西，經判定內含物是以葡萄酒醃製的半顆人腎，據研判摘自開膛手傑克的第四號冤魂凱瑟琳・艾道斯（Catherine Eddowes）。根據此信，另外半顆已被凶手油炸後吃掉。

勒斯克先升，

我從一個女人身上取甚臟淹好送你半棵令一半被我油炸吃了非常香。若你能等几天我說不定把取甚的血刀寄給你。

（簽名）
　　　有本事來抓我

　　　勒斯克先生

From hell

Mr Lusk

Sor
                I send you half the
Kidne I took from one women
prasarved it for you tother piece
I fried and ate it was very nise I
may send you the bloody knif that
took it out if you only wate a whil
longer

        Signed   Catch me when
                        you Can
                    Mishter Lusk -

上緊發條

**E · B · 懷特致納竇（Nadeau）
先生**
一九七三年三月三十日

作家 E · B · 懷特一生獲獎連連並非浪得虛名，誕生於一八九九年的他名列當代散文界巨擘之林，曾在《紐約客》和《Harper's》發表過無數影響深遠的文章。一九五九年，他與人合著《英文寫作風格的要素》（*The Elements of Style*）一書，擴充內容再版，長銷數百萬冊，廣獲好評。懷特也撰寫童書，其中多部成為經典，包括《小老鼠司徒特》（*Stuart Little*）和《夏綠蒂的網》（*Charlotte's Web*）。他也寫過數百封膾炙人心的信。

一九七三年三月，納竇先生對人類的未來萬念俱灰，懷特以這封架構四平八穩的信回應。

親愛的納竇先生：

只要世上尚存正直的男人一名，只要世上尚存溫情滿懷的女人一名，其影響力或許能擴散而出，人間世態未必炎涼。在困苦的時刻，希望仍留存於你我心中。我仍將在週日早晨起床，上緊時鐘發條，以增進秩序與常規。

航海人常說，天候是個唬人不眨眼的傢伙。我猜，同理也可驗證於人類社會——狀況再黑再晦暗，烏雲總有開展的一刻，屆時萬物皆變，有時轉變來得相當突然。人類把地球上的生活搞得烏煙瘴氣，這是眾所週知的事，然而你我心田裡極可能埋藏善籽，已蟄伏多時，靜候狀況理想之日發芽茁壯。人具有好奇心、創意、巧思、百折不撓的毅力，誤入今日之困境，當前僅能企盼同樣的人性特質能協助人類爬出深淵。

堅守立場吧。堅守你的希望。莫忘上緊時鐘發條，迎向嶄新的明日。

專此奉覆，
E · B · 懷特

我將遭處決

瑪莉·斯圖亞特（Mary Stuart）
致法王亨利三世

一五八七年二月八日

瑪莉·斯圖亞特人生最後二十年當中，大半時日不是遭囚禁，便是在英國受審，受盡表姑伊麗莎白一世擺布。瑪莉一生非比尋常，出生六天世襲為蘇格蘭女王，婚後才十七歲便守寡，甚至曾短暫成為法國王妃。瑪莉也曾覬覦英國王位，因此鑄下悲慘的命運。四十四歲的瑪莉在一五八七年二月八日凌晨寫下這封信，向第一任先夫的胞弟訣別，六小時後如信所述，在三百人面前遭斬首示眾。

譯自英譯本，原文為法文。

蘇格蘭女王
一五八七年二月八日

皇叔惠鑑，承蒙上帝旨意，或許基於私德缺失，我在表姑女王掌握下受苦受難近廿載，終遭女王與皇族賜死。我想立遺囑，奈何無紙可用，索求不得，始終無法取回可用之物，甚至無法脫身去隨心交代後事，無法請令姐故舊移靈回我有幸貴為女王之王國。

今夜晚餐後，我獲知刑罰：我將於明早八時如罪犯一般伏法。我無暇道盡事件全貌，但醫師與其他苦難僕役知情，你當可聆聽他們闡明真相，可得知謝天謝地我鄙視死神，雖貴為君主卻面對刑罰，誓言以清白之身面對。我遭判處極刑，乃因我篤信天主教並主張英國王位是天賜予我之權，當局卻唯恐干擾到新教而禁止我以殉教自居。明證在於當局禁神父見我，儘管神父在同一屋簷下，我仍無法徵求當局同意他入內聽我告解並賜予臨終聖禮。當局引進御用牧師，再三堅持我接受該牧師之勸慰輔導。此信之信使等人多為君之子民，能見證我赴義時之言行。在此向始終誓言關愛我的至尊法王、皇叔、故舊，尚請君明示善心，成全我以下所有心願：首先，代我清償積欠苦難僕役之薪資，唯有君能減輕我良心重擔。再者，請君為我向上帝禱告——曾加冕為至尊女王、死為天主教徒、身外之物被剝奪一空的我。至於吾兒，我將他託付予你，但依他意願而定，因我無法代言。恕我擅自送你驅病寶石兩枚，祝君長命安康，務請笑納親嫂之薄禮，臨終之嫂至死對君銘感。容我再度託付僕役予你。願請你指示，念我靈魂的份上，你欠我之債應償還部分，且念在耶穌基督之名，明日臨終時我將為君祈禱，願我身後尚餘足款可行天主教葬儀並依習俗善葬。星期三凌晨二時

真心敬愛君之嫂

瑪莉·R

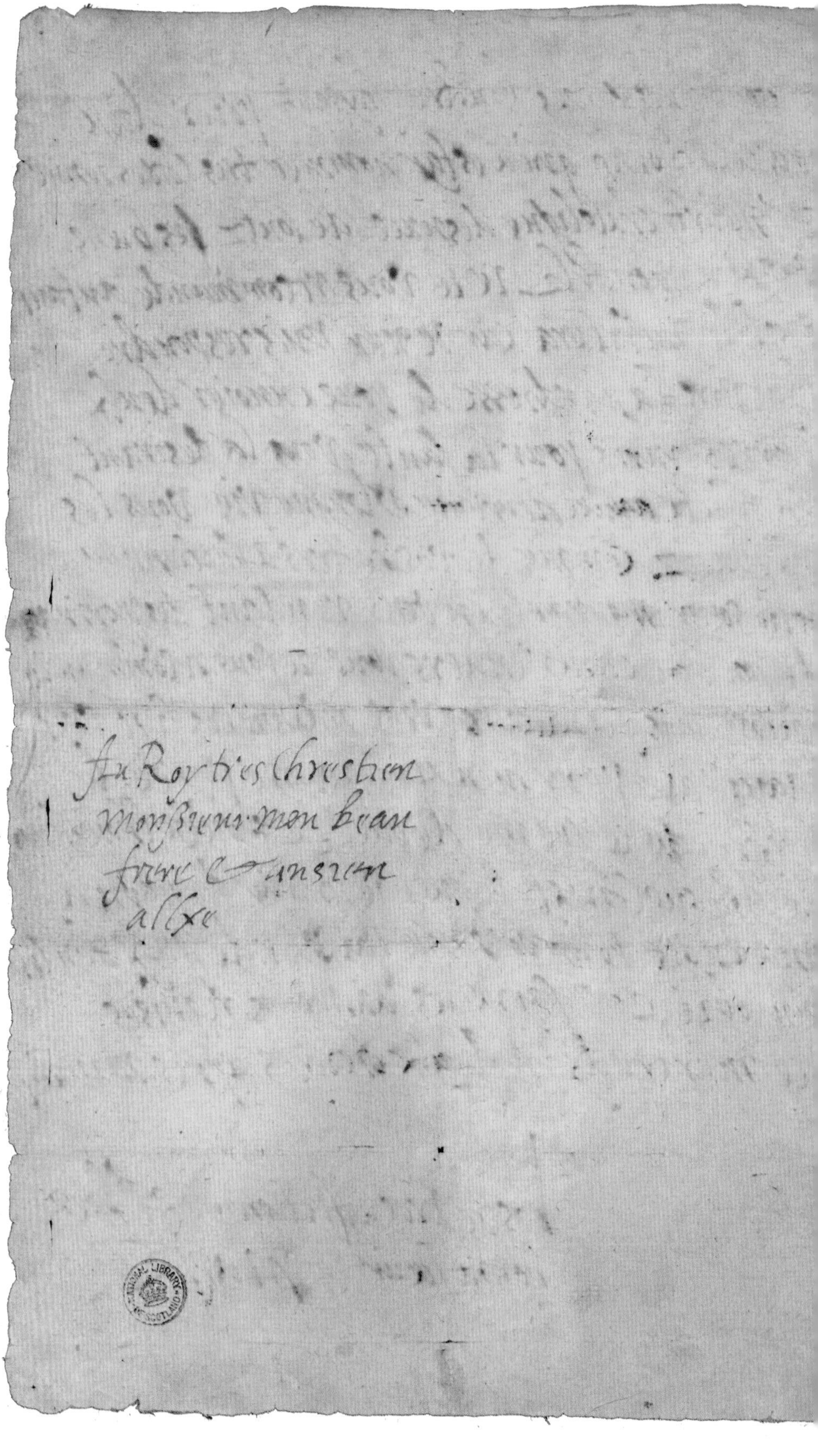

Au Roy tres Chrestien
Monsieur mon beau
frere cousin
a luy

Monsieur mon beau frere estant par la permission
de Dieu pour mes peschez comme ie croy venue
me iecter entre les bras de ceste Royne ma
cousine ou iay eu beaucoup dennuis & passe
pres de vingt ans ie suis enfin par elle & ses
estats condampnee a la mort & ayant demande
mes papiers par eulx ostez a ceste fin de fayre
mon testament ne nay peu rien retirer qui me
servist ny obtenir congie den fayre ung libre
ny quapres ma mort mon corps fust transporte
sellon mon desir en votre royaulme ou iay eu
lhonneur destre royne votre soeur & ancienne
allyee

ce iourdhuy apres disner ma este denonsee
ma sentence pour estre executee demain comme
une criminelle a huict heures du matin
ie nay eu loisir de vous fayre ung ample discours
de tout ce qui sest passe mays sil vous plaist
de croire mon medecin & ces aultres miens
desolez serviteurs vous oyrez la verite & comme
graces a dieu ie mesprise la mort & fidellement

proteste de la recepuoir innocentem<ent tant> ...
quant ie serois leur subiecte la religion chato<lique>
et le mayntien du droit que dieu ma donne
ceste couronne sont les deulx poincts de ma
condampnation et toutesfoys ilz ne me veu<lent>
permettre de dire que cest pour la religion <seule>
que ie meurs mays pour la crainte du cham<gement>
de la leur et pour preuue ilz mont oste mon
aulmonier lequel bien quil soit en la mayson
nay peu obtenir quil me vinst confesser <et>
communier a ma mort mays mont faict grand<e>
instance de recepuoir la consolation et doctri<ne>
de leur ministre ammene pour ce faict ce po<rteur>
et ia compaignie la pluspart de vos subiect<z>
vous tesmoigneront mes desportementz en
mon acte dernier il reste que ie vous supplie
comme. roy tres chrestien mon beau frere et anc<ien>
allye et qui mauuez tousiours proteste d<e>
maymer qua ce coup vous faysiez preuue en
toutz ces poincts de vostre uertu tant par
charite me soulageant de ce que pour des<char>
ger ma consçrance ie ne puis sans vous q<ui>
est de recompenser mes seruiteurs desolez

ayssant leurs gaiges lamiddre faysant prier dieu
sur une ϳorne qui a esté nommee tres Chrestienne
et meurt chatolique desnuee de toutz ses biens
quant a mon fylz ie le vous recommande autant
qu'il le meritera car ie n'en puis respondre
ϳ'ay pris la hardiesse le vous envoier deulx
pierres rares pour la santé vous la desirant
parfaicte avec heureuse et longue vie Vous les
receparez comme de vostre tres affectionnee
et le saeur mourante en vous rendant tesmoygnage
de son bon cueur envers vous ϳe vous recommande
encore mes serviteurs vous ordonnieres si il vous
plaict que pour mon ame ϳe soye payee de
partye de ce que me debuez et qu'en Chrestien
de Jhesus Christ lequel ie priray demayn a
ma mort pour vous me laisser de quoy fonder
un obit et fayre les aulmosnes requises
ce mercredy a deulx heures apres minuict

Vostre tres affectionnee et bien
bonne saeur   MARI R

信之 005

聽說你喜歡番茄濃湯

___

威廉・P・麥法蘭（William P. MacFarland）致安迪・沃荷

一九六四年五月十九日

身為金寶湯公司產品行銷經理，威廉・麥法蘭見到安迪・沃荷於一九六二年以精湛的畫筆首度開展，想必是樂翻天了。畫展在洛杉磯菲盧斯（Ferus Gallery）舉行，其中一幅作品為人津津樂道至今，一眼即知是金寶濃湯，以絲網印刷而成，總共三十二罐，排排站，每一罐的湯料互異。沃荷的作品有助於推廣波普藝術給大眾，引發藝術圈熱議，同時炒得特定濃湯品牌大放光明。一九六四年，沃荷的聲望水漲船高之際，麥法蘭決定以此信向畫家致謝，隨後以幾箱金寶罐頭相贈。

金寶湯公司
紐澤西州坎頓

一九六四年五月十九日

沃荷先生
紐約州紐約市
萊辛頓大道**1342**號

___

親愛的沃荷先生：

　　久仰您在藝術圈動態。您的大作在金寶湯公司獲得不少回響，原因可想而知。

　　我一度希望買下您的金寶湯商標畫作，可惜的是，現在價位已飆漲到我只能望畫興嘆了。

　　言歸正傳，本公司景仰您的作品，而我也得知您喜歡本公司的番茄濃湯，所以擅作主張送您兩箱番茄濃湯罐頭至此地址。

　　在此祝您屢創佳作，好運連連。

謹上，

威廉・P・麥法蘭
產品行銷經理

Campbell Soup Company

✤ ✤ ✤ ✤ ✤ ✤ ✤ **CAMDEN 1, NEW JERSEY** ✤ ✤ ✤ ✤ ✤ ✤ ✤

May 19, 1964

Mr. A. Warhol
1342 Lexington Avenue
New York, New York

Dear Mr. Warhol:

I have followed your career for some time. Your work
has evoked a great deal of interest here at Campbell Soup
Company for obvious reasons.

At one time I had hoped to be able to acquire one of
your Campbell Soup label paintings - but I'm afraid you
have gotten much too expensive for me.

I did want to tell you, however, that we admired your
work and I have since learned that you like Tomato Soup.
I am taking the liberty of having a couple of cases of our
Tomato Soup delivered to you at this address.

We wish you continued success and good fortune.

Cordially,

William P. MacFarland

William P. MacFarland
Product Marketing Manager

比爾・希可斯之言論自由論

比爾・希可斯（Bill Hicks）致某牧師

一九九三年六月八日

脫口秀諧星比爾・希可斯生前常針對最具爭議性的題材直言不諱，觀點強硬不屈，在流星般的舞臺生涯中屢次掀起話題。一九九三年五月，亦即他以三十二歲之齡死於胰臟癌前幾月，英國電視第四頻道錄影轉播他名為《啟示錄》（*Revelations*）的現場秀。不久後，一名牧師投書給電視臺抱怨該節目。從不逃避討論機會的希可斯閱畢，直接回函給牧師。

親愛的牧師，

您來信關切本人特別節目《啟示錄》，我閱信後覺得有義務親自回應，盼能針對您的高見澄清個人立場，或許能助你認清原原本本的我。

我來自美國，當地存在一種古怪的概念，稱為「言論自由」，許多人認為是人類智能發展史上的一大成就。我個人強力支持「言論自由權」，也相信如果大家明白言論自由的真諦，多數人也會支持。「言論自由」的意思是，別人發表你不認同的想法時，你照樣支持他的發言權。（反之，你不接受「言論自由」的道理，只接受你自信大家都接受的想法。）全世界的信仰信念何其多，硬要所有人信任何一種東西簡直是難如登天，若你能從這角度切入，你或許能漸漸領悟「言論自由」的概念多麼重要。這概念的基本要領是：「儘管我不認同、不想聽你的說法，我照樣支持你的發言權，因為這才能彰顯真自由。」

你說你覺得我的題材「引人反感」、「褻瀆神明」，我倒覺得有意思的是，你認為你的信仰被抹黑、受威脅，而我卻敢打賭，從未有人寫信抗議你的信仰，也未曾有人質疑你信仰的合法性。（假使你收過這種抗議信，執筆人絕不可能是我。）此外，我猜想，綜觀平日的每週電視節目表時，必定能信手挑出許多宗教節目，絕對多於［我的］節目——畢竟「特別節目」的定義就是［久久才上一次］節目。

我在《啟示錄》上做的，只不過是根據個人經驗，以個人言語發表看法，很類似電子媒體佈道人做節目的方式。多年來，我看過的宗教節目許多不合我胃口，也和我的個人信念相左，但我卻從未自認有權施展電檢法，頂多換個頻道，更好的做法是索性關掉電視不看。

接著是信中最令我困擾的部分。

為表達憤怒的立場，你假設一種情境：穆斯林人遇到他們也感冒的題材，產生「憤怒」的反應。我想問你的是：面對一群不識「言論自由」、不懂寬容、也許連基督教義也覺得陌生的惡棍，你默許他們進行血腥恐怖攻擊嗎？如果你暗示的是，他們無法見容相反思想是情有可原、值得讚賞、或許更勝於包涵與寬恕，那麼，我懷疑你真正信仰的東西究竟是什麼。

假使你從頭到尾看完我的節目，你會留意到，結尾時我強調個人信念，大聲疾呼各國政府少花一點錢作戰，多撥一點預算在食、衣、教育上，以救濟全球貧民難民……這份理念不能說和基督精神背道而馳吧？

總而言之，我的節目題材呼籲世人多一份諒解，少一份無知，以和平取代爭戰，多寬恕少譴責，以愛制懼。儘管這份訊息有可能（因我的語調）造成你認知的偏差，但我向你保證，我在英國巡迴演出時，有成千上萬的觀眾聽懂了。

我希望此信能回答你一部分的疑問。另外，我也希望你視此信為持續交流溝通的邀約。今後若有意見、想法或疑問，歡迎你不妨直接聯繫我。如果你不願保持聯絡，容我邀請你收看我即將上演的兩場特別節目《傻蛋穆罕默德》和《肥豬佛祖》。（玩笑話）

謹此

比爾・希可斯

你的好朋友約翰・K

約翰・奎克法魯西（John Kricfalusi）致阿米爾・亞夫尼（Amir Avni）
一九九八年

一九九八年，立志成為漫畫家的阿米爾才十四歲，決心寫信給電視動畫編劇家約翰・奎克法魯西。約翰的《任恩與史丁皮》（Ren & Stimpy）首開成人電視卡通的先河。阿米爾隨信附上自己畫的漫畫，較少為人知的幾個約翰自創的角色也包含在內。阿米爾接到回信驚喜不已，更發現約翰並非以草草兩三句敷衍他。

十幾年後，阿米爾表示，「我認為約翰對卡漫界新生代信心十足，而且希望新人接受完善的教育。他把新生代視為卡漫界未來的主人翁，所以才這麼大方，不擺架子。」

約翰的身段確實值得讚賞，也因此啟發至少一位粉絲踏上尋夢之路。阿米爾後來進加拿大薛立丹（Sheridan）學院研讀動畫並教書，二〇一三年為卡通頻道的新節目作畫至今。

親愛的阿米爾，

感謝你來信並附上漫畫供我參考。

可惜我們打不開你附上的 flash 檔，啟動播放器時只看見空白一片。我正請高手幫忙。如果還是打不開，可能要麻煩你上載到網路，然後傳網址給我。

你的漫畫相當不錯，佈局和接續尤其出色。你具有畫分鏡腳本的天份，有可能成為優秀的腳本畫家。我想寄給你一本普萊斯頓・布列爾（Preston Blair）教人畫動畫的好書，他是動漫大師泰克斯・埃富瑞（Tex Avery）旗下的動畫師，作品包括《熱辣小紅帽》（Red Hot Riding Hood）和無數角色。

想把卡通畫好，他的書能教你非常重要的基本竅門。

構圖。照 3D 物體素描，從中學習構圖。學著怎麼畫人的手，將手畫得有肉感。我要你照他書中的圖描一描。從第一頁開始。慢慢畫。仔細看。目測比例。一步一步描畫，照普萊斯頓的方式。

畫完那每一幅圖之後，仔細檢查書中的原圖。（如果你畫在描圖紙上，可以拿描圖紙覆蓋原圖，比對你哪裡畫錯，記錄在自己的圖上，然後再畫一遍，這一次修正剛才畫錯的部分。

再教你一個要訣：

製作動畫時，好的素描比其他任何東西都更重要，勝過點子、風格、故事。一切都從好的素描為起點。學著畫構圖，畫遠近配置。

接著，一切由你自由發揮。

附帶提一件事——舊卡通（特別是一九四〇年代的東西，比新卡通好。如果照新卡通去描，保證你學不到任何東西，只會養成一堆壞習慣。參考一九四七到一九五四年的湯姆貓和傑瑞鼠，或四

○和五○年代初的小獵人艾默和豬小弟（Elmer Fudd）＋（Porky Pig）。）

你對我們懂不少嘛，我很驚奇。你怎麼連大隻巴比（Bobby Bigloaf）都知道？居然還知道溫順男（Mildman）！

建議你上網看看吉米＋喬治酒品商行。唉，我猜你早知道了。

好了，兔崽子，該辦正事了。去畫吧！記得要慢慢畫。

有任何問題歡迎來信，我的電郵是 **CENSORED!** ——希望你沒有太多問題！我收到的電郵很多，很難全部回覆。

你的好朋友，

約翰・K

Dear Amir,

Thanks for your letter and all your cartoons to look at.

We're having trouble opening your flash-files, though; when I click the player it opens a blank screen. I have somebody trying to figure it out. If it doesn't work, maybe you can post them on the web and give me the URL.

Your comics are pretty good, especially your staging and continuity. You might have the makings of a good storyboard artist.

1

I'm sending you a very good how to draw
animation book by Preston Blair.
Preston was one of Tex Avery's animators.
He animated "Red Hot Riding Hood" and
many other characters.

His book shows you very important
fundamentals of good cartoon drawing,
Construction. Learn
how to construct your drawings
out of 3-dimensional objects.
Learn how to draw hands, so they
look solid.   this
                              not
                              this

2

I want you to copy the drawings in his book. Start on the first page, Draw slow. Look very closely. Measure the proportions. Draw the drawings step-by-step, just the way Preston does!

After you finish ~~the d~~ each drawing check it carefully against the drawing in the book. (if you do your drawings on tracing paper, you can lay the paper on top of the book to see where you made mistakes! On your drawing 3 write the mistakes!.

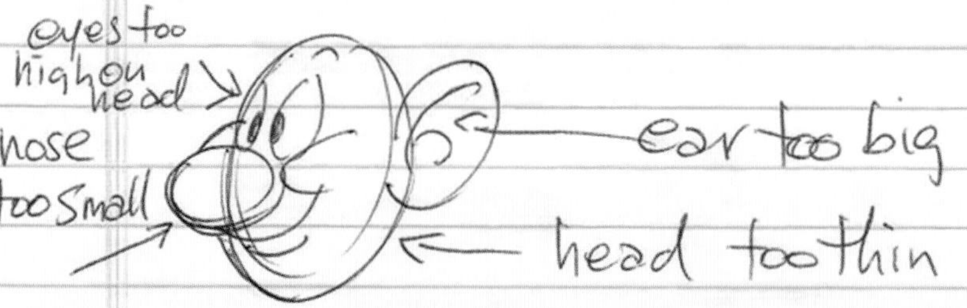

eyes too
high on
head

nose
too small

ear too big

head too thin

Then do the drawing again, this
time correcting the mistakes!.

Here's another important piece
of information for you:

Good drawing is more important
than anything else in animation.

More than ideas, style, stories!.

Everything starts with good drawing.

learn to draw construction.
perspective.

4

OK, now its up to you.

Oh, by the way — OLD cartoons (from the 1940's especially are better than new cartoons.

If you copy the drawings in new cartoons you won't learn anything — except how to get bad habits. Look at Tom and Jerry from 1947-1954 or Elmer Fudd + Porky Pig from the 40's + early 50's.)

5

6

I'm amazed at how much you know about us'. How do you know about BOBBY BIGLOAF? and MILDMAN!

You can see Jimmy + George Liquor on the Internet. Oh, I Guess you know that.

7

ALLRIGHT Bastard, let's get to work. Draw! and slow now.

My email address is [redacted] CENSORED! .com if you have any questions - not too many I hope! I get a lot of email and it's hard to answer it all.

Your pal,

JOHN K.

8

刊登於一八八六年十二月四日《泰晤士報》

象人

法蘭西斯‧卡爾─戈姆（Francis Carr-Gomm）致《泰晤士報》

一八八六年十二月四日

一八八六年十二月，倫敦醫院的院長法蘭西斯‧卡爾─戈姆投書《泰晤士報》，公開一名病例：二十四歲男子罹患怪疾，面目畸形，難以言喻，外表「恐怖」到被迫住進醫院閣樓單人小房間，以免嚇到人。院長描述的病患名叫喬瑟夫‧梅瑞克（Joseph Merrick），綽號「象人」，一八六二年誕生於英國萊斯特（Leicester），從幼年便出現異常發育的病狀，十幾歲時變得四肢腫脹，皮膚凹凸不平，言語不清，青春期特別難熬。不久後，他在倫敦露臉供人參觀，但為期不長。後來赴歐洲，慘遭毒打洗劫。梅瑞克回英國後，失業又身無分文，病弱又情緒低落，住進倫敦醫院，因此院長致函《泰晤士報》，請求民眾協助。

經報紙一披露，民眾熱烈回響，信件、贈禮、金錢如潮水湧現，來得突然又難以招架，基本上能支付梅瑞克住院生活費用，讓他安享生命的最後幾年。他過世未久，院長再投書《泰晤士報》。

致《泰晤士報》總編輯

主編先生，我經院方授權，請求貴報大力協助，希望社會大眾關注一項極為罕見的病例。本院閣樓區有一隱蔽的小病房住有一名病患喬瑟夫‧梅瑞克，年約二十七，萊斯特人，外表至為可怖，白天甚而無法外出至庭院。畸形嚴重的他被喚為「象人」。我在此不願詳述其病徵，以免嚇壞貴報讀者，僅能說他只有一手能運作。

約莫一年半前，他在白教堂路附近一房間展示，倫敦醫院外科醫師崔韋斯（Treves）先生見到可憐的他，當時他以舊窗簾遮身，湊著磚頭上的一盞油燈取暖，經紀守在門口，等路人投足錢幣，才叫苦兒梅瑞克掀開窗簾，顯露全身畸形的怪狀。展覽的淨收入由他與經紀對分，最後警方以有礙觀瞻為由，制止他曝露醜態。

無法在英國以身示眾的他聽人勸說，決定前往比利時，當地一名奧地利籍男子接納他，以其經紀人自居。梅瑞克靠此維生，攢足了近五十英鎊，但比利時警方也時時驅趕他，導致他居無定所，苦不堪言。後來有一天，奧地利人判定展覽已無油水可搾，遂搶走梅瑞克刻苦積蓄的五十英鎊，將走投無路的他拋棄在異國。幸虧梅瑞克找到當舖，籌足旅費回英國，因為他視倫敦醫院崔韋斯醫師為唯一朋友。梅瑞克每到一港一站，總吸引好奇的群眾圍觀尾隨，因此行動極為不便，抵達倫敦醫院時，他除了身上的衣服之外一無所有。雖然他罹患的是不治之症，本院仍接納他，如今面對的問題是將來如何照顧他。

他至為懼怕濟貧院，本院也不可能送他去缺乏隱私的地方住，因為他的外觀令所有人退避三舍。

儘管有足夠資金支付他今後費用，皇家絕症醫院與英國絕症之家仍雙雙拒收。

警方基於情理禁止他再露臉展示，而他也無法上街，因為他所到

之處總被人群團團包圍，無法動彈。為顧及他人，濟貧院也不便安置他於大通鋪。因此，即使他能出房門也如驚弓之鳥處處閃躲。（本院安排他住單人房，以最誠摯的善意對待他，他說他活到這麼大，首度嘗到寧靜、休閒的滋味。）由於他罹患不治之症，而本院屬於病患過多的綜合醫院，不適合照顧他。縱使本院願全額支付他的開銷，絕症醫院也拒收他，因此他何去何從的難題仍有待解決。

他的外貌嚇人，婦女、神經質的民眾一見他便驚惶奔逃，而他也無法循正常管道就業維生，但他的智力過人，讀寫無礙，生性文靜寡言，思想甚至可謂高雅。在本院，他活用厚紙板，以正常的一手製作小模型，消磨時光，作品致贈護士長、醫師、以及愛護他的民眾。浮沉人生苦海之際，他時時刻刻將慈母畫像帶在身邊，以顯示生母是面目可親的善良人，也以此懷念入院前的半生唯一善待他的人。入院後，本院外科醫師與他交誼融洽，護士也親切照料他。

身染怪疾，錯不在他。崔韋斯醫師向我斷言，他長命的機率微乎其微，他只盼餘生過得安寧而隱蔽。

在此懇請貴報讀者惠賜高見，推薦一個肯收容他的理想場所。一旦他獲得接納之後，我確信善人將挺身而出，讓我有能力提供膳宿。在尚未覓得理想場所之前，儘管本院不適合收留此一絕症病例，他在本院棉花區旁的小房間裡衣食無憂。聖殿教長在耶穌降臨節週日侃侃佈道，問及，「此人或其父母造過什麼孽，才害他出生就失明？」主的回應即為當日佈道的主題：造物者為何讓人天生殘障、終生無望，目的之一是藉此勾起世人憐憫心，激發那些不必背負十字架重擔的人慷慨救助他。

本院每年醫治七萬六千名病患，但院方從未授權我呼籲大眾關注特定病例，盼讀者相信本病例確實有異於常情。

讀者若有回響，可直接聯絡我本人或倫敦醫院祕書。

忠僕F・C・卡爾・戈姆，
倫敦醫院院長

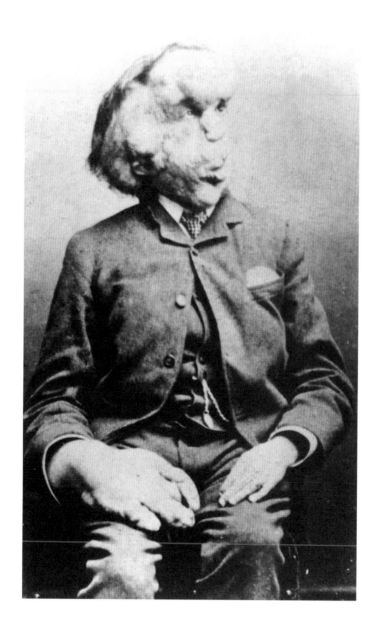

刊登於一八九〇年四月十六日《泰晤士報》

致《泰晤士報》總編輯

主編先生，在一八八六年十一月，本人投書藉貴報披露「象人」喬瑟夫‧梅瑞克的病例，引起社會關注這位奇特而不幸的患者。梅瑞克因外貌畸形可怖，無法見容於世人，找不到工作，僅能供好奇人士窺奇維生。本國警方基於情理，制止他在上街展示，因此他被奧地利探險家帶至海外，在歐陸巡迴展出，後來有一日，奧地利人竊走梅瑞克細心累積的所有存款，逃逸無蹤，任由他在異邦孤苦無依無友無力。

歷經萬難，他輾轉來到倫敦醫院門口，拜本院外科醫師之恩，得以暫住。但隨之而來的難題是他將何去何從。他被各地絕症醫院拒收，也畏懼濟貧院，更無法考慮住進缺乏隱私的場所，而本院屬於綜合醫院，礙於規定與必要性，資金與空間僅供醫治病患，再怎麼異常的絕症病例也恕難破例。進退維谷之際，我基於人性常理，不願驅逐他出院，不願任其流浪街頭，因此投書貴報，從此一切難題煙消雲散。該信引發眾人同情，雖然推薦的收容所無一合適，但各界捐款豐沛，在我支配之下，除了本院既有的資金外，總算能讓罹患絕症的他衣食無憂。本院委員會決議破例收留他，條件是每年收到相當於一張病床平均支出的款項。

因此，在本院中，苦兒梅瑞克得以在隱蔽舒適的環境裡，渡過三年半的餘生。本院主管、醫師、神父、修女、護士攜手合作，盡可能減輕他生命中的苦痛，他也漸漸習慣以病房為家，各界善心人士紛至沓來，其中不乏本國權貴。他也培養出多種興趣與嗜好：他飽讀群書，書籍由劇場界最艷麗的女士之一供應；他也學會編籃術，並且不只一次獲邀進劇場包廂看戲。

在本院神父教導下，他獲得不少宗教啟發。渥尚姆‧豪博士在擔任貝德福主教期間，也曾私下為他施堅信禮，他也能在聖具室等候，從旁參加教堂禮拜。梅瑞克死前數日，曾以此方式兩度做禮拜，早晨也參加聖餐禮。博士與他最後一次交談時，他對他在本

院蒙受的照顧表達深切的感激，也謝上帝施恩，引他進本院。每年，他能出院至一棟清幽的小木屋渡假六週，他過得愜意，但他回本院時總是開開心心，覺得又「回家」了。儘管眾人溺愛他，他仍寡言，不擺架子，非常感激大家對他的一切關照，凡事必定照規矩行事。

我認為資助他的捐款人想瞭解院方將錢用在何處，所以在此贅述。上週五午後，雖然外表上健康無異狀，他仍在睡夢中安祥辭世。

我手邊殘留一小筆資助他的款項，容我在此提議，以這筆錢付完賞金後，餘款可納入本院供日常支出。我相信此舉將能獲得捐款者一致贊同。

拜《泰晤士報》之賜，本人在一八八六年的投書才獲得回響，讓可憐病患的餘生過得舒適有保障，我願藉此機會表達誠摯的感激。

忠僕 F.C. 卡爾・戈姆

倫敦醫院委員會

四月十五日

信之 009

我喜歡文字

**羅伯特・畢若許（Robert Pirosh）
致電影界**
一九三四年

一九三四年，名叫羅伯特・畢若許的紐約人辭去待遇優渥的廣告文案撰稿工作，毅然前往好萊塢，決心追求夢想，立志成為電影腳本作家。抵達好萊塢後，他廣泛蒐集導演、製作人、電影公司主管姓名，寄履歷給他們，附上的自薦信寫得巧，堪稱史上最精彩、最有效的自薦信之一。他獲得三次面試的機會，因而得以進入米高梅電影公司擔任初級寫手。

十五年後，羅伯特・畢若許以戰爭片《戰場》（Battleground）的原著劇本榮獲金像獎，數月之後更勇奪金球獎。

敬愛的長官：

我喜歡文字。我喜歡肥滋滋、奶油油的文字，例如滲溢 ooze、卑劣 turpitude、膠黏 glutinous、諂媚 toady。我喜歡嚴肅、方正、古板的字，例如拘謹 straitlaced、執拗 cantankerous、一貧如洗 pecunious、告別演說 valedictory。我喜歡亂真、黑即白的字，例如殯儀業者 mortician、清算 liquidate、理容師 tonsorial、放浪形骸 demi-monde。我喜歡滑順帶 V 的字，例如催眠音樂家斯文加利 Svengali、窈窕 svelte、磅礴 bravura、氣勢 verve。我喜歡鬆脆、一折即斷、啪嚓裂開的字，例如碎片 splinter、搏鬥 grapple、纏打 jostle、硬皮 crusty。我喜歡慍怒、乖戾、擺臭臉的字，例如潛行 skulk、橫眉豎目 glower、下賤 scabby、乖僻 churl。我喜歡蒼天啊、我的天、看在天地份上的字，例如虞詐 tricksy、古胸衣 tucker、儒雅 genteel、怖畏 horrid。我喜歡優雅、花稍的字，例如夏眠 estivate、遊歷 peregrinate、樂土 elysium、富庶 halcyon。我喜歡蠕軟 wormy、鑽動 squirmy、粉蟲 mealy 的字，例如匍匐 crawl、肥厚 blubber、尖音 squeal、流淌 drip。我喜歡賊賊跑、嘿嘿笑的字，例如額前亂髮 cowlick、潺潺流 gurgle、冒泡 bubble 以及打嗝 burp。

腳本作家 screenwriter 和文案撰稿人 copywriter 這兩字，我比較喜歡前者，所以決定辭去我在紐約一家廣告公司的職位，前來好萊塢碰碰運氣，但在我驟換跑道前，我以一年的時間在歐洲進修、思考、閒晃。

我剛回美國，依然喜歡文字。

可否與我當面文字交心呢？

羅伯特・畢若許
紐約麥迪遜大道三八五號六一〇室
Eldorado 5-6024

星期二。

無法再戰

維吉尼亞‧吳爾芙致雷諾德‧吳
爾芙（Leonard Woolf）

一九四一年三月

影響深遠的小說家吳爾芙年方二十
二，就已精神崩潰兩次，據信是因
母親和同母異父姐姐兩年內相繼去
世而導致，父親幾年後也離開人
間。不幸的是，她的坎坷路還沒走
完。她終其一生憂鬱纏身，最後不
敵魔掌。

一九四一年三月某天晚上，她跳河
尋短未果，拖著濕漉漉的一身回
家。可惜她不肯放棄。幾天後，在
三月二十八日，她再試一次，終於
成功擺脫終生的身心病。

在她自盡當天，丈夫雷諾德遍尋不
著她的行蹤，只在家中壁爐架上找
到傷透人心的遺書。數週後，遺體
在烏斯（Ouse）河被尋獲，外套口
袋裡裝滿著大石頭。

至親，

我確定我又即將發狂。我覺得，我倆嘗到的辛酸太多了，無法再
續。而且這次我康復無望。我開始幻聽，無法專心。所以我打算
運用最佳的對策。你帶給我無窮極致的幸福。裡裡外外，你面面
俱到，仁盡義至。我認為世上沒有任何一對能比我們更幸福，是
這份惡疾壞了我們的好事。我無法再戰。我明白我擾亂你的生
活，也明白你沒有我，日子能照常過。我明白你能。唉，我連這
信都不能好好寫。我認不得字了。我想說的是，我今生的所有快
樂全歸功於你。你對我耐心到底，不可思議地善待我。我想這麼
說——而大家都知道。假如世上有誰能救我，那人非你莫屬。除
了你那堅定的善之外，一切都拋棄我而去。我無法繼續再破壞你
的日子了。

我認為世上沒有任何一對能比我們更幸福。

V.

回信沒錢可賺

葛勞裘·馬克斯（Groucho Marx）
致伍迪·艾倫（Woody Allen）
一九六七年三月二十二日

一九六一年，諧星馬克斯和電影人伍迪·艾倫相識，友誼就此延續十六年。馬克斯比艾倫年長四十五歲，對艾倫而言像「我們家族裡的猶太伯父，一個愛賣弄嘴皮子的猶太伯父，機智而諷刺。」馬克斯在一九七六年對艾倫的看法是，「當今最重要的喜劇人才。」有一陣子，艾倫苦等馬克斯回信已久，等得生悶氣，終於在一九六七年三月接到信。

親愛的 WW：

小艾（Goodie Ace）對我的一個失業朋友說，我一連幾年沒回你的信，搞得你失望或惱怒或高興或醉醺醺。你當然曉得，回信沒錢可賺——除非是瑞士寄來的信用狀或黑手黨來信。不情願之下，我提筆回你信，因為我知道你正在同時做六件事——五件，外加房事。你哪有空寫信？我搞不懂。

我相信，等我四月頭兩星期到紐約時，你的舞臺劇會繼續公演中。果真如此，劇評一定氣得直跳腳，因為如果我沒記錯，他們說你的戲寫得太好笑了，絕對演不下去。既然現在還在演，他們一定被氣得更火大。我兒子和鮑伯·費雪（Bob Fisher）合作的戲也有同樣的情形。心得是：別寫一齣能逗觀眾大笑的喜劇。

劇評的問題，早在我接受猶太成年禮時，也就是將近一百年前，就已經討論過了。偷偷告訴你一個祕密，我童年最後轉大人時，收到兩份禮物。一個有錢的伯伯送我一雙長統黑襪，一個祝我賺大錢的姨媽送我一個銀錶。禮物到手才三天，手錶飛了，原因是我哥奇戈（Chico）在撞球桌上不自量力，銀錶被他拿去八十九街和第三大道交叉口當掉了。有一天，我在路上漫無目標逛，發現銀錶出現在當舖櫥窗裡。要不是我的姓名縮寫刻在錶背，我一定認不出來，因為錶被日曬摧殘，變得和煤炭一樣黑。襪子被我穿了一星期沒洗，現在呈現參差不齊的綠色。我在世上存活了十三年，得到的獎賞就這麼多。

我遲遲不回信，簡而言之，原因就在這裡。我仍穿著同一雙襪子——不再是襪子了，已成為我的腿的一部分。

你來信說，你二月要來，我興奮得沖昏頭，買了好多熟食，花了一大疊鈔票，買回一大疊冷肉片。假如沒買，錢省下來，保證能在一九六七、六八年捐款給聯合猶太福利基金。

我考慮在紐約投宿聖瑞吉斯（St. Regis）大飯店。看在上帝的份上，求你不要再繼續成功了——快把我整瘋了。祝你和矮友小迪（little Dickie）好運。

葛勞裘

信之 *012*

劇如其名

伊恩・梅因（Ian Main）致喜劇與輕娛樂部門主管

一九七四年五月二十九日

約翰・克里斯與當時的妻子康妮・布思（Connie Booth）攜手撰寫一齣喜劇首集的腳本，寄給BBC電視臺。一九七四年五月，喜劇腳本編輯伊恩・梅因翻閱之後，顯然興趣缺缺，寫了一封反對到底的報告給BBC電視喜劇與輕娛樂部門的主管。幸好視聽大眾有眼福，而夫妻檔作者的奮戰不懈精神也是一大功臣，小編輯的意見最後被上司漠視。一年後，腳本演進為影集，成了史上最滑稽的電視節目之一，片名是《巔樓大酒店》（Fawlty Towers）。

克里斯在二〇〇九年提及這份報告，表示，「由此可見，狀況外是人之常情。」

發　自：電視部輕娛樂，喜劇腳本編輯

室號與樓碼：4009 TC

電話分機：2900

日　期：一九七四年五月二十九日

主　旨：「巔樓大酒店」，作者約翰・克里斯（John Cleese）與康妮・布思

收件人：H.C.L.E.

恕我直言，這篇內容跟劇名一樣顫巍巍。

劇情有點像旅館界的《王子復仇記》（*Prince of Denmark*），以陳腔濫調和刻板角色堆砌而成，我認為搬上電視只會引發災難一場。

CF

伊恩・梅因

From: Comedy Script Editor, Light Entertainment, Television

Room No. &
Building: 4009 TC   Tel. Ext.: 2900   date: 29.5.1974.

Subject: "FAWLTY TOWERS" BY JOHN CLEESE & CONNIE BOOTH

To: H.C.L.E.

I'm afraid I thought this one as dire as its title.

It's a kind of "Prince of Denmark" of the hotel world. A collection of
cliches and stock characters which I can't see being anything but a disaster.

CF   (Ian Main)

AS/20

信之 013

令我瞠目驚駭

狄更斯致《泰晤士報》
一八四九年十一月十三日

在一八四九年十一月十三日，南倫敦一所監獄外聚集多達三萬民眾，爭相目睹菲德瑞克（Frederick）與瑪莉·曼寧（Marie Manning）夫婦接受絞刑。妻子瑪莉的多金前男友派崔克·歐康納（Patrick O'Connor）遭兩人合夥謀財害命，被埋在曼寧家廚房，隨後兩人捲款逃逸，手法拙劣。在英國，由於夫妻一同接受絞刑是一百多年來首見，因此民眾反應熱烈，人稱「柏芒吉戰慄」（Bermondsey Horror），號稱是「世紀大絞刑」。事件場面之浩大，甚至引來作家狄更斯的注意。狄更斯觀察行刑過程與群眾喧囂後，投書《泰晤士報》，表達絕望透頂的心意。

德文郡臺路，
一八四九年十一月十三日星期二

編輯先生，

今晨我目睹馬販巷監獄外的處決。我想觀察圍觀的民眾反應，結果觀察的良機從夜裡持續至破曉，直到場面結束為止。我對此投書的重點不在於探討死刑存廢與否，也不願贅述正反雙方的立論。我只願將這次驚心動魄的經驗化為教化人心之舉，以最簡便而公開的方式引述內政大臣葛雷爵士在國會休會前的宣示：政府或能接受勸誘，支持極刑在監獄內部實施之政策，以力求隱蔽靜肅（並保證貫徹處決，毫不留情，以符合社會大眾期望）。本人更鄭重懇請葛雷爵士秉持社會公道，肩負終生使命，親自主導立法。今晨處決時萬頭鑽動，群心邪惡輕浮，其場景極難入目，必定無人能想像，也無法見容於普天下的蠻夷之邦。凶手再殘暴，絞刑架再驚駭，依我淺見，也遜色於圍觀群眾之氣勢、表情、言語。我於午夜時分抵達現場，喧譁叫囂聲此起彼落，宛如孩童聚會同樂之聲，令我心寒。連夜的嘶吼、歡笑、叫罵，蔚為大合唱的磅礴橋段，眾人模仿黑人旋律，將「蘇珊娜」改為「曼寧太太」，諸如此類。黎明時分，各路盜賊、低級娼妓、無賴、流氓群集而來，各種粗俗齷齪之舉盡出，打鬥、暈眩、口哨聲、損人笑話、模仿木偶劇駝背莽夫（Punch）之場面層出不窮。警方將暈厥女士拖離現場時，女士衣衫不整，更引發群眾猥瑣笑鬧，為整場娛樂活動增添新風味。旭日東昇，陽光普照，將抬頭望的成千上萬面孔鍍金，每一張臉是無法言喻的猙獰，人人以殘暴為樂，冷血無情，同為人類的人不得不為自身的形體汗顏，無地自容，因為這些人的嘴臉無異於撒旦。吸引群眾的鄙輩伏法，雙雙顱懸半空中之際，現場的情緒、憐憫、思想再也無關乎兩條人命已歸陰受審，淫言穢行再也無忌憚，猶如世人從未耳聞基督之名，猶如群眾將這兩人視為野獸。

最劣質的罪惡淵藪和貪污之多，我在國內見怪不怪，而倫敦生活圈的層面萬千，能令我稱奇的不多。我沉痛之餘相信，在同樣時

間內，在同一座城市裡，再高明的頭腦也無法如行刑示眾一般斬喪人性，令我在絞刑現場瞠目驚駭。今晨馬販巷監獄外的殘暴場景若呈現在善良公民的家門口，若眾人視若無睹，甚或過目即忘，我相信沒有任何群體仍能成長茁壯。佳節將臨，在吾人祈禱感恩中，向上帝謙卑表達掃除人間惡行之願望時，我想請求貴報讀者深思此惡行，並考慮根除之。

忠僕敬上

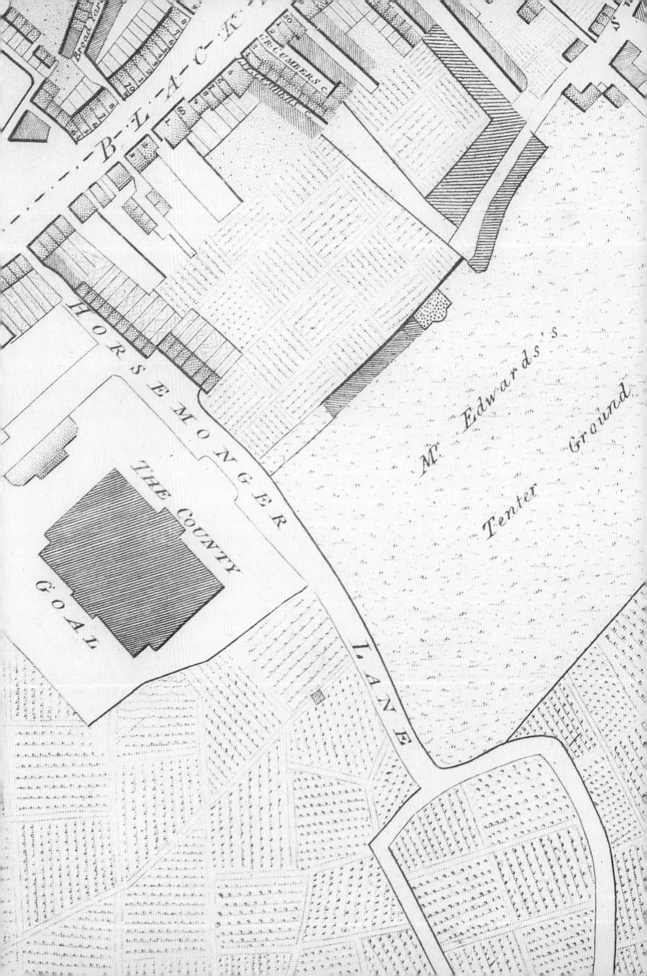

女神射手五十名
供您差遣

安妮・歐克理（Annie Oakley）
致麥金利（William McKinley）
總統
一八九八年四月五日

美國─西班牙戰爭於一八九八年四
月一觸即發時，知名神射手安妮・
歐克理決定效忠政府，以本信貢獻
人力物力給當時的美國總統。安妮
是水牛比爾旗下的藝人，名氣響
亮，可以說是全球史上首見的超級
女巨星。她以印刷精美的信紙，簡
單寫下她的心意：願以五十名「女
神射手」精兵投效軍方，各個在戰
場上是不可或缺的人才，全配備充
份彈藥。令她大感失望的是，她被
當權者婉謝拒絕。畢生愛國的安妮
不因此灰心，在第一次世界大戰爆
發前，再度向政府表達報國心意，
卻得到同樣的答覆。

全球各國一致轟動
安妮・歐克理
美利堅女國民神射手

紐澤西州納特利，四月五日

麥金利總統鈞鑑

敬愛的總統我個人深信您憑高超的判斷力能迴避戰爭帶領美國安
渡難關。

但如果戰爭無法避免我準備號召五十名女神射手供您差遣。全員
皆美國人而且槍彈自備因此政府之支出能減到最低。
誠心敬上

安妮・歐克理

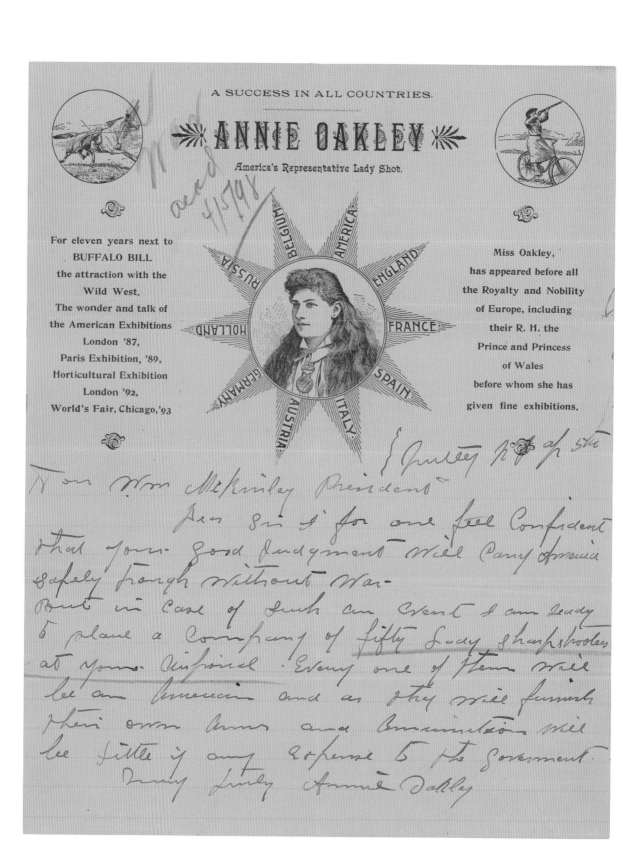

A SUCCESS IN ALL COUNTRIES.

ANNIE OAKLEY

America's Representative Lady Shot.

For eleven years next to
BUFFALO BILL
the attraction with the
Wild West.
The wonder and talk of
the American Exhibitions
London '87,
Paris Exhibition, '89,
Horticultural Exhibition
London '92,
World's Fair, Chicago, '93

BELGIUM · AMERICA · ENGLAND · FRANCE · SPAIN · ITALY · AUSTRIA · GERMANY · HOLLAND · RUSSIA

Miss Oakley,
has appeared before all
the Royalty and Nobility
of Europe, including
their R. H. the
Prince and Princess
of Wales
before whom she has
given fine exhibitions.

Hon Wm McKinley President

Dear Sir I for one feel Confident
that your good Judgment will carry America
safely through without War—
But in case of Such an event I am Ready
to place a Company of fifty Lady Sharpshooters
at your disposal Every one of them will
be an American and as they will furnish
their own Arms and Ammunition will
be little if any Expense to the Government.
Very Truly Annie Oakley

一九四二年三月三日
美利堅合眾國羅斯福總統尊鑑
華盛頓特區白宮

希特勒該死

派崔克・希特勒（Patrick Hitler）
致美國羅斯福總統
一九四二年三月三日

派崔克逃離納粹德國，定居紐約，一年後在一九四〇年，自願投效美國軍隊卻遭拒絕，原因奇特，因為他是希特勒的侄兒。兩年後他再接再厲，在希特勒對美國宣戰幾月後，他以這份陳情書逕向美國總統訴求從軍的願望。本信立刻被轉至FBI局長胡佛（J.Edgar Hoover），經FBI調查身家背景後，派崔克終於如願以償。

派崔克於一九四四年進入美國海軍，在四七年因戰傷而退伍，四十年後在紐約過世。

敬愛的總統先生：

　　恕我冒昧佔用您和白宮幕僚的寶貴時間。我明白國內正面臨緊要關頭，冒昧陳情僅因唯有位居高位的您能解決我的特殊困境。

　　容我簡述個人處境，若您過目後認為值得介入並裁示，問題應可輕易解決。

　　我是德國總理兼大統帥的侄兒，也是他唯一的後代，而惡名昭彰的他現在專橫跋扈，竟想奴役全球的自由民族和基督徒。

　　多虧您領導有方，世人不分信仰和國籍，衡量輕重之後，刻正奮力揮軍反抗，以決定將來能否繼續服侍上帝，遵循道德，安居樂業，反之則難逃遭蠻夷暴政奴役的下場。

　　目前全球人民必須捫心自問願意效忠哪一份理想。對信仰虔誠的自由人而言，答案僅有一個，出路僅有一條，能確保信念長守，能奮戰到底。

　　我是一介草民，但我能為這份偉大理想奉獻心力，不惜拋頭顱灑熱血，在眾人傾力下終能凱旋而歸。

　　我的所有親朋好友在星條旗領軍下，不久將邁向自由與禮教之路。為此，總統先生，我秉持崇敬心，呈遞這份陳情書，盼能獲准加入他們的行列，共同反抗暴政和壓制。

　　目前我遭拒，是因為我在一九三九年逃離德國時身為英國公民。我後來隨愛爾蘭籍母親移民美國，主要是想和這裡的親戚團圓。我在美國取得寫作和講課的合約，工作的壓力令我無暇爭取移民配額，因此以觀光名義入境。

　　我曾嘗試加入英軍，但由於我口才優異，政治演說時吸引廣大人潮，少有人能比，在波士頓、芝加哥等城市演說時，更常勞駕警方管制吵著要進場的民眾，英國當局因而對我敬而遠之。

　　英國民族性封閉，儘管態度和善有禮，但在我印象中，無論此印象是否錯誤，總覺得英方碰上與我同姓的人，長遠而言不太可能表現得太熱忱或同情。我唯一的辦法是循英國法律途徑改姓，無奈代價過高，超出我的財力。我也向加拿大陸軍詢問過能

否從軍，但軍方意願不高。依照目前的情況，在缺乏高層的指引下，我認為以希特勒侄兒之名從軍需要一份異於常人的勇氣，而我因缺乏任何等級，也無從取得任何單位高層的支持，如今苦無勇氣再續。

至於我為人是否正直，總統先生，我僅能說有紀錄可循，我也具有前瞻精神，與總統先生不無相近之處。總統先生用盡治國之巧思，向美國國會爭取武器，如今在危機中能提供完善的國防。反觀我本人，我也曾在安逸無知的風氣下挺身而出，以基督徒的身份為所應為。逃出蓋世太保魔掌後，我曾透過媒體警告法國，希特勒必定在該年侵法。我以同樣的方式警告英國人民，所謂的慕尼黑「方案」是無稽之談，後患無窮。我一抵達美國，立即知會媒體，希特勒即將釋放他的科學怪人，該年即將肆虐文明世界。雖然各界對我所言置若罔聞，我仍持續在美國演說寫作。現在，搖筆桿清談的時刻已過，我僅惦記美國給予家母和我的大恩大德，全心盼能儘快荷槍上戰場，藉此讓友人和袍澤接納我，視我為爭取自由大戰的同儕。

若總統能成全我的訴求，此舉必定能確保美國人民保持仁慈精神，而現在的我深切感到我是美國的一份子。我以最誠摯的心向您擔保，總統先生，本人秉持一貫的態度，未來也將竭盡一己之所能，不虛您善心義助之莫大光榮，因為我確信，本人將依循民主的偉大原則行事，至少能讓沒資格享受民主權益的美國人自慚形穢。因此，恕我斗膽盼望，總統先生，您能在亂世中明察，不至於因我無從更改的身家而拒絕我的訴求。

總統先生，對我而言，現在最大的榮耀是生活在美國，而且有幸效勞美國人民之救星。在美國人民的努力之下，您將獲後世政治史家推崇為苦難人類最偉大的解放者，我若有幸一同奮鬥，哪怕是角色渺小，我也將視之為莫大的恩惠。

若您需要進一步資訊，我願樂意奉上。在此恕我附上一份傳單，上面詳載我個人資料。

容我誠心預祝總統先生未來健康快樂，同時希望您不久將統御誠心為善的全體勇士，率眾勇往直前，打一場轟轟烈烈的勝仗。

派崔克・希特勒
秉持萬分敬意敬上

信之 016

感謝妳獻夢

羅爾德·達爾（Roald Dahl）
致小書迷艾咪·寇克蘭（Amy Corcoran）
一九八九年二月十日

一九八九年某週日午後下雨，七歲女童艾咪在父親鼓勵並大力協助下，決定寫信給知名作家。羅爾德·達爾不僅是史上最成功的童書作者之一，對艾咪更重要的是，艾咪最愛的一本書是他的傑作《吹夢巨人》（*The BFG*）——故事寫得奇幻而美妙，敘述一位友善的巨人專門蒐集美夢，趁兒童沉睡時吹進他們窗戶裡。小艾咪也想如法泡製，所以混合了油和金蔥粉，攪進加了顏料的水，連瓶帶信寄給達爾。這份禮物既恰當又寶貴，因為瓶裡裝著艾咪的夢。

從回信來看，達爾能充份體會她的心意。

吉普西之家
白金漢郡大彌森登
HP16 0BP
一九八九年二月十日

親愛的艾咪，

　　我必須特別提筆寫信感謝妳送我一瓶好夢。在妳之前，全世界沒有人送過我這種禮物，令我感觸很深。我也很喜歡妳送的夢。今晚我打算下山進村子，趁某個小孩在睡覺，對著臥房窗戶把夢吹進去，看看有沒有效。

　　　愛妳的

　　　羅爾德·達爾

10th February 1989

Dear Amy,

I must write a special letter and thank you for the dream in the bottle. You are the first person in the world who has sent me one of these and it intrigued me very much. I also liked the dream. Tonight I shall go down to the village and blow it through the bedroom window of some sleeping child and see if it works.

With love from,

Roald Dahl

信之 017　　一九三三年三月十五日

我多麼盼望進貴社上班！

尤朵拉・韋爾蒂（Eudora
Welty）致《紐約客》
一九三三年三月十五日

一九三三年三月，二十三歲的尤朵拉・韋爾蒂想應徵寫作的工作，寫了這封迷人至極的信給《紐約客》雜誌社，以輕巧坦誠的筆法侃侃自介。能以親和的方式介紹個人專長並不容易，很難想像有誰能比她寫得更討喜，但令人錯愕又失望的是，寫得四平八穩的這封信竟石沉大海。幸好後來《紐約客》知錯能改，韋爾蒂順利進雜誌社，撰寫數篇文章，陸續獲得多項大獎，並在一九七三年以小說《樂觀者的女兒》（*The Optimist's Daughter*）榮獲普立茲獎，七年後更榮獲總統自由獎章。

紳士們，

　　與其讀應徵貴社的信，看人耍把戲變魔術大概比較有意思吧？可惜常理是，最想要的東西最要不到。

　　我今年二十三歲，在紐約闖蕩六星期了。其實，一九三〇—三一年之間，我當了一整年的紐約客，在哥大商學院進修廣告課程。我是南方人，家鄉在全國最落後的密西西比州，人脈包括沃特・H・裴吉，都怪我運氣欠佳，他已離開 Doubleday-Page 出版社，甚至連社名都改了。我曾就讀威斯康辛大學，主修英語，日子過得無憂無慮，取得文學學士學位（二九年）。過去一年半的時間，我在密西西比州賈克森（Jackson）的電臺上班，過著苦哈哈的生活，撰寫節目串場詞、戲劇、騾飼料廣告、耶誕老公公講稿和壽險短劇；我已經辭職了。

　　我能為貴社做的是——我最近常逛藝廊，常看十五分錢的電影，多到不像話，能以我往常事不干己的好態度寫評語吧，我想；事實上，我最近去瑪莉・哈里曼藝廊欣賞馬諦斯的新作，發明了一個能概括他作品的新詞：鳳梨情婦（concubineapple）。這能顯示我腦筋的運作模式——快而不準。我嗜書如命，而且讀完後能揮灑見解。由於我買了一塊印度花布和一大批唱片——老闆是專門收集這些東西的努斯邦姆先生——我也有一幅一英吋長的塞尚弄潮圖（希望由此可見我是康明斯的詩迷），因此我想要一小臺手提式留聲機，更迫切想買一間公寓。我多麼盼望進貴社上班！假如貴社無法僱我朝九晚五，那麼找我每早寫一小段，每晚寫一小段也好，只不過我工作起來會像奴隸一樣賣命。我的畫工也不輸桑伯先生，如果他掛了，可以找我接手。我研讀過花卉畫。

　　如果貴社不錄取我，我不曉得何去何從；我知道您聽了這話會滿不在乎，但請深思我的另一條出路：北卡大學想找人吟唱韋切爾・林賽的《剛果》詩，以十二美元的酬勞找我去跳舞，我剛果然走下去（I congo on）。到此別不多說了。重申：我是個賣命的工作者。

尤朵拉・韋爾蒂　誠心敬上

'音樂即'人'生

路易斯·阿姆斯壯（Louis Armstrong）致准下士韋列克（Villec）

一九六七年

在一九六七年，駐越南的一名美國海軍陸戰隊士兵寫信給爵士音樂界傳奇樂手路易斯·阿姆斯壯，他不久以這封坦蕩溫馨的信回覆歌迷。這封信怎麼看也不像兩人素昧平生，因為阿姆斯壯在第一段就欣然提起他最愛服用的通便劑瑞士快適（Swiss Kriss），然後遙想童年與耳濡目染的音樂，接著提及最近動手術切除腫瘤的妻子，文字詼諧，溫情洋溢。他甚至在信尾附上一首歌。整體而言，綽號書包大嘴（Satchmo）的他個性迷人灑脫，信寫得妙，更奇特的是他獨門的標點符號用法，不熟悉他文筆的人絕對會被他迷得一愣一愣。基於不為人所知的因素，他常在文句裡攙加眾多大寫、縮寫撇號、引號、破折號、底線等等，而且通常加在一般人不會加的地方。這封信是絕佳的例子。

親愛的准下士，韋列克」

我想 '佔一兩 '分鐘告訴你，得知你是 '爵士樂迷而且和 '我們 '一樣恍神在旋律中，我 '多麼「爽」啊。「老弟——我帶著一本 '唱片簿，'裝滿 '專輯—— '曲子很 '長的那種。當我 '刮鬍子時，或 '坐在 '寶座上，滿肚子 '瑞士快適'時，那音樂真能 '拉出那種 '即興調調'，'隨著我 '每晚或上床前 '吃的 '瑞士快適一起流瀉。'爽啊。我用那些 '唱片給自己一場 '音樂會。'音樂即 '人 '生。'世上如果沒有 '好音樂，那還得了？管它是 '什麼音樂都好。

音樂 '全來自 '神聖的老 '教堂。我記得，'好久好久 '以前在路易西安納州 '紐奧良'，在 '我的故鄉，我差不多 '十歲大那年，我母親常帶我上 '教堂，神父（'也就是牧師'）常用那種既老又 '好的 '讚美詩 '帶頭炒氣氛。不知不覺中，'整群 '信徒哇哇叫起來，'瘋了似的 '高歌，'聽起來好 '美。'我 '是個什麼都「愛」，見人就「愛」的小鬼頭，進 '教堂 '樂翻天，特別是在「神父」（牧師）講道講到 '一半的時候 '修女們鬼叫到靈魂出竅啦。'哇塞那些 '教會 '修女會開始 '大呼小叫的，叫到 '襯裙 '掉下來。當然囉 '執事急忙 '衝過去抱人，'摟住她，對著她的臉 '煽風煽到 '她 '醒。

另外呢也有「洗禮式——也就是有人加入 '教會搞宗教，想改信我們的教，所以要被洗禮。'懂嗎——我記得有個 '禮拜天，'教會來了一個 '大傢伙想 '洗禮，所以 '執事全 '站在河裡—— '水淹到腰、鑽進 '白 '袍。他們已經為 '一些 '女人和幾個 '男人 '施洗—— '拯救他們的 '靈魂。沒想到這個當兒，有個 '大塊頭的 '壯漢 '罪人 '冒出來'，走到隊伍前面，所以呢—— '這些個 '執事們一個個 '力氣也 '很大，他們 '抓住這頭 '老虎，一面 '壓他進水下，一面問他——」老兄，你 '信不信」？大塊頭不 '吭聲，只瞪著他們看。於是呢，他們再把他 '按進河水裡，'只不過 '這次讓他多泡 '幾分鐘。然後呢，'執

事直直看著他的眼睛，問他——」你‘信不信’？這傢伙終於‘回答了——他說，「信——我相信你們這群‘狗娘養的想‘淹死‘我。」

　　P.S. 我猜你會把我當‘瘋子。‘不是‘不是。我‘提這些事件是因為它們全以‘音樂為‘主軸。事實上，‘全是音樂。「你‘懂嗎？我們在‘老家‘紐奧良’也做‘同樣的事——那些‘喪葬隊伍等等的。*Why Gate‘韋列克，我們‘行進中的‘彈奏全靠發自‘內心的‘真情。‘一路彈奏到墓園——當然是’銅管樂隊囉。在前進墓園的路上，‘小鼓手會在‘響弦裡夾一條‘手帕，增加鼓聲的‘死氣——」像鳥一樣逃走。」不過牧師的「灰歸‘灰、‘塵歸‘塵」一說出嘴巴，「小鼓手會‘拉掉手帕，會敲起‘長音滾奏’，以‘聚集所有人，包括‘死人‘別墅——或‘俱樂部裡的成員。‘然後我們會‘回總部，‘彈奏「迷途知返」（Didn’t he Ramble）或「聖徒到」（When the Saints Go Marching In）。‘看到沒？‘還是音樂。

　　扯了‘這堆東西，全是希望你做事時把‘音樂‘同樣放在‘心上，絕對錯不了啦。‘我和我的‘明星隊’正在‘哈洛德（Harrods）‘俱樂部（雷諾市）‘駐唱‘三禮拜，有‘妻子‘露西兒（Lucille）‘陪伴。休息一下對她好處多多。差不多在‘七月‘中，她被‘開刀治‘腫瘤，現在康復的‘非常‘快。手術‘大夫在紐約‘貝斯‘以色列（Beth Israel）醫院’告訴她——’她可以去‘雷諾待一陣子，條件是‘妳（露西兒）+妳‘丈夫（大嘴）‘保證守‘規矩，不准動歪腦筋‘做「囂」（「意思是‘行房）。我‘說——」大夫啊，我‘保證——不過我每天‘早上會‘輕輕‘摸它一把——以確定它‘還在不在‘那裡。‘哈‘哈。‘人生多‘美好。想想看，‘露西兒的‘小‘障礙解決掉啦——「不久就能「變得健康快樂——能恢復‘嬌滴滴‘小‘可愛的原來的她啦。一‘想到這裡，我就‘樂到不行。

　　‘好了，‘韋列克‘老弟，我猜我該‘歇‘筆，該‘睡一點覺了。現在時間已經算‘凌晨了。我‘剛‘下‘班。我‘累到

'眼 '皮都 '睜不開了。嘻嘻。這樣吧，我就用這首小詩送你：

當你 '穿越 '暴風雨——
昂 '首挺 '胸——
'別怕 '黑——
因為 '暴風雨 '結束後——
'天光 '金一亮——
'雲雀扯銀鈴嗓——
歡唱甜美的 '歌——
'往前' ——走，迎著風——
'往前' ——走，冒著雨——
縱使 '夢被「吹垮 '擊倒——
'往前' 走——'往前' 走——
心懷 '希望——
'你一路——不——孤獨——
一路——不——孤獨——
（重複一次）
往前走——往前走——心懷希望——一路——不——孤獨
——一路——不——孤獨——。了不了？

　　代我向連裡的弟兄問候。其他弟兄也一樣。現在，我要照 '馬鈴薯 '農夫的做法——現在 '種你下去，以後挖你出來玩。我要停筆了。真的很 '高興 '寫信給——' 你。

「滿肚瑞士快適的」

書包大嘴
路易斯・阿姆斯壯

致我前奴主

喬頓・安德森（Jourdon
Anderson）致派崔克・亨
利・安德森（Patrick Henry
Anderson）

一八六五年八月七日

黑奴喬頓服侍主人長達三十二年後，於一八六四年趁北軍解放他不辭辛勞服務的農場時，帶著妻子逃脫奴役生活。夫婦使勁把握良機，趕緊移居俄亥俄州。喬頓找到工作，以薪水養家，兒女逐漸成群，再也不回頭。一年後，在南北戰爭結束不久後，喬頓接到一封措辭焦急的信，寄件人是他以前的主人派崔克・亨利・安德森。主人要求他回田納西州工作，以拯救告急的農場事業。

喬頓接到信後，在家於八月七日口述回信，請人代筆，內容句句大快人心，後來更獲得多家報社轉載。喬頓始終不回田納西州大泉鎮。他在一九〇七年去世，享年八十一，六年後妻子也西歸，葬在丈夫旁，兩人總共養育了十一名子女。

致我的前奴主安德森上校，田納西州大泉鎮

上校：我收到你的來信，很高興你沒忘記喬頓也希望我回歸，你也承諾將比任何人更加善待我。你常讓我忐忑不安。我本以為，北方人老早把你吊死了，因為你在家裡窩藏南軍。北軍把一個士兵留在馬丁上校家的馬廄裡，你去馬丁家要他的命，想必北軍未曾耳聞此事。我離開你時，你對我開兩槍，但我不願得知你受傷，因此慶幸你仍健在。若能重回溫馨的老家，若能再看看瑪麗小姐、瑪莎小姐、艾倫、伊莎、葛林、里伊，該有多好。請代我問候大家並轉告他們，今生若無緣再見，但願來生能重逢。我本來在納什維爾醫院工作，本想回去見大家，但有鄰居告訴我，如果亨利逮到機會，一定會槍斃我。

我特別想知道你願提供的良機是什麼。目前的我生計尚可果腹，月薪二十五元包括伙食和衣著，居家舒適，曼蒂被大家尊稱安德森夫人，小孩米莉、珍、葛倫迪都上學了，學習很認真，老師說葛倫迪憑頭腦可望成為牧師。他們也上主日學，曼蒂和我勤上教堂，獲得親切的待遇。有時候我們旁聽別人說，在田納西州「那些有色人種當過奴隸」，我家小孩聽見後傷心，但我告訴他們，在田納西，主人是安德森上校，不足羞恥。我從前以你為主人，覺得光榮，換成其他黑人，他們也會有同感。如果你願回信告知未來支薪的數字，我可考慮回去是否對我有利。

你信上承諾給我自由，但我已於一八六四年獲自由之身，有納什維爾市政府憲兵司令的證書為憑。曼蒂說，在你保證以公正、善意的態度對待我們之前，她害怕回去。我們討論後決定要求你先清償我們服務多年累欠的薪資，以測試你的誠意，我們也會因而忘卻過往，不計前仇，未來全仰仗你的公義和友誼。我忠心效勞你三十二年，曼蒂二十年，若以我月薪二十五元、曼蒂週薪兩元計算，夫妻薪資總計一萬一千六百八十美元。歷年累欠薪資生息，扣掉服裝費用、我三度求醫的醫藥費、曼蒂拔牙一顆的費

用，加減後的數字可顯示我們合理的所得。這筆款項請透過亞當斯氏快遞支付，由俄亥俄州戴頓的Ⅴ·溫特斯紳士轉交。若你不願支付我們往年忠心苦勞的薪水，我們對你許諾的將來也不會抱存太大的信心。我們深信，萬能上帝已敞開你的心眼，教你認清你和父祖虧待我和父祖的一切，認清你強迫我們歷代無償的辛苦付出。在這裡，我每週六領薪，但在田納西州，黑人一如牛馬，從無薪餉日。對僱請勞工卻無故不支薪的人而言，結算日總有一天將來臨。

米莉和珍已長大為亭亭玉立的少女。你回信時，請表明她們的安全是否有保障。瑪蒂達和凱瑟琳當年多悽慘，你應知道。我寧可待在這裡挨餓，甚至不惜餓死，也不願坐視女兒因少爺們的暴行劣舉而蒙羞。此外也請你表明居家附近是否有學校願收有色人種兒童。我現在人生一大心願是讓兒女接受教育，培養道德情操。

代我向喬治·卡特問好，感謝他在你舉槍射我時奪走手槍。

老僕喬頓·安德森

信之 *020*

我的好朋友羅斯福

少年卡斯楚致美國羅斯福總統

一九四〇年十一月六日

卡斯楚在一九五三年發動革命，最後推翻古巴獨裁巴蒂斯塔（Fulgencio Batista），但在十三年前，亦即一九四〇年十一月，十四歲的卡斯楚謊稱十二歲，寫了一封有點調皮的信給當時的美國總統羅斯福，叫他寄一張十元美鈔。過了一段時日，小卡斯楚收到官方制式的回信，但信裡不見美鈔。他知道古巴最大鐵礦在哪裡，願向總統指出地理位置，但回信對此同樣漠不關心。一九七七年，經過國家檔案資料署的專家鑑定後，小卡斯楚這封無價之寶終於重見天日。

聖地亞哥德古巴市

一九四〇年十一月六日
致美國總統羅斯福先生

我的好朋友羅斯福我懂少的英文，但我懂的英文足夠寫信給你。我喜歡聽收音機，而且我是非常快樂的，因為我聽電臺說，你將成為總統新（任期）。

我是十二歲的。我是一個男孩但我非常多的思想但我不曾想過我會寫信給美國總統。

如果可以的話，回信附一個十元美金鈔票，因為從來我沒見過十元美金鈔票而我非常想要一個。

我的地址是：

> 費德爾・卡斯楚一世
> 東古巴聖地亞哥德古巴市
> 多洛勒斯學院

我懂少的英文但我懂非常多的西班牙文而我猜你懂少的西班牙文但你懂非常多的英文因為你是美國人但我不是美國人。
　　（非常感謝你）
　　在見。你的朋友，

　　　　費德爾・卡斯楚

如果你想要鐵造舟大船我能帶你去找國內最大的鐵（壙）。它們在東古巴馬亞里。

COLEGIO DE DOLORES
APARTADO 1
SANTIAGO DE CUBA
—

Santiago de Cuba.
Nov 6 1940.
Mr. Franklin Roosvelt,
President of the United
States.

My good friend Roosvelt
I don't know very En-
glish, but I know as much
as write to you.
I like to hear the radio, and
I am very happy, because
I heard in it, that you will
be President for a new
(período)
I am twelve years old.
I am a boy but I think very
much but I do not think
that I am writing to the

President of the United S
tates.
If you like, give me a
ten dollars bill green american, in the letter, because
never, I have not seen a
ten dollars bill green american and I would like
to have one of them.
My address is:
      Sr. Fidel Castro
   Colegio de Dolores.
    Santiago de Cuba
      Oriente. Cuba.
I don't know very English
but I know very much
Spanish and I suppose
you don't know very Spa-
nish but you know very
English because you
are American but I am
not American.

(Thank you very much)
Good by. Your friend,

Castro
Fidel Castro

If you want iron to make
your skeaps ships I will
show to you the bigest
(minas) of iron of the land.
They are in Mayari. Oriente
Cuba.

人一定不能無足輕重

亨特·湯普森（Hunter S.
Thompson）致休姆·羅根
（Hume Logan）
一九五八年四月二十二日

二十歲那年，亨特·湯普森仍在美國空軍服役，接到友人休姆·羅根的來信請教指引人生方向。他於一九五八年四月回覆，行文智慧深長。十年後，湯普森才因勇於潛入地獄天使幫採訪一年而聲名大譟。不久後，他最知名的作品之一《賭城風情畫》（*Fear and Loathing in Las Vegas*）出版，以他為宗的「荒誕新聞派」（Gonzo journalism）也漸成氣候。二〇〇五年，他因健康問題尋短自盡，留下一封遺書給妻子，標題是《美式足球季結束了》：

「不再有賽事。不再有炸彈。不再走路。不再享樂。不再游泳。六十七。是五十過後十七年。比我需要或想要的歲數多十七。乏味。我向來愛發牢騷。任何人都覺得我無趣。六十七。你愈來愈『貪婪』了。認份吧（老頭）。放輕鬆──不會痛的。」

親愛的休姆，

　　你想聽我的建議──這種行為太人類、太危險了吧！為什麼？被人請教人生何去何從時，如果提供建議，等於自曝一種近乎自大狂的心態。指向正道，指向最終目標──比著顫抖的指頭指向**正確**的方向，這種事只有傻瓜會攬在身上。

　　我不是傻瓜，但我尊重你徵求我建議的誠意。不過，我請你聆聽我的說法，請你記住所有忠言全是建議者的片面之詞。某人視為真理的東西如果硬套在另一人身上，可能導致災難一場。我不經由你的眼睛看人生，你也不透過我眼睛望天下。如果我硬塞**確切**的建議給你，豈不太像是盲人導盲？

> 「問題在於：死或活何者為佳：忍受厄運矢石弓箭的磨難，或對萬難宣戰，心靈能否因而更高尚……」
>
> （莎士比亞）

　　問題確實在這裡：是隨波漂流好呢，或是泳向目標呢？走到人生某一階段，人人在有意無意中，都必須如此抉擇。明白這一點的人少之又少！在你做過的抉擇當中，影響到將來的抉擇有哪幾個能全然跳脫我提起的這兩種：漂或游。我不一定對，但我很難想見漂或游之外的抉擇。

　　然而，如果你沒目標，何不乾脆漂流呢？這又是另一個問題。與其無所適從亂游，倒不如享受漂流，樂趣絕對更高。那麼，人如何找到目標？目標不是星辰中的一座城堡，而是伸手可觸及的真事物。人怎知自己追求的不是「冰糖高山」呢？怎知目標不是引人垂涎的糖果，而是味薄又沒營養的冰糖？

　　答案──就某種意義而言，人生的悲劇──在於，我們致力於理解目標，而不去理解人。我們設定目標，而目標要求我們做某些事：所以我們乖乖做這些事。我們隨一個概念的要求而調整，而這概念**不可能**站得住腳。以你童年的志向來說，假設你想當消防隊員，我敢篤定說，現在的你不再想進消防隊了。為什

麼？因為你的人生觀（perspective）變了。變的不是消防隊員，而是你。遇事反應累積成的經驗總和才構成一個人，人人都是如此。隨著你體驗到的事物多元化，經驗增加，你會變成不一樣的人，人生觀也跟著生變。這種現象持續不斷。每一種反應都是學習的過程；每一種重大經驗都能改變你的人生觀。

既然看待目標的角度天天變，為了達成這目標而改變生活，豈不太傻了嗎？除了變得神經兮兮之外，我們還能奢望成就什麼大事？

因此，答案根本不在目標身上，至少和明確的目標毫無關聯。這題材很廣泛，想闡述得淋漓盡致，勢必耗掉一疊又一疊的紙。以「人生意義」為主題的書何其多，只有天知道；多少人思考過這題材，也只有天知道。（我寫「天知道」無關宗教，純屬慣用語。）要我化繁為簡向你建議，我覺得沒什麼道理，因為我承認自己最清楚我完全沒資格把人生意義縮簡成一兩段文字。

我不想沾上「存在主義」這詞，但你可以把它記在心中參考。你也可以試一試尚—保羅・沙特（Jean-Paul Sartre）的《存在與虛無》（*Being and Nothingess*）；你也可以試試看另一個小東西《存在主義：從杜斯妥也夫斯基到沙特》（*Existentialism: From Dostoyevsky to Sartre*）。這些純屬建議。如果你真心滿意於現狀，那就對這兩本書敬而遠之。（狗睡得好好的，別去吵牠。）言歸正傳。如我所說，如果潛心追求確切目標，說得好聽一點是不智。所以我們不應該立志成為救火員，不應立志從事銀行業、警察、醫生。**我們應該立志做自我。**

不過，你可別誤解我的意思。我指的不是我們不能**做**消防隊員、銀行業者或醫生——我指的是，我們應該叫目標向個人看齊，而不是叫個人向目標看齊。先天遺傳和後天環境交互作用後，能在每人身心創造某些能力和欲望——包括一種深植人心的渴望，渴望以行動為人生賦予**意義**。人非當個某某人不可；人一定不能無足輕重。

照這麼說，依我所見，我擬出一道公式：人必須挑選一條能發揮**能力**到極限的路，以滿足個人的**欲望**。走上這條路後，他能滿足一份渴望（以既有的模式追求既有的目標，讓自己有所認同）；他能避免潛能受挫

（選擇的道路能讓自我發展無窮盡）；接近目標時，如果發現目標凋零或魅力盡失，他也能避免惶恐（並非扭曲自我以迎合志向，而是扭曲目標以配合個人能力與欲望）。

簡而言之，他尚未為了達成預設目標而奉獻終生，而是選上他**自知**將來會喜歡的一條人生道路。目標絕對是次要的：重要的是［朝目標邁進］的動作。誰說人**必須**照自己抉擇的模式去運作呢？這話未免太荒唐了吧。因為，讓別人界定你的個人目標，等於是放棄人生最富寓意的層面之一──意志力的行使。唯有發揮意志力，人才算是獨立的個體。

假設你認為你有八條路可選（全是預設道路，當然）。假設你左看右看，怎麼也看不出這八條路的哪條有道理。**這時候**──我目前為止所言的精髓在此──你**必須尋找第九條道路**。

說來容易，做起來並不一定輕鬆。你走過的人生道路比較窄，人生比較像垂直線，而非水平線，因此不難理解你為何彷徨。然而，拖延不**抉擇**的人終將被情勢剝奪抉擇權。

所以，如果現在你自我歸類為幻滅一族，那你別無選擇，只好接受現實，否則應該認真尋找其他東西。但尋找［目標］時切記：尋找人生之道。先決定你想過什麼生活，然後再看看那條人生道路的**週邊**能找到什麼維生之道。不過你說，「我不知道往哪裡找；我不知道該找什麼。」

癥結就在這裡。為了尋找更好的東西就放棄手上的東西，值得嗎？我不知道。除了你，誰能判定呢？然而，即使只是**決定尋找**，你也朝抉擇之路邁出一大步了。

我再不停筆，恐怕要寫成書了。乍看之下，我寫的東西很紊亂，希望不是有理說不清。請你務必記住，這是**我個人**看待事物的角度。我覺得我這角度大致能普遍適用，但你可能不以為然。人人必須自創信條──而我碰巧信這一條。

如果你覺得信裡哪些地方沒道理，儘管告訴我。我並不是想叫你「動身」去追尋北歐神話天堂瓦爾哈拉（Valhalla），只想指出，人生際遇丟給你的抉擇，你不一定要照單全收。抉擇多的是──沒有人**非得**一輩子做他不想做的事。但話說回來，如果你做的是非做不可的事，那就盡量勸自己接受**非做不可**的命運吧。將來，和你一樣的人多著呢。

到這裡收筆吧。等你回信再敘。我依然是

你的朋友……
亨特

我求你收我兒

多位母親致託孤院（Foundling Asylum）

一八七○年代

在一八六○年代末，紐約爆發棄嬰潮，殺嬰案例也增加，更令人憂心。為此，艾琳·費茲吉本（Irene Fitzgibbon）修女鼓吹奔走，最後在格林威治村成立託孤院，以收養市內棄嬰為宗旨。託孤院於一八六九年開張，門階擺著一座白搖籃，立刻為棄嬰提供庇護所。成立頭兩年，兩千五百名棄嬰湧入，通常伴隨一張手寫的信，說明棄養父母的心酸。其中許多信已由紐約歷史學會保存至今。

一百四十年後，今名為紐約託孤所的託孤院仍運作如常，為當地家庭提供寄養等救濟服務。

善心修女們

　　妳們將發現一個小男孩他明天滿月他父親不想養他而他是一個可憐小男孩他母親必須工作養活三個其他小孩她養不起他性名是沃特·庫柏還沒受洗請妳們好心施洗他我不願他沒受洗就死他母親也許哪天領他回家我結婚五年嫁進好人家我不認為丈夫是壞人我不得不離開他我不能把幾個小孩交給他我現在不知道他在哪裡他還沒見到這個小孩我想給他錢但身上一元也沒有我希望妳們能留他三四個月如果一直沒人認領八成他母親養不起他我以後或許能寄一點錢給他不要忘記他性名

庫柏夫人敬上

1703
admitted as James Fisk
2-21-71

New York tuesday

Kind Sisters

You will find a little boy
he is a month old to morrow it Father
will not do anything and it is a poor little
boy mother has to work to keep 3 other
and can not do anything with this one
it name is walter Cooper and he is not
christen yet will you be so good as to
do it I should not like him to die
with out it his mother might claim
him Some day I have been married 5
years and I married respectfuly and I
did not think my husband was a bad
man I had to leave him and I could
not trust my children to him now
I do not know where he is and he has
not Seen this one yet I have not a
dollar in the world to give him or I
would give it to him I wish you would
keep him for 3 or 4 month and if he
is not claimed by that time you may be
Sure it mother can not Support it I
may Some day send Some money to him
do not forget his name.

Yours Respectfuly

Mrs Cooper

女院長

　　我是一個苦命女，他成諾娶我卻騙我；我目前無力養我兒，也無親氣可依靠。因此我求妳看在上帝份上收下我兒，等到狀況許可，我有足夠能力自己養活他。我希望妳好心接下我兒，我將向上帝為妳祈禱。

　　謙卑僕人

　　　　　　　泰瑞莎‧培拉佐

　　　　　　　紐約一八七四年十二月三日

Sister Superioress.

I am a poor woman and I have been deceived under the Promis of marriage; I am at Present with no means and without any relations to nurse my babey Therefore I beg you for god sake to take my child; untill I can find a situation and have means so I can bring up myself I hope that you will so kind to accept my child and I will pray god for you
I remain umble servant

Teresa Peruzzo

New york Dec 3rd 1874

乖乖吃蔬菜！

約翰・W・詹姆士三世致美國總統尼克森
一九七三年七月十二日

一九七三年七月對美國總統尼克森而言，日子並不好過，因為水門事件的風波愈演愈烈，橢圓形辦公室密錄對話錄音帶曝光，讓原本霧裡看花的內幕更加撲朔迷離，七四年導致尼克森下臺。在七三年七月中旬，尼克森忙得不可開交，肺炎偏偏來攪局，迫使病弱的他躺在醫院病床上，無奈觀看電視轉播的聽證會。幸好至少有一位小朋友為他加油。八歲大的約翰・詹姆士三世懂得將心比心，寫了一封可愛的信，向已康復一半的受難總統獻計。總統閱信大為感動，返回白宮後竟朗讀給幕僚聽。

親愛的尼克森總統，

我聽說你得了肺炎。我也得過肺炎，昨天剛出院，希望你不是被我傳染到的。你要聽話，乖乖吃蔬菜，跟我住院時一樣！如果你吃藥兼打針，就能跟我一樣，八天就能出院。

敬愛你的
約翰・W・詹姆士三世
八歲
（完）

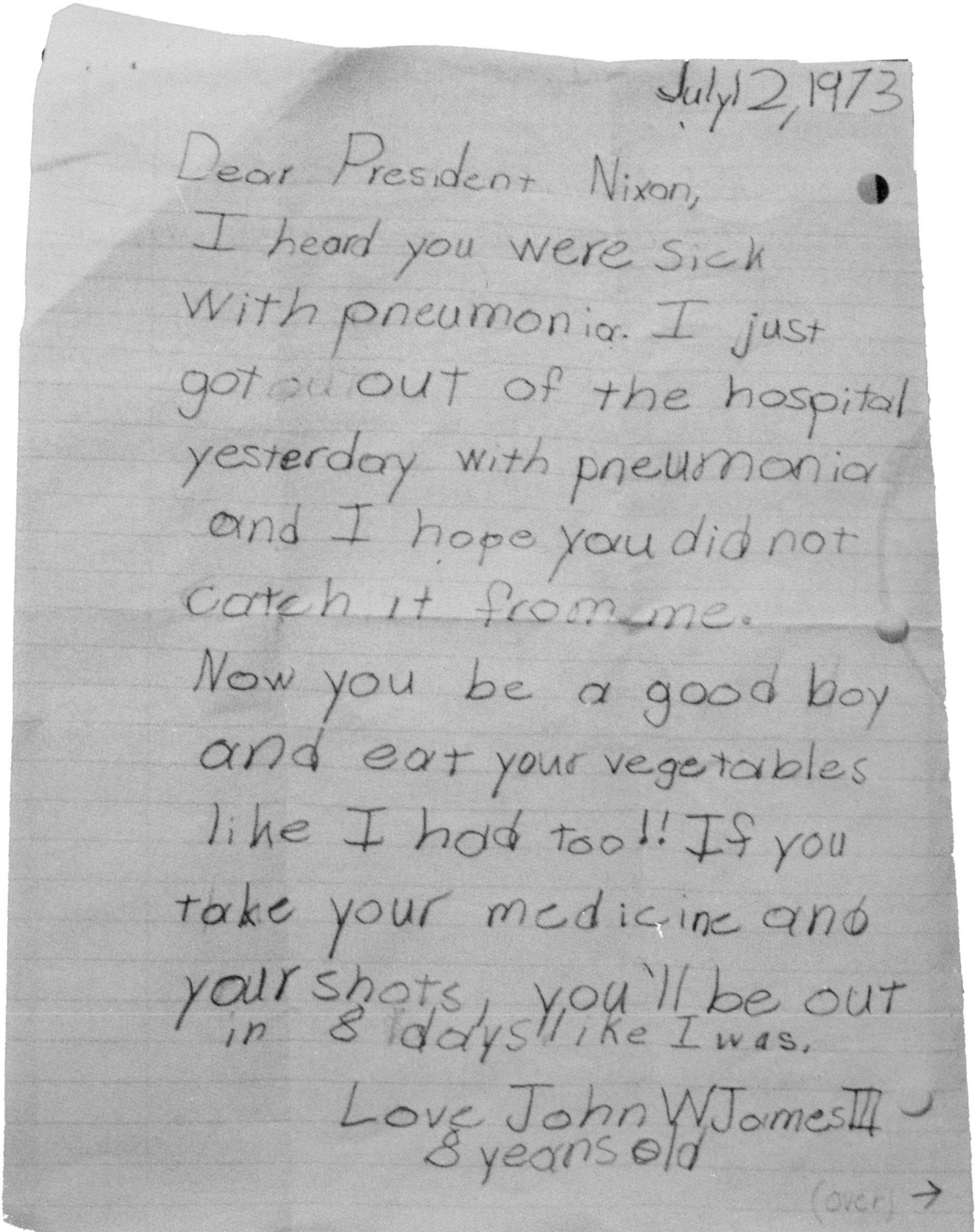

July 2, 1973

Dear President Nixon,
I heard you were sick
with pneumonia. I just
got out of the hospital
yesterday with pneumonia
and I hope you did not
catch it from me.
Now you be a good boy
and eat your vegetables
like I had too!! If you
take your medicine and
your shots, you'll be out
in 8 days like I was.
        Love John W James III
        8 years old

                    (over) →

來自史提夫·馬汀的親筆信

史提夫·馬汀（Steve Martin）
致傑瑞·卡爾森（Jerry Carlson）

一九七九年

星運看漲的名人會碰到的難題是，原本粉絲信函如細水涓流而來，最後會暴增至一整棟房子裝不下。面對這些加油支持的訊息，原本每週撥兩三小時就能應付，轉眼間回信變成一份全職工作。極少數名人奮勇迎戰，決心不辭辛勞代價，有信必回，不願拖延；但多數名人以一封制式回信附簽名應萬信，輕鬆又近人情。這種回函缺乏親近感，也讓粉絲微微感到失望，但有回信總勝過石沉大海。

長青笑將史提夫·馬汀當然走第二條路，但多虧他回信時多加一點恰到好處的幽默，仍應得不少讚賞。當年的他印好一堆制式的回信，以「來自史提夫·馬汀的親筆信」為標題，信裡留幾個空格，依照每位粉絲來信內容填寫，克漏字寫得笑點滿載。這一封信於一九七九年寄給十七歲影迷傑瑞·卡爾森，當年史提夫·馬汀的《大笨蛋》（*The Jerk*）剛上映，咸認是他最逗趣的電影之一。

山楊集團

山楊電影學會
山楊錄音學會
山楊商品
山楊演藝經紀

來自史提夫·馬汀的親筆信

親愛的傑瑞，

很高興接到你的來信。雖然我的行程排得很滿，我仍決定抽空回一封親筆信給你。

有太多演藝人員跟觀眾愈隔愈遠，不把他們當成一回事，但我認為我永遠不變成那種藝人。你認為我會嗎，<u>傑瑞</u>？我不知道未來何時會在你家附近登臺，不過你家如果有雙層床空著，請把寢具整理好，說不定哪天我會去<u>富林特市</u>（Flint）。

史提夫·馬汀敬上

P.S. 我永生珍惜我倆在里約共度的一下午，漫步在沙灘上，欣賞<u>石頭</u>。

The Aspen Companies

Aspen Film Society
Aspen Recording Society
Aspen Merchandising
Aspen Artist Management

A PERSONAL LETTER FROM STEVE MARTIN

DEAR _Jerry_,

WHAT A PLEASURE IT WAS TO RECEIVE A LETTER FROM YOU. ALTHOUGH

MY SCHEDULE IS VERY BUSY, I DECIDED TO TAKE TIME OUT TO WRITE YOU

A PERSONAL REPLY.

TOO OFTEN PERFORMERS LOSE CONTACT WITH THEIR AUDIENCE AND BEGIN

TO TAKE THEM FOR GRANTED, BUT I DON'T THINK THAT WILL EVER HAPPEN TO

ME, WILL IT _Jerry_? I DON'T KNOW WHEN I'LL BE APPEARING

CLOSE TO YOU, BUT KEEP THAT EXTRA BUNK MADE UP IN CASE I GET TO

Flint.

SINCERELY,

Steve Martin

STEVE MARTIN

P.S. I'LL ALWAYS CHERISH THAT AFTERNOON WE SPENT TOGETHER IN RIO,

WALKING ALONG THE BEACH, LOOKING AT _rocks_.

生為華人難道是一種恥辱？

瑪麗·臺普（Mary Tape）致舊金山教育董事會

一八八五年四月八日

一八八四年九月，舊金山市民喬瑟夫·臺普與妻子瑪麗做了一件看似稀鬆平常的事——帶著八歲大的女兒梅咪（Mamie）去學校辦入學手續。梅咪的朋友就讀當地的春谷（Spring Valley）小學，她也想去，可惜當時是一八八四年，梅咪雖然在美國出生，父母卻是華人移民，因此立刻被校長珍妮·赫利（Jennie Hurley）拒收。臺普夫婦氣不過，採取史無前例的行動，不顧微乎其微的勝算，一狀告上法院，最後竟然勝訴。學校董事會面對首創先河的判決，臨時變通，另闢一所學校給當地華人學童就讀，包括梅咪·臺普，進展遲緩而痛苦。

一八八五年四月，因校方繼續避重就輕，梅咪的母親寫了這封信給學校。

舊金山葛林街1769號

一八八五年四月八日

致教育董事會——

親愛的諸君：

我發現你們用盡百般借口，就是不讓我家小孩進公立學校。親愛的諸君，求求你們給我一個說法！生為華人難道是一種恥辱？我們難道不全是上帝造的嗎！！！你們憑什麼因為她是華裔就禁止她入學。除了這一點之外，我想不出還有什麼理由。我想你們星期天全去教堂做禮拜吧！強迫我家幼兒大老遠去上特製學校，你們還有臉自稱基督徒。我家小孩的穿著不像其他華人。我家小孩和華人小孩站在一起，看起來跟華人穿唐裝站在白種人之間一樣滑稽。何況，假如我想送小孩去上華人學校，我兩年前早就送去了，何苦惹這麼大的麻煩。單單為了一個小可憐蟲，你們竟然浪擲那麼多公帑。從她能爬能走開始，她的玩伴全是白人。如果她配跟他們一起玩！難道她不配跟他們坐同一間教室一同用工嗎？你們最好過來親自看一看。看看臺普家小孩是不是和其他白人家庭一樣，不同的只是長相。看來，無論華人過什麼樣的生活穿什麼樣的衣服，只要你知道他們是華人，你就一視同仁仇恨他們。他們沒有任何權利，也爭不到公道。

你們見過我丈夫和小孩。你們告訴他，你們拒絕的不是梅咪·臺普。如果你們拒絕的不是梅咪·臺普，當初怎麼不讓她就讀離家最近的學校！居然搬出接二連三的借口，硬是不讓她入學。我認為牟德先生跟八歲大的梅咪·臺普有宿怨。我知道沒有一個小孩願意上你們那間公立華人學校，沒有一個華人小孩願意！但願你牟德先生將來不會淪落到被欺壓，像小梅咪·臺普的下場一樣。梅咪·臺普絕不就讀你們蓋的那種華人學校！休想！！！種族歧視者當權，世上還有什麼公道，我打算讓世人見識。只因她是華裔，而不是因為她的服裝不像你們，她和你們穿的衣服一模一樣。只因她的生父母是華人。和你們這些不準她接受教育的多數人比較起來，我倒覺得她比較像美國人。

瑪麗·臺普夫人

O.M.G.

費雪男爵（John Arbuthnot Fisher）致丘吉爾
一九一七年九月九日

綽號賈基（Jacky）的費雪於一八五四年從軍，在英國皇家海軍服役長達六十年，功勳彪炳。十三歲的他於一八五四年進入海軍軍校，於一九〇五年達到官階巔峰，晉昇為海軍元帥，總共在四場戰爭中擔任要角。但是，他最了不起的成就其實出現在一九一七年致丘吉爾的信裡。溫斯頓·丘吉爾當時仍未當上英國首相。費雪在信中寫著目前時興、當時沒人用過的縮寫字 O.M.G.。根據牛津英語辭典，O.M.G. 在此之前從未出現在文獻上。

我親愛的溫斯頓，

　　我來這裡多待幾天，改天再去勝利之家（Victory House）與我的「智者」兄弟會合——

　　　　　　「忘卻人世煩憂，
　　　　　　　被煩世遺忘！」

　　閱報見到幾道標題，卻把我氣得直跳腳！可惡啊！
　　「德艦隊將輔助波羅的海登陸戰」
　　「德陸軍在瑞渥爾（譯註：Reval，愛沙尼亞首都舊名）以南登陸」
　　在海上，我軍比敵軍強五倍，現在殺出了一個小艦隊，幾分鐘就能被我軍生吞活剝，竟然在重大海戰中幫陸軍登陸敵軍後門，還可能從海路攻下俄羅斯首府！
　　簡直把「維持秩序」的口號變本加厲！
　　大帝國盛景，我們真的無力維護？
　　難道又要成立一個以 O 起頭的動爵團嗎？我聽說國會正審議中，團名正是 O.M.G.（哇！我的天！）——讓榮光照耀海軍本部吧！

　　　　　　　　　　　　　　　　　　費雪敬上
　　　　　　　　　　　　　　　　　　9/9/17

P.S. 作戰要講究「**出奇制勝**」。想「**出奇制勝**」，要靠「**想像力**」和「**勇往直前**」配對共枕。

唯有成年人會惶恐

娥蘇拉・諾斯崇（Ursula Nordstrom）致某小學圖書館員
一九七二年一月五日

童書繪本作家莫里斯・桑達克（Maurice Sendak）獲獎無數，著作包括精彩的《野獸國》（*Where the Wild Things Are*）。他在一九七〇年發表《廚房之夜狂想曲》（*In the Night Kitchen*）時掀起軒然大波，原因是名為米奇（Mickey）的幼童主角幾度裸身見讀者。部分家長與圖書館員不願視若無睹，為米奇畫上尿布遮羞，更有人為了省事，乾脆燒掉整本書，免得敗壞風俗。該書出版兩年後，抵制風潮愈演愈烈，作者的優秀編輯娥蘇拉・諾斯崇看不下去了，寫信給焚書的圖書館。

親愛的（刪）：

　　你的信寄到本社位於賓州斯官頓的部門，輾轉才送來我桌上，很抱歉現在才回覆你針對桑達克《廚房之夜狂想曲》的感想。

　　聽說你在一九七二年燒掉一本書，我心實在感嘆。我們真正感嘆的是，你居然認為那本書不適合小學生閱讀。我猜，令你感冒的是書中小男童赤身裸體吧。其實說真的，兒童才不會為了裸體而傷神！桑達克先生是文創藝術工作者，是不折不扣的天才，作品能講進兒童的心坎。兒童——至少是十二、三歲以下的兒童——通常本身創意滿點。你我成年人懷抱偏見和神經質，對這類圖書的感想最好留在心裡，不應對兒童灌輸，以免妨礙文創藝術者和兒童讀者之間的交流，成人干預時應格外審慎，不是嗎？我身為童書編輯兼發行人，職責很多，這是最重大、最艱苦的職責之一。相信我，我們絕不怠忽職守！我認為，幼童讀到《廚房之夜狂想曲》，反應永遠是喜悅，也會激發他們的創意和健全心態。只有成年人會對桑達克的作品感到惶恐。

　　近日我將寄幾則本書引發的佳評給你，希望你過目，也盼你能給貴校學生閱讀桑達克先生作品的機會。

（簽名）

敬上

哼，被我一分，
就分到底了

雷蒙‧錢德勒（Raymond
Chandler）致艾德華‧衛克斯
（Edward Weeks）
一九四七年一月十八日

在一九四七年一月，知名小說家雷
蒙‧錢德勒致函《大西洋月刊》編
輯艾德華‧衛克斯，主要是討論一
篇投稿──稿子翌年獲刊載，標
題是「好萊塢奧斯卡之夜」（Oscar
Night in Hollywood），但這封信鞭
闢入裡的部分在後半，其中一句後
來成為錢德勒最為人津津樂道的名
言之一。作者請編輯將信的內容傳
達給社內審稿人，編輯代轉後，名
為瑪嘉烈‧莫奇（Margaret Mutch）
的審稿人回信給作者，作者則以一
篇妙趣橫生的打油詩回應，由本書
收錄在此信之後。

加州拉荷亞市
沿海公路六○○五號
一九四七年一月十八日

親愛的衛克斯先生：

　　你把我搞糊塗了。我以為「好萊塢的鬼神崇拜」這標題棒透
了，怎麼也看不出為何要跟刑案推理扯在一起。不過，畢竟你是
老大。我書寫文人的時候，你並沒有想到這一點。我考慮過的標
題很多，例如「好萊塢的銀行夜」、「蘇特（Sutter）的堅守」、
「黃金偷窺秀」、「只缺大象」、「贓物讓步賽」、「輕歌舞喜劇所
到之處必死」，諸如此類的爛標題。可惜，沒有一種能討你歡
心。對了，有勞你代我問候你那崇尚文法的審稿人，告訴他或
她，我的筆法有點像胡拼亂湊的土語，類似瑞士服務生的措辭，
而且我用分離不定式（譯註：to和原形動詞之間加副詞，例如to slowly write，計較
文法的人會改成to write slowly）的時候，哼，不定式被我一分，就分到底
了，休想再合體。請轉告審稿人，我的東西寫得文謅謅時，若我
在滑順如絨布的行文突然穿插幾句酒吧粗話，我並非瞇著眼亂
寫，我神智雖鬆懈卻不至於失神。這種寫法並非十全十美，卻是
我使出渾身解數的寫法。我認為你的審稿人好心想攙扶我站穩，
儘管我感激這份熱忱，其實，只要馬路和兩旁人行道都讓給我
走，我真的有辦法不撞到別人。

　　我想到其他東西時再發電報給你。

　　　　　　　　肺腑敬意
　　　　　　　　（簽名）

致不分不定式之女

瑪嘉烈·莫奇小姐舉杖
以波士頓腔咆哮，
戳吾眼嘶吼道，
「汝為耶魯高才生，文法詒人笑。」

「汝為普林斯頓高才生，關係子句最傷我眼！
汝為哈佛高才生，
再高尚的幼蟲也不吃你的語癌。

公立小學老師教你勿流口水
（P和S照規定大寫），
你唾液照流，shall、will不分，
如今面目可憎！」

她蠻吼一聲，戳他一眼，
他痛得哀嚎，遭她揶揄。
他抱傷逃逸波士頓公園。
養病數週，投靠衛克斯療癒。

「親愛的莫奇小姐勿舉杖，
且饒新義眼珠！
學府再高
也教不動me、I不分之蠢豬

文法再重
也砸不醒才疏學淺之輩。
To加原形動詞，出自我手
副詞動不動插隊。

本人文筆至為拙劣
因我習作之地為酒吧。
側車調酒杯杯灌，
言不及義請笑納。

拙作多處極粗俗，
因吾家無待嫁小姑。
親愛的莫奇小姐，且放尊手，勿再緊抓韋氏西裝褲！

待詩人安息之日，
文法師將傳授吟唱之術。
金科玉律明晰，我認同，
但文法為何物？

葬儀社薄暮悠悠，
蒼蒼殯儀師彎腰頷首。
文法寫在重寫本上最合適，
或刻印捕鯨艇之船頭？

難道文法如針織
由端坐愛椅之祖母縫紉？
難道文法如暴徒就義
傾灑於碎木之血痕？

親愛的莫奇小姐，放下手杖，且讓妳我開瓶酒敘。
如我之鄙人，今生不為亞里斯多德捐軀。

小而美的註腳死不足惜，
我將以磨光利刃，
且讓妳我歡慶，
我將宰分不定式，由喉至跟。

分號改打卻不打，
逗號閒置，任其枯褸。
任撇號如太妃糖延展，
再以句號終結全句。

與＆號攜手同行乎
從容不迫，
有適位星號發微光
徹夜漫遊。

馨夜心雀躍，
妳我杯觥交織，
以淺笑迎戰
虛懸分詞！」

她蹙眉瞪人，
被他的詞形變化氣得發抖。
他倏然驚恐，臉色唰白
句法更形怯弱優柔。

「親愛的莫奇小姐，放下手杖！」
腦海空白的他驚嘶。

她冷漠以對，獻上墓誌銘：
印刷廠之訛誤長眠於此。

我等你

木村重成之妻致木村
一六一五年

江戶時代武士木村重成年方二十
二，幾月前才率兵在今福之役大
勝，號稱「舉國無雙英雄」，此時
再次整軍，即將出兵圍攻大阪城。
儘管木村自信滿滿，其妻深知我軍
寡不敵眾，因此決定先走一步，以
此信向英勇的丈夫訣別。不出所
料，木村在戰場上壯烈成仁，並遭
斬首，而妻子早已踏上絕路。

有道是兩旅人同在一樹下避雨，共飲一江解渴，緣全由前世註
定。這些年來，你我夫妻共枕，本可白頭偕老，而我也委身於
你，如影隨形。我如此相信，亦認你也有同感。

但如今，我得知你已決心赴最後一役，縱使我無法與你共度輝煌
時刻，我仍能銘感喜悅。據說，中國名將項羽於最後一役前夕，
驍勇善戰的他為離開虞姬而無限哀痛。而在我國，向夫人告辭的
木曾義仲將軍亦有濃濃愁緒。如今我已斷念，結髮無能共度餘
生，念及古人之例，我已決心趁你揮軍時踏上絕途，願在黃泉路
盡頭等你。

秀賴當主多年來賜予之恩德如山高海深，我倆皆應萬世謹記。

九六年十月二十一

謬思女神非馬也

**尼克‧凱夫（Nick Cave）致
MTV頻道**
一九九六年十月二十一日

尼克‧凱夫與壞種籽（Bad Seeds）
樂團第九張專輯在一九九六年發行
時，獲得各界樂評讚譽，銷售量也
高於前幾張。《謀殺歌謠》（*Murder
Ballads*）專輯的樂風空靈淒美，時
而令人膽寒，不僅大受歡迎，也榮
獲MTV獎最佳男歌手提名，令凱
夫格外不自在，因此他在同年十月
以妙筆寫了這封信，令主辦單位不
知如何是好。

致MTV全體人員，

首先，我想感謝各位近年來對我的支持。獲得最佳男歌手提名，
我既感恩也受寵若驚。最新專輯《謀殺歌謠》裡收錄我與凱莉‧
米洛、P. J.哈維的二重唱獲得貴頻道播放，我也銘感在心，因此
再次在此誠摯感謝各位。

話雖這麼說，我必須請求各位撤銷我的提名，今後的提名與獎項
也敬請頒發給其他人。頒獎典禮具有競爭性，別人或許較能泰然
自若以對，但我不然。我總認為，我的音樂獨一無二，個體性很
強。有人喜歡把事物化簡為量度，但我的音樂自外於這種範疇。
我與世無爭。

即使在最密切的時刻，我和謬思女神的關係也吹彈即破。我認為
我的職責是保護她，讓本性脆弱的她免受外界侵擾。

她捧著歌曲登門送我，我理應以她應得的尊重回報，換言之，我
不應強迫她面對評判與競賽的負面效應。我的謬思女神並非一匹
馬，而我也非賽馬騎師。假使她真是一匹馬，我也不會逼她拉送
一輛血淋淋的死囚馬車——裡面裝滿斷頭和亮晶晶的獎座——因
為她可能受驚！可能被嚇跑！可能拋棄我，一去不回頭！

因此，我再次感激MTV諸君對本專輯傾心厚愛，我真心在此說
聲謝謝你們，並且再說一次：心領了⋯⋯謝謝你們。

尼克‧凱夫敬上

我們的法蘭克

康乃爾（Connell）家致齊伍拉（Ciulla）家

一九九二年

一九八八年十二月二十一日晚間，泛美航空前往紐約的一○三號班機因炸彈爆炸而粉碎，殘骸如雨灑落在蘇格蘭小鎮洛克比（Lockerbie），乘客加機組人員共兩百五十九人，全數罹難，地面居民十一人也喪生。乘客之一是四十五歲的法蘭克・齊伍拉，搭上該班機返鄉，想和紐澤西州的妻子與三名子女共度耶誕節。康乃爾夫婦瑪格瑞和修（Margaret and Hugh）在沃特貝克（Waterbeck）鎮有一座小農場，距離墜機地將近八英哩，夫婦卻在自家農場尋獲法蘭克的大體。

事隔將近四年，齊伍拉家終於鼓起勇氣前往蘇格蘭，拜訪民斯卡（Minsca）農莊，與康乃爾家相處，認識至親法蘭克長眠的安寧地，遠離混亂的洛克比墜機現場。得知噩耗至今，齊伍拉家壓著許多問題迫切想問，如今終於能一吐為快。拜訪完回美國後，齊伍拉家收到康乃爾夫婦捎來的一封用心至深的信。悲劇屆滿七年，洛克比紀念碑在阿靈頓（Arlington）落成時，這封信在儀式中當眾朗讀。兩家人至今仍往來密切。

我親愛的路易、瑪麗露和家人，

我幾乎不敢相信我正寫信給你們。這是我自一九八八年十二月二十一日以來一直渴望做的事。當你們的至親從夜空降臨我家時，我們驚恐不敢置信，內心更是哀悽悲愴。你們說過，能親赴現場，心境因此大為改觀，而我們也有相同的感觸。法蘭克原本是一個空有姓名的人，和其他人毫無關聯。如今，我們終於能將他擺進一個溫馨的家庭裡。事發後和相見之間，我有時會停下手邊的事，不禁想到，「他的親人現在能否節哀，近況如何？」

有人告訴我們，部分家屬可能永遠不會來。我們也擔心，你們即使來蘇格蘭，也不會想聯絡我們。但你們終究來了，也問了你們一直想問的所有問題。你們終於找到一個能填充那最後幾小時解答，拼對了總是擺不對位子的那塊拼圖。最能引發困惑和苦楚的是「不知」。人的想像力無窮盡，能在你我的腦海裡作怪。我相信，各位的心靈必定飽受許多難言的悽苦和憂慮。

能和你們當面相識是美事一樁。我們也有和各位相談的必要。誠如你們所言，我們將能透過你家認識法蘭克。對我們而言，他從來不僅僅是「死者之一」。頭幾個月，我們以「我們的男孩」稱呼他，後來得知他姓名，我們才改喚「我們的法蘭克」。請相信我，他的來訪影響我們至深。見到英俊完整的他躺在那裡，見到生命在轉瞬間飄逝，當時的心情，我們永生難忘。我們才剛渡過難以接受的階段。

當時我們只能把他留在原地，徹夜有警方和醫師前來檢視，隔天早上，我們才再回去現場。他是血肉之軀，在最令人沉痛的情況下前來我們家。如今，藉由他的引介，各位常在我們心中。今後如果你們想來，我們隨時歡迎，請各位務必知道這一點。

康乃爾家

我不怕機器人，怕的是真人

雷・布萊伯利（**Ray Bradbury**）
致布萊恩・希布利（**Brian Sibley**）
一九七四年六月十日

一九七四年，英國作家布萊恩・希布利寫信給他最愛的科幻小說家雷・布萊伯利。布萊伯利最為人稱道的作品是《華氏 451 度》（*Fahrenheit 451*）。希布利藉信誠摯仰慕布萊伯利作品，熱切關注迪士尼的他也向布萊伯利請教幾個關於迪士尼的問題。

「如果我沒記錯，」希布利解釋，「我曾針對迪士尼樂園裡的語音機器人（Audio-Animatronic）表達疑慮。在當時，我仍未參觀過迪士尼主題樂園，或許讀了太多科幻小說──其中當然少不了布萊伯利的大作──唯恐真人世界被機器人佔領，也將機器人視為有害無益的實驗。然而，見識淺薄的偏見被辭藻大師破解，是多麼暢快的事啊。他竟能撥冗點燃破解偏見的引信，是多麼美妙的事，而引爆後的餘波竟是長達三十餘年的友誼，可謂是蔚為奇蹟！」

布萊伯利回信確實寫得精妙，內容的質量與用心皆屬上乘，而且在後記裡，他以布萊伯利體，藉詩意優雅的文句，質疑希布利為何畏懼機器人。

親愛的布萊恩・希布利：

抱歉，這封信只能短不能長，因為我忙著寫劇本《闇夜嘉年華》（*Something Wicked This Way Comes*），而且沒有祕書，更從來沒請過祕書：所以，信全由我自己寫：一星期兩百封！！！

迪士尼先生是個夢想家和實踐者：早在世人空談著未來，他就已經著手打造。他藉迪士尼樂園教我們市街規劃、群眾動線、舒適度、人性等等，勢必影響下一世紀的建築業者、建築師、都市計劃人。由於他，我們必能讓都市人性化，將小鎮規劃得讓大家和以往一樣更親近，使得民主的運作更具創意，因為我們將**熟識**候選人。他超前時代之多，我們再過五十年才有希望追上。你**一定**要來迪士尼樂園參觀，一看就能收回成見，嚥下疑慮。現代社會裡多數建築師非混帳即笨蛋，罵完老大哥政權，回頭卻建造監獄，把我們全關進去：以這種現代環境來窒息、摧毀我們。被貼保守派標籤的迪士尼，反而成了高瞻遠矚、積極建樹的偉人。

夠了。你快來吧。我想把你拋進「叢林河舟」上，用火車載你前進明日、昨日、更遙遠的時空。

祝你好運，不要再隔空評判事物了。你還不夠格。迪士尼生前充滿謬誤矛盾，但他也活力滿檔、美與灼見兼俱。這些描述語，不也能涵蓋我們所有人嗎？我們全是光影形成的謎團。世上沒有徹底的保守派、自由派等等。世上只有人。

　　　　　　　　　　　　　　　　　　雷・布萊伯利敬上

P.S. 我針對迪士尼寫過一封信，被刊在雜誌裡，忘記是《國家》或《新共和》了，找不到就是找不到。重點是，我說如果布萊船長覺得迪士尼樂園已經很不錯了，那我也有同感。我第一次去迪士尼樂園玩，是查爾斯・洛頓夫妻帶我去的，最先玩的就是叢林河舟，洛頓兩三下就懂得操作，忙著嘲笑身邊其他船上的遊客！我玩鬧得不亦樂乎。以這種方式開始和迪士尼樂園交往，多麼暢快！RB

P.S. 你怕迪士尼機器人，我忍不住想囉唆幾句。碰到書，你怎麼不怕呢？其實自古至今，恐書的人多的是。書是人的衍生物，而非人類本身。任何機械，任何機器人，端賴你我如何使用它。自動攝像的器材何其多，而這種器材裡具備的複製功能何其多，例如電影院裡的投影機，你為什麼不去打倒它們？電影投影機是一臺不具人形的機器人，能重述人類灌入的事實。它不具備人性嗎？不具備。它常能投射人性現實真理，能把我們演得更有人性嗎？能。

有些書濫不卒睹，所以該燒掉所有書，這種歪理或許說得通。

駕駛開車肇事，所以所有的車子都該被搗毀。

有些電影是爛片，浪費時間，所以應該燒掉所有戲院。

最後談到你說你怕的機器人。何苦怕東怕西呢？為何不化懼怕為創意？為何不把機器人設計成老師，教一些**人人**都覺得索然無味的科目？為何不設計一臺柏拉圖機器人，坐進希臘文的課堂，盡情回答關於《理想國》的問題？我倒有興趣往這方向實驗。我不怕機器人。我怕的是人，人，人。我要人類保持人性。我能借重書籍、電影、機器人以及我的手腦和心，來幫助人類保持人性。

我怕天主教徒殺害新教徒，反之亦怕。

我怕白人殺害黑人，反之亦怕。

我怕英國人殺害愛爾蘭人，反之亦怕。

我怕年輕人殺害老人，反之亦怕。

我怕共產黨員殺害資本主義分子，反之亦怕。

怕不怕機器人呢？天啊，愛都來不及了。我能秉持人性善用它們，為它們灌輸以上理念。它們的嘴傳達的是我的心聲，語音將動聽得不得了。

RB 敬上

RAY BRADBURY
AUTHOR
CHARLES ROME SMITH
DIRECTOR
JOSEPH STECK
PRODUCER
MICHAEL SHERE
SCENIC AND LIGHTING DIRECTOR
MARK S. KRAUSE
PRODUCTION STAGE MANAGER
PHIL N. LATTIN
ASSOCIATE PRODUCER
PETER LYNCH
ASSISTANT PRODUCER
DONALD C. MITCHELL
PROMOTION
JOE MUGNAINI
ART DESIGNER
ROBERT CABEEN
ART DESIGN ASSISTANT
DOUG TRUMBELL
DESIGN CONSULTANT
KAREN ARTHUR
ASSISTANT TO THE DIRECTOR
MARION CLINE
ADMINISTRATIVE ASSISTANT
TRI-ARTS INC.
GRAPHICS
SAMUEL GOLDWYN PRODUCTIONS

P.O. Box 2099
Hollywood Station
Los Angeles, CA 90028
(213) 851-2099

JUNE
10, 1974

Dear Brian Sibley:

This will have to be short. Sorry. But I am deep into my screenplay
on SOMETHING WICKED THIS WAY COMES and have no secretary, never have
had one..so must write all my own letters..200 a week1!!!

Disney was a dreamer and a doer..while the rest of us were talking
ab out the future, he built it. The things he taught us at
Disneyland about street planning, crowd movement, comfort, humanity, etc,
will influence builders, architects, urban planners for the next
century. Because of him we will humanize our cities, plan small towns
again where we can get in touch with one another again and make
democracy work creatively because we will KNOW the people we vote for.
He was so far ahead of his time it will take us the next 50 years
to catch up. You MUST come to Disneyland and eat -your words, swallow
your doubts. Most of the other architects of the ;modern world were
asses and fools who talked against Big Brother and then built
prisons to put ;us all in..our modern environments which stifle
and destroy us. Disney the so-called conservative turns out to
be Disney the great man of foresight and construction.

Enough. Come here soon. I'll toss you in the Jungle Ride River
and ride you on the train into tomorrow, yesterday, and beyond.

Good luck, and stop judging at such a great distance. You are kkkk-
simply not qualified. Disney was full of errors, paradoxes, mistakes.
He was also full of life, beauty, insight. Which speaks for all of
us, eh? We are all mysteries of light and d-ark. There are
no true ;conservatives, liberals, etc, in the world. Only people.

Best,

    P.S. I can't find that issue of THE NATION, or the NEW REPUBLIC, which ever
it was, with my letter in it on Disney. Mainly I said that if Disneyland was
good enough for Captain Bligh it was good enough for me. Charles Laughton
and his wife took me to Disneyland for my very first visit and our first
ride was the Jungle Boat Ride, which Laughton immediately commandeered,
jeering at customers going by in other boats! A fantastic romp for me and
a hilarious day. What a way to start my assocation with Disneyland! R.B.

Pandemonium II Productions

P.S. Can't resist commenting on your fears of the Disney robots. Why aren't you afraid of books, then? The fact is, of course, that people have been afraid of books, down through history. They are extensions of people, not people themselves. Any machine, any robot, is the sum total of the ways we use it. Why not kknock down all robot camera devices and the means for reproducing the stuff that goes into such devices, things called projectors in theatres? A motion picture projector is a non-humanoid robot which repeats truths which we inject into it. Is it inhuman? Yes. Does it project human truths to humanize us more often than not? Yes.

The excuse could be made that we should burn all books because some books are dreadful.

We should mash all cars because some cars get in accidents. because of the people driving them.

We should burn down all the theatres in the world because some films are trash, drivel.

So it is finally with the robots you say you fear. Why fear something? Why not create with it? Why not build robot teachers to help out in schools where teaching certain subjects is a bore for EVERYONE? Why not have Plato sitting in your Greek Class answering jolly questions about his Republic? I would love to experiment with that. I am not afraid of robots. I am afraid of people, people, people. I want them to remain human. I can help keep them human with the wise and lovely use of books, films, robots, and my own mind, hands, and heart.

I am afraid of Catholics killing Protestants and vice versa.

I am afraid of whites killing blacks and vice versa.

I am afraid of English killing Irish and vice versa.

I am afraid of young killing old and vice versa.

I am afraid of Communists killing Capitalists and vice versa.

But...robots? God, I love them. I will use them humanely to teach all of the above. My vo-ice will speak out of them, and it will be a damned nice voice.

Best, R.B.

起而行

索羅・勒維特（Sol LeWitt）致
依娃・赫斯（Eva Hesse）
一九六五年，四月十四日

一九六〇年，走在時代尖端的美國藝術家索羅・勒維特認識了依娃・赫斯，兩人一拍即合，迅速培養出深厚情誼，延續長達十年，期間討論無數話題，意見交流豐富，深具啟發意義。的確，直到一九七〇年五月，兩人維持密切無間的友誼。後來依娃罹患腦癌，悵然離世，得年僅三十四歲。

一九六五年，友誼之路走到一半時，依娃面臨創意瓶頸，走不出缺乏自信的死胡同，因此向索羅傾吐。幾星期後，勒維特以這份藝術品回覆。這封忠言信寫得精闢，直如無價之寶，後來被全球藝術工作者傳頌，更被貼在世界各地畫室成為座右銘。

親愛的依娃，

　　離妳上次寫信給我，已過將近一個月了，妳大概忘了當時的心境（但我很懷疑）。妳似乎和往常一樣，恨透了妳自身一切。千萬不要！學著偶爾罵全世界「去你的」。權利握在妳手裡。不要再思考、擔憂、緊張回頭望、納悶、懷疑、恐懼、心痛、期盼輕鬆解脫的機會、掙扎、抓著最後一根稻草、迷惑、心癢、抓癢、嘟噥、結巴、發牢騷、喪氣、踉蹌、麻木囉唆、胡言亂語、亂賭一通、跌跌撞撞、畫柔和線條、亂畫線條、亂扯話題、亂畫影線、碎碎念、唉聲嘆氣、呻吟、抱怨、糾纏、鬼扯屁、挑剔、雞蛋裡挑石頭、灑尿滴尿、愛管閒事、摳屁眼、戳眼珠、指責別人、躲暗巷、漫長等候、不敢邁大步、毒眼瞪人、搔背、搜尋、徘徊、污損、蹉跎、蹉跎、蹉跎自己的青春。停下來，

起而行

　　從妳的描述，從我對妳以前作品和妳的能力得知，妳正在創作的東西聽起來非常好「畫畫——清爽——素淨卻瘋狂如機器，更大也更大膽……不折不扣的亂來。」聽起來的確是優質、美好——不折不扣的亂來。多做一點這種事。更加無俚頭，更瘋狂，更多機器，更多胸部，更多陰莖，陰戶，隨便什麼都行——讓它們洋溢著無俚頭。盡量刺激妳內心，激發妳的「怪幽默」。妳內心最私密的地方才是妳的歸屬。別擔心酷不酷，儘管做一些不酷的東西。創造妳個人專屬的東西，妳專屬的世界。如果妳恐懼，讓恐懼推妳一把——素描彩繪出妳的恐懼和焦慮。不要再煩惱一些深重的大事，例如「決定人生目標和方針，以貫徹一致的心態追求不可能的理想，甚至追求憑空捏造的理想。」妳務必多多練習傻勁、愚昧、無思想、放空心靈。然後妳才有辦法

Dear Eva,   April 14

It will be almost a month since you wrote to me and you have possibly forgotten your state of mind (I doubt it though). You seem the same as always, and being you, hate every minute of it. Don't! Learn to say "Fuck you" to the world once in a while. You have every right to. Just stop thinking, worrying, looking over your shoulder wondering, doubting, fearing, hurting, hoping for some easy wayout, struggling, grasping, confusing, itching, scratching, mumbling, bumbling, grumbling, humbling, stumbling, numbling, rambling, gambling, tumbling, scumbling, scrambling, hitching, hatching, bitching, moaning, groaning, honing, boning, horse-shitting, hair-splitting, nit-picking, piss-trickling, nose sticking, ass-gouging, eyeball-poking, finger-pointing, alleyway-sneaking, long waiting, small stepping, evil-eyeing, back-scratching, searching, perching, besmirching, grinding, grinding, grinding away at yourself. Stop it and just

DO

起而行

即使在妳自我折磨的當兒，我仍對妳有信心，看重妳的作品。盡量做一些**爛**作——盡量爛到底，看看結果如何，但最主要還是放輕鬆，讓天下大亂——妳無須把世界扛在肩膀上——妳只需對妳的作品負責——所以，**起而行**吧。

別認為妳的作品必須從俗，不必符合既有的形式、構想或風格。妳可以隨心所欲創作。反過來說，假如說停止創作，對妳比較輕鬆——那就停止創作吧。不要懲罰自己。然而，我認為，妳根深蒂固的觀念是

起而行

我大概能稍微認同妳的態度，因為我偶爾也會經歷類似的階段，會「忍痛再三評估」自己作品，能改的地方全部修改——然後恨自己改過的一切，盡量改進，做一些截然不同的東西。也許這種階段對我有必要，能鞭策我不停向前走，自覺我能改進我剛做的爛東西。也許妳需要苦悶，才能完成妳的作品。也許苦悶能誘導妳進步。但這種過程非常痛，我很清楚。比較好的做法是，妳擁有「做了再說」的自信，連想都不用想就做。難道妳無法拋開「外界」和「**藝術**」的束縛，無法戒除自我驕縱的自大心嗎？我知道，妳（或任何人）不可能全天候創作，一有空閒會胡思亂想。但在妳創作時或創作之前，妳一定要讓腦袋淨空，專注於眼前的正事。做了一件事之後就算了，不要回頭計較。過一陣子，妳就看得出，有些作品比較好，但妳也能察覺自己的走向。我相信這些道理妳全懂。妳也必須知道，妳不必為自己的作品辯白——甚至不必為了作品而跟自己吵嘴。妳知道我非常仰慕妳的作品，無法理解妳為何對它們心存疙瘩。然而，妳看得出接下來的作品，我看不出。妳也非相信自己的能力不可。我認為妳有這份自信。所以，嘗試一些妳認為最狂妄的東西——震撼自己一下。自由發揮的權力握在妳手裡。

我想觀摩妳的作品，但也只能乖乖等到八九月再說。在露西那裡，我見到幾張湯姆新作的相片，非常亮眼——特別是形式較嚴謹的那幾個，比較簡單的那幾個。我猜他以後會再寄一些。藝展情況之類的東西記得告訴我。

妳走後，我的作品變了，比以前好多了。我將在五月四日到二十九日辦展，地點是東六十四街十七號的丹尼爾斯藝廊（艾默瑞奇那裡），希望妳也能來。祝福你倆。

索羅

From you description, and from what (2)
I know of your previous work and
you ability, the works you are doing
sounds very good. "Drawings – clean – clear
but crazy like machines, larger, bolder... –
real nonsense." That sounds fine,
wonderful – real nonsense. Do more.
more nonsensical, more crazy, more
machines, more breasts, penises, cunts,
whatever – make them abound with
nonsense. Try and tickle something
inside you, your "weird humor". You
belong in the most secret part of you.
Don't worry about cool, make your
own uncool. Make your own, your own
world. If you fear, make it work
for you – draw + paint your fear + anxiety.
And stop worrying about big, deep things
such as "to decide on a purpose and
way of life, a consistant approach to
even some impossible end or even an
imagined end." You must practice being
stupid, dumb, unthinking, empty. Then
you will be able to

DO

I have much confidence in you and ③
even though you are tormenting yourself the work you do is very good. Try
to do some BAD work - the worst you
can think of and see what happens but
mainly relax and let everything go to
hell - you are not responsible for the
world - you are only responsible for
your work - so DO IT. And don't think
that your work has to conform to any
preconceived form, idea or flavor. It
can be anything you want it to be. But
if life would be easier for you if you
stopped working - then stop. Don't punish
yourself. However, I think that it is so
deeply engrained in you that it would
be easier to

DO

It seems I do understand your attitude ①
somewhat, anyway, because I go through
a similar process every so often. I have
an "Agonizing Reappraisal" of my work and change
everything as much as possible—and hate
everything I've done, and try to do something
entirely different and better. Maybe that kind
of process is neccessary to me, pushing me
on and on. The feeling that I can do better
than that shit I just did. Maybe you need
your agony to accomplish what you do.
And maybe it goads you on to do better.
But it is very painful I know. It would
be better if you had the confidence just to
do the stuff and not even think about
it. Can't you leave the "world" and "ART" alone
and also quit fondling your ego. I know
that you (or anyone) can only work so much
And the rest of the time you are left with
your thoughts. But when you work or
before you work you have to empty
your mind and concentrate on what you
are doing. After you do something it is
done and that's that. After a while you
can see some are better than others but
also you can see what direction you are

going. I'm sure you know all that. ⑤
You also must know that you don't have
to justify your work — not even to yourself.
Well you know I admire your work greatly
and can't understand why you are so bothered
by it. But you can see the next ones & I can't.
You also must believe in your ability. I think
you do. So try the most outrageous things you
can — shock yourself. You have at your power
the ability to do anything.

I would like to see your work
and will have to be content to wait until
Aug or Sept. I have seen photos of some of Tom's
new things at Lucy's. They are very
impressive — especially the ones with
the more rigorous form; the simpler
ones. I guess he'll send some more
later on. Let me know how the
shows are going and that kind of
stuff.

My work has changed since you
left and it is much better. I will
be having a show May 4-29 at the Daniels
gallery 17 E 64th St (where Emmerich was). I wish
you could be there. Much Love to you both
Sol

你剛說什麼？
我沒聽見……

凱瑟琳‧赫本（Katharine
Hepburn）致亡夫史賓塞‧崔西
（Spencer Tracy）
一九八五年前後

一九六七年六月十日，史賓塞‧崔
西心臟病發作，在家中猝逝，同居
人是曾多次榮獲奧斯卡最佳女主角
的凱瑟琳‧赫本。崔西自己也曾九
度獲得奧斯卡最佳男主角提名，演
藝生涯璀璨。兩人同居二十六年，
過程坎坷，尤其是因為崔西一直
未離婚，兩人的關係大半生潛伏地
下。崔西去世後大約十八年，赫本
寫信給他。

親愛的史賓塞，

我居然會寫信給你，誰想得到呢？你早在一九六七年六月十
日過世了。天啊，史賓塞，十八年了。好漫長。你終於快樂了
嗎？是不是終於能好好睡個飽了呢？長年輾轉難眠，終於能一次
補齊了吧？你知道嗎，你說你睡不著，我始終不相信。我以為，
唉，少來了，你怎可能沒睡？人不睡會死的。一定會累壞。接著
我想起那一夜——唉，我記不清楚了——你的心情很不安定。我
說，還是上床吧——去睡覺。我就躺地上，講話給你聽，一直講
一直講，讓你聽到無聊，最後保證你慢慢睡著。

所以呢，我進臥房，拿來一個舊枕頭，叫老狗洛波過來。我
躺著看你撫摸老狗。我講著你的事，提到我們剛殺青的電影——
《誰來晚餐？》——講到我的電影公司、你的新花呢西裝、花園
等等的催眠話題，也提烹飪、無聊閒言，但你還是翻來覆去，一
下子躺左邊，一下子躺右邊，枕頭換不停，拉扯著被單，停不
住。終於——真的是到最後了——不只是當時——你安靜下來。
我等一陣子，然後溜出臥房。

你講的真是實話，對不對？你是真的睡不著。

我那時候常納悶——為什麼？我現在還想不透。你服藥。藥
性相當強。我猜你會說，不然根本完全睡不著。對你而言，活著
並不容易，對不對？

你以前有什麼嗜好？你熱愛帆船，特別是狂風暴雨的時候。
你熱愛馬球。可惜後來威爾‧羅傑斯墜機罹難，你再也不打馬球
了，一次也沒有。網球、高爾夫球呢？你不太熱衷，打幾次而
已，身手平平。你好像從未呼過高爾夫球桿。「呼」的用法對
嗎？游泳呢？呃，你不喜歡冷水。散步呢？不合你胃口。做有些
活動時，你可以同時想東想西，散步就屬於這種活動。史賓，你
想什麼東西呢？想著人生當中特定的事物嗎？例如強尼耳聾，或
是身為天主教徒的你自覺不夠虔誠？找不到慰藉，找不到慰藉。
我記得西科里克神父對你說，你淨想著宗教帶給你的壞處，完全
不往好的一面去想。你想的一定是非常基本、怎麼揮也揮不去的

東西。

　　另外就是一個不可思議的事實。你真的是最成功的電影演員。我這麼說，是因為我相信如此，而且我也聽過這一行的重量級人物如此稱讚你，從奧力佛到李‧斯特拉斯伯格到大衛‧連，不勝枚舉。再難的事，你都辦得到，而且做得直截了當，簡潔俐落：想做就做得到。你無法進入自己的世界，卻能搖身一變，成為別人。你能扮演凶手、牧師、釣客、體育記者、法官、報社從業人員，瞬間變身。

　　你幾乎不必事先做功課，臺詞一下子就背起來。你能暫時變成別人，心情多輕鬆啊！你不是你──你安全了。你愛笑，對不對？你不願錯過單人脫口秀諧星：吉米‧杜蘭特、菲爾‧西爾沃斯、範妮‧普萊斯、弗蘭克‧麥休、米基‧隆尼、傑克‧班尼、伯恩斯與艾倫、史密斯與戴爾，以及你最喜歡的伯特‧威廉斯。你能講趣聞，講得精彩。你能自我嘲笑。你非常重視友誼，仰慕坎寧斯、法蘭克‧辛納屈、伯基與貝蒂、喬治‧庫寇爾、維克‧弗蘭明、史丹利‧克雷姆、甘迺迪夫婦、杜魯門、魯‧道格拉斯等朋友。和他們在一起時，你很風趣，也玩得開心，覺得安全自在。

　　再把鏡頭轉回人生的苦難。唉，喝一杯嘛──好，不要，也許。隨即停止喝酒。這方面你很內行，史賓。你能說停就停。我多麼敬重你這一點。非常不尋常。

　　你談過這話題：除非躺進地下七呎，否則絕對不安全。可是，逃生口有什麼用處呢？為什麼逃生口總是開著──你是想擺脫出色的你嗎？

　　怎麼了，史賓？我本想問你。到底怎麼了，你知道嗎？

　　你剛說什麼？我沒聽清楚……

砍

查爾斯・M・舒茲（Charles M. Schulz）致伊麗莎白・史威姆（Elizabeth Swaim）
一九五五年一月五日

一九五四年十一月三十日，《史努比》漫畫才四歲，廣受喜愛，夏樂蒂・布隆恩（Charlotte Braun）在這天新登場，幾乎做盡了討人厭的事。夏樂蒂・布隆恩號稱乖乖女，其實是長舌婆，態度咄咄逼人，主觀意識很強，一出場就惹毛了死忠《史努比》迷。一九五五年二月一日，才和讀者見面十次的她又在故事中現身一次，從此消失。事隔四十五年，《史努比》作者查爾斯・M・舒茲去世後，女讀者伊麗莎白・史威姆捐了一封舒茲親筆信給美國國會圖書館。在信裡，舒茲以逗趣的文字，回應伊麗莎白對夏樂蒂的怨言。這封信寫好，才過一個月，夏樂蒂便無疾而終。舒茲在信中同意砍掉夏樂蒂的角色，並提醒伊麗莎白，她可要為漫畫人物之死負責。在信尾，舒茲畫夏樂蒂頭挨斧頭砍的圖。

親愛的史威姆小姐，

　　我虛心接受妳針對夏樂蒂・布隆恩的建議，決定總有一天會把她變走。假如她再現身，那是我在接到妳的信之前已畫好的作品，也可能是另有讀者來信支持她。話雖這麼說，妳可要記得，一個無辜的小孩就這樣死翹翹，妳和妳朋友會良心不安喔。妳準備承擔這樣的責任嗎？

　　感謝妳來信，期望未來發表的作品能博得妳的歡心。

　　　　　　　　　　　　查爾斯・M・舒茲敬上

Jan. 5, 1955

Dear Miss Swaim,

I am taking your suggestion
regarding Charlotte Braun, & will eventually
discard her. If she appears anymore it will
be in strips that were already completed before
I got your letter or because someone writes in
saying that they like her. Remember, however,
that you and your friends will have the death
of an innocent child on your conscience. Are
you prepared to accept such responsibility?

Thanks for writing, and I hope that
future releases will please you.

Sincerely,

Charles M. Schulz

The Ax

吾愛吾妻。吾妻已死。

理察・費曼（Richard Feynman）
致亞琳・費曼（Arline Feynman）
一九四六年十月十七日

理察・費曼是同世代最知名、最具影響力的物理學家之一，一九四〇年代曾參與原子彈研發計劃。一九八四年，羅傑斯委員會調查挑戰者號太空梭爆炸案，費曼擔任要角，追究事發原因。一九六五年，他與兩名同事榮獲諾貝爾獎，得獎理由是「為量子電動力學奠定基礎，對基本粒子物理學影響深遠。」費曼不僅人緣極佳，在專業領域的成就也數不清，學術功勳的深度是我一輩子也難以理解。

一九四五年六月，高中時期的女友、髮妻亞琳因肺結核病逝，得年二十五。十六個月後，也就是一九四六年十月，費曼寫下這封感人肺腑的情書給亡妻，裝進信封裡封起來，直到一九八八年去世時才重見天日。

親親亞琳，

我愛妳，甜心。

我知道妳多麼喜歡聽這句話──但我不只因妳喜歡而寫──我寫這句話是因為，寫給妳令我通體暖洋洋。

離我上次寫給妳已經好久了──將近兩年了。但我知道，妳會原諒我，因為妳瞭解我是怎樣的一個人──固執而講求實際。我本來認為，寫信沒人讀也是白寫。

但現在，親愛的妻子，我知道我該做我拖欠太久的事，做我以前常做的事。我想告訴妳，我愛妳。我想妳。我會永遠愛妳。

我發現，妳死後，愛妳的意義何其大，我理智上難以理解──但我仍想安慰妳，照顧妳。而我也要妳愛我，照顧我。我想找妳討論難題──想和妳合作一些小工程。直到最近，我才想到我倆能這樣合作。應該做什麼。我們以前開始一起做衣服──或學中文──或買一部電影投影機。難道我現在不能做嗎？不行。沒有妳，我孤零零一個人。妳在世時是「點子女王」，是我倆所有狂野歷險記的總策劃師。

妳病倒時，妳好擔心，怕妳無法給我一些妳想給我的東西──妳以為我需要的東西。妳其實過慮了。正如我那時告訴妳，我真的不需要什麼，因為我愛妳的方式太多了，太深了。現在，同樣的道理顯然更加真切──如今妳什麼也無法給我，我卻照樣愛妳，乃至於妳擋住我愛其他人的機會──但我要妳繼續擋。死去的妳勝過任何活人千百倍。

我知道，妳會笑我傻，會叫我全力追求幸福，不想妨礙到我。兩年了，我連一個女友都沒有交（除了妳之外，甜心），我敢打賭妳會感到意外。但妳無能為力，親愛的，我也一樣。我不懂，因為我結識許多女孩，其中不乏條件非常好的女孩，而我不想繼續單身──然而約會兩三次之後，她們全像死灰。留存我身邊的僅有妳。妳才是真的。

我親愛的妻子，我好愛妳。

吾愛吾妻。吾妻已死。

瑞奇

P.S. 我不寄這封信，請原諒我，因為我不知道妳的新地址。

你的親切度不如前

一九四〇年六月二十七日

克蓮坦・丘吉爾（Clementine Churchill）致溫斯頓・丘吉爾
一九四〇年六月二十七日

在一九四〇年六月，丘吉爾首度榮登英國首相寶座才幾個月，二次大戰愈演愈烈，這月丘吉爾三度進下院，發表重大演說，在局勢緊繃的情況下鼓舞民心。但在幕後，丘吉爾承受的負荷沉重，周遭的人全看得出來，也感受得到。在六月二十七日，妻子克蓮坦看不下去了，寫信給他，基本上是勸他放輕鬆，善待幕僚。

我親愛的，

有件事我覺得你非知道不可，藉此告訴你，盼你見諒。

你的一位幕僚（盡心的朋友）來找我，告訴我說，由於你的態度狂妄刻薄又傲慢，同事和部屬恐將一致排斥你——據說你的私人祕書團已協議出一項對策，模仿學童的「擺爛」心態，表面上逆來順受，逃離你身邊之後聳聳肩不理。在政府高層，如果你的態度繼續如此輕慢，今後將沒有人願意（在開會時）獻計。我聽了很詫異，也很難過，因為這些年來，和你合作、為你效勞的人無不敬愛你，我已習以為常了。我如此告訴那位幕僚，他說，「肯定是壓力太大了」——

我親愛的溫斯頓——我必須坦承，我注意到你的舉止確有惡化之趨勢，你的親切度不如前。

你有權發號施令，如果命令執行不力——除了英王、坎特伯里大主教、議長之外——你能開除任何人。由於你掌握如此大的權威，你的言行應攙加文雅與親和，可能的話也多加一點神定。你以前常引述法文：「沉著鎮定，方能駕馭萬心。」效忠英國與首相的人若不敬愛尊重你，我實難忍受——

更何況，暴躁無禮得不到最佳成果，只會滋生憎惡或一種奴隸心態——（正值戰時，所以叛變是絕不可行！）

請原諒盡心愛你關照你的克蓮坦

我上週日在契克斯閣寫完信後撕毀，現在再寫一次。

對，維吉尼亞，世上真有耶誕老人

維吉尼亞‧歐罕倫（Virginia O'Hanlon）致紐約《太陽報》主編

一八九七年

一八九七年，八歲大的維吉尼亞‧歐罕倫在父親建議下，寫了一封短信，向紐約的報社主編發問。這家報紙名為《太陽報》，目前已停刊。她想確認耶誕老公公是否存在。主編法蘭西斯‧P‧丘吉（Francis P. Church）很快就透過社論回覆她，標題是「世上真有耶誕老人嗎？」蔚為英語史上流傳最廣的社論，也連帶產生幾種改編版本。

維吉尼亞後來當上老師，終其一生持續接到這封童稚信激起的回響。她在一九七一年去世，享壽八十一。

親愛的主編，

我今年八歲。我有一些小朋友說，世上沒有耶誕老公公。爸爸說，「如果《太陽報》這麼寫，那就錯不了。」請告訴我真相，世上真的有耶誕老公公嗎？

維吉尼亞‧歐罕倫。
西九十五街一一五號

維吉尼亞，妳的小朋友們錯了。猜疑時代瀰漫猜疑氣氛，他們被感染了。除非親眼看見，否則他們一概不信。他們以為，他們的小腦筋無法理解的事物一概不存在。維吉尼亞，無論大人小孩，所有人的心智都小。在浩瀚的宇宙裡，人類的智識和無垠的世界相比，和理解所有真理知識的智能相比，是區區一隻蟲蟻。

是的，維吉尼亞，世上真有耶誕老人。世上有愛、有寬容、有奉獻，當然也有他，而且多不勝數，為妳的生活帶來最高境界的美與樂。唉，倘使沒有耶誕老人，這世界多麼枯燥啊，就像世上沒有**維吉尼亞**一樣枯燥，童真的信念將不復存在，也沒有詩歌，沒有浪漫，今生將何其痛苦難熬，視覺和感官之外的享受也蕩然無存，兒童照亮天下的永明燈也將熄滅。

不信世上有耶誕老公公！乾脆連小仙女都一起懷疑吧！妳可以請爸爸花錢找人，在耶誕前夕看守所有煙囪，抓住耶誕老人。即使他們沒看見耶誕老人鑽煙囪下來，那又能證明什麼？沒人見過耶誕老人，又不能證明耶誕老人不存在。世上最真切的事物往往是大人小孩都看不見的東西。妳見過小仙女在草坪上跳舞嗎？當然沒有，但這不能證明仙女不存在。世上看不到、無人見過的神奇事物多的是，沒有人能憑空捏造想像所有東西。

嬰兒的手搖玩具會發聲，妳可以拆開來，看看裡面有什麼東西，但看不見的世界蒙著一面薄紗，力氣再大的人也揭不開，甚至古今所有大力士一同出力也難揭穿，唯有信念、遐思、詩詞、愛、浪漫情懷，方可撥開簾幕，一窺至高無上的美麗與光輝。這全是真的嗎？啊，維吉尼亞，在這世界上，沒其他事物比這更真切、更永恆了。

耶誕老人不存在？謝天謝地！他不但存在，而且永生不死。一千年後，維吉尼亞，不對，一萬年後，他仍然將繼續取悅童年之心。

我剛寫給你一封長信

艾菲德・D・溫妥（Alfred D. Wintle）致《泰晤士報》主編
一九四六年二月六日

艾菲德・D・溫妥中校的主觀意識很強，頭腦聰穎，個性勇敢，極具娛樂性，是個不折不扣的「性情中人」。負傷住院的他為了重回戰場，曾打扮成女護士，不料單眼鏡令他穿幫，逃脫不成。二次大戰期間，他在法國淪為戰俘，不滿獄卒「儀容邋遢」，竟絕食抗議兩星期。幾年後，戰爭結束了，有一天他搭火車，發現頭等車廂位子不夠坐，於是坐進駕駛艙，奪取操控權，霸佔到問題解決為止。他在沒有律師的情況下，和一位黑心律師纏訟三年，最後告進上院，在一九五八年勝訴，開創司法史新頁。他的傳奇事跡不勝枚舉。

一九四六年，他寫這封信給《泰晤士報》，被報社保存至今，供人景仰。

致《泰晤士報》主編。

主編先生，

　　我剛寫給你一封長信。

　　寫好後再讀一遍，被我扔進廢紙簍。

　　希望此舉能獲得你的認可，

　　忠僕（簽名）敬上

四六年二月六日

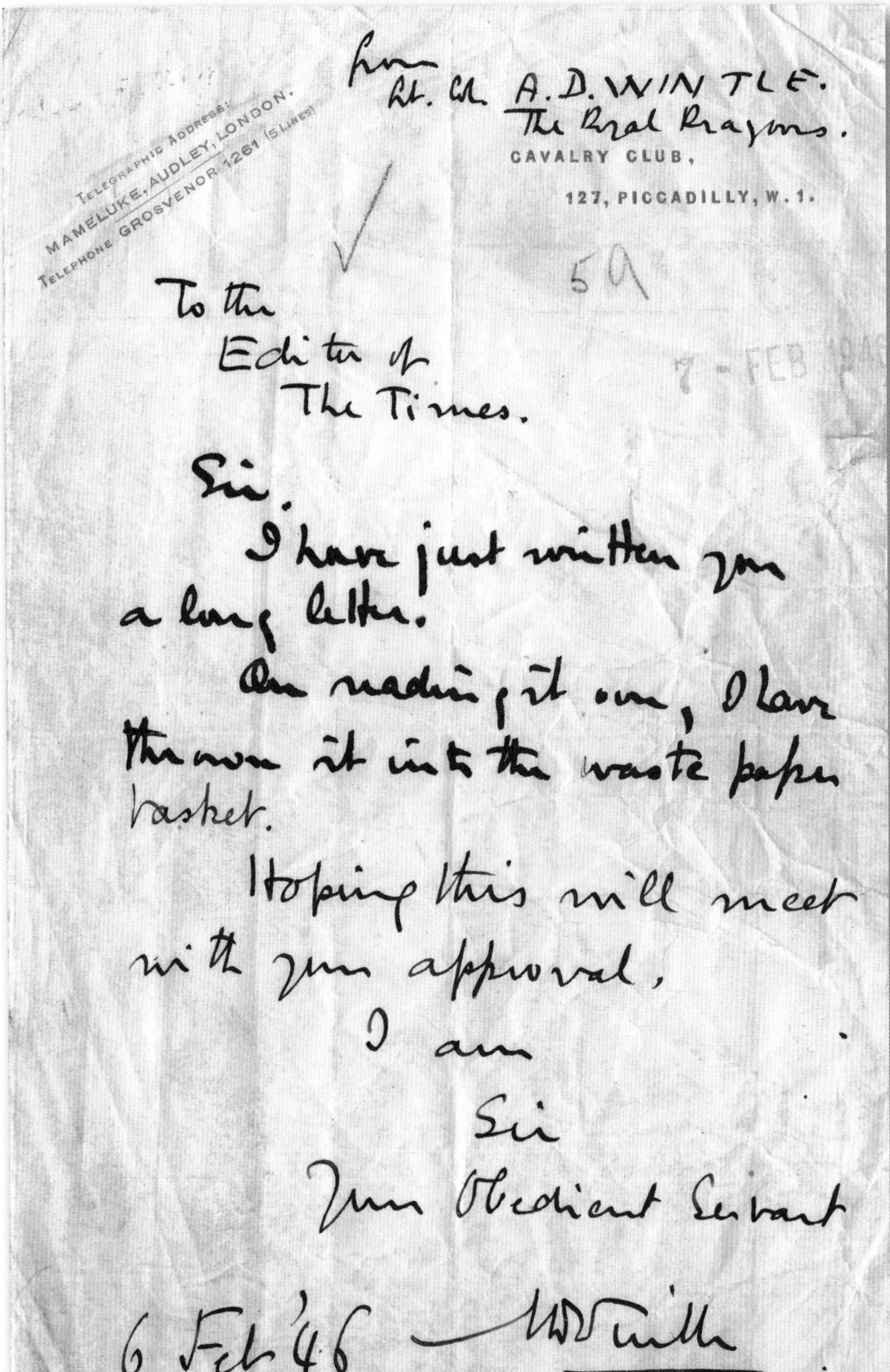

Telegraphic Address:
MAMELUKE, AUDLEY, LONDON.
Telephone GROSVENOR 1261 (5 Lines)

From
Lt. Col. A. D. WINTLE.
The Royal Dragoons.

CAVALRY CLUB,

127, PICCADILLY, W.1.

59

7 - FEB 1946

To the
Editor of
The Times.

Sir,

I have just written you
a long letter.

On reading it over, I have
thrown it into the waste paper
basket.

Hoping this will meet
with your approval,

I am

Sir

Your Obedient Servant

6 Feb '46   A D Wintle

信之 *040*

老公，快來

**艾瑪・郝克（Emma Hauck）致
馬克・郝克（Mark Hauck）**
一九〇九年

在一九〇九年二月七日，三十歲、
育有二子的艾瑪・郝克因被診斷出
早發失智症，住進德國海德堡大學
醫院精神科病房。這種病今名精神
分裂症。由於病情好轉，她住院
一個月之後出院，幾週後病情卻
加劇，只好再入院治療。可惜這
次病況持續惡化，同年八月，院
方研判她已「病入膏肓」，痊癒無
望，家人因此將她轉至衛斯洛克
（Wiesloch）精神病院。她待了十
一年後去世。

她死後，海德堡醫院才在舊檔案
裡發現一批椎心刺骨的親筆信，
全是她在一九〇九年二度入院時
拚命寫的，據說那段時期她不停提
起家屬。每一封信寫得萬分焦急，
對象是缺席的丈夫馬克，每一頁爬
滿重疊的文字，有幾頁濃密得難
以辨識。有幾頁反覆以德文寫著
「Herzensschatzi komm」（老公，快
來）。另有幾封只重複懇求著「快
來快來快來」，不下幾千遍。

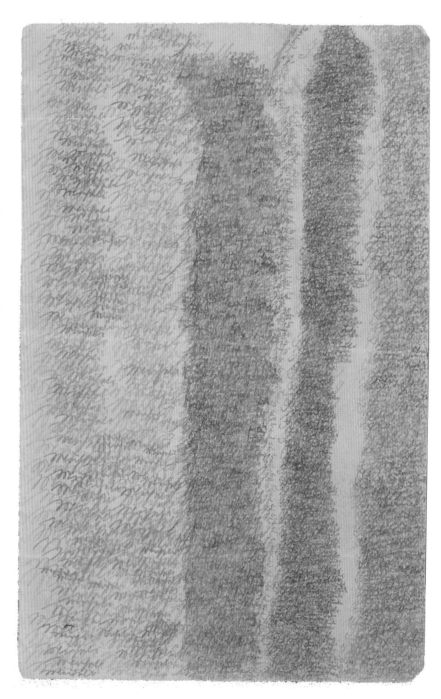

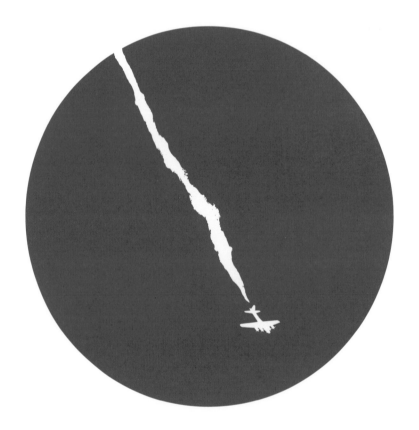

信之 *041**

不枉我成仁

久野正信中佐致兒女
一九四五年五月二十三日

在一九四五年五月二十三日晚間，久野正信在知覽町家中坐下，撰寫這封訣別書給五歲大的兒子正憲和兩歲大的女兒紀代子。隔天，他駕駛滿載火藥的飛機升空，蓄意衝向一艘同盟軍戰艦。當時正值沖繩島戰役，在一九四〇年代，久野中尉的自殺行動並無特殊之處。除了他之外，二次大戰期間，另有大約四千名神風特攻隊飛行員選擇代表日本人捐軀。神風特攻隊的策略確實奏效了，在二戰期間摧毀盟軍數十艘戰艦，導致數千名軍人喪生。

*譯註：原文以幼童讀得懂的片假名書寫。

親愛的正憲和紀代子，

縱使你們看不見我，我將永永遠遠守望你們。你們長大後，願你們依循心之所向，長成優秀日本男女。勿欽羨他人之父親。你們的父親將成神，近身守望兩小。你們兩個要用功讀書，幫母親分擔家事。我無法扮馬讓你們騎著玩，但你們兩個將成好玩伴。心情愉悅的我駕駛大轟炸機，收拾所有敵軍。盼你們長大後不輸父親，不枉我成仁。

別碰他的頭髮

三名貓王迷致美國總統艾森豪
一九五八年

一九五八年三月二十四日是貓王迷的「黑色星期一」，因為二十二歲的搖滾歌王艾維斯・普列斯萊進入美國陸軍服役，許多粉絲痛不欲生。直至今日，貓王仍是全球最知名的藝人之一。比入伍更糟糕的是，貓王將遠赴重洋至德國服役，兩年之後才退伍。想當然爾，貓迷驚恐不已，終日揣測他的未來，有些人甚至打高射砲，直接寄特急件給白宮，希望讓貓王全身而退。這封信只是眾多貓迷信之一，由三名女粉絲共筆，於一九五八年寄給艾森豪總統。信中，她們似乎認定入伍的命運已難挽回，所以退而求其次，期望軍方至少不要亂改貓王的造型。

親愛的艾森豪總統，

　　我和兩個閨密從搖遠的蒙大拿寫信給你。我們認為，爭召貓王入伍已經夠糟糕了，如果你連他的鬢角都剃掉，那我們一定死翹翹！你不知到我們對他用情多深，我真不了解為何非逼他從軍不可，但我們求你，拜託拜託不要把他剃成美國大兵頭，拜託拜託不要啦！一剃下去，我們會少掉半條命！

　　　　　　　　　　　　貓迷

　　　　　　　琳達・凱立
　　　　　　　雪莉・弁恩
　　　　　　　米姬・麥森

普列斯萊
普列斯萊
是我們的隊呼
P-R-E-S-L-Y

Box 755
Noxon, Mont

Jill

Dear President Eisenhower,

My girlfriend and I are writting all the way from Montana, We think its bad enough to send Elvis Presley in the Army, but if you cut his side burns off we will just die! You don't no how we fell about him, I really don't see why you have to send him in the Army at all, but we beg you please please don't give him a G.I. hair cut, oh please please don't! If you do we will just about die!

Presley
Presley
IS OUR CRY
P-R-E-S-L-E-Y

E. P.
Lover

Elvis Presley
Lovers

Linda Kelly
Sherry Bare
Micke Mattson

致我的遺孀

羅伯特·史考特致凱瑟琳·史考特
一九一二年

在一九一二年一月十七日，經過幾年來的籌備，英國探險家羅伯特·法肯·史考特與四名隊員抵達南極，成就驚人，但他們攻抵目的地不久卻發現，南極在四週前已被洛德·阿蒙森（Roald Amundsen）率領的挪威探險隊搶先抵達。史考特與團員既氣餒又疲憊，不久啟程，踏上八百英哩的返鄉路。一個月後，路即將走完一半時，隊員之一艾格爾·伊凡斯（Edgar Evans）因跌倒導致腦振盪而死亡。一個月後，隊員勞倫斯·歐茨（Lawrence Oates）凍瘡嚴重，為避免拖累全隊，毅然走進暴風雪輕生。未久，剩下三人在帳篷裡遭凍斃，遺體和物品於一九一二年十一月十二日尋獲。據信，包括史考特在內的最後三人死於三月二十九日。

到最後幾天，史考特已有最壞的打算，於是寫了一封感人肺腑的信給「遺孀」凱瑟琳，信中也提及兩歲兒子彼得·史考特的胞姐演員艾緹（Ettie）、好友桑德斯特（Sandhurst）夫人（艾蓮諾·渥德豪斯 Eleanor Wodehouse）以及發人瑞吉諾·史密斯、以及開導史考特有功的探險家克列蒙茲·馬坎姆（Clements Markham）。凱瑟琳·史考特以雕塑為業，前往紐西蘭迎接探險隊榮歸的途中得知噩耗，後來為丈夫塑造一座銅像，立於倫敦的滑鐵盧廣場至今。

致我的遺孀

至親——本隊目前情況危急，我懷疑這一關可能難過了。我利用短暫的午餐時間，藉著一小許溫暖寫幾封信交代後事——第一封當然是寫給妳，因為無論走路或睡覺，縈繞我腦海的泰半是妳。若我遭不測，希望妳明白妳在我心中的地位多重要，我將帶著甜美回憶離世——

在此告知妳幾件事實以寬慰妳——我走時將不受任何苦痛，了無羈絆，健康與活力俱在——我們已決定，當食糧用罄之時，我們將在下一補給站容易抵達之距離內止步。因此，妳切勿把此事胡思亂想成大悲劇——我們數週以來固然憂心如焚，但生理機能健全，食慾良好，足以掩蓋所有不適。冷風刺骨，時而引人惱怒，所幸有難能可貴的熱食可吃，讓我們在享受口福之餘得以再挺進。

自從寫完以上那段後，本隊狀況惡化許多。可憐的歐茨走了——他的情況很糟——其他人繼續前進，遐想著我們可望渡過難關，但寒天硬是不肯放暖——我們現在離補給站只二十英哩，但油糧所剩無幾。

親愛的老婆，我盼妳理性看待這整件事，而我相信妳必能理性以對——兒子將成妳的慰藉——我本期望助妳撫養他長大，但在妳羽翼下的他能平安成長，我就心滿意足了。我認為，你們母子倆皆應受政府特別照顧，畢竟我們全為國奉獻生命，精神堪稱典範——寫完這封信後，我將在這筆記本最後幾封信詳述這一點，希望妳為我代寄。

我必須寫一短信給兒子，等他長大後閱讀。我家祖傳的惡習是怠惰——這是他最須防範、妳最須避免他養成的惡習。務必把他教養成活力充沛的男子漢。我自幼強迫自己多多活動，妳也知道——我一直有偷懶的傾向，我父親也懶，導致許多困擾。

至親妳知，對於妳再婚一事，我不是多愁善感的那種無聊人——妳若遇到合適的貴人，應回歸快樂的自我——我是個不合格

的丈夫，但我盼妳讓我好的一面長駐妳心頭。婚姻走到盡頭，妳無須羞慚，我希望兒子能及早再受好教養，日後或能引以為榮。

　　親愛的，天寒地凍，寫字不易——零下七十度，避寒物唯獨帳篷——妳知我始終愛妳，妳知我心常念妳，唉，妳必須知道，此刻最苦的念頭是我倆將無緣重逢——必然的結果無法閃躲——妳叫我擔任此行領隊，而我知妳認為此行危險——我全程領隊了，不是嗎？願上帝保祐妳，我親愛的老婆，我以後會再多寫一些——接著寫在背頁。寫完前面之後，我們逼近到補給站以外不到十一英哩，剩一天份的熱食和兩天份的口糧。我們本可挺過這難關，奈何遇到駭人的暴風雪，滯留四天——我認為本隊已錯失求生良機，大家決定不自戕，反而是朝補給站勇往直前至援絕為止。但在奮力前進之中，無痛的絕路即將來臨，妳勿擔憂。我在這筆記本的單數頁寫了幾封信，妳可以代我寄嗎？現在的我為妳和兒子的將來著急——盡妳所能讓兒子對博物學感興趣，總比體育來得好。有些學校鼓勵學生打球賽。我知道妳會盡量叫他從事戶外活動——盡量教他信神，信神有撫慰心靈的作用。唉我親愛的我親愛的，我對他的將來懷抱多少美夢，我的愛妻啊，我知妳將強顏面對事實——妳和兒子的畫像將在我懷抱中被人尋獲，另有巴克斯特夫人送的摩洛哥小紅盒裡的那張。我在南極立一面國旗，其中一片收藏在我的私人工具包，另有阿蒙森的黑旗和雜物——送國王一小片，也送亞歷山德拉王后一小片，剩下留著——卑微的戰利品給妳！此行的經歷之豐富，我多想告訴妳。能在家中舒服坐臥著，該有多好——多希望妳能將我的見聞轉告給兒子，可惜唉代價未免太高了——無緣再見妳那親之又親的臉龐——親愛的妳記得善待老母。我在這本裡寫給她幾句話。另外記得和艾緹和其他人保持聯繫——唉但妳對外界必定會故作堅強——我只求妳不要自尊太強而拒絕接受外人對兒子的好意——他以後應從事好職業，對社會有所貢獻。我沒時間寫給克列蒙茲爵士——對他說他常在我心中，他命令我前來南極探險，我從不曾後悔接受——代我向巴克斯特夫人和桑德斯特夫人道別，繼續和她們往來，因為兩位待我親切，也向瑞吉諾・史密斯夫婦*

*編按：信件至此完結。

To my widow

Dearest darling — we are in a very tight corner and I have doubts of pulling through — In our short lunch hours I take advantage of a very small measure of warmth to write letters preparatory to a possible end — The first is naturally to you on whom my thoughts mostly dwell waking or sleeping — If anything happens to me I shall like you to know how much you have meant to me and what pleasant recollections are with me as I depart —

I should like you to take what comfort you can from these facts also — I shall not have suffered any pain but leave the world fresh from harness + full of good health + vigour — this is decided already when provisions come to an end we simply stop unless we are within easy distance of another depot Therefore you must not imagine a great tragedy — we are very anxious of course + have been for weeks but our splendid physical condition and our appetites compensate for all discomfort The cold is trying + sometimes angering but here again with the

hot food which turns it forth in
so wonderfully enjoyable that one
would scarcely be without it
We have gone down hill a good
deal since I wrote the above
Poor Titus Oates has gone - he was
in a bad state - the rest of us
keep going and imagine we have
a chance to get through but the
cold weather doesn't let up at
all - We are now only 20 miles
from a depot but we have very little
food & fuel

Well dear heart I want you to take
the whole thing very sensibly as
I'm sure you will - The boy will
be your comfort - I had looked
forward to helping you to bring him
up but - it is a satisfaction
to feel that he is safe with you
I think both he and you ought
to be specially looked after by the
country for which after all we
have given our lives with
something of spirit which makes
for example - I am confident

letters on them [...] in the [...]
of the book, will you [...] them
to their various destinations

— I must write a little letter for
the boy if time can be found
to be read when he grows up
He inherited vice from my side
of the family is indolence —
above all he must guard & you
must guard him against that —
Make him a strenuous man
I had to force myself into being
Strenuous as you know — had
always an inclination to idleness
My father was idle [...]
brought much trouble

— Dearest heart you know !
Cheerily no sentimentality about
about re marriage — When the
right man comes to help you to
life you ought to be free
happily self again ———— I would
be very good husband but I
hope I shall be a good [...]
certainly the had or nothing
for you to be ashamed of

and I like to think that the boy will have a good start in the parentage of which he may be proud

Dear it is not easy to write because of the cold – 40° below zero and nothing but the shelter of our tent – You know I have loved you, you know my thoughts must have constantly dwelt on you and oh dear me you must know that quite the worst aspect of this situation is the thought that I shall not see you again – The inevitable must be faced – You urged me to be leader of this party and I know you felt it would be dangerous – I've taken my place throughout, haven't I?

God bless you my own darling I shall try & write more later – I go on across the back pages

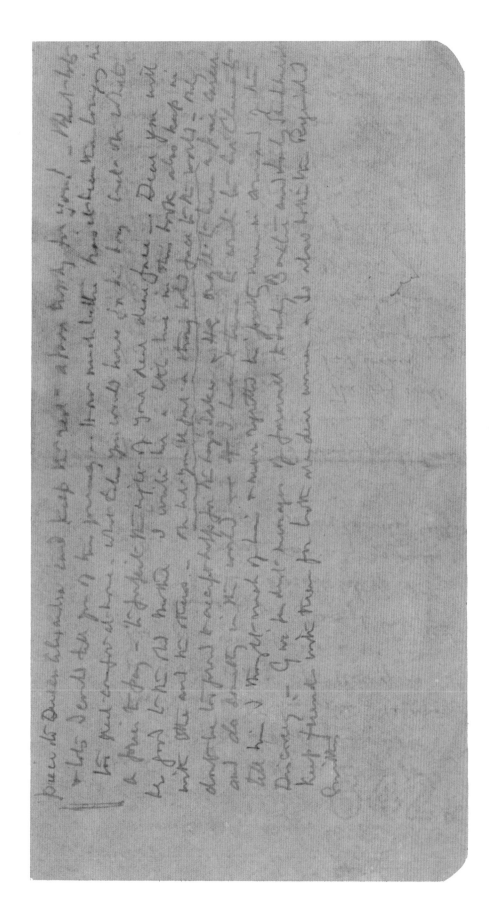

卯足勁寫信吧！

傑克・凱魯亞克（Jack Kerouac）致馬龍・白蘭度（Marlon Brando）

一九五七年前後

一九五七年末，垮世代作家傑克・凱魯亞克甫發表小說《在路上》（On the Road），佳評如潮，振筆寫信給好萊塢巨星馬龍・白蘭度，積極將原著推上大銀幕。《在路上》是作者的個人寫照，長篇描寫公路行旅見聞，記錄薩爾・帕瑞岱斯（Sal Paradise）和迪恩・默理亞提（Dean Moriarty）的旅程與友誼，兩人其實是凱魯亞克和作家尼爾・卡薩迪（Neal Cassady）的化身。白蘭度始終沒回信。

十二年後，凱魯亞克去世。《在路上》改編為電影《浪蕩世代》，於二〇一二年上映。

傑克・凱魯亞克
佛羅里達州奧蘭多市
科勞瑟街一四一八半號

親愛的馬龍

我祈禱你會買下《在路上》的製片權，拍成電影。別擔心小說的架構，我懂得稍微壓縮重組情節，改成完全適合大銀幕的架構：把書裡縱橫東西岸的幾趟旅程統合為涵蓋全程的單一路線，改成紐約、丹佛、舊金山、墨西哥、紐奧良、紐約的來回旅程。依我憧憬，鏡頭可架在車子前座，拍攝路途（不分晝夜），畫面一定美不勝收，讓蜿蜒的馬路直闖擋風玻璃內的鏡頭，薩爾和迪恩則在一旁嗑牙。我希望你能飾演迪恩，因為（你也知道）迪恩不是只懂改裝車的傻漢，其實是個知識豐富的（耶穌會）愛爾蘭裔。你演迪恩，我演薩爾（華納兄弟示意由我飾演薩爾）。我可以教你揣摩現實生活裡的迪恩，因為不見逼真的模仿無法想像他的言行。事實上，我可以帶你去舊金山拜訪他，也可以找他過來洛杉磯。他仍是一隻忙亂的貓，但最近比較安份了，陪伴最後一任妻子，晚上和兒女一同唸主禱文……你讀過《垮世代》劇本一定能想見。我的目標是為我和老母籌足一份無後顧之憂的信託基金，好讓我能盡情週遊世界，書寫日本、印度、法國等等……我想我手寫我心，能在我的小朋友喊餓時有錢餵飽他們，能不必為老母擔憂。

附帶一提，我的下一部小說《地下人》（The Subterraneans）明年三月在紐約發表，主題是白種男人的一段異族戀，故事非常新穎，有些人物你在村裡認識過了（史丹利・古德？等等），很容易改編成劇本，比《在路上》更簡單。

我的心願是改造美國劇場界和電影圈，為它們增添即興的色彩，不再設定「情境」，讓臺上的人像現實生活一樣盡情亂扯。舞臺劇正應該這樣演：無特定劇情，無特定「涵義」，只呈現人類本性。寫作時，我總想像我和天使重返地球，以沉痛的目光看著炎涼百態。我知道你能認同這些點子。附帶一提，法蘭克・辛納屈的新電影也以「即興」為基調——「即興」本來就是**唯一**的做法嘛，無論在演藝圈或現實生活都一樣。三〇年代法國片仍遠勝我國電影，因為法國人真的讓演員演自己，文人不會主觀認定

電影觀眾多聰明而跟電影人吵架，們*有話直說（*譯註：the是they之誤），大家一聽就懂。等我終於有錢了，我想在美國拍幾齣精彩的法國片……目前，美國劇場和電影是一頭趕不上時代的恐龍，不能跟最優質的美國文學同步演進。

如果你真想合作，你下次去紐約時可以約我，你來佛羅里達也可以找我，不過，我們是真的應該討論這事，因為我有預感，這將帶動大風潮。反正我最近閒得發慌，沒事想找事做——小說愈寫愈覺得太容易了，劇本也一樣，我花二十四小時就把劇本寫好了。

快加入吧，馬龍，卯足勁寫信吧！

稍後再聊

傑克·凱魯亞克　敬上

Jack Kerouac
1418½ Clouser St
Orlando,Fla

Dear Marlon
  I'm praying that you'll buy ON THE ROAD and make a movie
of it. Dont worry about structure, I know how to compress and
re-arrange the plot a bit to give perfectly acceptable movie-type
structure: making it into one all-inclusive trip instead of the
several voyages coast-to-coast in the book, one vast round trip
from New York to Denver to Frisco to Mexico to New Orleans to New York
again. I visualize the beautiful shots could be made with the camera
on the front seat of the car showing the road (day and night) unwinding
into the windshield, as Sal and Dean yak. I wanted you to play the
part because Dean (as you know) is no dopey hotrodder but a real
intelligent (in fact Jesuit) Irishman. You play Dean and I'll play
Sal (Warner Bros. mentioned I play Sal) and I'll show you how Dean
acts in real life, you couldnt possibly imagine it without seeing a
good imitation. Fact, we can go visit him in Frisco, or have him
come down to L.A. still a real frantic cat but nowadays settled
down whth his final wife saying the Lord's Prayer with his kiddies
at night...as you'll seen when you read the play BEAT GENERATION.
All I want out of this is to be able to establish myself and my
mother a trust fund for life, so I can really go roaming around the
world writing about Japan, India, France etc. ...I want to be free
to write what comes out of my head & free to feed my buddies when
they're hungry & not worry about my mother.

  Incidentally, my next novel is THE SUBTERRANEANS coming
out in N.Y. next March and is about a love affair between a white
guy and a colored girl and very hep story. Some of the characters
in it you knew in the Village (Stanley Gould? etc.) It easily could
be turned into a play, easier than ON THE ROAD.

  What I wanta do is re-do the theater and the cinema in
America, give it a spontaneous dash, remove pre-conceptions of
"situation" and let people rave on as they do in real life. That's
what the play is: no plot in particular, no "meaning" in particular,
just the way people are. Everything I write I do in the spirit
where I imagine myself an Angel returned to the earth seeing it with
sad eyes as it is. I know you approve of these ideas, & incidentally
the new Frank Sinatra show is based on "spontaneous" too, which is
the only way to come on anyway, whether in show business or life.
The French movies of the 30's are still far superior to ours because
the French really let their actors come on and the writers didnt
quibble with some preconceived notion of how intelligent the movie
audience is, the talked soul from soul and everybody understood at once.
I want to make great French Movies in America, finally, when I'm rich
...American Theater & Cinema at present is an outmoded Dinosaur
that aint mutated along with the best in American Literature.

  If you really want to go ahead, make arrangements to
see me in New York when next you come, or if you're going to Florida
here I am, but what we should do is talk about this because I
prophesy that it's going to be the beginning of something real
great. I'm bored nowadays and I'm looking around for something to do
in the void, anyway----writing novels is getting too easy, same with
plays, I wrote the play in 24 hours.

  Come on now, Marlon, put up your dukes and write!

    Sincerely, later, *Jack Kerouac*

務必再明白我拒婚之心

愛蜜莉亞・埃爾哈特（Amelia Earhart）致喬治・普特南（George Putnam）
一九三一年二月七日

在一九三二年五月，三十四歲的劃時代女飛行員愛蜜莉亞・埃爾哈特，駕駛洛克希德 Vega 5B 單引擎飛機，從紐芬蘭至北愛爾蘭，以十四小時五十六分鐘橫渡大西洋，成為史上首位單獨飛越大西洋的女飛行員。她一生志向遠大，寫下無數航空史新頁。埃爾哈特個性極為獨立自主，不願讓任何事——包括婚姻在內——攔阻她的畢生志向。在橫越大西洋的前一年，在與她深愛的經紀人結婚當天早上，她寫下這封極不尋常的信。

這一對的婚姻雖美滿卻也短暫。一九三七年，埃爾哈特在環繞地球之旅的過程中消失在太平洋上空，遺體一直未被尋獲。

康州諾昂克（Noank）

丘吉街方塊屋

親愛的 GPP

在你我結婚之前，有些事應書面寫明白，多數是我們討論過的問題。

你務必再明白我拒婚之因。以事業為重的我認為，結婚將擊碎我事業上的良機。我此時覺得，此舉是我做過最愚昧的事。我知道，犧牲或許將有補償，但此時的我無心前瞻。

今後我倆共處，我要你明白，我不會逼你遵守中古世紀的貞節規範，我也不願受同樣的束縛。若你我能坦誠相向，定能避免萬一今後你或我另有心上人（或一時迷戀）時產生的糾葛。

請勿讓我倆干涉彼此工作或遊樂，也勿讓外界看見兩人世界裡的喜悅或歧見。在這份關係中，恕我或許有時想獨處，因為我無法保證我能忍受牢禁的苦悶，縱使是困在美侖美奐的籠子裡也受不了。

我必須強求一件事，請你成全：若我倆攜手找不到幸福，請你一年之後放我走。

我將在各方面盡我所能，把你所知所求的我的一面獻給你。

A.E.

                                        Noank
                                        Connecticut

                    The Square House
                    Church Street

    Dear GPP

            There are some things which should be writ before
    we are married -- things we have talked over before -- most of
    them.

            You must know again my reluctance to marry, my
    feeling that I shatter thereby chances in work which means most
    to me. I feel the move just now as foolish as anything I
    could do.   I know there may be compensations but have no heart
    to look ahead.

            On our life together I want you to understand I
    shall not hold you to any midaevil code of faithfulness to me
    nor shall I consider myself bound to you similarly.   If we can
    be honest I think the difficulties which arise may best be avoided
    should you or I become interested deeply (or inpassing) in anyone
    else.

            Please let us not interfere with the others' work or
    play, nor let the world see our private joys or disagreements.
    In this connection I may have to keep some place where I can go to
    be myself, now and then, for I cannot guarantee to endure at all
    times the confinement of even an attractive cage.

            I must exact a cruel promise and that is you will let
    me go in a year if we find no happiness together.

            I will try to do my best in every way and give you that
    part of me you know and seem to want.

                                        A.E.

我願繼續當好兵

**艾迪‧斯洛衛克（Eddie Slovik）
致艾森豪將軍**

一九四四年十二月九日

在一九四四年十月，二次大戰期間，二十四歲的美國兵艾迪‧斯洛衛克駐紮法國，被砲火嚇呆，無法在前線作戰，因而逃兵。當時美國陸軍的逃兵多達兩萬餘人。斯洛衛克申請改調單位，但被駁回。三個月後，於一九四五年一月三十一日上午十點過幾分，斯洛衛克因逃兵罪遭射擊隊處決，成為美國自一八六〇年代以來首位伏法逃兵。行刑前兩個月，斯洛衛克擔心死期將近，寫了一封求情信給艾森豪將軍，但軍方不領情，這位未來的美國總統不久後下達處決令。

親愛的艾森豪將軍：

我是軍籍編號三六八九六四一五的陸軍兵艾迪‧斯洛衛克，在一九四四年十一月十一日停戰日被軍法審判定罪，即將因逃兵罪接受死刑。

在定罪期間或定罪之前，我決對無意逃兵。假如我真的有意逃兵，我就不會自首了。我對美國陸軍完全沒有反對的意思，只想轉調前線以外的單位。我回來後，曾問直屬長官是否有轉調的基會，因為任務太危險我無法承擔，而且我的神經也無法承受。我承認我的神經非常翠弱，這種情形我認為很常見。結果上級拒決調我走。

我必須詳述我的生平。我猜你握有我年少犯罪的前科。我曾入獄服刑五年，然後假釋兩年。在假釋的那兩年，我找到一份好工作，因為我被歸類4-F級，陸軍當時根本不想要我。所以我出獄五個月後，決定結婚，現在有一個很棒的老婆，家庭生命美滿。結婚近一年半，我學乖了，不再被人帶壞。我被關的原因就是交到壞朋友。接著，我收到徵兵令。陸軍來找我時，我其實可以朵回監獄，但被關久了我很厭煩監獄生活，所以我決定從軍。我去徵兵處的時候，他們告訴我，陸軍想試試我的原因只有一個，因為我出獄差不多兩年，結婚了，一直守法。就我所知將軍，我在過去兩年沒有犯法。從軍以後，在我惹這麻煩之前，我也一直是個好軍人，盡量做軍方叫我做的事，直到我第一次跑掉，或者我應該說脫離營隊。

如我第一次口供所言，我不相信那次算逃兵。我以遞補兵的身份被調來法國，敵軍一開始轟炸，我嚇壞了，神經受不了，嚇得我爬不出散兵坑。我猜我一直沒基會克服我對砲彈的恐懼。隔天，美軍全不見了，我只好向加拿大憲兵自首，他們設法聯絡我的單位。我猜他們大概花了六星期才追上美軍。將軍我歸建之後，把事情經過和我的遭遇報告給直屬長官聽，然後我要求轉調，結果被他拒決。然後我寫自白書。後來上級說，如果我願意回前線，自白書可以銷毀。但是，如果我拒決回前線，他們會對

我不利。果然。

　　我為我犯的錯太惶恐遺憾了。我那時候一時糊塗，不曉得逃兵罪多嚴重。也不清楚被判死刑的茲味。我深切乞求將軍，念在我愛妻的份上，念在家鄉的母親，對我法外開恩。就我所知，我婚後行為良好，從軍後也是。我想繼續當好兵。

　　我迫切等候你回音，誠心期待好消息，願上帝保祐你，祝我方凱旋：

　　我仍遵從將軍命令，

兵艾迪・D・斯洛衛克

信之 *047*

伽利略的衛星

伽利略（Galileo Galilei）致
里奧納多‧東納托總督
（Leonardo Donato）
一六一〇年

根據知名物理學家史蒂芬‧霍金，
伽利略「催生現代科學居功厥
偉。」伽利略是義大利哲人，是物
理學、數學、天文學專家，在荷蘭
見到初具雛形的望遠鏡，研究其結
構，在一六〇九年自行設計製作望
遠鏡，度數更強，後來以這望遠鏡
觀天，發現無數新事物。一六一〇
年一月，他致函威尼斯總督里奧納
多‧東納托，先描述望遠鏡本身，
接著首度描繪他剛發現的木星最大
四顆衛星。附圖為底稿。

至上王侯。

　　伽利略俯首跪拜殿下，眼觀四面，意願滿懷，於帕度瓦鑽研
數學疑難之餘，決定致函報告此遙視鏡筒（「Occhiale」）將對海
陸探險大有助益。臣向殿下保證，此新發明僅呈殿下，不對外公
開。此鏡筒可極精準研判遠物，能在肉眼看見敵艦兩小時前發現
敵蹤，更能辨識敵艦質量，判斷軍力，以利我軍決定是否驅逐
之、對抗之或逃避之。或者在曠野亦能俱細靡遺辨認動靜與運
籌。

Ser.mo Prin̄cipe.

Galileo Galilej Humiliss.o Seruo della Ser:ª Vª inuigilan=
do assiduam.te, et co ogni spirito p̄ potere nõ solam̄ satisfare
alcarico che tiene della lettura di Matematica nello stu=
dio di Padoua,

Scriuere d'auere determinato di presentare al Ser.mo Prin̄cipe
l'Ochiale et ↑ p̄ essere di giouamento inestimabile p̄ ogni
negozio et impresa marittima o terrestre stima di tenere que=
sto nuouo artifizio nel maggior segreto et solam̄ a dispositione
di S. Ser:ª L'Ochiale cauato dalle più recõdite speculazioni di
prospettiua hà il uantaggio di scoprire Legni et Vele dell'inimico
p̄ due hore et più di tempo prima c̄ egli scuopra noi et distinguendo
il numero et la qualità dei Vasselli giudicare le sue forze
p̄ allestirsi alla caccia al combattimento o alla fuga, o'pure anco
nella cãpagna aperta uedere et particolarm̄ distinguere ogni suo
moto et preparamento.

Adi 7. di Gennaio
Gioue si uedde cosi   ℥ * ori:
Adi 8 cosi   ori * ⊛ * *   ℥   10.   11.
                                        ⊛ * ** ⊛ * * *
℥ ⊛ * * * *   era duq̄ diretto et nõ retrogrado   ori ori:
Adi 12. si uedde in tale costituzione * * ⊛ *   oci:
Il 13 si ueddero uiciniss.e à Gioue 4 stelle * ⊛ * * *   o'meglio cosi
Adi 14 è nugolo   * ⊛ * * *
Il 15 ⊛ * * * *   oci: * la prossª à ℥ era la minñ la 4ª era di=
stante dalla 3ª il duppio ĩcirca   ⊛ * * * *
Lo spazio delle 3 ocidẽtali nõ era   ⊛ * * * *
maggiore del diametro di ℥ et e=   ⊛ * * *
rano in linea retta.   *   ℥ long. 71. 38 Lat. 1. 13

信之 *048*

樺樹皮信

**蓋瓦瑞・坡森亞（Gavril Posenya）
致親戚**

一三五〇年前後

一九五一年七月二十六日，在俄國古城諾夫戈若德（Novgorod），考古學家妮娜・費德洛夫納・阿庫羅瓦（Nina Federovna Akulova）挖掘出一項重大古物：一片雕刻著個人書信的樺樹皮。據研判，其年代可遠溯至一四〇〇年左右，用語屬於古東斯拉夫語系的諾夫戈若德方言。古信出土後，由考古學家

阿特米・阿奇科夫斯基（Artemiy Artsikhovsky）率領的團隊在同地陸續發現超過一千則樹皮信，多數是商業或個人書信，年代從十一至十五世紀不等，生動描繪俄羅斯中世紀東斯拉夫民族的語言與生活。這一封寫在一三四〇至一三六〇年代之間，於一九七二年出土。

我是蓋瓦瑞・坡森亞，此致吾姐烏莉姐與姐夫——戈利果里之教父。若你倆能依諾言前來本鎮，我心將歡愉。願上帝賜福予你倆。我們將不會忘記你們的承諾。

信之 049

致頂尖科學家

丹尼斯‧卡克斯（Denis Cox）
致頂尖科學家
一九五七年十月二十八日

（急件）

一九五七年，十二歲學童丹尼斯‧卡克斯聽見蘇聯宣佈發射史潑尼克一號衛星成功並超前美國，他趕緊寫信給澳洲空軍位於武默拉（Woomera）的火箭試射場，想把祖國送進太空競賽圈。遺憾的是，

這封信石沉大海──事隔五十二年，在二○○九年，他這封信獲得澳洲國家檔案館網站介紹，躍上新聞。在媒體關注下，丹尼斯終於接到回信。丹尼斯長大後不再醉心火箭科學，而是投身環保永續研究。

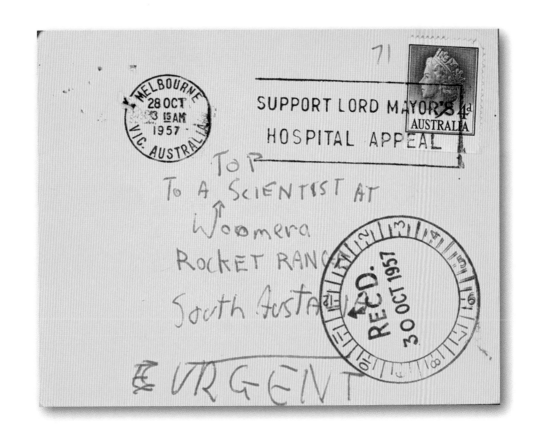

我的火箭　　　　　　　澳大利亞國徽

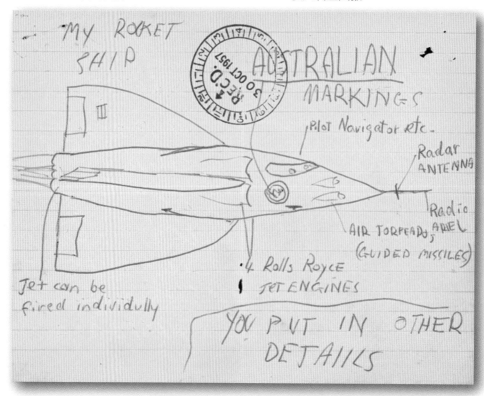

飛行員、領航員等

雷達天線

無線電天線

飛彈（導彈）

四個勞斯萊斯噴射引擎

其他細節由你加

噴射引擎可單獨運作

請回信給我。

這是我設計的火箭
作者丹尼斯·卡克斯
維多利亞省莫里亞洛克丘特街二十六號

回信
澳大利亞政府
國防部
國防科學與科技組織

丹尼斯‧卡克斯先生

〇九年八月二十八

親愛的卡克斯先生，

你的信在一九五七年十月二十日抵達，主旨是個人設計的火箭，在此我向你致謝，並為延遲回覆向你道歉。請你務必諒解，由於你指名「**武默拉火箭試射場**」的「**頂尖科學家**」閱信，你的信過了好一陣子才轉給我。另外，我們也花了一些時日慎重考慮你的點子。

別不多談。最近本單位的HIFiRE計劃試射特超音速火箭成功，我附上一張相片給你參考，你或許看得出，你的設計裡有多處確實可圈可點。成品的尾翼比你的設計稍小，而且尚未進步到能照你建議載人升空。但說也奇怪，大家至今仍照你信中建議，嘗試著火箭引擎和渦輪機並用的概念。這種引擎現在稱為火箭基複合循環發動機（Rocket Based Combined Cycle Engines），功能似乎不輸一九五七年！我也對機身的形狀很感興趣，你的設計確實長處多多！

我認為，最有意思的一句是「**其他細節由你加**」，可見你有朝一日會成為優秀的計劃召集人，懂得尊重專業，給專家自由揮灑。再者，你把「**澳大利亞國徽**」放在最顯著的地方，顯示你懂事物的優先順序。

記得我小時候也曾設計火箭和飛機，當時和寫信的你年齡差不多。不知怎麼的，我的運氣居然夠好，坐上現在的職位，能領導一組人員設計飛機和引擎，不久能以八馬赫飛行，相當於時速九千公里。這些飛機將照你指示，每一架都顯示「**澳大利亞國徽**」，你應該與有榮焉才對。我唯一的心願是，希望我們尚屬稱職，能啟發多年前你信裡傳達的靈感、夢想和希望。

我再次感謝你來信。

（簽名）

亞蘭‧保羅，科學學士、工程科學碩士、科學博士
應用特超音速研究長
航空載具科
DSTO—布里斯本

噁心感排山倒海而來

露西‧瑟斯敦（Lucy Thurston）
致么女瑪麗
一八五五年十月二十九日

在一八一九年十月，二十三歲小學老師露西‧瑟斯敦隨丈夫艾沙（Asa）遷離麻州的家，加入基督傳教會首度前進夏威夷群島的團隊。瑟斯敦夫婦利用下半生教育當地人，協助興學建教堂，甚至翻譯《聖經》。他們育有五名子女，分別是珀西絲‧谷戴爾、露西‧谷戴爾、艾沙‧谷戴爾、瑪麗、哈伍、湯瑪斯‧蓋德納。一八五五年，露西定居夏威夷三十六年了，被診斷罹癌，唯一的療法是切除左乳房。手術本身已經夠痛苦了，更慘的是她不能接受任何形式的麻醉，只能咬牙忍受全程。一個月後，她寫信給么女，描述過程。手術結果很成功，露西有幸多活了二十一年。

我親愛的女兒瑪麗：

　　我九月接受手術，以為妳即將返家，因此迄今不願寫信告知手術經歷，既然妳近日不回家，我在此詳盡描述那些日子的刻骨試煉。六月底開完大會後，妳父親回凱魯亞，留我在檀香山與泰勒先生家人同住，由福特醫師照顧，也找席爾布蘭德醫師會診。八月下旬，他們決定動刀，因此請瑟斯敦先生前來檀香山。我擔心回不了凱魯亞，所以託他帶來一些我要的物件。那時海風強勁，有一艘船被吹垮，從凱魯亞可遙見。另有一艘在前來檀香山途中險些沉沒，折返後報銷。我們想不出其他辦法，只見腫瘤急速惡化，已接近表皮，顯現一團黑暈。萬一破皮成潰瘍，腫瘤的惡性將危害到全身機能。妳哥艾沙說，再等下去，父親還不來，後果他不願承擔。珀西絲也有同感。星期六下午，醫師會診，建議立即動手術，時間訂在翌週星期四（九月十二日）上午十時。醫師將此歸類為「頭等手術」。有鑑於我曾患癲瘓症，兩位醫師一致建議不施氯仿麻醉。我慶幸他們准我使用我的感官。妳姐珀西絲想讓我用她的客廳，妳哥艾沙也願意讓出新娘房供我使用，但我寧可待在茅草屋裡，以圖僻靜。妳弟湯瑪斯把他的物品全搬至幾步遠的房間裡，屋內徹底打掃過，裝修精緻。一位女士稱讚說，好像被人施法，房子變漂亮了。星期一入夜，福特先生上門查看是否一切準備就緒。有兩張整理過的躺椅，一張掛著白蚊帳，另一張瑰紅。有一張坐臥式躺椅，一張手術器具桌，一座洗手臺上有水盆、海綿、水桶。架子上有二十幾條毛巾，有一桌精選興奮劑與補藥，另外也有一桌擺《聖經》和讚美詩。

　　當晚，家人全回自己家睡覺去，我第一次獨守這間房子。在幽靜的暗夜時分，我在寬廣的門院裡來回踱步不休。惡疾纏身、頹廢、無助的我釋然了，將身心託付給聖主，遵照主的指示、智慧、力量行事。總算與天地無羈絆，總算心寧了，我才平心靜氣躺上枕頭，安睡一晚。晴朗的一天降臨。我的心情自然、愉悅、高昂。我信主所言：「你的日子如何，你的力量也必如何。」我

帶著堅定不移的心，求上帝支持賜力。在為手術著裝之前，我特地去拜訪愛倫，因為她一星期前甫分娩。我倆暢談甚歡，態度如常，因她不知今日大事。我接著準備迎接醫師登門。賈德醫師提早到。我帶他去艾沙房間，與艾沙、莎拉坐談片刻，等其他醫護人員騎馬前來。賈德起身外出，我也是。妳哥艾沙說，「妳最好別出去。他們還沒喚妳。」我回應：「我想搶先站好位子，以免倒栽蔥。」我抵達房間，發現福特先生已經來了。他介紹我給檀香山的霍夫曼醫師認識，也介紹當時進港的美國海軍軍艦布雷登醫師。隨後，手術器具平攤桌上，有封阻動脈用的線，有縫傷口用的針，黏合石膏被切成帶狀，繃帶被擺出來，唐椅被他們放在雙扉正門口。一切準備妥當，獨缺大夫一名。所有人站屋內或門廊上。責任落在福特醫師身上，他在門院裡踱步走著。我與其他人站在屋內，閒聊著往事，許久才有人請我坐下，我回應：「因為待會兒一躺就躺很久，我現在寧可站著。」布雷頓醫師事後表示，居然發現即將接受手術的女士同大家站著，令他**至感震驚**。

席爾布蘭德醫師抵達，表示行動的時刻到了。珀西絲與我走進布幕裡，我摘掉帽子，脫下晨衣，穿上白長裙現身，披著一八一八年購買的白邊披肩，在椅子坐下。珀西絲和艾沙站我右側，由珀西絲負責遞給我補藥，艾沙負責在我自制無方時施力。賈德醫師站我右肘邊，用意相同。我拉掉披肩，左臂、胸與腰裸露。福特醫師教我伸左臂至極限，緊握椅子扶手，右手握住右扶手，雙腳緊貼椅腳。指示完畢，一切就緒。福特醫師直視我臉，以甚為鄭重的語氣問：「妳是否決定切除腫瘤？」「是的，大夫。」「妳是否準備好了？」「是的，大夫；不過，開始時請讓我知道，讓我有心理準備。刀子已在你手中嗎？」他攤開手讓我看，說，「我現在要開始了。」隨即，一道深長的傷口從乳房一側劃至另一側，噁心感如排山倒海而來，早餐被迫湧出，極度暈眩感緊接而來。痛苦不再局限，如今充斥渾身上下。我覺得全身每一吋骨肉皆有衰竭之勢。手術全程中，我能自我控制全身與言語。珀西絲與艾沙全力以赴照料我，使用強心劑、阿摩尼亞，為我擦洗太陽穴等等。我有強烈意願見證手術過程。但如今回想，每次我一瞥僅見醫師血淋淋的右手，手腕以下全是血。事後他告訴我，動脈血一度飛濺至他的眼，使他一時看不見。他以近一個半小時的時間，切除全乳房、切除腋下腺、結紮動脈、拭血、縫合傷口、敷上黏合石膏、覆以繃帶。

那一小時的情境與感覺如今歷歷在目。我在切除的過程中開始講話。我感覺跳脫周遭人群而至另一地，此感令我心無拘無束。我因此有感而發：外子不在身旁，令我心實難承受，但朋友如此之多，耶穌基督

也在，他其實不需前來。他以左手枕我頭，右手扶持擁抱我。我願意受苦。我願意死。我不怕死。我不怕地獄。我期待至福永生。請告訴外子，我心寧如江河。

> 「吾眼仰望天，
> 助吾者唯上帝，
> 上帝造天，
> 創大自然造地。
> 上帝為塔
> 我飛翔而去
> 聖恩鄰近
> 時刻皆在。」

上帝對我試煉，但祂溫柔待我。我一度說，「我知道你能忍受我。」艾沙回應，「我想，該忍受我們的人是妳。」醫師切除全乳房後，對我說，「我想從妳腋下再多切除一些。」我回應，「你想做就做，我唯一要求是請你動手前通知我，好讓我有心理準備。」有人說，傷口看似長達超過一英呎。十一條動脈被切斷，開始縫合時，珀西絲說，「母親，醫師的手藝真好，勝過妳一生縫過的所有東西。」「珀西絲，針插進去時告訴我，好讓我有心理準備。」「來了——來了——來了，」諸如此類。「對，告訴我，妳是個乖女兒。」縫十針，每針在傷口兩側各戳一孔。手術完成後，福特醫師與艾沙將我椅移至房間後面，扶我進躺椅。布雷頓醫師來到我身旁，握我一手說，「能如妳那般承受者，千人之中找不到一個。」

到這階段，一切皆記憶猶新。當天午後與夜裡，我僅記得傷口劇痛不止，只願躺在原位。聽說福特先生午後曾來探望，夜裡再來一次，珀西絲與艾沙照顧著我。據說這階段我受苦的程度幾乎與手術期間不相上下。傷口不斷滲冷水。我後來告訴珀西絲，「我認為醫師給我鴉片樟腦酊，我變得迷茫茫。」他卻說，「一滴也沒給妳。」「那我何以不記得經過？」「因為妳痛得氣若游絲了。」晨曦初露，痛停止了。以外科醫師的術語而言，此時傷口進入「第一期癒合」。

那天早上，我又回想往事。我躺在躺椅上，虛弱無助，睜眼見天明。艾沙捧著《聖經》，正走過房間，見我醒，在我附近坐下，朗讀片段，然後祈禱。

接下來數日，狀況幾度急轉直下，為期數小時。受難第三日，星期

四夜，湯瑪斯騎馬近兩英哩，遠赴村子找醫師，一次是晚間七八點，另一次是十一時。醫師兩度前來探望。當晚凌晨二時，他第三度前來，令人意外。第二次探望時，他對珀西絲說：「明早為妳母親煮雞湯。她挨餓夠久了。」（醫師擔心我發高燒。）珀西絲立即喚醒湯瑪斯去抓雞、生火、三時未到已開始熬湯。翌日星期五，在葡萄酒與雞湯幫助下，我稍微恢復精神。下午，妳父親到了。手術後至今，他終於出現，我情緒激動到所剩的半條命也將散盡。手術當天，他從凱魯亞岸上見到一船經過，趕緊划獨木舟出海搭便船，總算啟程。迄今，珀西絲、艾沙、湯瑪斯不分晝夜，充當我僅有的護士。醫師叮囑過，除了照顧者之外，不准閒人入內。

手術後數星期，我機能衰弱無比，僅能藉調羹餵食，情同嬰孩。期間，我歷經無數險境。某日，我眼前的人各個伴隨分身，萬物皆伴隨孿生子。十六年前，我罹患癱瘓症也有同樣幻覺。手術後三星期，妳父親首次扶我仰躺四十五度角，動作緩之又緩，唯恐害我喪失知覺似的。約莫此時，我的狀況逐日長足改善，乃至於困守病榻進入第四週的我在旁人攙扶下已能坐進馬車，幾乎每天與妳父親同行。他在工作空檔，無須負擔家事時，必定全心照顧我，隨時朗讀簡單趣聞給我聽，舒緩氣氛，為我加油，讓我從無度日如年之感，此心意對我至為重要。隨伺在側六星期後，他返回凱魯亞，留我讓醫師與四兒女照料。

幾星期後，母親、泰勒先生、珀西絲、湯瑪斯、露西、瑪麗與喬治告辭艾沙與莎拉，也向他倆的黑眼珠小男娃羅伯特告別，一行人橫渡洶湧海峽，前進老家園。此後，妳父親不再獨自用餐，一家三代同堂進食。

如今，妳母親又如常忙著迎戰日常家務事。再會。縱然我們看不見天主，縱然在病痛纏身之際天主不拭我輩額眉，請天主心神與意念常伴我們左右。

愛妳的母親

他仍在世，生龍活虎，
永遠難忘

史都華・史騰（Stewart Stern）
致溫斯洛（Winslow）**夫婦**
一九五五年十月十二日

加州好萊塢四六
米勒巷一三七二號
一九五五年十月十二日

在一九五五年九月三十日，詹姆
斯・狄恩駕駛保時捷，高速撞車
身亡，年僅二十四。事隔不到一
個月，《養子不教誰之過》（*Rebel
Without a Cause*）上映，觀眾對其
經典級表演激賞不已。告別儀式
在印第安納州費爾芒（Fairmount）
舉行，數千人到場致意，地點離
他童年老家不遠。狄恩母親過世
後，姑媽歐恬絲（Ortense）與姑
丈馬可斯（Marcus）・溫斯洛在此
地農莊撫養狄恩長大。喪禮結束後
幾天，百萬民眾持續為英年早逝的
他哀悼之際，這封悼念信寄到溫斯
洛家，作者是狄恩朋友史都華・史
騰，《養子不教誰之過》腳本也出
自他之筆。

親愛的馬可斯與溫斯洛夫人：

我永生難忘艷陽高照的那天，全鎮靜悄悄。我永生難忘人行
道上的行人步履多謹慎，彷彿唯恐鞋跟倏然磨地聲會吵醒熟睡的
男孩。肅穆的告別式期間，兩位可曾記得誰人提高嗓門，以高過
低語的音量開口？我記得是沒有。全鎮啞然無言，全鎮的咽喉被
愛哽住，全鎮怨嘆未能及時把握時光將愛散佈出去。

印度聖雄甘地曾說，假若廣島民眾仰頭望那架原子彈飛機，
假若大家在心中齊聲嘆息，飛行員就不會投彈了。會或不會，我
們不得而知。但我確定，我確信，我知道——告別式當天從費爾
芒騰空而起一股溫情巨浪，必然緊緊擁抱著那縷難以抗拒的幽
魂，永不鬆手。

我也難忘他生長的故土、他垂釣的溪流，也難忘那些正直、
剛柔的鎮民——他離鄉後百提不厭，往往談至深夜方休。見證過
半部美國史的曾祖父母、他的祖父母與父親、以及他摯愛的你們
三位，總計四代如彈簧的螺旋鐵絲，長達九十年的活歷史，種
籽、耕耘、苗芽，週而復使。他的背景紮實，令人羨慕。彈簧一
放開，他被彈進我們的世界，旋即又被彈出，在他的藝術史上留
下永難磨滅的烙印，如同義大利演員杜絲在世時改變天下。

一顆星在大氣層之外撒野——一顆黑星在看不見的冰冷宇宙
誕生，觸及大氣層。快看！看得見了！星星著火，弧形的身影灼
亮，隨即化為灰燼與記憶，但視覺暫留讓流星映入心眼，讓你我
能一再欣賞。因為它罕見。而且美。我們感謝上帝與大自然將它
送至大家眼前。

能發光的事物不多。美的事物也少得可憐。我們的世界似乎
無能挽留光輝燦爛。唯有嘗過苦，方能體驗極樂的滋味。唯有醜
陋的襯托，美才存在。有戰火在先，世人方能珍惜和平。但願人

間僅有善而無惡。可惜，一缺乏周遭的惡對比，善也消失無蹤，猶如積雪上的一塊白大理石。在爾虞我詐、混搭合成、單調充斥的世界上，吉米昂然獨樹一幟。他來世上，重新組合世人的分子結構。

除了鞋底的乾土，以及一粒玉米種籽，我沒有吉米的遺物。土來自他成長的農莊。我僅有這些東西，別無所求。我仍能感受他的手溫，因此無須碰觸他碰過的東西。他對我有信心，毫無疑問，毫無保留——他曾說，他願演出《養》片是因他知我要他演。另有一次，他曾找《生活》雜誌讓我為他立傳。他告訴我，他覺得我瞭解他，如果雜誌社不讓我為丹尼斯拍攝的相片寫文字說明，他會拒讓雜誌社跨頁刊載相片。我知道《生活》雜誌只派社內編輯撰文，勸他接受，但我永難忘他託付一生於我的感覺。最後，他送我一份厚禮——他的藝能。我的文字，我的一景一幕，藉由他的詮釋演繹，比近代任何演員更傳神。我認為，他另有其他禮物待贈——對象是大家。他的影響力不隨著斷氣而終止，而是與大家同行，深滲大家看待事物的眼光。從吉米身上，我領悟到分秒必爭的價值。他生前愛他的分秒，我從此也將愛我的分秒。

這些文字不夠明確，但總勝過我上週能對兩位表達的心意。

我藉拙筆傳達肺腑的謝意——感謝吉米觸動我人生，開放我視野；感謝兩位以愛灌溉培養他；感謝兩位發揮人性光輝與雅量，在悲慟之餘接納我這陌生人，視我為友。

當我駕車離去之際，暮色泛黃，幾株大樹挺立在天邊。夜空降臨，覆蓋新墳的眾多鮮花跟著黯淡，色澤不敵夕陽。我當時心想，這裡才是他的歸宿——上有漸暗的蒼穹，四處飄送著如山泉般解渴的空氣，有一世紀的家族圍繞他，玉米田簇擁著他常在的牧草地。但他不在牧草地裡。他在玉米中，冬季獵兔，夏季釣鯰魚。他一手放在小馬克肩上，冷不防吻你倆。他教我的精彩笑話引我與他一同歡笑——他仍在世，生龍活虎，永遠難忘，調皮搗蛋的他豈肯長眠？

對兩位與小馬克獻上愛與感激

（簽名）

思念我最大的一顆心

艾蜜莉・狄金生（Emily Dickinson）致蘇珊・吉柏特（Susan Gilbert）

一八五二年六月十一日

一八八六年，美國詩人艾蜜莉.狄金生過世後，親友才發現她寫過多少詩，才瞭解她的才情多麼高深。在藏詩曝光前，大家僅能透過她詩意盎然的書信一窺其才華。她去世四年後，詩集出版，讀者暴增，書信集接著在一八九四年問世，最常通信的對象是蘇珊・杭廷頓・吉柏特。今人認為，啟發狄金生熱情辭藻的人大半是她。蘇珊是她的紅粉知己，在一八五六年更成為她嫂子。狄金生寫給她的信親暱，情意濃厚，不斷引發外人對女女關係的遐想。（這封信提到的雯尼是狄金生胞妹樂雯尼亞[Lavinia]。）

蘇，在六月今日午後，我僅有一念，念念不忘的是**妳**。祈願時，我僅為一人祈願，親愛的蘇，為**妳**。但願妳與我，依心之所趨，**攜手**如童悠遊樹林原野，忘卻過往，忘卻煩憂，兩人再成稚童——這是我的心願，蘇。每當我放眼找妳卻發現四週無人，我再因妳而嘆，小小的嘆息，嘆了也無法喚回妳的嘆息。

妳不在的每一日，我對妳的需求愈來愈深，而大千世界變得日益寬廣，親友變得愈來愈少——我思念我最大的一顆心；我心去流浪了，尋覓蘇——親密不可分之友伴太少了，不久他們將遠去妳我難尋之地。我們千萬不可遺忘這些景況，因為**現在**記住它們，在日後**來不及**愛它們時，才不會心傷連連！

蘇，原諒我，親愛的，因為我每一字——我心充滿著妳，腦海非妳不想，但當我想對妳訴說不足為外人道之語，我卻苦思不出字。假使妳在這裡——若妳真的在，蘇，我倆毋須對話，我倆的眼眸能互訴心語，我手緊握妳手，兩人毋須語言——我試著引妳接近，追逐著時日，追到它們遠邊，想像妳已來臨，而我穿越綠巷相迎，我心雀躍奔馳，結果煞費周章才把心追回，教它沉住氣，耐心等候親愛的蘇到來。三星期——不可能過不完，因為它們終將追隨光陰兄姐，前往西天的長屋！

在相逢之日來臨前，我將愈來愈沉不住氣，因為在這之前，我僅為妳而**哀悼**，現在我開始**盼望**見到妳。

親愛的蘇，我絞盡腦汁思索能寄何物討妳歡心——最後見我的小紫羅蘭求我釋放它們，於是它們進了信封，幾縷騎士草也乞求隨行指引。它們雖小，蘇，而且恐怕如今花香無存，且它們能代轉我在家的心意，能傳達「永不盹睡」的赤誠——將它們壓在枕頭下，蘇，妳將夢見藍天、家園、以及「美好的鄉野」！等妳回家，妳與我將找「艾德華」與「愛倫・密鐸頓」共度一小時——我們將發現某些家事是否屬實。如果是，妳我未來將如何發展！

蘇，行筆至此，再會了。雯尼向妳致意，母親亦然，而我獻上羞怯的一吻，以免被人瞧見！別讓旁人看見，**好嗎**，蘇？

艾蜜莉——

前赴輝格黨大會的代表為何不是我？——難道我不懂丹尼爾‧韋伯斯特、關稅、法律？話說回來，蘇，大會空檔，我見得到妳——但我絲毫不喜歡這國家，也不願在此地再待片刻！美國必滅，麻州必滅！

謹慎開啟我

I

MISS

MY

BIGGEST

HEART

你死期將近

匿名者致黑人民運領袖金恩博士
（**Martin Luther King, JR**）
一九六四年十一月

由於金恩與史丹利・李文森（Stanley Levison）合作聽取政治建言，而後者曾任美國共產黨黨魁，FBI 唯恐金恩將引發國內動盪，因此於一九六四年十一月寫匿名信給金恩，內容粗鄙，語帶脅迫，附上一捲錄音帶，聲稱竊聽自金恩與多名女子開房間的過程。FBI 監聽行動的策劃人是威廉・C・蘇利文（William. C. Sullivan），為期九個月。不出意料，金恩將這封措辭強硬的信視為誘他自盡的詭計。FBI 逼他自殺的另一項證據是一九七六年提出的一份調查報告，由「聯邦眾議員刺殺陰謀調查小組委員會」執筆，內容表示在 FBI 助理局長蘇利文檔案裡起獲一封信的副本，認定該信「顯然暗示自戕是金恩博士適合採取的行動。」

金恩，

有鑑於你層次低……我不屑為你的姓冠上先生、牧師或博士。你的姓只令人聯想到亨利八世國王……

金恩，你捫心反省一下。你自知是個徹頭徹尾的騙徒，是我們全體黑人同胞的一大累贅。我國白種人已有夠多的騙徒了，但我相信，目前他們最可惡的騙徒也難和你抗衡。你不是神職人員，你有自知之明。我再說一遍，你是個天大的騙子，而且是個邪惡、狠毒的騙子。你不可能信上帝……至於私德原則，你一條也不信。

金恩，你和所有騙徒一樣，死期將近。你本來可望成為我們最偉大的領袖。即使在早年，你就已經缺乏領袖風範，只不過是個放蕩失常的缺德低能兒。現在，我們只好仰賴年長的領袖，例如人品高尚的衛金斯，感謝上帝我們還有他這種人。可是，你完了。你的「榮譽」學位，你的諾貝爾獎（胡鬧嘛），再多獎也救不了你。金恩，我再說一遍，你完了。

沒有人能辯得倒事實，連你這種騙徒也沒辦法……我再說一遍──雄辯也扳不倒事實。你完蛋了……他們有些人竟冒充牧師散佈福音。撒旦也瞠乎其後。邪惡到這種程度，難以想像……金恩你完了。

美國民眾和一直幫助你的教會──新教、天主教、猶太人，將認清你的真面目──一個邪惡、變態的野獸。曾支持你的其他人也將覺醒。你完了。

金恩，你只有一條路可走。你自知是哪一條。給你三十四天考慮（這數字有特定原因，具有重要的實用性。你完了。你只剩一條出路。這條路你最好自己走，以免你那齷齪、變態、造假的一面被公諸於全國。*

*編按：信件至此完結

KING,

   King, look into your heart. You know you are a complete
fraud and a great liability to all of us Negroes. White
people in this country have enough frauds of their own but I
am sure they don't have one at this time that is any where near
your equal. You are no clergyman and you know it. I repeat you
are a colossal fraud and an evil, vicious one at that.

   King, like all frauds your end is approaching. You could
have been our greatest leader.

   But you are done. Your "honorary" degrees, your Nobel
Prize (what a grim farce) and other awards will not save you.
King, I repeat you are done.

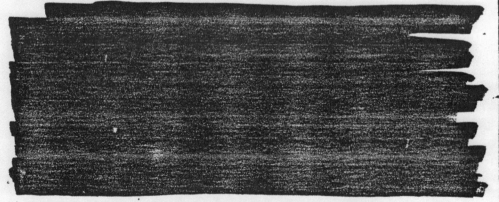

   The American public, the church organizations that have been
helping - Protestant, Catholic and Jews will know you for what
you are - an evil, abnormal beast. So will others who have backed
you. You are done.   #2

   King, there is only one thing left for you to do. You know
what it is. You have just 34 days in which to do (this exact
number has been selected for a specific reason, it has definite

至為重大的發現

法蘭西斯·克里克（**Francis Crick**）致兒子

一九五三年三月十九日

科學家法蘭西斯·克里克發現DNA結構，趕在對外宣佈前幾週，興高采烈在一九五三年三月十九日寫信向寄宿學校的兒子報告。DNA是生物體內負責代代相傳基因的分子，其構造是現代科學界最重大的發現之一，克里克向十二歲兒子解釋DNA是「一種基本的複製機制，能讓物種生生不息。」儘管DNA早在一八六〇年代已由弗雷德里希·米歇爾（Friedrich Miescher）分析出，但今日眾所週知的雙螺旋結構卻直到一九五〇年代初，才由克里克與同事詹姆斯·華生（James Watson），延續前人莫里斯·威爾金斯（Maurice Wilkins）、羅莎琳·佛蘭克林（Rosalind Franklin）以及雷蒙·戈斯林（Raymond Gosling）的成果，確立其模型。一九六二年，克里克、華生與威爾金斯獲頒諾貝爾獎。

二〇一三年四月間，這封信以五百三十萬美元拍賣成交，一躍成為史上身價最高的信。

我親愛的麥可，

　　吉姆·華生和我可能做出一項至為重大的發現。我們研究去氧核糖核酸（發音要謹慎），簡稱DNA，從中建立其結構的模型。你可能記得，附有遺傳因子的染色體基因由蛋白質和DNA組成。

　　我們發現的這結構非常美。DNA大抵可視為長長的一串鏈子，表面有很多扁平的小東西凸出。這些扁平的小東西稱為「基」，公式大致如下。

這種鏈子有兩條，互相纏繞——兩條都呈螺旋狀。由糖和磷組成的鏈子在<u>外面</u>，基全在<u>裡面</u>。我畫得不太好，不過它長得像這樣。

（雙螺旋圖示）

模型比這圖好看<u>幾倍</u>。

振奮人心的是，雖然基有<u>四種</u>，我們卻發現四種未必能配對。這四種基的名字分別是腺嘌呤、鳥嘌呤、胸腺嘧啶、胞嘧啶（Adenine, Guanine, Thymine, Cytosine），簡稱A、G、T、C。我們研究出可配對的組合──也就是一條鏈子的一個基和另一條鏈子的另一個基連接在一起，配對只能是

　　A和T
　　G和C。

就我們所知，一條鏈上的基可以照任何順序排列，但如果排序〈固定〉，那麼另一條鏈上的排序也是固定的。舉例來說，假設第一條鏈如下，那麼第二條鏈〈必定〉也是

$$
\begin{array}{l}
A\!-\!-\!-\!-\!-T \\
T\!-\!-\!-\!-\!-A \\
C\!-\!-\!-\!-\!-G \\
A\!-\!-\!-\!-\!-T \\
G\!-\!-\!-\!-\!-C \\
T\!-\!-\!-\!-\!-A \\
T\!-\!-\!-\!-\!-A
\end{array}
$$

這就像一組符碼。如果你拿到一組，就能寫下排序。

　　另外，我們相信DNA<u>確實</u>是一種符碼。換句話說，基（字母）的排序讓各基因互不相同（正如印刷品的每一頁都不一樣）。現在，你看得出大自然<u>複製基因</u>的方法。因為，如果兩條鏈分開來，各自獨立，如果每一條隨後另找一條鏈來結合，那麼，由於A一定和T配對，而且G一定和C配對，原本的東西現在就被複製成兩份。

　　例如

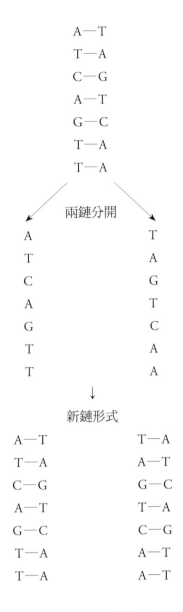

換言之，我們認為，我們發現了生命繁衍不息的複製機制。我們的模型美就美在形狀特別，〈唯有〉這幾種配對能結合，只不過如果它們分開，自由活動，也能以其他方式配對。我們有多麼興奮，你應該能理解。我們過一兩天必須寫信給《自然》雜誌。

　　仔細讀這封信，讀到懂為止。等你回家，再拿模型給你看。

　　　　　　　　　　　　　愛你愛不完的爹地

19 Portugal Place
Cambridge.
19 March '53

My Dear Michael,

Jim Watson and I have probably made a
most important discovery. We have built a model for
the structure of des-oxy-ribose-nucleic-acid (read it
carefully) called D.N.A. for short. You may remember
that the genes of the chromosomes — which carry the
hereditary factors — are made up of protein and
D.N.A.

Our structure is very beautiful. D.N.A.
can be thought of roughly as a very long chain
with flat bits sticking out. The flat
bits are called the "bases": The formula is rather

like this

```
              Sugar ——— base
                |
              phosphorus
                |
              sugar —— base
                |
              phosphorus
                |
              sugar —— base
                |
              phosphorus
                |
              Sugar —— base
                ⋮
              and so on.
```

Now we have **two** ~~the~~ of these chains winding

round each other — each one is a helix — and

the chain, made up of sugar and phosphorus, is

on the _outside_, and the bases are all on the

inside. I can't draw it very well, but it looks

like this

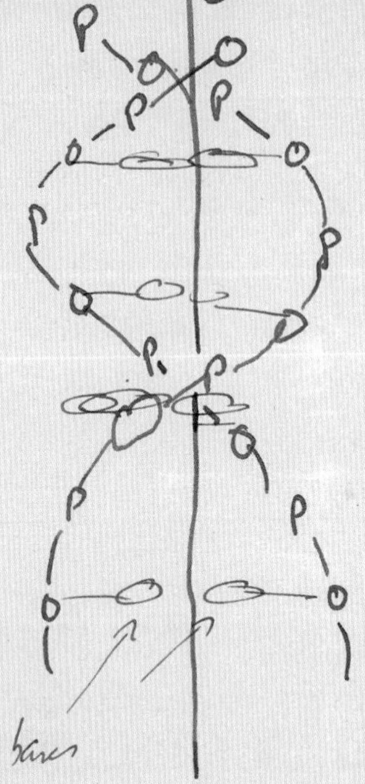

③

bases

The model looks much nicer than this.

Now the exciting thing is that while there
are 4 different bases, we find we can only
put them certain pairs of them together. The
bases have names. They are Adenine, Guanine,
Thymine + Cytosine. I will call them A, G, T
and C. Now we find that the two pairs

we can make — which have one base from
one chain joined to one base from another — are
only   A   with T
        and   G   with C.

Now   on one chain, as far as we can see,
one can have the bases in any order, but if that
order is fixed , then   the order on the other
chain is also fixed. For example , suppose the
first chain goes ↓   then the second must go

A	T
T	A
C	G
A	T
G	C
T	A
T	A

It is like a code. If you ~~cannot~~ are given one set of letters you can write down the others.

Now we believe that the D.N.A. <u>is</u> a code.

That is, the order of the bases (the letters) makes one gene different from another gene (just as one page of print is different from another).

You can now see how Nature <u>makes copies of the genes</u>. Because if the two chains unwind into two separate chains, and if each chain then makes another chain come together on it, then because A always goes with T, and G with C, we shall get two copies where we had one before.

For example

```
A — T
T _ A
C _ G
A _ T
G _ C
T _ A
T _ A
```

← chains separate ↘

```
A                    T
T                    A
C                    G
A                    T
G                    C
T                    C
T                    A
                     A
```

↓ new chains form

```
A — T        T — A
T — A        A — T
C _ G        G — C
A — T        T — A
G — C        C — G
T — A        A — T
T — A        A — T
```

In other words & we think we have found the basic copying mechanism by which life comes from life. The beauty of our model is that the shape of it is such that only these pairs can go together, though they could pair up in other ways if they were floating about freely. You can understand that we are very excited. We have to have a letter off to Nature in a day or so.

~~Read~~ Read this carefully so that you understand it. When you come home we will show you the model.

Lots of love,

Daddy.

達文西的技能

達文西（Leonardo Da Vinci）致米蘭公爵

一四八三年前後

一四八〇年代初，在達文西畫出舉世聞名的《蒙娜麗莎》之前許多年，這位義大利博學者曾向相當於米蘭君主的司甫薩（Ludovico Sforza）公爵遞履歷表。達文西明白公爵想延請軍武工程師，於是擬妥一封應徵信，明示個人似乎不勝枚舉的工程技能，以表列式寫下個人十大專長（接近結尾時才暗示藝術天賦）。本書附上的這封信是定稿，咸信出自專業寫手，而非達文西親筆寫成。後來，他果然受聘，苦心沒有白費。十年後，公爵出資請他畫《最後的晚餐》。

我最敬仰的公爵尊鑑，

在下遍覽並剖析自詡為軍武製作大師巧匠之成就，發現其研發與性能其實無異於尋常器具，因此斗膽在此向公爵獻計，意不在詆譭任何人，而在展現私人機密，今後供公爵差遣，在適當時機運用。個人專長簡述如下：

一、在下構想出一種攜帶式橋樑，質輕堅固，可應用于追討敵軍，有些情況下更能用于逃離敵軍等人，構造強韌，不忌火焚，在戰場上刀槍不入，提抬放置簡便。在下也有燒燬破壞敵軍橋樑之計。

二、包圍敵方之際，在下懂得流放護城河之水，能搭造無限量之橋樑、活動掩體、攀牆梯等器具，以應戰時之需。

三、砲擊過後，包圍某地之際，若礙于斜堤高度或礙于其方位之強度，我方無法進擊，在下也有攻破所有堡壘工事之法，但地基若為岩地則另當別論。

四、在下也有幾種大砲，移動與使用俱便，能拋射小石子，製造近乎劇降冰雹的破壞力，砲煙也能讓敵方聞之色變，唯恐導致巨災大亂。

五、在下也有辦法鑽礦坑，無聲無息打造蜿蜒地道，即使護城河或任何江川在前，也能鑽地底而過。

六、在下亦能製作安全的覆頂車輛，百攻不破，能直搗敵軍與砲兵軍團，再強的武裝勇士也難以阻擋，我方步兵隨後跟進，全員無傷，暢行無阻。

Hauedo S.mo S.re uisto & considerato horamai ad sufficientia le proue di tutti quelli chi se reputono maestri & compositori de instrumenti bellici : et che le inuentione & operatione di dicti instrumenti no sono niente aliene dal comune uso : mi exforzero no derogando a nessuno altro farmi intende da vostra Excellentia : aprendo a quella li secreti mei : & appresso offerendoli ad ogni suo piacimento i tempi oportuni operare cum effecto circa tutte quelle cose che sub breuita saranno qui disotto notate : & ancora in molte piu secondo le occurrentie de diuersi casi

1 Ho modi de ponti leggerissimi & forti & acti ad portare facilissimamente : Et cum quelli seguire & alcuna uolta fuggir li inimici & altri securi & inoffensibili da foco & battaglia : facili & comodi da leuare & ponere : Et modi de ardere & disfare quelli de inimici

2 So in la obsidione de una terra togliere uia l'aqua de fossi : et fare infiniti ponti ghatti & scale & altri instrumenti pertinenti ad dicta expeditione

3 Item se per altezza de argine op. per forteza de loco & di sito no si potesse in la obsidione de una terra usare l'officio de le bombarde : ho modi di ruinare omni forte o altra forteza se gia no fusse fondata in su el sasso

4 Ho anchora modi de bombarde comodissime & facile ad portare : Et cum quelle buttare minuti saxi ad similitudine quasi di tempesta : & cum el fumo di quella dando grande spauento al inimico cum graue suo danno & confusione

5 Et quando accadesse essere in mare ho modi de molti istrumenti actissimi da offende & defende : e navili che faranno resistentia al trare de omni grossissima bombarda : e poluere & fumi

6 Item ho modi per caue & strette & distorte facte senza alcuno strepito peruenire ad uno certo e dicto loco bisognando passare socto fossi o alcuno fiume

7 Item faro carri coperti securi & inoffensibili e quali intrando intra li inimici cum sue artiglierie no e si grande multitudine de gente che no rompessero Et dietro a questi poteranno seguire fanterie assai illesi & senza alcuno impedimento

8 Item occurrendo di bisogno faro bombarde mortari & passauolanti di bellissime & utile forme fora del comune uso

9 Doue mancasse la operatione de le bombarde componero briccole mangani trabuchi & altri instrumenti di mirabile efficacia & fora dal usato : Et in somma secondo la uarieta de casi componero uarie & infinite cose da offende & defende

10 Et quando accadesse essere in mare ho modi de molti instrumenti actissimi ad offendere & defendere & navili che faranno resistentia al trare de omni grossissima bombarda

11 In tempo di pace credo satisfare benissimo ad paragone de ogni altro in architectura in compositione de edificii & publici & priuati & in conducere acqua da uno loco ad uno altro

12 Item conducero in sculptura di marmore di bronzo & di terra : similiter in pictura cio che si possa fare ad paragone de ogni altro & sia chi uole

13 Anchora si potra dare opera al cauallo di bronzo che sara gloria immortale & eterno honore de la felice memoria del Signor uostro patre & de la inclyta casa Sforzesca

Et se alcuna de le sopradicte cose a alcuno paressino impossibile & infactibile me offero paratissimo ad farne experimento in el parco uostro o in qual loco piacera a vostra Excellentia a la quale humilmente quanto piu posso me recomando

七、在下亦能應需求，研製砲彈與輕火砲，設計精美實用，風格
　　獨具。

八、砲彈不適用時，在下能組裝弩砲、射石機、投石機等不常用
　　之器具，效率一流。簡言之，在下能視各種狀況所需，製作
　　種類無限多的攻防品。

九、若遇海戰，在下備齊多種器具，可攻可守，遭逢再重的砲火
　　煙塵也能設法解圍。

十、承平時期，在下自信在設計建造公私房舍、引水流通方面定
　　能包君滿意。

除此之外，在下也能以大理石、銅、黏土雕塑作品。同理，在繪
畫方面，敝人的作品也不輸任何人。

再者，在下亦能製作銅駒塑像，以緬懷公爵父之永恆光輝、永世
榮耀並紀念司甫薩世家。

倘使任何人認為上述任何一點不可行或不適用，在下願在公爵所
屬或指定的公園，竭盡鄙能示範之。

六一年三月二十八

我感到震驚

富蘭納瑞‧歐康納（Flannery O'Connor）致某英文系教授
一九六一年三月二十八日

某校英文系教授代表學生，在一九六一年致函作家富蘭納瑞‧歐康納，請她解釋短篇小說《好男人難覓》（*A Good Man Is Hard to Find*），因班上學生苦思不出合宜的詮釋。

教授在信中寫著，「我們煞費苦心，想出幾種可能的詮釋來辯論，可惜無一能讓所有人滿意。大致而言，我們相信，〈怪胎〉（Misfit）出現具有虛幻的意味，不如小說前半部來得真實。我們相信，怪胎的出現來自貝利（Bailey）的想像，而這份想像源於出遊前一晚、以及在路邊餐廳歇腳時發生的事。我們進一步相信，貝利認同怪胎本人，因此在故事後半段的想像世界一人分飾兩角。但我們絞盡腦汁，仍無法判定現實淡出成幻景的關鍵點。車禍真有其事嗎？或者是貝利做的夢？請相信我，直接向妳請教並非我們想抄捷徑化解難題。我們深愛妳的故事，經過再三檢視不得其解，堅信是我們漏看妳有意讓讀者理解的重點。請妳務必針對以上詮釋表示意見，也請妳進一步說明撰寫《好男人難覓》的用意，我們感激不盡。」
以下是作者的回信，看得出她不以為然。

你的九十位學生和三位老師詮釋得盡善盡美了，已經是儘可能貼近我的用意。若說這份詮釋是正統詮釋，這則故事豈不淪落為語文遊戲，唯有研究變態心理學的人才會感興趣。我對變態心理學沒興趣。

故事前半進入後半時，怪胎登場，張力生變，但真實度並未縮減。我寫這則故事，當然無意把它寫成喬治亞州民眾日常生活的寫照，而是酌情美化扭曲，即使內涵嚴肅，寫法也偏向於笑鬧。貝利的唯一重要性在於，他是聽老媽話的乖兒子，是這輛車的駕駛。最擔心碰到怪胎的人是祖母，率先認出怪胎的人也是她。故事情節有點類似角力戰，一方是祖母和她膚淺的觀念，另一方是怪胎對基督言行的內心感受。這份感受顛覆了怪胎的人生觀。

一則故事的涵義應隨讀者而定，應該讓讀者愈想愈豐富才對，但涵義無法以單一詮釋來闡明。如果老師習慣以解題的方式看待故事，以為任何答案只要是不太顯而易見就值得採信，那麼，我認為學生將永遠無法享受讀小說的樂趣。太多詮釋絕對比太少來得糟。故事讀完若無感，若想以理論取代讀後感，那可行不通。

我無意用罵人的語氣回信。我感到震驚。

富蘭納瑞‧歐康納

無任所聯邦探員

貓王致美國總統尼克森
一九七○年十二月二十一日

人稱搖滾樂之王的貓王酷愛收藏警察徽章，範圍遍及全美警政單位數十種，獨缺最難到手的一個——緝毒署探員徽章。他苦求多年不得，居然在一九七○年十二月搭機前往白宮，親交這封在班機上寫的信。在信裡，他巧言願意效勞緝毒署，擔任「無任所聯邦探員」，對抗毒品。親訪白宮的絕招奏效了。才到幾小時，他就得到尼克森總統接見，匆匆合照後，致贈總統一支科特.45手槍，並索取夢寐以求的徽章。總統答應了，兩人也合影留念，隔天貓王返回自家雅園（Graceland）。

事由奇特的這次會面，相片後來成為國家檔案館史上詢問度最高的一項館藏。

親愛的總統先生：

　　首先容我自介，我是艾維斯‧普列斯萊，久仰您大名，對您領導的政府至為尊敬。三星期前，我在棕櫚泉市與副總統艾格紐（Agnew）面晤，表達個人對我國時局之關切。毒品風氣、嬉皮文化、民主社會學聯（SDS）、黑豹幫等團體**不把我當成他們的敵人**，也不認為我是他們口中的「體制」——<u>我稱之為美國</u>，是我熱愛的對象。總統先生，我可以也願意盡一己所能，為國效勞。我別無顧忌，也無誘因，只想效勞國家。因此，我不奢求頭銜或官位。如果我擔任無住所聯邦探員，我可以也願意造福國家，更願意和各年齡層民眾交流，促進社會進步。我主要是個藝人，目前只欠缺聯邦單位的認證。喬治‧莫菲參議員與我同行，和我在飛機上探討我國當前面臨的問題。

　　總統先生，我即將化名約翰‧布洛斯，投宿華盛頓大飯店五○五—六—七號房，兩位幫手的姓名是傑瑞‧緒凌和桑尼‧威斯特。此行我將待到取得聯邦探員認證才走。我深入研究過毒品濫用問題以及共黨的洗腦詭計，而我置身這兩大問題當中，可以並願意發揮最大助力。

　　我有心效勞國家，但求此事嚴格保密。總統可吩咐部屬或任何人打電話找我，今天、今夜或明天隨時都可以。我入選明年的美國十大傑出青年，即將在一月十八日在我家鄉田納西州孟斐斯頒獎。我將附上一則個人事跡簡介，好讓總統明瞭我此舉的用心。如果總統不是太忙，我希望能見個面，即使只說聲嗨也好。

　　　　　　　　　　　　　　艾維斯‧普列斯萊　敬上

P.S.我相信總統先生也名列美國十大傑出人士之林。

此外我也有一件私禮，願當面致贈，總統若暫時不便收下，我願代為保管。

AmericanAirlines

In Flight...

Altitude;

Location; *O*

Dear Mr. President:

First I would like to introduce myself.
I am Elvis Presley and admire you
and Have Great Respect for your
office. I talked to Vice President
agnew in Palm Springs 3 weeks and
expressed my concern for our Country.
The Drug Culture, The Hippie Elements,
The SDS, Black Panthers, etc do not
consider me as their enemy or as they
call it the Establishment. I call it america and

I Love it. Sir I can and will be of any Service that I can to help the country out. I have no concern or motives other than helping the country out. So I wish not to be given a title or an appointed, position I can and will do more good if I were made a Federal agent at Large, and I will help out by doing it my way through my communications with people of all ages. First and Foremost I am an entertainer but all I need is the Federal credentials. I am on this Plane with

AmericanAirlines

In Flight...　　③

Altitude;

Location;

_____

Sen. George Murphy and we
have been discussing the problems
that our Country is faced with.
So I am Staying at the Washington
hotel Room 505-506-507- I have
2 men who work with me by the
name of Jerry Schilling and Sonny
West. I am regestered under the name
of Jon Burrows. I will be here
for as long as it takes to get
the credentials of a Fedual agent.
I have done an in depth study of
Drug Abuse and Communist Brainwashing

Techniques and I am right in the middle of the whole thing, where I can and will do the most good. I am glad to help; just so long as it is kept very Private. You can have your staff or whoever call me anytime today tonight or Tomorrow I was nominated the coming year one of America's Ten most outstanding young men. That will be in January 18 in my Home Town of Memphis Tenn. I am sending you the short autobiography about myself so you can better understand this

AmericanAirlines

In Flight...

Altitude;

Location; 5

_____

~~approach~~

approach. I would love to meet you just to say hello if you're not to Busy.

Respectfully

Elvis Presley

P.S. I believe that you Sir were one of the Top Ten Outstanding Men of America also.

I have a personal gift for you also which I would like to present to you and you can accept it or I will keep it for you until you can take it.

勿為我哀愁

杜斯妥也夫斯基（Fyodor Dostoevsky）致兄長米克海爾（Mikhail）

一八四九年十二月二十二日

在一八四九年四月，俄國小說作者杜斯妥也夫斯基遭逮捕，罪名是祕密研討被沙皇尼古拉斯一世查禁的書刊，同時入獄的人是培托雪夫斯基（Petrashevsky）文學社的多名知識分子。八個月後，在十二月二十二日，杜斯妥也夫斯基等人被押至聖彼得堡的賽門諾夫操場（Semyonov Place），其中三人被蒙頭綁在柱子上，射擊隊舉起步槍瞄準，全場鴉雀無聲。不久，劃破寂靜的並非扣扳機聲，而是上級下令槍手收槍稍息。原來，在最後一刻，行刑被喊停，文學社成員改服有期徒刑。

同一天後來，杜氏寫信給胞兄米克海爾，描述當天經過，預測未來遭遇，並問候親友。將近五年後，杜斯妥也夫斯基才從西伯利亞的歐姆斯克（Omsk）勞改營獲釋，後來寫出《罪與罰》和《卡拉馬助兄弟》等經典作品。

彼得與保羅堡壘
一八四九年十二月二十二日

米克海爾·米海洛維奇·杜斯妥也夫斯基，
涅瓦大道，葛利亞茲尼街對面，
內司林德之家

兄，我寶貴的好友！一切解決了！我被判勞改四年，地點是堡壘裡（我相信是在歐倫堡），爾後將服兵役。今天，十二月二十二日，我們被押至賽門諾夫操場，得知我們所有人被判處死刑，必須親吻十字架，我們的劍在我們的頭上被折斷，我們進行最後盥洗（白衫）。隨後，三人被綁束於柱，等候處決。我排在第六。被叫出列的人以三人為一組，因此我被歸在第二組，僅存不到一分鐘的活命機會。當時我惦記著你，兄，惦記你的一切；在那最後一刻，唯有你在我心頭，別無他人，我倏然領悟我多麼愛我親愛的兄！普列斯切耶夫和杜洛夫站立我身旁，我設法擁抱他們，向他們道別。最後，撤退號響，宣讀赦免我們性命之聖旨，被綁束柱上的死囚被押回牢籠，隨後改判徒刑。獲赦免刑期的人唯獨坡姆，他歸建陸軍編制。

親愛的兄，我甫得知，我們今明將動身。我要求見你。但獄方告知辦不到，僅准我寫此信，盼你儘快回覆。我擔心你或許已得知我們被判死刑。在前往練兵場途中，我從囚車窗見到大批民眾聚集，也許你聽見消息了，為我憂心忡忡。現在你總算能寬心了。兄！我並未意志消沉，也未情緒低落。生命無處不在，生命自在你我心中，不在身外。人即使在最遠的地方，自有其他人在我身旁，而身為人群中的一人，身為永永遠遠的一人，不會意志消沉，遇到再大的打擊仍隨遇而安──這才是人生，才是人生的重任。我已有這份領悟。這想法已滲進我血肉深處。對，這是事實！曾能產生創意的那顆頭，曾伴隨最高境界的藝術人生的那顆頭，曾領悟並習於性靈最高需求的那顆頭，早已從我身上被砍下。尚在的是記憶，以及由我憧憬但仍未實現的影像。它們未來將撕裂我，這是事實！然而，猶存我體內的是我心，是同樣的血肉，仍能愛，能受苦，能渴望，能記憶，而這一切終究是人生。套句法文的說法是：「我們能見天日！」好了，再會吧，兄！勿為我哀愁！

接下來談實事：我的書（《聖經》尚在）與手稿裡的幾頁──劇本和小說（以及完稿的短篇《一童之故事》[*A Child's*

Tale]）的大綱被沒收了，最後可能歸於你。若你能派人來拿，我也留下大衣和舊衣物。兄，我日後可能須長途跋涉，需要錢。我親愛的兄，當你收到此信，如果你能籌到一<u>些</u>錢，請立刻寄給我。比起空氣，現在的我更需要錢（有一特定用途）。也寫幾句話寄給我。如果來自莫斯科的錢寄到了，記得我，勿拋棄我。好，交代完了！我有債，別無他法。

吻吻你的妻小。持續在他們面前提及我，勿讓他們遺忘我。也許，我們將來仍有機會相見！兄，好好照顧你自己和家人，平靜謹慎度日。思考你小孩的未來……。活得樂觀一點。在精神生活方面，我從未如此富足過。但我的肉身能否堅持不懈？我不知道。我罹患瘰癧，即將帶著病身離去。但切勿掛念！兄，我受過的苦難無數，幾乎沒有任何事物能嚇倒我。再苦的日子儘管來吧！下次一有機會，我將向你表達自我。代我向麥科夫夫婦道別，致最後敬意，轉告他們，我感激他們對我時時刻刻關切。代我問候尤金妮亞‧培妥夫斯納，語氣盡你可能溫馨一些。我祝她幸福快樂，對她的感激與敬意常在我心。代我按一按尼克雷‧阿波羅諾夫奇與阿波隆‧麥科夫之手，也按一按其他所有人的手。去找顏諾夫斯基，按按他的手，感謝他。最後，按按所有仍記得我的人的手。至於已忘掉我的人，也代我提醒他們。吻吻弟弟科亞。寫信給弟弟奧德瑞，告知我的近況。也寫信給叔父母。我衷心請你也代我問候他們。寫給妹妹們：我祝福她們快樂。

也許，有朝一日，我們將能重逢，兄！好好保重，念在上帝份上，繼續生活，直到重逢那一日。也許有朝一日，我們將互擁，重溫兒時黃金歲月，重溫年少光景與願望——在此時，我淌血掏心挖除它們埋葬之。

是否有那麼一天，我將無法提筆？我認為，經過四年勞改後不無可能。假使今後仍能寫，天啊，我每寫必寄給你。何其多的想像由我親身體驗過，由我創思，日後即將凋零枯萎，即將在我腦內滅絕，即將在我血脈裡如毒藥一般裂解！沒錯，假如我被禁止寫作，我將凋零枯萎。若能一筆在手，我寧可服刑十五年！

再勤寫信給我，寫更多細節，更多更多事實。每一封都詳述各式各樣的家事、瑣事，要記得。如此能帶給我希望，賦予我生命力。但願你知你信帶給堡壘裡的我多大鼓舞。過去兩個半月以來，收發信被禁止，我的日子非常難熬。你目前無法寄錢給我，也為我憂心，在在顯示你個人也捉襟見肘！再次吻吻小孩；他們可愛的小臉蛋不曾脫離我心。啊，願他們快樂！你自己也要快樂，兄，要快樂！

切勿哀愁，看在上帝份上，勿為我哀愁！要相信我並未意志消沉，要記得希望並未棄我而去。四年後，我的命運必能好轉。我將成為軍人，——不再是階下囚。請記住，有朝一日我將擁抱你。今天，我在死神魔掌中渡過四十五分鐘，靠著這念頭硬撐過來。走過最後一刻的我現在重獲新生！

如果任何人對我心懷芥蒂，如果我曾與任何人爭吵，如果我在任何人腦海留下壞印象，若你見到他們，請他們忘掉往事。我的心靈不含宿怨或惡意；在此當兒，我渴

望至深的是擁抱任何與我曾交好的朋友。今天在鬼門關前，我向親友道別時，曾感受到這份寬慰。我當時以為，處決的噩耗必使你痛不欲生。如今我仍健在，願你寬心。我將活下去，有朝一日兄弟能互擁的念頭常在我心。目前我僅有此念。

你正在忙什麼？你今天忙著思考什麼？你知道我們的遭遇嗎？今天真冷！

啊，但願我這封信能儘速寄達，否則我將四個月無你音訊。近兩月來，你寄錢的信封上有你親筆寫的地址，見你仍安康，我心雀躍。

每當我回首往事，想到浪擲光陰何其多，想到自己因妄想、犯錯、怠惰、不懂生活道理、不珍重時光、時常反心靈之所欲而行——愈想心愈痛！人生是一份禮，人生是快樂，每一分鐘可以自成一生一世的快樂。法文有道是：「青春見真章！」如今我人生有所轉折，我以新型態再生。兄！我對你發誓，我永不絕望，永保心與靈之純淨。我將脫胎換骨，變得更好。這是我僅有的願望，僅有的慰藉！

監獄生活已斷絕我肉身不甚純潔之雜念；在此之前的我不太重視自身。現在，匱乏擊不倒我，切勿擔心我會被物質上的困境擊垮。不可能！啊！身體健康多好！

再會了，再會，我兄！我何時能再寫信給你呢？我將寫信儘可能詳述一路上的經歷。但求我身體保持健康，萬事必能迎刃而解！

好了，再會吧，再會，兄！我緊緊擁抱你，緊緊吻你。把我記在心裡，無痛。勿哀愁，我求你，勿為我哀愁！下一封信裡，我將告知我近況。接到我下一封信時，你要記得我說過的話：好好規劃人生，不要浪擲生命，勿隨命運擺布，為小孩著想。唉，能見到你該多好！再會了！現在的我硬將自己剝離我摯愛的一切，忍痛揮別一切！痛心的是將自己一分為二，一心切成兩半。再會了！再會！但我深信，我倆將再相見——我希望。勿變，要愛我，勿讓記憶冷卻，兄弟之情常在我心，將成為我人生最美的一部分。再會了，再向你道別一次！所有人，再會！

——弟
菲爾度・杜斯妥也夫斯基
一八四九年十二月二十二日

我遭逮捕時，有幾本書被沒收，其中僅有兩本是禁書。其他的書給你，你願去取用嗎？但我有一份要求：其中一本是《瓦雷瑞恩・梅科夫作品集》（*The Work of Valerian Maikov*），是他的評論文——是尤金妮亞借我的，她視之如珍寶。我遭逮捕時，曾請警官還書給她，並告知地址，不知警官是否已歸還。代我詢問一下！我不願她痛失珍寶。再會了，再次向你道別！

——你的 F・杜斯妥也夫斯基

咖啡豆豆滿載公司（**Chock Full o'Nuts**）

一千七百萬黑人無法靜待人心轉變

傑基·羅賓森（Jackie Robinson）致美國總統艾森豪
一九五八年五月十三日

傑基·羅賓森是一位球技過人的籃球選手，在一九四七年打破籃球界不成文規定，成為首位進軍大小聯盟的非裔球員，隨後六度躋身世界大賽，贏得許多獎項，並在一九六二年榮登籃球名人堂。在一九五七年，他從籃壇退休換換跑道，積極參與政治活動，打擊種族隔離與其他不公義的現象。一九五八年，艾森豪總統演說呼籲爭取民權的非裔美國民眾戒急用忍，羅賓森以此信回應。

紐約州紐約市一七
勒辛頓大道四二五號
一九五八年五月十三日

致總統
華盛頓特區
白宮

親愛的總統先生：

昨天在黑人領袖高峰會上，您勸我們應該忍耐，我也在觀眾席上，當時我多想跳起來說，「不會吧！又來了。」

容我提醒總統先生，我們是最有耐心的族群。當您說，我們應保有自尊，我聽了懷疑，我們怎能經年累月忍受不公平待遇，卻同時保有尊嚴。

一千七百萬黑人無法遵照您的建議靜待人心轉變。我們認為，黑人和全體美國人一樣，有權享受權利，現在就要。其他族群在一百五十多年前已爭取到權利，除非我們現在積極爭取，否則恐難達成心願。

您作為我國最高行政長官，恕我明言，您在無意中打壓黑人的自由心，屢次呼籲黑人忍耐，對著反黑派領袖輸送希望。種族隔離派領袖如佛布斯州長，甚至想奪走我們目前僅有的自由。由您個人與佛布斯州長交手的經驗足以證明，隱忍、族裔不融合才是種族隔離派領袖的目標。

依我淺見，去年秋您和佛布斯州長交手時，曾以行動支持斬釘截鐵的宣言，如果您能再展現相同的魄力，定能宣示美國有決心，近期將賦予黑人在憲法保障下的自由。

傑基·羅賓森敬上

425 LEXINGTON AVENUE
New York 17, N. Y.

May 13, 1958

The President
The White House
Washington, D. C.

My dear Mr. President:

I was sitting in the audience at the Summit Meeting of Negro
Leaders yesterday when you said we must have patience. On
hearing you say this, I felt like standing up and saying, "Oh
no! Not again."

I respectfully remind you sir, that we have been the most
patient of all people. When you said we must have self-
respect, I wondered how we could have self-respect and remain patient considering the treatment accorded us through
the years.

17 million Negroes cannot do as you suggest and wait for the
hearts of men to change. We want to enjoy now the rights
that we feel we are entitled to as Americans. This we cannot do unless we pursue aggressively goals which all other
Americans achieved over 150 years ago.

As the chief executive of our nation, I respectfully suggest
that you unwittingly crush the spirit of freedom in Negroes
by constantly urging forbearance and give hope to those pro-
segregation leaders like Governor Faubus who would take
from us even those freedoms we now enjoy. Your own experience with Governor Faubus is proof enough that forbearance and not eventual integration is the goal the pro-
segregation leaders seek.

In my view, an unequivocal statement backed up by action
such as you demonstrated you could take last fall in deal-

ing with Governor Faubus if it became necessary, would let
it be known that America is determined to provide -- in the
near future -- for Negroes -- the freedoms we are entitled to under the constitution.

Respectfully yours,

Jackie Robinson

Jackie Robinson

JR:cc

信之 *060*

十一員倖存……需小船……甘迺迪

約翰 · F · 甘迺迪致盟軍
一九四三年八月

二次大戰期間，在一九四三年八月二日，未來美國總統甘迺迪擔任 PT-109 魚雷艇指揮官，遭日軍驅逐艦天霧號撞擊，瞬間一分為二，兩名隊員當場殉國。六天後，倖存的弟兄滯留於所羅門群島，甘迺迪在椰殼上刻寫求救信，交給兩名土著彪庫 · 賈沙（Biuku Gasa）與伊洛尼 · 庫馬納（Eroni Kumana），請他們划獨木舟，轉送至三十五海浬外最近的盟軍基地。兩人達成了使命，甘迺迪一行人不久後獲救。

事後，甘迺迪以塑料封存椰殼，於總統任內將椰殼作為橢圓形辦公室裡的紙鎮。

諾魯島指揮官
土著知方位
他能導引
十一員生還
需小船
甘迺迪

剛那顆炸彈掉哪了？

史派克・密里根（Spike Milligan）致史蒂芬・賈德（Stephen Gard）

一九七七年二月二十八日

在一九七七年二月，教師史蒂芬・賈德寫信給英國長青喜劇演員史派克・密里根，詢問不少問題，對密里根的新書《蒙提》（*Monty*）特別感興趣。密里根計劃一連發表七本回憶錄，《蒙提》是第三冊，以密里根在二次大戰軍中生活為主軸。賈德接到一封妙得冷若冰霜的回信。賈德解釋：

「我以影迷身份寫信給他，不過信裡實在是問太多問題了，全是從小到大收聽《呆瓜秀》（*Goon Show*）產生的疑問。惹惱他的問題想必是：『《呆瓜秀》有很多集，例如〈男衫逸事〉那集，總對軍人懦弱的主題百提不厭？其中有一句：「戰俘營裡關滿了誓死不願被俘虜的英國軍官，」引來聽眾大笑，你為何在這句之後走向麥克風說，「感謝同樣是懦夫的各位！」？是因為你自己也被人這樣罵過嗎？』「當然，密里根的下一本回憶錄說明的正是這件事：他被炸到，精神大受震撼，身心症狀交攻，卻又被搞不清楚狀況的指揮官惡行惡狀虐待。我確實也發牢騷說，《蒙提》裡的呆瓜秀風格未免太濃了一點。我的原意是想進一步瞭解他的情

史派克・密里根

一九七七年二月二十八日
倫敦 **W.2.**

歐爾姆巷九號
史蒂芬・賈德紳士
班納盧東公立小學，
泰拉路，
via. MOAMA. 2739.

親愛的史蒂芬，

問題這麼多啊——如果你對我的書《蒙提》失望，我也一樣。我一定比你更失望，因為我花了整整一年蒐集資料，是用來出書好呢，或用來做西裝，令我有點難取捨。

本書裡有許多「單句笑點」，不過話說回來，人一旦碰到德軍猛砸熱呼呼的大鐵球，只講得出單句。其實，這本書應該只寫以下的單句：

「操，慘了」
「小心」
「天啊又來一顆」
「剛那顆掉哪了」
「我的軍卡著火了」
「老天啊，伙食兵死了」。

你應知道，一本書如果只收錄這些單句，絕對沒戲唱，所以我書中的單句笑點是這些短句的延伸。

另外，你煩惱我回憶錄還沒寫到我先後認識瑟康姆和塞勒斯。這嘛，因為《蒙提》最後的時間點還不到我認識這兩人的那年。我認識瑟康姆是在義大利，會出現在第四冊，而我約彼得・塞勒斯在倫敦見面，寫在第五冊的第七十八頁。抱歉我無法讓時空倒轉，不能在一九四一年認識瑟康姆。告知這些資訊後，你又會對我感到失望，恕我無能解消失望之情。

讓你不爽的另一件事是「在敵軍面前展現懦弱」。其實呢，重點是，大戰從頭到尾，我一見到敵軍的臉，懦弱症馬上發作——不只是在敵軍面前，連我見到敵軍的腿、手肘、手腕都怕。

spike milligan

28th February, 1977

9 Orme Court,
LONDON. W. 2.

Stephen Gard Esq.,
Bunnaloo East Public School,
Thyra Road,
via. MOAMA. 2739.

Dear Stephen,

Questions, questions, questions - if you are disappointed in my
book 'MONTY', so am I.   I must be more disappointed than you
because I spent a year collecting material for it, and it was a
choice of having it made into a suit or a book.

There are lots of one liners in the book, but then when the German
Army are throwing bloody great lumps of hot iron at you, one only
has time for one liners, in fact, the book should really consist
of the following:

> "Oh fuck"
>
> "Look out"
>
> "Christ here's another"
>
> "Where did that fall"
>
> "My lorry's on fire"
>
> "Oh Christ, the cook is dead".

You realise a book just consisting of those would just be the end,
so my one liners are extensions of these brevities.

Then you are worried because as yet I have not mentioned my meeting
with Secombe and later Sellers, well by the end of the Monty book
I had as yet not met either Secombe or Sellers.   I met Secombe
in Italy, which will be in vol. 4., and I am arranging to meet
Peter Sellers on page 78 in vol. 5, in London.   I'm sorry I can't
put back the clock to meet Secombe in 1941, to alleviate your
disappointment ≛ hope springs anew with the information I have
given you.

Another thing that bothers you is "cowardice in the face of the
enemy".   Well, the point is I suffer from cowardice in the face
of the enemy throughout the war - in the face of the enemy, also

況。他接著出的幾本回憶錄敘述比較直接了當，讀者較能瞭解這麼有趣、這麼複雜的一個人。

「我也想藉此聲明，接到他這封妙語如珠的信後，我趕緊回信說我多麼仰慕他和他的作品，也拙劣套用呆瓜幽默，附上一張內人和家貓的合照，以證明我的誠意。這封信他沒有回，我也不指望他再回信。」

有一次在前線，一顆迫擊砲在我頭旁邊爆炸（或是我的頭被砲彈炸開？），把我嚇得半死，兩年後發生重度口吃，講話結結巴巴，渾身打顫，有時還驚喊「媽媽」，另外還有痢疾流暢我全身，使得我能退出前線，體檢被降級到B.2.。若非我當時演技精湛，這封信勢必從義大利墳墓寄到你手裡。

你膽敢再發問，我倆的交情就此斷絕。

史派克‧密里根敬上

- 2 -

```
in the legs, the elbows, and the wrists, in fact, after two years
in the front line a mortar bomb exploded by my head (or was it
my head exploded by a Mortar bomb), and it so frightened me, I
put on a tremendous act of stammering, stuttering, and shivering
this mixed with cries of "mother", and a free flow of dysentry
enabled me to be taken out of the line and down-graded to B.2.
But for that brilliant performance, this letter would be coming
to you from a grave in Italy.

Anymore questions from you and our friendship is at an end.


                    Sincerely,



                    Spike Milligan.
```

登月若釀禍

收：哈德門
發：威廉・薩法爾

一九六九年七月十八日

在一九六九年七月十八日，全球屏息等候阿波羅十一號平安降落月球表面之際，專為總統撰寫講稿的威廉・薩法爾（William Safire）擬好這篇用語講究的講稿，註記是：「登月若釀禍」，準備在登月遇突發狀況時由尼克森總統宣佈。實難想像有哪篇備忘錄比這篇更令人心寒。預想狀況是，萬一太空人阿姆斯壯和艾德林受困月球，無法生還，總統將對噓唏遺憾的民眾發表這篇講稿以及其他宣示。如大家所知，這份備忘錄是白寫了，但它仍能隱隱提醒今人，登陸月球喪命的機率不是沒有，政府高層早有最壞的打算。

登月若釀禍：

命運之神已決定，和平探索月球的太空人將安詳長眠月球。

兩位英勇的太空人尼爾・阿姆斯壯與艾德溫・艾德林已明瞭獲救無望，但他們也知，犧牲自己性命可為全人類帶來希望。

兩人捨己追求的是人間最崇高的理念：追尋真理與理解。

親友將哀悼他們，舉國上下將哀悼他們，全球民眾將哀悼他們，敢把兩兒送上虛空的大地也將哀悼他們。

兩位在探索過程中，鼓舞了全球，萬眾齊心期待；兩位壯烈犧牲時，全人類的兄弟情誼更加緊扣。

古人望夜空，在星辰中描摹英雄輪廓。在現代，今人也有類似行徑，不同的是，我們的英雄是史詩型、有血有肉的好漢。

日後，其他人將跟進，必定能安然歸來。人類的探索必將無止境。這兩位勇士是先鋒，將成為你我心中的典範。

未來仰頭望月的人們將知道，天外的一隅有人跡，永遠屬於人類。

總統宣佈之前：
總統應電告即將成為寡婦的兩位。

總統宣佈之後，在NASA結束與兩人通訊之際：
神職人員應循海葬習俗，將兩人靈魂委託給「最深邃的海底」，最後以《主禱文》完結。

To : H. R. Haldeman

From: Bill Safire   July 18, 1969.

IN EVENT OF MOON DISASTER:

Fate has ordained that the men who went to the moon to explore in peace will stay on the moon to rest in peace.

These brave men, Neil Armstrong and Edwin Aldrin, know that there is no hope for their recovery. But they also know that there is hope for mankind in their sacrifice.

These two men are laying down their lives in mankind's most noble goal: the search for truth and understanding.

They will be mourned by their families and friends; they will be mourned by their nation; they will be mourned by the people of the world; they will be mourned by a Mother Earth that dared send two of her sons into the unknown.

In their exploration, they stirred the people of the world to feel as one; in their sacrifice, they bind more tightly the brotherhood of man.

In ancient days, men looked at stars and saw their heroes in the constellations. In modern times, we do much the same, but our heroes are epic men of flesh and blood.

Others will follow, and surely find their way home. Man's search will not be denied. But these men were the first, and they will remain the foremost in our hearts.

For every human being who looks up at the moon in the nights to come will know that there is some corner of another world that is forever mankind.

PRIOR TO THE PRESIDENT'S STATEMENT:

The President should telephone each of the widows-to-be.

AFTER THE PRESIDENT'S STATEMENT, AT THE POINT WHEN NASA ENDS COMMUNICATIONS WITH THE MEN:

A clergyman should adopt the same procedure as a burial at sea, commending their souls to "the deepest of the deep," concluding with the Lord's Prayer.

信之 *063*

最美的絕期

赫胥黎妻致赫兄夫婦
一九六三年十二月八日

以傑作《美麗新世界》刻劃烏托邦
亂象的阿道斯・赫胥黎，一九六〇
年撰寫《島》（*Island*），以烏托邦
美景呼應舊作，不料罹患喉癌。赫
胥黎在一九五三年接觸毒品麥斯卡
靈，著迷於幻覺毒品的效應。一九
六三年十一月，臨終的赫胥黎要求
結婚七年的妻子蘿拉給他LSD，妻
子順從了。赫氏在妻子摯友維金妮
亞・菲弗（Virginia Pfeiffer）家過
世。同年十二月，蘿拉從菲弗家中
致函赫氏兄長朱立安（Julian）和
嫂子茱莉葉，以感性的筆調詳載
丈夫在世最後幾天，信裡提及的
親友包括赫氏與元配所生的獨子
馬修、馬修之妻愛倫（Ellen）、以
及老友羅莎琳・洛丘坡（Rosalind
Rajopal）。這則底稿由毒品教育中
心 Erowid 的 Stolaroff 資料庫提供。

加州洛杉磯市二八，
穆荷蘭公路六二三三號
一九六三年十二月八日

至親朱立安與茱莉葉：

　　阿道斯在世最後一星期有很多情形我想告訴兩位，特別是臨
終那天。那段期間發生的事不僅有必要讓親友知道，也幾乎可算
是他作品的完結篇，更貼切的說法是他作品的延續，因此有必要
公諸於世。

　　首先，我必須向兩位證實，以我全然主觀的斷定，直到阿道
斯過世當天，他理性上遲遲未正視死期將近的事實。潛意識裡，
死的陰影到處都有，兩位有機會自行判斷，因為我在十一月十五
日到十一月二十二日之間錄下阿道斯大部分言談。有這些錄音
帶，我知道我們所有人將至為慶幸。阿道斯向來不太願意捨筆改
口述，也不願以錄音代筆。他使用過速記機，但僅止於讀詩或讀
文學片段，在睡前的幽靜時刻放出來聽。我有一臺錄音機，用很
多年了，有時候想拿出來讓他用，但這臺太笨重了，尤其是現在
成天待在臥房裡，床周圍擺了好多醫藥器材。（我和他商量過，
想另買一臺，但市面上電晶體錄音機充斥，多數品質極差，我也
沒空閒研究，結果買錄音機的事耽擱下來，和我們打算做的許多
事一樣。）十一月初，阿道斯住院後，我的生日到了，所以金妮
仔細研究過所有錄音機種，送我最好的一型——體積小，操作簡
易，簡直不會被人注意到。我自己練習操作幾天，然後拿給阿道
斯看，他非常滿意，於是我們從十五日起，每天錄一小段，記錄
他的夢境，記載將來寫作的素材。

　　在我認為，從十五日到二十二日，阿道斯的思想極為活躍。
那時已開始逐次縮減鎮定藥物的劑量——每天四次一種叫做
Sperine的藥，據我所知近似Thorasin。劑量縮減到趨近零了，只
用Percodon之類的止痛藥，加一點Amitol和治噁心的藥。他也被
注射幾針Dilaudid，一次〇點五CC，是嗎啡的衍生藥，對他造
成多夢的副作用，有些夢的內容收錄在錄音帶裡，兩位可以聽聽

6233 Mulholland Highway
Los Angeles 28, California
December 8, 1963

Dearest Julian and Juliette:

There is so much I want to tell you about the last week of
Aldous' life and particularly the last day. What happened is
important not only for us close and loving but it is almost a
conclusion, better, a continuation of his own work, and there-
for it has importance for people in general.

First of all I must confirm to you with complete subjective
certainty that Aldous had not consciously looked at the fact that
he might die until the day he died. Subconsciously it was all
there, and you will be able to see this for yourselves because
beginning from November 15th until November 22nd I have much of
Aldous' remarks on tape, For these tapes I know we shall all be
immensely grateful. Aldous was never quite willing to give up
his writing and dictate or makes notes on a recorder. He used a
Dictagraph, only to read poetry or passages of literature; he
would listen to these in his quiet moments in the evening as he
was going to sleep. I have had a tapes recorder for years, and
I tried to use it with him sometimes, but it was too bulky, and
particularly now when we were always in the bedroom and the bed
had so much hospital equipment around it. (We had spoken about
buying a small one, but the market here is flooded with transis ter
tape recorders, and most of them are very bad. I didn't have time
to look into it, and this remained just one of those things like
many others that we were going to do.) In the beginning of
November, when Aldous was in the hospital, my birthday occurred,
so Jinny looked carefully into all the machines, and presented me
with the best of them – a small thing, easy manageable and practically unnoticeable. After having practiced with it myself a few
days, I showed it to Aldous, who was very pleased with it, and
from the 15th on we used it a little every day recording his
dreams and notes for future writing.

The period from the 15th to the 22nd marked, it seems to me, a
period of intense mental activity for Aldous. We had diminished
little by little the tranquillizers – he had been taking four
times a day a drug called Sperine which is akin, I understand, to
Thorazin. We diminished it practically to nothing – only used
painkillers like Percoden – a little Amitol, and something for
nausea. He took also a few injections of 1/2 cc of Dilaudid,

看。醫生說，這藥有微量的嗎啡。

言歸剛才主題，在他做的夢裡，在他有些日常對話中，顯而易見的是，他在潛意識裡知道自己快死了，然而，他一次也不曾明講。他有些朋友說，他避不談死，是唯恐我傷心，但我認為不是這麼一回事，因為阿道斯從來就不會演戲，一次也不曾說謊；他缺乏說謊的本性。此外，假如他想避免我傷心，他大可對金妮明講。

在最後那兩個月，我幾乎天天給他暢談死亡的機會，但這種機會當然總可以從生死兩個方向擇一談起，而他總是選生不選死。他讀完里瑞（Leary）醫生從《生死書》（*The Book of the Dead*）萃取而來的整本手冊。他本可開玩笑說，別忘了提醒我，但他卻只朝里瑞醫生進行LSD療法的方向去談，說半死的人經過治療後，能被醫生引回今生。他的確有時會說類似這種話：「如果我能挺過這一關，」他就能把新的寫作構想付諸紙筆，想著是否能恢復寫作的氣力，何時才能恢復。他的頭腦非常活躍，大腦的某個部位似乎被這個Dilaudid刺激到了，他這部位以前不太常被刺激到。

在他過世的前一夜（星期四晚上），大約八點，他忽然產生一個念頭。他說，「親愛的，我剛想到，金妮家有兩個小孩，我病這麼重，住在她家，該不會強人所難吧。我覺得真的是強人所難。」金妮當時不在家，所以我說，「好啊，等她回來，我會告訴她的。保證會逗得她大笑。」他聽了，以罕見的堅持語氣說，「不行，我們應該想辦法。」我回應，口氣保持輕鬆，「好吧，可以，你下床吧，我們去旅行。」他說，「不行。認真一點。我們非想辦法不可。屋裡這麼多護士進進出出。我們不妨租一間公寓，渡過這段時期。只過了這段時期就好。」他的含意非常明確，明確無誤。他以為，他可能還會病個三四禮拜，然後就能痊癒，恢復正常生活。重新過正常日子的念頭常常產生。在最後三四星期裡，他數度為自身的羸弱而心驚，因為他發現自己失去太多活力了，要多久才能復原。在星期四晚上，他以少見的活力提到租屋養病一事，但幾分鐘後，整個晚上，我覺得他開始走下坡，迅速失守。進食幾乎是不可能的事。他只喝了幾匙流質和果

which is a derivative of morphine, and which gave him many dreams, some of which you will hear on the tape. The doctor says this is a small intake of morphine.

Now to pick up my point again, in these dreams as well as sometimes in his conversation, it seemed obvious and transparent that subconsciously he knew that he was going to die. But not once consciously did he speak of it. This had nothing to do with the idea that some of his friends put forward, that he wanted to spare me. It wasn't this, because Aldous had never been able to play a part, to say a single lie; he was constitutionall unable to lie, and if he wanted to spare me, he could certainly have spoken to Jinny.

During the last two months I gave him almost daily an opportunity, an opening for speaking about death, but of course this opening was always one that could have been taken in two ways - either towards life or towards death, and he always took it towards life. We read the entire manual of Dr. Leary extracted from The Book of the Dead. He could have, even jokingly said - don't forget to remind me - his comment instead was only directed to the way Dr. Leary conducted his LSD sessions, and how he would bring people, who were not dead, back here to this life after the session. It is true he said sometimes phrases like, "If I get out of this," in connection to his new ideas for writing, and wondered when and if he would have the strength to work. His mind was very active and it seems that this Dilaudid had stirred some new layer which had not often been stirred in him.

The night before he died, (Thursday night) about eight o'clock, suddenly an idea occurred to him. "Darling," he said, "it just occurs to me that I am imposing on Jinny having somebody as sick as this in the house with the two children, this is really an imposition." Jinny was out of the house at the moment, and so I said, "Good, when she comes back I will tell her this. It will be a nice laugh." "No," he said with unusual insistence, "we should do something about it." "Well," I replied, keeping it light, "all right, get up. Let's go on a trip." "No," he said, "It is serious. We must think about it. All these nurses in the house. What we could do, we could take an apartment for this period. Just for this period." It was very clear what he meant. It was unmistakeably clear. He thought he might be so sick for another three or four weeks, and then he could come back and start his normal life again. This fact of starting his normal life occurred quite often. In the last three or four weeks he was several times appalled by his weakness, when he realized how much he had lost, and how long it would take to be normal again. Now this Thursday night he had remarked about taking an apartment with an unusual energy, but a few minutes later and all that evening I felt that he was going down, he was losing ground quickly. Eating

菜漿。事實上，每次他進食，必定會開始咳嗽。星期四晚上，我打電話給柏恩斯坦醫生，告知病人的脈搏非常快——一百四，而且有點發燒，我的直覺是死期近在眼前。然而，護士和醫生都否定。他們說，如果我想請醫生來，醫生願意當晚前來看他。後來我回到阿道斯房間，我們決定給他注射一針Dilaudid。那時大約九點，打完針他睡著了，我請醫生明早才來。阿道斯睡到凌晨兩點左右，再挨一針，我早上六點半再來看他。我再次覺得生命力正逐漸流失，總覺得哪個地方比平常更不對勁，但我也說不出哪裡不對勁。不久後，我發電報給你們、馬修、愛倫、和我妹。後來，大約早上九點，阿道斯情緒開始煩躁，身體很不舒服，說穿了是心煩到極點。他一直叫我幫他動一動身子。怎麼移都不對勁。柏恩斯坦醫生這時候來了，決定打一針以前打過一次的藥，藉點滴，非常緩慢，花了五分鐘才打完。這種藥能舒張支氣管，讓呼吸順暢一些。

以前打這種藥，他很不舒服，應該是三週前的星期五，那時他情況告急，我寫信告訴過你們。雖然不舒服，那次的藥仍然對他有幫助。但這次卻很糟糕。他雖無法自我表達，一看就知道他感覺糟透了，渾身不對勁，換什麼姿勢都不對勁。我問他怎麼了。他言語困難，勉強說，「單單是講話，情況就更加惡化。」他不斷叫我幫他移動身子。「移動我。」「移動我的腿。」「移動我的手臂。」「移動我的床。」他躺的是那種按鈕昇降床，頭腳都可以提高放下。我忙著按鈕，一下子提高，一下子又放下，按個不停，總算似乎能稍微消除不適，但效果非常非常之小。

大概在十點左右，突然間，他幾乎講不出話，他說他想要寫字板，首度寫下——「如果我死了……」寫出他的遺願。我懂他的意思。我一星期前告訴過你們，他已經在遺書上簽名。這一份遺書把壽險受益人從我轉給馬修。我們討論過轉移事宜，前一陣子請保險公司寄文件過來，居然就在那前幾分鐘派專人送到。寫字對他來說非常非常辛苦。羅莎琳和柏恩斯坦醫生也在場，盡量揣摩他的心意。我對他說，「你的意思是，你想確定壽險從我轉給馬修嗎？」他說，「對。」我說，「轉移的文件剛到，你想簽名的話可以現在簽，不過你沒必要簽名，因為你已經在遺囑裡讓轉移成立了。」不必簽名，他如釋重負嘆一口氣。我前一天要求他

was almost out of the question. He had just taken a few spoonsful of liquid and puree, in fact every time that he took something, this would start the cough. Thursday night I called Dr. Bernstein, and told him the pulse was very high – 140, he had a little bit of fever and my whole feeling was one of immanence of death. But both the nurse and the doctor said they didn't think this was the case, but that if I wanted him the doctor would come up to see him that night. Then I returned to Aldous' room and we decided to give him an injection of Dilaudid. It was about nine o'clock, and he went to sleep and I told the doctor to come the next morning. Aldous slept until about two a.m. and then he got another shot, and I saw him again at six-thirty. Again I felt that life was leaving, something was more wrong than usual, although I didn't know exactly what, and a little later I sent you and Matthew and Ellen and my sister a wire. Then about nine a.m. Aldous began to be so agitated, so uncomfortable, so desperate really. He wanted to be moved all the time. Nothing was right. Dr. Bernstein came about that time and decided to give him a shot which he had given him once before, something that you give intravenously, very slowly – it takes five minutes to give the shot, and it is a drug that dilates the bronchial tubes, so that respiration is easier.

This drug made him uncomfortable the time before, it must have been three Fridays before, when he had that crisis I wrote you about. But then it helped him. This time it was quite terrible. He couldn't express himself but he was feeling dreadul, nothing was right, no position was right. I tried to ask him what was occurring. He had difficulty in speaking, but he managed to say, "Just trying to tell you makes it worse." He wanted to be moved all the time – "Move me." "Move my legs." "Move my arms." "Move my bed." I had one of those push-button beds, which moved up and down both from the head and the feet, and incessantly, at times, I would have him go up and down, up and down by pushing buttons. We did this again, and somehow it seemed to give him a little relief. but it was very, very little.

All of a sudden, it must have been then ten o'clock, he could hardly speak, and he said he wanted a tablet to write on, and for the first time he wrote – "If I die," and gave a direction for his will. I knew what he meant. He had signed his will as I told you about a week before, and in this will there was a transfer of a life insurance policy from me to Matthew. We had spoken of getting these papers of transfer, which the insurance company had just sent, and that actually arrived special delivery just a few minutes before. Writing was very, very difficult for him. Rosalind and Dr. Bernstein were there trying also to understand what he wanted. I said to him, "Do you mean that you want to make sure that the life insurance is transferred from me to Matthew?" He said, "Yes." I said, "The papers for the transfer have just arrived,

簽一些重要文件，他說，「再等一小陣子吧。」順帶一提，這句話是他這階段的口頭禪，意思是他沒辦法做。進食的時間到了，他會說，「再等一小陣子吧。」星期四，我要他簽一份很重要的東西時，他又說——「再等一小陣子吧。」他想寫信給你們——「尤其是對茱莉葉的書的心得，寫得很美。」他說過好幾遍。我提議代他寫時，他會說，「好，再等一小陣子吧。」他的語氣極為疲憊，和他平常判若兩人。所以當他聽我說簽名沒必要，一切都妥當了，他才如釋重負嘆氣。

「如果我死了。」這是他首度指涉到**當前**。他寫下這句。我知道也意識到，他首度正視死亡。有一位精神科醫生名叫席尼・科恩，是LSD療法的名醫，在他寫下這句的半小時之前，我問醫生是否曾對如此病重的病人注射LSD，他說他其實只做過兩次，其中一次讓病人稍微接受死亡的命運，另一次毫無影響。我問他能否教我如何對病重的阿道斯投藥。我告訴醫生，這兩個月來，我多次問他想不想要LSD，他總回答，等到病情好轉再說。這時科恩醫生說，「我不曉得。我認為不適合。妳認為呢？」我說，「我也不知道。不如我問問他要不要？」醫生說，「如果由我問他，我會以迂迴的方式問，『你想不想改天再試試看LSD？』」我請教過這領域的幾個醫護人員：「你在病危的情況下會用LSD嗎？」得到的回應都像這醫生，總是模稜兩可。就我所知的指涉當中，《島》是唯一明確的一個。我大概在九點半和科恩醫生通電話。阿道斯的情況惡化到痛苦不堪，神智混沌，情緒激動到講不清他要的是什麼，而我也搞不懂。他一度講了一句話，在場無人能向我解釋他說了什麼，他說，「誰拿著我的碗吃東西？」我當時不懂這話的含意，現在仍猜不透。我問他。他擠出微弱的悠悠一笑，說，「沒什麼意思啦，說笑而已。」後來，我覺得有必要多瞭解他一點，好讓我能盡一些力，他以氣人的口吻說，「在這個當兒，能分享的東西太少了。」我當下明白，他自知他快走了。然而，無以表達自我的情形只是肌肉不聽使喚而已——他的腦筋很清楚。另外我也覺得，當時他的頭腦激烈運轉中。

後來，我忘了是幾點了，他要我遞寫字板給他，寫下，「試LSD一百微克，肌肉注射。」照這份影印本雖然看不太清楚，但

if you want to sign them you can sign them, but it is not necessary because you already made it legal in your will. He heaved a sigh of relief in not having to sign. I had asked him the day before even, to sign some important papers, and he had said, "Let's wait a little while." This, by the way, was his way now, for him to say that he couldn't do something. If he was asked to eat, he would say, "Let's wait a little while," and when I asked him to do some signing that was rather important on Thursday he said, "Let's wait a little while." He wanted to write you a letter – "and especially about Juliette's book, is lovely," he had said several times. And when I proposed to do it, he would say, "Yes, just in a little while." in such a tired voice, so totally different from his normal way of being. So when I told him that the signing was not necessary and that all was in order, he had a sigh of relief.

"If I die." This was the first time that he had said that with reference to NOW. He wrote it. I knew and felt that for the first time he was looking at this. About a half an hour before I had called up Sidney Cohen, a psychiatrist who has been one of the leaders in the use of LSD. I had asked him if he had ever given LSD to a man in this condition. He said that he had only done it twice actually, and in one case it had brought up a sort of reconciliation with Death, and in the other case it did not make any difference. I asked him if he would advise me to give it to Aldous in his condition. I told him how I had offered it several times during the last two months, but he always said that he would wait until he was better. Then Dr. Cohen said, "I don't know. I don't think so. What do you think?" I said, "I don't know. Shall I offer it to him?" He said, "I would offer it to him in a very oblique way, just say 'what do you think about taking LSD?'" This ~sometimes again?~ vague response had been common to the few workers in this field to whom I had asked, "Do you give LSD in extremes?" ISLAND is the only definite reference that I know of. I must have spoken to Sidney Cohen about nine-thirty. Aldous' condition had become so physically painful and obscure, and he was so agitated he couldn't say what he wanted, and I couldn't understand. At a certain point he said something which no one here has been able to explain to me, he said, "Who is eating out of my bowl?" And I didn't know what this meant and I yet don't know. And I asked him. He managed a faint whimsical smile and said, "Oh, never mind, it is only a joke." And later on, feeling my need to know a little so I could do something, he said in an agonizing way, "At this point there is so little to share." Then I knew that he knew that he was going. However, this inability to express himself was only muscular – his brain was clear and in fact, I feel, at a pitch of activity.

Then I don't know exactly what time it was, he asked for his tablet and wrote, "Try LSD 100 mgs intramuscular." Although as you see from this photostatic copy it is not very clear, I know that this is what he meant. I asked him and he confirmed it. Suddenly something became very clear to me. I knew that we were

我懂他的意思。我問他，他證實了。霎然間，我頓悟了一件事。近兩個月來，我倆交談起來很折騰人，見他如此寫，我知道我倆又心靈契合了。我當下明白，我知道該怎麼辦。我趕緊去柏恩斯坦醫生的房間，電視剛宣佈甘迺迪遇刺的新聞。我從那房間的碗櫥取出 LSD，說，「應他要求，我想為他打一針 LSD。」醫生情急了一陣，因為你們很清楚，醫界對這種藥還沒有定論。然後他說，「好吧，病到這階段，沒差別了。」無論醫生怎麼說，再強勢的權威、甚至出動一支威權部隊，當時都攔不住我。我回阿道斯的房間，手裡多了一小瓶 LSD，準備針筒。醫生問我，要不要讓醫生注射，也許是我手在抖，他看見了。經他這麼一問，我才察覺手抖的現象，我說，「不用了，我打就好。」我穩定自己情緒，注射時，雙手變得非常堅定。隨後，不知怎麼的，我倆感覺卸下心頭的巨石。第一次為他注射一百微克，時間應該是十一點二十。我坐在他床邊，說，「親愛的，等一會兒，我自己也來一針吧。你要不要我待會兒也來一針？」我說「待會兒」是因為我自己也不清楚何時能用藥，事實上，由於身旁的情況一直很亂，我至今仍無法用藥。他聽了表示，「好。」請記住，到這階段，他的言語非常非常少。接著我說，「你要不要馬修也陪你來一針？」他說，「好。」「那愛倫呢？」他說，「好。」接著我提到兩三個接觸 LSD 的人，他夾雜義大利文說，「不，不，夠了，夠了。」接著我說，「金妮呢？」他加強語氣說，「好。」之後我們不語。我默默坐著，半晌不開口。阿道斯的肢體不再那麼煩躁了。他似乎──我隱隱覺得他知道，我倆都知道我們在做什麼，這總讓阿道斯大為釋懷。在他病倒後，我多次見到他情緒很沮喪，直到他想到自己該怎麼辦，情緒才好轉。後來，即使是遇到手術或拍 X 光，他會徹底轉變，莫大的鬆懈感會籠罩他，讓他完全不擔憂即將面臨的事，他會說，動手吧，而我們就動手，他活像獲得解放。現在我也有同樣的感受──決定了，他再度明快做決定。忽然，他接受了死的事實；他接受了他信服的解放藥。他正在實踐他寫在《島》裡的理念，而我覺得，他感興趣、如釋重負、安寧。

過了半小時，他的表情開始略有變化。我問他是否感覺到 LSD 的藥效，他表示沒有。話雖這麼說，我認為某種作用已開始發威。這是阿道斯的特點之一。無論任何藥，即使藥效相當明顯

together again after this torturous talking of the last two
months. I knew then, I knew what was to be done. I went quickly
into the cupboard in the other room where Dr. Bernstein was, and
the TV which had just announced the shooting of Kennedy. I took
the LSD and said, "I am going to give him a shot of LSD, he asked
for it." The doctor had a moment of agitation because you khow
very well the uneasiness about this drug in the medical mind.
Then he said, "All right, at this point what is the difference."
Whatever he had said, no"authority," not even an army of
authorities could have stopped me then. I went into Aldous' room
with the vial of LSD and prepared a syringe. The doctor asked me
if I wanted him to give him the shot - maybe because he saw that
my hands were trembling. His asking me that made me conscious of
my hands, and I said, "No, I must do this. " I quieted myself, and
when I gave him the shot my hands were very firm. Then, somehow,
a great relief came to us both. I believe it was 11:20 when I gave
him his first shot of 100 microgrammes. I sat near his bed and
I said, "Darling, maybe in a little while I will take it with you.
Would you like me to take it also in a little while?" I said a
little while because I had no idea of when I should or could take
it, in fact I have not been able to take it to this writing because
of the condition around me. And he indicated "yes." We must keep
in mind that by now he was speaking very, very little. Then I said,
"Would you like Matthew to take it with you also?" And he said,
"Yes." "What about Ellen?" He said, "Yes." Then I mentioned
two or three people who had been working with LSD and he said, "No,
no, basta, basta." Then I said, "What about Jinny?" And he said,
"Yes," with emphasis. Then we were quiet. I just sat there
without speaking for a while. Aldous was not so agitated physically. He seemed - somehow I felt he knew, we both knew what we
were doing, and this h₂s always been a great relief to Aldous. I
have seen him at times during his illness very upset until he knew
what he was going to do, then even if it was an operation or
X-ray, he would make a total change. This enormous feeling of
relief would come to him, and he wouldn't be worried at all about
it, he would say let's do it, and we would go to it and he was
like a liberated man. And now I had the same feeling - a decision
had been made, he made the decision again very quickly. Suddenly
he had accepted the fact of death; he had taken this moksha
medicine in which he believed. He was doing what he had written
in ISLAND, and I had the feeling that he was interested and
relieved and quiet.

After half an hour, the expression on his face began to change
a little, and I asked him if he felt the effect of LSD, and he
indicated no. Yet, I think that a something had taken place
already. This was one of Aldous' characteristics. He would
always delay acknowledging the effect of any medicine, even when
the effect was quiet certainly there, unless the effect was very, very
stong he would say no. Now, the expression of his face was
beginning to look as it did every time that he had the moksha

了，他總習慣拖延一段時間才承認藥已生效，除非效果非常非常強，否則他一概說，還沒效果。現在，他的表情開始像他每次接受解放藥後的模樣，愛和極樂的神態充滿整張臉，但這次不同。不過，和兩小時之前相比，他的表情已有轉變。我再等半小時，然後決定再給他一百微克。我對他說我要打針了，他默許。針打完後，我開始對他講話。他現在變得非常安靜；他非常安靜，兩腿愈來愈冷，紫紺的範圍愈升愈高。接著，我開始對他說，「輕盈，自由。」在最後那幾星期，晚上我常在他睡前講一些話助眠，這時我在語氣裡加重說服力，說得更迫切──「去吧，去吧，放開手，親愛的；向前，向上。你正要向前向上走。你正走向光明。你有意願也有意識地走，有意願也有意識。你的表現非常棒；你做得很棒──你正走向光明；你正走向更浩瀚的愛；你往前走，往上走。好輕鬆，好優美。你做得好輕鬆，好優美。向前，向上。你帶著我的愛，正投向聖母愛的懷抱。你正走向你今生從未體驗過的大愛。你正走向最高深、最浩瀚的愛，好輕鬆，好輕鬆，而且你的表現好棒。」我開始講這些話時，大概是下午一兩點的事。我很難注意時間。護士在房間裡，羅莎琳和金妮和兩位醫生──奈特醫生和科特勒醫生也在場。他們離床鋪有點遠，我則是非常非常接近他的耳邊，希望我講得清晰，容易理解。我一度問他，「你聽得見我嗎？」他捏捏我手。他聽得見。我本想多問幾句，但早上他求我不要再問了，整體的感覺是對勁了。我不敢問，不敢打擾，所以只問一個問題：「你聽得見我嗎？」也許我該多問幾句，但我沒問。

後來，我問相同問題，但他不再動作。從兩點到他去世──五點二十，在這段期間，一切平靜無事，只有在大約三點半或四點，我見到他下唇開始掙扎。他的下唇動起來了，彷彿他拚命想喘氣。這時候，我加強對他下的指令。「做起來很輕鬆，你做得很棒，做得有意願，有意識，全然自覺，全然自覺，親愛的，你正走向光明。」在最後三四小時，我重複這幾句或類似的話。偶爾，我的情緒激動到無法言語，我會立刻離開床邊兩三分鐘，情緒平復之後才重回床邊。下唇抽抖的現象只維持一會兒，似乎完全在呼應我說的話。「輕鬆，輕鬆，你做得很棒，有意願，有意識──你往前往上走，輕盈，自由，向前向上走向光明，走進光輝裡，進入徹底的愛。」抽抖停了，呼吸變得愈來愈慢，絲毫不

medicine, when this immense expression of complete bliss and love would come over him. This was not the case now, but there was a change in comparison to what his face had been two hours ago. I let another half hour pass, and then I decided to give him another 100 mg. I told him I was going to do it, and he acquiesced. I gave him another shot, and then I began to talk to him. He was very quiet now; he was very quiet and his legs were getting colder; higher and higher I could see purple areas of cynosis. Then I began to talk to him, saying, "Light and free." Some of these things I told him at night in these last few weeks before he would go to sleep, and now I said it more convincingly, more intensely - 'go, go, let go, darling; forward and up. You are going forward and up; you are going towards the light. Willing and consciously you are going, willingly and consciously, and you are doing this beautifully; you are doing this so beautifully - you are going towards the light; you are going towards a greater love; you are going forward and up. It is so easy; it is so beautiful. You are doing it so beautifully, so easily. Light and free. Forward and up. You are going towards Maria's love with my love. You are going towards a greater love than you have ever known. You are going towards the best, the greatest love, and it is easy, it is so easy, and you are doing it so beautifully." I believe I started to talk to him - it must have been about one or two o'clock. It was very difficult for me to keep track of time. The nurse was in the room, and Rosalind and Jinny and two doctors - Dr. Knight and Dr. Cutler. They were sort of far away from the bed. I was very, very near his ears, and I hope I spoke clearly and understandingly. Once I asked him, "Do you hear me?" He squeezed my hand. He was hearing me. I was tempted to ask more questions, but in the morning he had begged me not to ask any more question, and the entire feeling was that things were right. I didn't dare to inquire, to disturb, and that was the only question that I asked, "Do you hear me?" Maybe I should have asked more questions, but I didn't.

Later on I asked the same question, but the hand didn't move any more. Now from two o'clock until the time he died, which was five-twenty, there was complete peace except for once. That must have been about three-thirty or four, when I saw the beginning of struggle in his lower lip. His lower lip began to move as if it were going to be a struggle for air. Then I gave the direction even more forcefully. "It is easy, and you are doing this beautifully and willingly and consciously, in full awareness, in full awareness, darling, you are going towards the light." I repeated these or similar words for the last three or four hours. Once in a while my own emotion would overcome me, but if it did I immediately would leave the bed for two or three minutes, and would come back only when I could dismiss my emotion. The twitching of the lower lip lasted only a little bit, and it seemed to respond completely to what I was saying. "Easy, easy, and you are doing this willingly and consciously and beautifully -

見攣縮、掙扎的現象，只見呼吸愈來愈慢，愈來愈慢，愈來愈慢。五點二十分，呼吸停止。

那天早上，有人對我預警，病人死前可能有攣縮的現象，肺可能攣縮，會冒出聲響，令人不忍卒睹。有些人以為死前肢體會出現某些可怕的反應，想對我做好心理建設，幸好慘狀全沒發生，呼吸停止的過程完全不見波濤，因為過程非常緩慢，非常輕柔，好像一首曲子剛以柔美的尾音結束。我當時覺得，最後一小時的呼吸其實是人體的制約反射動作，動了六十九年，動了幾億萬次，不會說停就停。聽人說，嚥下最後一口氣時，靈魂會脫離肉身，我倒沒有感覺到，只覺得靈魂在最後四小時輕輕飄離。在房間裡，最後四小時有兩位醫生、金妮、護士、羅莎琳·羅傑·葛坡。你們知道她是克里希那穆提大師的摯友，也是加州歐海那所學校的校長，阿道斯對那學校盡過不少心力。他們似乎沒聽見我說的話。我以為我的音量夠大，但他們說他們沒聽見。羅莎琳和金妮偶爾靠近床邊，握握阿道斯的手。這五人全說，這樣走最安詳、最美。兩位醫生和護士說，他們從未見過類似病況的病人走得這麼平靜，完全無痛無掙扎。

是否真是如此，這是不是我們一廂情願的想法，我們永遠無從得知，但從外在跡象與內心感受判斷，他走得確實是優美、安詳、輕鬆。

我獨處的這些日子以來，較不受外人心情的轟炸，最後那天對我的意義愈來愈明晰，也愈來愈重要。《島》裡的東西不被認真看待，讓阿道斯大為感冒（我覺得是）。雖然書被視為科幻小說，內容卻不是虛構的，因為他描寫的每一種生活方式都不是他想像出來的產物，而是在某地真正實行過的生活，有些甚至引用我們的日常生活。如果阿道斯的死法公諸於世，或能喚醒世人，讓他們知道此事，更能讓他們接受書中描述的許多事實可能出現在現世裡。阿道斯臨終要求解脫藥，表示他對個人著作的信心更堅定，因此此事不僅對我們重要，對世人也很重要。沒錯，日後有些人會批評說，他一輩子毒癮纏身，以毒品結束生命，但史上不爭的事實是，人間眾多的赫氏被無知攔阻之前，赫氏會先制止無知。

going forward and up, light anf free, forward and up towards the
light, into the light, into complete love." The twitching
stopped, the breating became slower and slower, and there was
absolutely not the slightest indication of contraction, of struggle.
it was just that the breathing became slower - and slower - and
slower, and at five-twenty the breathing stopped.

I had been warned in the morning that there might be some
up-setting convulsions towards the end, or some sort of contraction
of the lungs, and noises. People had been trying to prepare me for
some horrible physical reaction that would probably occur. None
of this happened, actually the ceasing of the breathing was not a
drama at all, because it was done so slowly, so gently, like a
piece of music just finishing in a sempre piu piano dolcemente.
I had the feeling actually that the last hour of breathing was
only the conditioned reflex of the body that had been used to
doing this for 69 years, millions and millions of times. There
was not the feeling that with the last breath, the spirit left.
It had just been gently leaving for the last four hours. In the
room the last four hours were two doctors, Jinny, the nurse,
Rosalind and Roger Gopal - you know she is the great friend of
Krishnamurti, and the directress of the school in Ojai for which
Aldous did so much. They didn't seem to hear what I was saying.
I thought I was speaking loud enough, but they said they didn't
hear it. Rosalind and Jinny once in a while came near the bed
and held Aldous' hand. These five people all said that this was
the most serene, the most beautiful death. Both doctors and nurse
said they had never seen a person in similar physical condition
going off so completely without pain and without struggle.

We will never know if all this is only our wishful thinking,
or if it is rea l, but certainly all outward signs and the inner
feeling gave indication that it was beautiful and peaceful and
easy.

And now, after I have been alone these few days, and less
bombarded by other people's feelings, the meaning of this last
day becomes clearer and clearer to me and more and more important.
Aldous was, I think (and certainly I am) appalled at the fact
that what he wrote in ISLAND was not taken seriously. It was
treated as a work of science fiction, when it was not fiction
because each one of the ways of living he described in ISLAND was
not a product of his fantasy, but something that had been tried
in one place or another and some of them in our own everyday
life. If the way Aldous died were known, it might awaken
people to the awareness that not only this, but many other facts
described in ISLAND are possible here and now. Aldous' asking
for moksha medicine while dying is a confirmation of his work,
and as such is of importance not only to us, but to the world.
It is true we will have some people saying that he was a drug
addict all his life and that he ended as one, but it is history
that Huxley's stop ignorance before ignoracne can stop Huxleys.

即使在我們通信討論病情之後，我仍覺得保密不讓他知道病情非常不妥。我總覺得，他寫了這麼多、談過這麼多以死亡為題的論述，任他懵懵懂懂走向死亡，對他似乎不太公平。而他對我的信心堅定不移——可能認定，如果死期將近，我必然會告訴他、幫助他。因此，他能猛然覺醒並迅速調適，令我大大鬆了一口氣。你們是否也有同感？

　　至於他這種走法為的只是讓我們寬心安慰，或者也希望造福其他人，你們有何見解？

8

Even after our correspondence on the subject, I had many doubts about keeping Aldous in the dark regarding his condition. It seemed not just that, after all he had written and spoken about death, he should be let to go into it unaware. And he had such complete confidence in me - he might have taken it for granted that had death been near I certainly would have told him and helped him. So my relief at his sudden awakening at his quick adjusting is immense. Don't you feel this also.

Now, is his way of dying to remain our, and only our relief and consolation, or should others also benefit from it? What do you feel?

信之 064

水壩怨言 *

地主致水土管理局

一九九八年一月六日

一九九七年十二月，密西根州水土管理局接獲民眾申訴，對迪夫瑞斯（DeVries）先生發出這封措辭嚴厲的警告信函，迪夫瑞斯是房客，所以把信轉給房東史蒂芬·提韋登（Steve Tvedten）。水土局指稱，他的土地上有一條溪流通過，他「未經核可」建造兩座「危險」水壩，限他六星期之內拆除，否則訴諸法律。地主立即回信，詼諧的措辭躍上地方新聞，水土局不久後表示不予追訴。

*譯註：屋主回應內容裡「水壩」（dam）一詞全可置換為「該死的，天殺的，去你的（damn）。」

密西根州
一九九七年十二月十七日
存證信函

親愛的迪夫瑞斯先生：

主旨：環境品質部檔案編號97-59-0023-1 T11N, R10W, Sec.20，蒙特康郡

據環境品質部瞭解，上述土地最近出現未經核可的活動。經查證，臺端依法是地主或建商或兩者皆是，涉及從事以下未經核可之行為：

在春泉池外流的溪流上建築並維護兩座廢木水壩。此類工程進行前必須先申請核可。經本單位調查，此工程並未獲得核可。

有鑑於此，本單位判定此工程違反天然資源與環境保護法案內陸湖泊河川法第三〇一條、一九九四年公共法案第四五一條、密西根編纂法規註解之324.30101至324.30113。本單位獲知，近日降雨時，該水壩之一或全數有半毀的現象，導致下游地區廢物阻塞並淹水。本單位發現，此類型水壩本身具有危險性，無法發照施工，因此下令臺端在此處即刻停止所有未經核可之活動，並移除阻塞流水之所有木頭與樹叢，將溪流恢復固有之流動性。限臺端於一九九八年一月三十一日之前完成修復工作，並請修復完成後通知本單位，以便本單位安排日期派員前去驗收。若臺端不從，若臺端未經核可在同地進一步違建，本單位將請更高機關取締之，敬請臺端全力配合。

如有任何問題，請不吝至本單位指教。

（刪除）
敬上
水土管理局區域代表

九八年一月六日

（刪除）
水土管理局區域代表
大湍流區辦事處

親愛的（刪除）：

主旨：環境品質部檔案編號97-59-0023-1 T11N, R10W, Sec.20，蒙特康郡

你九七年十二月十七日的存證信函已轉交我手，由我回覆。你寄了許多複寫本給很多人，但你卻忘了附上他們的地址，因此你只好影印我的回信寄給他們。

首先，萊恩‧迪夫瑞斯依法不是密西根州皮爾森鎮戴格特路二〇八八號的地主或建商或其中之一，那塊地是我的，土地上有一對河狸，正在春泉池的溢流溪上（未經州府核可）建造並維護兩座「廢木」水壩。我並未付錢請牠們施工，也未准許牠們造壩，而牠們善用天然建材居然被你斥之為「廢木」，我想牠們會覺得大受侮辱。我願代牠們向你下戰帖，看你有沒有能耐把水壩蓋得比牠們更高明，時間地點由你自選。我能信心滿滿地說，你再厲害，和牠們的水壩技巧、水壩巧思、善用資源、堅忍不拔、決心毅力、敬業精神相比，你絕對望塵莫及。

你說築水壩之前，河狸必須填妥相關申請表，而我第一條水壩疑問是：你是想歧視我家春泉池河狸，或是想要求全州所有水壩河狸遵守上述的水壩要求？如果你並非歧視我家這一對河狸，請把其他相關河狸水壩許可證的影本全寄給我瞧瞧，如此一來，或許我們能研究看看是否真有水壩觸犯了天然資源與環境保護法案內陸湖泊河川法第三〇一條、一九九四年公共法案第四五一條、密西根編纂法規註解之324.30101至324.30113。

我最關切的是，水壩河狸難道無權延請水壩律師嗎？春泉池河狸貧困潦倒，無錢聘請水壩律師，因此州府必須代請公設水壩律師。環境部憂心說，近日降雨，水壩之一或全數故障，導致水壩氾濫，這足以證明我們不應招惹春泉池造壩河狸，不應該騷擾、謾罵牠們。如果你希望「恢復」水流的流動性，你自己去聯絡水壩河狸們。不過，如果你準備逮捕牠們（牠們不懂英文，顯然不理會你寄的水壩信），你可別忘了先宣讀水壩人權給牠們聽。

至於我本人，我不準備干擾這些水壩建築工，以免造成更多水壩洪災或雜物阻塞。如果你想對這些水壩河狸不利，請記得，我影印你的水壩信和這封回信各一份，正想寄給善待動物協會PETA。如果你那水壩環境部真的認定此類水壩本質上具有危險性，真的不願允許這類水壩存在於本州，我誠摯希望你不要選擇性執法，否則我與春泉池

河狸將再度齊聲喊冤！

依我淺見，只要天藍、草綠、水往低處流，春泉池河狸就有權造壩。我有權住春泉池，享受春泉池，牠們比我更有水壩權。因此，就我和河狸而言，這件水壩案儘管請上級執法取締吧。幹嘛等到九八年一月三十一日呢？等到一月底，河狸可能被水壩冰封住了，你或你的水壩部屬也沒法子聯絡／騷擾牠們。最後，我盼望你去關切一種真正有損環境品質（健康）的問題：熊真的在我們的樹林裡便溺。我堅持主張你去取締隨地便溺的熊，少煩水壩河狸。如果你想調查河狸水壩，走路可要當心喔！（熊隨地撇條，不看風水喔！）

由於我無法順從你的水壩要求，也無法透過你的水壩答錄機聯絡你，所以寄這封信到你的水壩辦事處去。

史蒂芬・L・提韋登
副本抄送：PETA

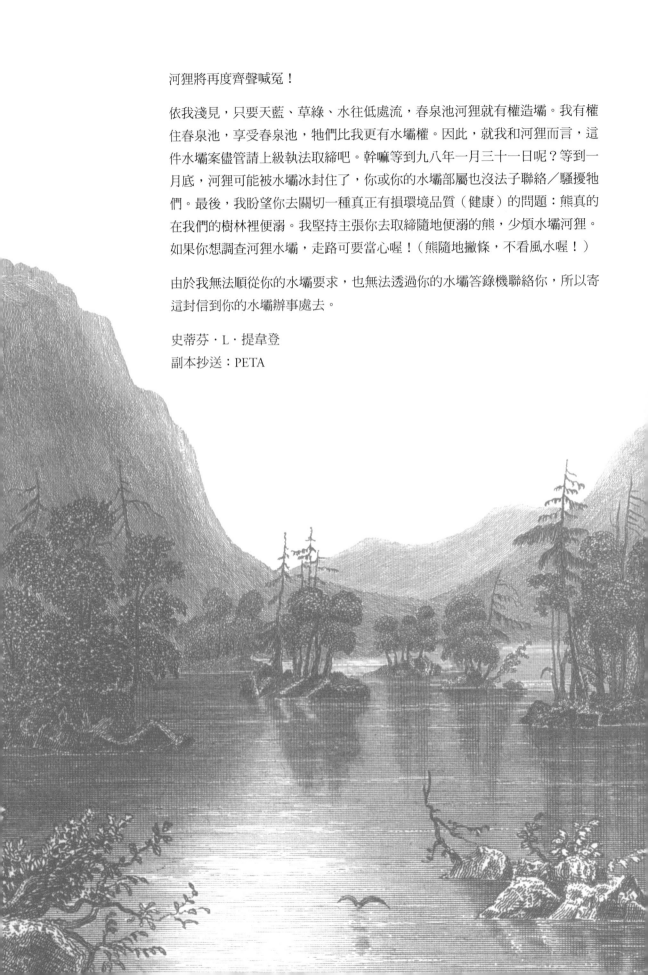

何必探索太空？

航太主管致修女
一九七〇年五月六日

在一九七〇年，尚比亞修女瑪麗·裘昆達（Jucunda）致函美國航太總署，馬歇爾太空飛行中心科學主任恩斯特·史都凌格（Ernst Stuhlinger）博士接到信。修女在信中詢問太空人探索火星的必要性，更質疑火星計劃的經費高達數十億美元，怎能棄當前全球無數飢童不顧？主任以思慮周詳的長篇語句娓娓解釋，並附上一幅經典太空圖——一九六八年太空人威廉·安德斯（Anders）從月球上空拍攝的地球初昇照。主任的回信廣獲同事稱讚，後來航太總署決定以《為何探索太空》為標題公諸於世。

親愛的瑪麗·裘昆達修女：

我每天接到許多信，您的信是其中一封，但它帶給我的感受比其他信更深，因為它來自求知心深處，出自於人性關懷，誠摯深刻。我在此竭盡我所能回答您的疑問。

但首先我想說的是，我極為欽佩您與無數勇敢的修女，因為妳們貢獻終生履行人類最崇高的理念：義助困苦的世人同胞。

您信中質疑，當前全球餓到瀕死的兒童多不勝數，為何我竟然提議耗資數十億美元，送太空人升空去探索火星。我大可回答說，「唉，我不曉得有兒童快被餓死了，好，從今以後，我不再推動任何太空研究計劃，等全人類解決飢餓問題再說！」但我知道您要的並非這種回答。其實，早在我知道探索火星在技術上行得通之前，我就已經知道世上有飢童問題。然而，我和我許多朋友的共識是，前進月球、然後再前進火星與其他行星，是我們應即刻著手進行的計劃，而我甚至相信，長遠來看，如果想解決地球上的嚴峻考驗，太空計劃比救濟方案的貢獻更深遠。很多救濟提案年復一年爭辯不休，進程遲緩如流沙，實質成果不彰。

在我詳述太空計劃如何協助地球化解難題之前，我想簡述一則據信是真的故事，或許能藉這故事支持我的論點。大約四百年前，德國小鎮住著一位善心伯爵，常捐出大半收入來濟助鎮裡的貧民，鎮民對他很感激，因為在中世紀飢民遍野，瘟疫經常肆虐。有一天，伯爵遇見一名陌生人，見他在家中闢一小間實驗室，也有一臺工作桌。這人平日辛勤賣力做工，好讓自己每天晚上能進實驗室裡玩幾小時。在實驗室裡，男子將玻璃碎片琢磨成小鏡片，將鏡片裝進管子兩端，用來細看小之又小的物體。伯爵特別讚嘆的是，鏡片的放大作用很強，能用來觀察他從未見過的微小生物。伯爵請男子將實驗室遷移到城堡裡，男子成為伯爵家的一員，以特聘員工的身份，全神專注於開發改良光學器材。

鎮民發現伯爵竟把錢浪費在這種無用的小玩意上，忿而批判，「我們受瘟疫之苦，而他居然出錢給那人培養一個沒用的嗜好！」但伯爵意志堅定。「我已經盡能力幫助你們了，」他說，「但我也想支持這人的工作，因為我知道總有一天，成品一定有用處！」

成品確實大有用處，而其他地方由別人開發出的類似成品也同樣能造福人類：顯微鏡。眾所週知，在醫學史上，顯微鏡的貢獻超越任何一種發明。此外，瘟疫和多數傳染惡疾絕跡，顯微鏡加持的研究也居功厥偉。

伯爵將部分捐款保留下來，轉用於研發，對消除世人苦難的貢獻遠大於全額濟助瘟疫災民。

我們今日面對的情況和小鎮伯爵有很多相似之處。美國總統每年預算支出大約兩千億美元，花在保健、教育、福利、市區更新、公路、運輸、援外、國防、環保、科學、農業，以及許多國內外設施。以今年而言，國家預算大約百分之一點六分給太空探索之用。太空預算涵蓋阿波羅計劃，以及許多較小型的太空物理學、太空天文學、太空生物學、行星研究、地球資源、太空工程等計劃。為了促成以上太空計劃，平均年收入一萬美元的美國納稅人支付大約三十元，其餘的九千九百七十元花在個人衣食住行、娛樂、存款、其他支出，繳其他稅。

您或許想問：「既然美國納稅人平均花三十元在太空計劃上，為什麼不從裡面扣一元或三元或五元，用來幫助飢童？」在回答這問題前，我必須簡短解釋我國經濟如何運作。美國經濟的運作和其他國家非常相似。政府下分為幾個部（內政部、司法部、健康部、教育福利部、交通部、國防部等等），下面分出更多單位（國家科學基金會、國家航太總署等等），所有部會每年依其既定任務統整預算數字並提出，由國會裡的相關委員會嚴審，而且必須承受來自總統和預算局的高壓。預算通過審核後，國會終於撥款下來了，錢只能用在預算裡被核准的詳細項目。

航太總署的預算當然只能用在與航太直接相關的事項上。如果這筆預算被國會否決了，這筆錢不會被挪用在其他地方，而是從一開始就不會向納稅人徵收，除非其他單位的預算獲准提高，如此一來，未能用在太空研究的款項會被這項預算吸收。美國以援外的方式，其實已慷慨幫助飢童了。但從這段簡短的解釋可知，若想額外再濟助飢童，唯有靠相關部會在提出預算報告時多加這麼一筆，而且這一筆必須通過國會的審核。

您或許會接著問，我個人是否贊成我國政府這麼做。我不但舉雙手贊

成，而且也不介意每年多繳幾元，以便政府把多出來的稅金拿去餵飽國內外的貧童。

我知道，所有朋友和我都有同感。然而，單單是扼殺火星計劃，並不能促成濟助飢童的方案，其實停止火星計劃的效果將適得其反。我甚至相信，我如果繼續在太空計劃上努力，不但能對飢童問題做出間接貢獻，最終更可望解決全球貧窮飢荒等重大問題。造成飢荒的基本因素一是糧食生產，二是糧食分配。糧食生產於農業、牧業、海洋漁業等大規模營運活動，在部分地區的產量很有效率，但在許多地區亟待加強。舉例來說，地球上有廣大區域的土地欠缺水土保持、施肥、氣象預報、肥料評估、農場規劃、原野選擇、種植習慣、農作物抽樣、收成計劃，也不注重栽種時機，如果能改進這些缺點，土地的運用將更具效率。

無庸置疑的是，改善以上缺點的最佳工具是人造衛星。環繞地球、居高臨下的衛星能在短時間內遍覽廣大土地，也能觀察測量繁多的因素，得知農作物、土壤、乾旱、降雨、積雪等等的現狀，進而將得到的資訊以電波傳給地面善用。據估計，即使是一小群人造衛星搭配地球資源和感應器，只要能配合一套全球農業改進措施，必能讓農作物年產量暴增數十億產值。

將糧食運到飢民手裡，又是完全不同的一種問題。這問題的癥結不在於出貨量，而是必須靠各國攜手合作。大國捐大批糧食，等著送給小國，小國國君可能非常為難，唯恐外國勢力隨著糧食入侵。遺憾的是，想有效掃除飢荒，必須先化解國與國之間對峙的情勢。我不信太空計劃能在一夕之間創造奇蹟並解決糧荒問題。然而，在破除糧荒的方法中，最具潛力和效力的推手之一就是太空計劃。

且讓我一提最近阿波羅十三號差點釀成悲劇一事。在太空人即將返回大氣層的關鍵時刻，蘇聯為避免干擾到阿波羅計劃的無線電，下令全蘇聯停止使用同一頻率，也派遣蘇聯艦艇守在太平洋和大西洋，以利失事時就近搶救。假如太空人座艙掉在蘇聯艦艇附近，蘇聯鐵定不計代價，一視同仁，把重返地球的美國太空人視為蘇聯人看待。如果蘇聯太空人也遇到類似緊急狀況，美國人無疑也會伸出援手。

藉由空照評估提高糧食產量，改善國際關係以促進糧食配送，這只是太空計劃大幅改善地球生活的兩例。我想再舉兩個例證：太空計劃能刺激科技發展並創新科學知識。

建造升月太空船，組件不僅高精密，更容不下一絲差錯，其要求之嚴苛，在工程學史無前例。為了符合高標準，人類被迫研發新材料和新管道，發明更高超的技術與製造程序，設法延長儀器的壽命，甚至因此發現新的大自然定律。

這些新近技能也能應用於地球科技上。太空計劃產生的新科技當中，每年有大約一千種應用在地球科技上，改良了廚房用品、農場器材、縫紉機、無線電、船艦、飛機、氣象預報、劇烈天候預警、通訊、醫學儀器、器皿和日常生活工具。您大概會接著問，為什麼要先為登月太空人研發維生系統呢？為何不能先為心臟病患研發遠程感應器？答案很簡單：技術問題的重大突破，往往不是來自直接埋頭研究，而是先放遠目標，把挑戰設定得更高深，這樣才能強化創新的動機，點燃想像力，鞭策人類使出渾身解數。將挑戰設定得更高更遠，也能觸發週邊的連鎖反應。

太空飛行無疑能扮演這種角色。航向火星絕對無法直接為飢民變出糧食，卻可望引發許許多多新科技和技術，應用之後物超所值不知千萬倍。

若想改善地球人類生活，除了追求新科技之外，科學界更持續渴望追求新的基礎知識，舉凡物理學、化學、生物學、生理學，尤其是醫學，都需要更多知識以對抗威脅人命的問題：飢荒、疾病、飲水糧食污染、環境污染。

我們需要更多青年男女以科學為志業，需要更大力支持有天資、有決心的青年投身成果豐碩的研究工作，必須提供他們更具挑戰性的研究目標，為研究計劃提供更豐富的人力物力。太空計劃提供絕佳機會，讓科學人深究月球、行星、物理學、天文學、生物學、醫學之奧祕，幾乎是一種近乎完美的觸媒，能觸發以下三種因素的交互作用：一、科學研究的動機，二、觀察振奮人心的自然現象的機會，三、實現研究所需的人力物力。

美國政府主導、控制、資助的所有活動當中，太空計劃絕對是能見度最高，可能也是最受爭議的一種，而太空計劃才佔全國總預算百分之一點六，相當於國民生產毛額不到百分之〇點三三。太空計劃既能刺激觸發新科技，更能帶動基礎科學研究，其價值讓其他預算項目望塵莫及。由此看來，我們甚至可以說，太空計劃取代了三、四千年以來戰爭所扮演的角色。

假使全球各國能放下武器，不再以火箭和戰機炸得你死我活，改以登月太空船一較高下，這樣做能減輕多少人間的苦難啊！在太空計劃上互別苗頭，出線者日後不僅前途無量，這種競爭更不會導致落敗者流離失所，導致復仇，導致新一輪的戰爭。

表面上看來，太空計劃把目標指向日月星辰，遠離地表，實際上，我相信這些天體受到的關注遠不及地球。地球明天會更好，不只因為所有新科技、新科學知識將應用在改善生活上，也因為我們正對地球、人生、人類培養出更深的一份感念。

我附上的相片拍攝於一九六八年耶誕節，是阿波羅八號繞月時拍攝的地球照。太空計劃至今產生的佳績多如繁星，最重要的一個或許是這張令人大開眼界的相片：你我因此明瞭，在浩瀚無邊際的虛空之中，地球是一座價值無限的美麗島，你我別無其他地方可住，只能在薄薄的地球表面存活，外圍全是黝暗真空。很多人看到這相片才恍然大悟：地球多麼渺小，破壞生態平衡是一件多麼危險的事。自從這張相片首度曝光以來，愈來愈多人大聲疾呼正視當代重大問題——污染、飢荒、貧窮都市生活、糧食生產、水資源管制、人口爆炸等等，呼聲愈來愈高。絕非意外的是，初生的太空時代讓我們首度正視我們所在的行星，我們才開始面對當前的艱鉅任務。

幸好，太空時代不僅舉鏡子讓地球人照照自己，更提供了科技、挑戰、動機，甚至讓讓你我樂觀自信迎戰難題。我相信，我們從太空計劃學習到的新知，完全能佐證史懷哲名言的真諦：「放眼未來，我帶著憂心，但也懷抱美好的希望。」

願最誠摯的祝福永遠伴隨您與兒女。

恩斯特·史都凌格

科學部副主任

一九七三年十一月十六日

真實的血肉之軀

馮內果（Kurt Vonnegut）致校區委員長
一九七三年十一月十六日

科幻作家馮內果的半自傳式穿越小說《第五號屠宰場》（*Slaughterhouse 5*）於一九六七年出版，儘管受各界推崇為傑出現代小說之一，卻至今仍被全球學校和圖書館列為禁書，常見的原因是內容「猥褻」。但在一九七三年，北達科他（Dakota）州卓瑞克（Drake）中學二十六歲英文老師布魯斯·歇沃里（Bruce Severy）決定拿來當輔助教材用，令學生大為高興，卻惹惱了校區委員長查爾斯·麥卡錫（Charles McCarthy）。委員長下令，班上三十二本書全應扔進學校裡的火爐燒掉。很多學生抗議，有些甚至拒絕把書交出去，可惜剛正的立場被校方漠視。

一九七三年十一月十六日，馮內果失望憤怒之餘，寫信向委員長傳達心聲，擲地有聲的這封信卻無回音。

親愛的麥卡錫先生：

我寫這封信針對的是你在卓瑞克校區擔任委員長的職權。你在學校焚書出名了，我是那些書的美國作者之一。

貴社群的部分人士指稱我的作品有邪性，對我造成莫大侮辱。卓雷克校區的這則新聞傳出後，令我意識到，書和作者對你們而言是非常虛幻的東西。我寫這封是想讓你們知道我有多真實。

我也想讓你們知道，卓雷克校區傳出這件噁心的新聞後，我和出版商都無意趁機炒作話題，不會互擁拍拍背慶賀這新聞會帶動多少書熱賣。我們拒上電視，也寫了措辭嚴厲的信投書報社民意版，拒絕接受長篇專訪。我們既憤慨、反感而沉痛。這封信僅此一封，沒有副本寄給其他人。你手裡的這份是絕無僅有的，是由我個人發給卓雷克校區的私信。貴校區殘害我個人名譽，先是在學童心目中作賤我，然後在全世界面前凌遲我。你們有沒有勇氣，有沒有常理心，敢把公開這封信給民眾看呢？或者會直接把信扔進爐子裡燒掉？

我閱報看電視大致得知，我和其他作者被你想像成鼠輩，專靠毒害少年心牟利。我其實是五十一歲的高壯男人，兒時在農場幹過不少活，擅長使用修繕工具，育有子女六名，其中三個是親身骨肉，另三個領養，各個都是正直的年輕人，其中兩個務農。我是二次大戰步兵戰鬥師的退伍軍人，曾獲頒紫心勳章。我的財產全是我辛苦掙來的。我從未被逮捕，從未被人告上法院。一般年輕人非常信任我，而在我任教的愛荷華大學、哈佛大學、紐約市學院裡的學生也是，每年有至少十幾封邀請函請我去高中大學向畢業生演講。在世的美國小說作者中，比我的作品更常進入課堂的人可能寥寥無幾。

如果你有空讀我的書，如果你肯表現得像受過教育的人，你就會發現，我的作品談的不是性愛情趣，也不鼓吹任何形式的胡搞。我的書其實懇求人們更親切相處，加強責任感。沒錯，有些角色言語粗俗，這是因為真實生活裡有些人言語粗俗，尤其是軍人和靠勞力過活的人，即使是被呵護得無微不至的兒童都明白這一點。此外，大家都知道，粗人講粗話，對兒童造成的傷害其實不大。你我小時候也聽過粗話，幼小的心靈並未因此遭踐踏。真正能傷害幼小心靈的是惡行和謊言。

我說了這麼多，相信你仍準備回應：「對是對啦，不過，我們仍有權有責決定社群裡的兒童被規定讀什麼書。」這當然有道理。但不爭的事實是，如果你行使這份權利、肩負這份責任時懷抱的是無知、苛刻、違背美國精神的態度，那麼人民有權罵你們是劣等國民，罵你們笨蛋。即使貴校區裡的兒童都有權如此罵。

我閱報得知，此事在全美掀起反對聲浪，令貴校區民眾感到困惑不解。你們應該已發現，卓瑞克校區屬於美國文明的一部分，而美國同胞無法忍受你們如此不文明的行徑。也許你們由此事件學習到，自由人以書為尊是天經地義的事，而且自古至今，恨書焚書的國家經常被討伐。如果你是美國人，你必須允許所有思想在校區自由流通，而不是以你的思想為準。

如果貴委員會已決定展現誠意，願憑智慧與成熟心行使教育兒童權，那麼你們應承認，在自由社會裡，詆毀並焚毀書籍——你們根本沒展閱過的書籍——對年輕人是一種錯誤示範。你們也應決心讓兒童接觸五花八門的意見與資訊，把他們訓練成更能妥善決策、生存力更強的人。

再重複：你侮辱到我了，我是個好國民，我非常真實。

馮內果

一九〇五年十一月二十日

三十三級大白痴

致 **J**·**H**·陶德
加州三藩市
韋伯斯特街一二一二號

**馬克·吐溫（Mark Twain）致
藥商**

一九〇五年十一月二十日

以《哈克歷險記》（*Adventures of
Huckleberry Finn*）一書聞名的美國
作家馬克·吐溫一生見證過不少
惡疾。一八七二年，他才十九個
月大的兒子朗登（Langdon）因白
喉夭折。一八九六年，女兒蘇西
（Suzy）因腦膜炎去世。一九〇四
年，妻子奧莉維亞因心臟衰竭撒手
人寰。成為鰥夫才一年後，他收到
藥商來信，裡面附有一份簡介書，
推銷「仙丹」，吹噓該藥能治百
病，喪事連連的大文豪看了忿而向
祕書依莎貝爾·里昂（Isabel Lyon）
口述，由祕書代筆，本書收錄的是
回信的初稿。

親愛的先生，

　　對我而言，你的信令我百思不得其解。你的筆跡公整，顯示
人格相當端正，而你的文句甚至隱約透露著學識，然而隨信而來
的廣告卻自稱出自同一人之手。撰寫廣告之人無疑是全地球在世
人類裡最無知的一個，也是白痴一個，是高達三十三級的白痴，
是代代白痴相傳而下的後裔，遠祖是人類進化史上「失落的環
節」。令我疑惑的是，同一手為何能寫出這封信與這份廣告。疑
惑令我膽寒，疑惑令我惱火，疑惑令我氣急敗壞。疑惑總在我心
中撩起一種稍縱即逝的薄情，想修理引我疑惑的人。片刻之後，
這份憎惡勢必消散一空，而我甚至可能為你祈禱，但我想及時祝
你誤服一帖你自己的毒藥，迅速淪落地獄，去和其他害人不眨眼
的專利藥商會合，因為你們無怨無悔爭取到此當仁不讓的良機。

　　　　再會、再會、再會！

　　　　　　　　　　　　　　　　　馬克·吐溫

Nov. 20. 1905

Jos. H. Todd.

12½ Webster St.

San Francisco
Cal.

Dear Sir

Your letter is an insoluble
puzzle to me. The hand writing
is good & exhibits considerable
character, & there are even
traces of intelligence in what
you say, ~~it~~, yet the letter
& the accompanying adver-
tisements profess to be the
work of the same hand.

The person who wrote the
advertisements is without doubt the
most ignorant person now
alive on the planet; also without doubt he is an idiot; an
idiot of the 33rd degree, &
scion of an ancestral procession
of idiots stretching back to the
Missing Link. It puzzles me
to make out how the same
hand could have constructed

...your letter & your advertisements.

Puzzles fret me, puzzles annoy me, puzzles exasperate me; & always, for a moment, they arouse in me an unkind state of mind toward the person who has puzzled me. A few moments from now my resentment will have faded & passed, & I shall probably even be praying for you; but while there is yet time I hasten to wish you may take a dose of your own poison by mistake, & enter swiftly into the damnation which you & all the other patent medicine assassins have so remorselessly earned & do so richly deserve.

Adieu, adieu, adieu!

Mark Twain

堅持下去

伊吉・帕普（Iggy Pop）致女歌迷
一九九五年二月

二十歲歌迷洛倫絲（Laurence）寫信給伊吉・帕普，他拖了九個月才回覆，時機卻巧得不能再巧。回信寄到女歌迷巴黎家中的那天早上，全家剛被房東趕走。洛倫絲回憶當時情況：

「我讀到最後淚崩。伊吉・帕普不但收到我九個月前寄的信——假如他晚一天回信，我就可能永遠收不到了——而且他居然讀了整整『他媽的』二十頁，更讀到我的那件愛迪達洋裝（我『半天真』的影射）和其他所有東西：我描述我是父母失和而離婚，碰到一連串社工、律師、貪財的家具拍賣商、殺到門口遞拘票的法院人，也寫到心中的恐懼、憤怒、挫折感、愛。」

雖然巨星的回信簡短，親筆字卻能將心比心，以翩翩丰采與文筆正視歌迷的難題。

親愛的洛倫絲，

　　妳的文筆好，信寫得真情流露，感謝妳照亮我灰暗的人生。我讀完了他媽的整封信，親愛的。當然，我也多想看妳穿黑洋裝搭配白襪的模樣，但我最想見的是妳深呼吸，盡妳所能活下去，找到妳能愛的東西去有樣學樣。妳的小腦袋顯然是他媽的靈光，心胸也開放，我想對妳說聲（遲來的）二十一歲生日{快樂快樂快樂}，祝妳興高采烈。在我二十一歲生日那天，我也悲哀到極點，過得很辛苦。那時我在臺上被人噓，借住別人家，心裡好害怕。一路走來，路途雖然漫長，但今生的壓力永遠不會結束。附帶一提，「穿孔問題」對我而言也代表說，無論我們想開創什麼樣的人生，坑坑洞洞是免不了的。所以，堅持下去吧，吾愛，長得更高更壯，懂得承受打擊，繼續前進。

對一個真正美的女孩獻上所有的愛。
　　　　　　這女孩就是妳洛倫絲。

　　　　　　　　　　　　　　　　伊吉・帕普

Dear Laurence,

thank you for your gorgeous
and charming letter, you brighten up
my bim life. i read the whole
fucking thing, bear. of course, i'd
love to see you in your ~~black~~ dress
+ your white socks too. but most
of all i want to see you take a
~~deep breath~~ breath + do whatever
you must to survive + find
something to be that you can love.
you're obviously a bright fucking
chick, w/ a big heart too + i want
to wish you a (belated) HAPPY
HAPPY HAPPY 21st b'day +
a happy spirit. i was very miserable
+ fighting hard on my 21st b'day, too. people
booed me on the stage, + i was staying
in someone else's house and i was scared.

its been a long road since then,
but pressure never ends in this life.
'perforation problems' by the way
means to me also the holes that
will always exist in any story
we try to make of our lives.
so hang on, my love, + grow big
+ strong + take your hits + keep going,
all my love to a really beautiful
girl

That's you Laurence!

我寫了一本叫做
《教父》的書

《教父》作者致馬龍·白蘭度
一九七〇年一月二十三日

在一九七〇年，在卡波拉坐上導演
椅之前，《教父》作者馬里歐·普
佐（Mario Puzo）寫信給馬龍·白
蘭度。如同先前的傑克·凱魯亞
克（詳見信之四十四），普佐也力
邀馬龍·白蘭度主演他新作翻拍的
電影，飾演維多·柯里昂尼（Vito
Corleone）一角。雖然白蘭度強力
爭取擔綱，可惜電影公司回絕作者
的請求，最大的原因是白蘭度素有
脾氣火爆的風評，常對人頤指氣
使，而且票房號召力一年不如一
年。後來卡波拉執導，請白蘭度試
鏡扮演大家長，然後請派拉蒙公司
高層鑑賞，高層立刻改變心意。
《教父》上映後打破多項票房紀
錄，獲獎連連。白蘭度的演技精
湛，也榮獲奧斯卡最佳男演員獎。
他拒收，成為傳世話題。

馬里歐·普佐
紐約州紐約市 **11706**
長島灣岸莊園巷八六六號

一月二十三

親愛的白蘭度先生

　　我寫了一本叫做《教父》的書，銷售成績不俗，我想你是飾演教父角色的不二人選，因為你能演活那份沉默威武而諷刺的模樣（這書的主旨是反諷美國社會）。我期望你翻閱後喜歡並盡你所能爭取扮演主角。

　　抱著姑且一試的心，我也致函派拉蒙，意思差不多一樣。

　　我知道，冒昧向你訴求是我太狂妄，但我能為本書略盡的微薄心意是姑且一試。我真的認為你極適合演主角。不消說，我久仰你爐火純青的演技。

　　　　　　馬里歐·普佐

你朋友傑夫·布朗也認識我，地址是他給的。

The book is an ironical comment
on American society

North
Carolina
platform

MARIO PUZO
866 MANOR LANE
BAY SHORE, LONG ISLAND
NEW YORK, N. Y. 11706

516-
555-1712

Jan 23

Dear Mr Brando

I wrote a book called
THE GODFATHER which
has had some success and I
think you're the only actor
who can play the Godfather
with that ~~fast~~
quiet force and irony the part
requires. I hope you'll read
the book and like it well enough
to use whatever power you can to
get the role.
    I'm writing Paramount to
the same effect but whatever good
that will do
    I know this seems presumptuous of
me but the least I can do for the book is
try. I really think you'd be tremendous.
Needless to say I've long been an admirer of your art.

Mario Puzo

A mutual friend, Jeff Brown, gave
me your address

信之 *070*

後果將不堪設想

火箭工程師致主管
一九八五年七月三十一日

在一九八六年一月二十八日，挑戰者太空梭升空才七十三分鐘，百萬人眾目睽睽下，於佛羅里達上空爆炸解體，七位太空人全數罹難。經調查判定，肇事主因是O形環故障。O形環基本上是固態火箭推進器的一個橡皮密封墊，故障的原因之一是發射當天嚴寒導致。但並非相關人員全體都對失事感到詫異。在失事前六個月，固態火箭推進器製造廠商莫頓希爾科（Morton Thiokol）的一名工程師羅傑·波伊斯丘利（Roger Boisjoly）寫下這封備忘錄，寄給公司副總裁，預測到問題，警告太空梭面臨「最嚴重的災難。」

工程師的警告無人理會。太空梭升空之前，他再試圖攔阻，可惜又沒成功。失事六個月後，他挺身揭發此事，提供這份備忘錄給政府召集的失事調查小組，他因而遭同事排擠，不久後辭職。

公司內部限閱
莫頓希爾科股份有限公司
瓦薩奇分部
內部備忘錄
一九八五年七月三十一日
2870：FY86：073
致：工程副總裁 **R.K. Lund**
副本：**B.C. Brinton, A.J. McDonald, L.H.Sayer, J.R. Kapp**
發自：**R.M.Boisjoly**，應用機械，分機 **3525**
主旨：**SRM O** 形環蝕損／恐釀成嚴重故障

本人提筆寫這封信的用意是站在工程立場上，確定主管完全知悉 SRM 接頭的 O 形環目前出現蝕損的現象，後果嚴重。

當前的錯誤共識是不顧接頭故障之威脅，逕行起飛，只需事前進行一系列的設計評估以求取解決之道，或者最低限度也能大幅減輕蝕損問題。如今，由於 SRM 16A 噴嘴接頭蝕損了次要 O 形環，而首要 O 形環無法密封，此立場如今已劇變。

萬一區域接頭發生上述情況（不無可能發生），接頭能否生效仍在未定之天，因為次要 O 形環無法回應 U 形接頭開放速（clevis opening rate），或許也無法加壓，其結果將鑄成最嚴重的災難──葬送人命。

一組人員組成非正式小組（界定小組任務的通知書從未公佈）在一九八五年七月十九日成立，在組長帶領下，負責化解長期與短期問題。目前，此一非正式小組根本不存在。依本人之見，上級應正式授權給此一小組並交付責任，以利在不干擾正事的情況下執行要務（專職排除問題，直到問題解決為止）。

誠心惶恐的我個人認為，如果我們不立即採取行動，若不組成專案小組解決區域接頭問題，若不視之為頭等大事，我們恐將痛失太空梭以及所有發射臺的設施。

R·M·波伊斯丘利

應用機械經理 J.R. Kapp 附議

MORTON THIOKOL, INC.

Wasatch Division

Interoffice Memo

31 July 1985
2870:FY86:073

TO: R. K. Lund
                Vice President, Engineering

CC: B. C. Brinton, A. J. McDonald, L. H. Sayer, J. R. Kapp

FROM: R. M. Boisjoly
                Applied Mechanics — Ext. 3525

SUBJECT: SRM O-Ring Erosion/Potential Failure Criticality

This letter is written to insure that management is fully aware of the seriousness of the current O-Ring erosion problem in the SRM joints from an engineering standpoint.

The mistakenly accepted position on the joint problem was to fly without fear of failure and to run a series of design evaluations which would ultimately lead to a solution or at least a significant reduction of the erosion problem. This position is now drastically changed as a result of the SRM 16A nozzle joint erosion which eroded a secondary O-Ring with the primary O-Ring never sealing.

If the same scenario should occur in a field joint (and it could), then it is a jump ball as to the success or failure of the joint because the secondary O-Ring cannot respond to the clevis opening rate and may not be capable of pressurization. The result would be a catastrophe of the highest order — loss of human life.

An unofficial team (a memo defining the team and its purpose was never published) with leader was formed on 19 July 1985 and was tasked with solving the problem for both the short and long term. This unofficial team is essentially nonexistent at this time. In my opinion, the team must be officially given the responsibility and the authority to execute the work that needs to be done on a non-interference basis (full time assignment until completed).

It is my honest and very real fear that if we do not take immediate action to dedicate a team to solve the problem with the field joint having the number one priority, then we stand in jeopardy of losing a flight along with all the launch pad facilities.

R. M. Boisjoly

Concurred by:

J. R. Kapp, Manger
Applied Mechanics

天下淑女都愛鬍鬚

少女致林肯
一八六〇年十月十五日

十一歲少女葛雷絲·貝德爾（Grace Bedell）見到共和黨總統候選人林肯和搭檔漢姆林（Hannibal Hamlin）的相片，決定在一八六〇年秋寫信給美國總統競選人，提供一項絕對能討選民歡心的建議。令她驚喜的是，不久林肯回信了。更棒的是，幾個月後，總統當選人林肯搭火車前往華府時，竟然接見她——而且早已接納她的建議。

少女事後回憶，「他下車，陪我坐在月臺邊緣。他說，『小葛，看看我的鬍子。我為妳留的。』說完，他親我一下。我只見過他這一次。」

敬 **A · B · 林肯**

親愛的先生

　　我父親剛去園遊會，帶回家一張你和漢姆林先生的合照。我是一個小女孩才十一歲，但我非常盼望你當選美國總統所以我希望你不會嫌我厚顏寫信給你這麼一個大人物。你家有沒有和我一樣大的小女孩。如果有，請代我問候她，如果你沒空回信，請她寫信給我。我有四個哥哥，其中幾個打定主意想投給你，如果你留鬍鬚，我會盡量說服其他哥哥，叫他們也投你一票有鬍子的你會變得更好看幾倍因為你的臉好瘦。天下淑女都愛鬍鬚，她們會吵著要丈夫投票給你，這樣你就能當選總統了。我父親準備投你一票，如果我是男人我也會投你一票不過我會盡力向所有人拉票，我認為你相片裡的鐵路圍牆把相片襯托得好漂亮，我有一個小妹妹她才九週大鬼靈精怪得不得了。你回信請寄給紐約州西田查托夸郡的葛雷絲·貝德爾。

　　我不能再寫下去了趕快回我信再見

葛雷絲·貝德爾

93   Grace Bedell

Westfield Chatauque Co
NY
Oct 15 1860

Hon A B Lincoln
                    Dear Sir

My father has just home from the fair and brought home your picture and Mr. Hamlin's. I am a little girl only eleven years old, but want you should be President of the United States very much so I hope you wont think me very bold to write to such a great man as you are. Have you any little girls about as large as I am if so give them my love and tell her to write to me if you cannot answer this letter. I have got 4 brothers and part of them will vote for you any way and if you will let your whiskers grow I will try and get the rest of them to vote for you you would look a great deal better for your face is so thin. All the ladies like whiskers and they would tease

their husbands to vote for you and then you
would be President. My father is a going to
vote for you and if I was a man I would
vote for you to but I will try and get
every one to vote for you that I can I think
that rail fence around your picture makes it
look very pretty I have got a little baby
sister she is nine weeks old and is just as
cunning as can be. When you direct your letter
diret to Grace Bedell Westfield
Chatauque County New York
I must not write any more answer
this letter right off Good bye
Grace Bedell

葛雷絲・貝德爾小姐

我親愛的小小姐

　　妳十五日寫的信寄到了，我讀了喜上心頭——我必須告知，很遺憾我家沒有女兒——我有三個兒子，分別是十七歲、九歲、七歲。再加上他們的母親，這組成我們全家——
至於鬍鬚，我從未蓄鬍過。妳認為，如果我現在開始留，會不會被人譏嘲說是可笑的討喜之舉？

誠摯敬祝妳安好的
A・林肯

Springfield, Ills. Oct 19. 1860

Miss. Grace Bedell

My dear little Miss.

Your very agreeable letter
of the 15th is received—

I regret the necessity of saying I
have no daughter— I have three
sons— one seventeen, one nine, and
one seven, years of age— They, with
their mother, constitute my whole family—

As to the whiskers, having never worn
any, do you not think people would
call it a piece of silly affection
if I were to begin it now?

Your very sincere well-wisher

A. Lincoln.

美國哥德製片股份有限公司

擔心創意受制於前人

一九八七年二月十三日
萊斯里·巴瑞尼先生
醜陋（**Ugly**）出版國際

詹姆士·卡麥隆（James Cameron）致特效師經紀人

一九八七年二月十三日

《異形》是電影史上最成功的續集之一，第二集籌拍之際，特效專家H·R·蓋格（H. R. Giger）沒有接到續聘通知，他錯愕之情可想而知：因為在第一集裡，蓋格的特效獲得廣大回響並贏得奧斯卡獎。《異形》中的外星怪物鮮活嚇人，就是知名瑞士籍設計師蓋格在一九七〇年代末構思出來的。他透過經紀人萊斯里·巴瑞尼（Leslie Barany）致函續集導演詹姆士·卡麥隆。三個月後，卡麥隆以此信帶歉意明述決定不續用的理由。兩人始終不曾合作過任何一部電影。

親愛的巴瑞尼先生：

礙於《異形二》籌拍的高壓，請原諒我至今才回你在八六年三月十一日代你客戶H·R·蓋格先生寄的信。

你在信中表示，蓋格先生自認對電影裡的怪物和設計懷抱強烈的創始感（有道理），如今《異形二》開拍，他未接到續聘書，令他「起初感到失望」。諷刺的是，最初令我有興趣接拍續集的原因，正是蓋格先生為《異形》創造的潛意識光景，既光怪陸離又含肉慾的底蘊。然而，由於我執導之前曾擔任製片設計，我認為我必須為續集蓋上個人特色的戳印，否則對我電影生涯的現階段意義不大，因為如果我不接《異形》續集，我另有幾個原創概念等我開發，酬勞相當，創始感甚至更高。

我覺得，拍攝續集難以平衡的兩種意念是，一方面想在全新的畫布上重新恣意揮灑，另一方面又需兼顧第一集，不得不適度援引套用。在《異形》中，蓋格先生的視覺創意戳印強烈而廣泛（我相信這是該電影成功的一大功臣），因此我擔心，如果續聘他，他會認為比我更應主導續集走向，我會因而受制於他的創意。

由於二十世紀福斯公司喜歡我提議的故事，他們給我機會以筆創作我想像的世界。我接受這機會，延攬和我合作過的特效設計師、雕塑師、技術人員，以確保進度順暢，預算合度，這是天經地義的事。

不續聘的另一項因素是，蓋格先生參與《鬼追魂》（*Poltergeist II*）的製片產生衝突，遺憾未能像《異形》一片善用他的願景。

透過道歉和解釋，我希望蓋格先生能雅量寬恕我綁架他的「第一胎」。如果他能原諒，我倆今後或許能相敬如賓，合作拍攝全新的非續集電影，屆時他必能盡情發揮高人一等的想像力。

我景仰他的作品，一向是他的粉絲（珍藏著《異形》拍攝期間委製的異形蛋簽名平板印刷畫）。

詹姆士·F·卡麥隆　敬上

JC：lw

AMERICAN GOTHIC PRODUCTIONS, INC.

February 13, 1987

Mr. Leslie Barany
UGLY PUBLISHING INTERNATIONAL

Dear Mr. Barany:

I regret that the intense pressure to complete "ALIENS" did not
afford me the time to reply to your letter of 3/11/86, which was
on behalf of your client, Mr. H.R. Giger.

In that letter you describe Mr. Giger's 'initial sense of
disappointment' at not being contacted for "ALIENS" in view of
his, quite correct, intense sense of authorship of the creatures
and designs. Ironically, it was the production design of
"ALIEN", with its bizarre, psycho-sexual landscape of the
subconscious as created by Mr. Giger, that initially attracted me
to the project of a sequel. However, having been a production
designer myself before becoming a director, I felt I had to put
my own unique stamp on the project. Otherwise, it would have had
little meaning for me at that point in my career, when I had a
number of original concepts and creations which I could have
pursued, with equal financial reward and an even greater degree
of authorship.

I found that creating a sequel can be an uneasy exercise in
balancing creative impulses, the desire to create a whole new
canvas, with the need to pay proper hommage to the original. Mr.
Giger's visual stamp was so powerful and pervasive in "ALIEN" (a
major contributor to its success, I believe) that I felt the risk
of being overwhelmed by him and his world, if we had brought him
into a production where in a sense, he had more reason to be
there than I did.

Because 20th Century Fox liked the story I presented to them,
they gave me the opportunity to create the world I had seen in my
mind as I wrote. I took that opportunity, and enlisted the aid
of special effects designers, sculptors and technicians with whom
I had worked before which, of course, is a natural course when
one must guarantee a schedule and budget.

An additional deciding factor was Mr. Giger's conflicting
involvement in "POLTERGEIST II" which unfortunately did not
utilize his vision nearly as well as "ALIEN".

2

I offer all this commentary by way of apology and explanation in
the hope that Mr. Giger can find it possible to forgive me for
abducting his 'first-born'. If so, there may come a time when we
can collaborate in mutual respect on some completely new and
original project where the only limitation is his superb
imagination.

I am, first and always, a fan of his work (a signed litho of the
alien egg commissioned during "ALIEN" is one of my prized
possessions).

Sincerely.

JAMES F. CAMERON

JC:lw

信之 073

你怎能早走我一步？

遺孀致李應台
一五八六年六月一日

一九九八年，考古人員在南韓安東市挖掘古墓，發現一具十六世紀男性乾屍，姓名是李應台，得年三十歲，是古韓固城李氏家族成員，胸前擺著一封致遺腹子之父的信，執筆人是懷孕的遺孀。同一古墓出土的是一雙草鞋，以麻皮和妻子的頭髮編製而成，放置在古屍頭旁邊。

此發現在南韓造成轟動，故事也被改編為小說、電影、歌劇。李應台的懷孕遺孀雕像如今立在古墓附近。

致煥之父
一五八六年六月一日

你總說，「親親，讓我們活著白頭偕老，在同一天死去。」你怎能棄我先走呢？我和小兒子今後該聽誰，該怎麼過日子？你怎能先走一步呢？

當初你是如何以你心相許，我是如何以我心相許？每當你我共枕，你總告訴我，「親親，別人也和我們一樣相愛相惜嗎？別人真的也像我們嗎？」你怎麼拋棄一切，先走一步？

沒有你，我真的活不下去。我只想投奔你。請帶我一起走。對你的情懷，我今生無以淡忘，對你的愁緒也永無止境。如今我心何去何從？幼子無你，我日子將如何過？

請看這封信，託夢詳細回答我。因為我想聽你託夢詳細訴說，所以寫妥這封信入土。請仔細閱信，託夢予我。

我腹中嬰兒出世後，該喊誰父親？我心惶惶，誰能明瞭？天底下找不到比這更慘的悲劇。

你只不過是魂在遠方，不像我陷入哀慟深淵。我的哀傷無邊際無止境，所以文筆潦草。請詳讀這封信，託夢予我，栩栩如生見我，向我傾吐。我相信我能在夢中見到你。幽幽來見我，對我現身。我想說的言語無窮盡，就此歇筆。

信之 074

法老王之卑僕

阿亞布王致法老王

約西元前一三四〇年

十九世紀末，埃及阿馬爾那
（Amarna）民眾在古城阿肯那唐
（Akhetaten）廢墟找到幾片黏土硬
化的石板，上面刻滿一種神祕文
字，後經研究證實是失傳的中東古
文阿卡德（Akkadian）楔形文，最
遠可溯至西元前兩千六百年，由古
人印在未乾的黏土上。這些石板據
信是遠古外交信函，各國王侯藉以
和鄰邦官員互通訊息。至今出土的
石板有三百八十二片。本書收錄的
這片寫於西元前一三五〇至一三三
五年之間，作者是迦南地區阿塔圖
（Atartu）市的阿亞布王，對象是古
埃及第十八朝代的法老王阿門霍德
普（Amenhotep）四世。

正義之戰

致尊主法老王。

卑僕阿亞布之訊息。

臣跪拜尊主足前七次加七次。臣乃尊主法老王之卑僕，足前之塵
土。臣已聽聞尊主法老王透過阿塔馬亞傳達之聖旨。誠然，臣已
悉心捍衛尊主法老王之眾城。再者，奪走三城者乃哈蘇拉之頭
目，請尊主明鑑。自臣聽聞此事並證實迄今，討伐其人之戰頻
起。誠然，願尊主法老王明察，並請尊主法老王常記卑僕。

我將常相左右

南北戰爭少校致髮妻
一八六一年七月十四日

在一八六一年，美國南北戰爭即將開打，三十二歲的律師蘇利文‧巴魯（Sullivan Ballou）加入北軍，留下妻子和兩子，官拜陸軍少校。同年七月十四日，少校深知即將爆發的戰事凶多吉少，因此寫下這封信給妻子，淒美感人，向妻預警他面臨的險境，洋洋灑灑訴說他對家與國的愛。信沒寄，寫完信後兩星期，蘇利文連同九十三名弟兄戰死於第一場布爾淵（Bull Run）之役。南北戰爭延續四年，最後犧牲超過六十萬人性命，布爾淵是首場激戰。後人在遺物裡發現這封信，代寄給遺孀，但原文已失散。這一份據信是由親戚抄寫，現存於林肯總統圖書博物館。

少校與莎拉結婚五年，戰死時妻子才二十四歲，妻子為他守寡一生，八十歲去世，與丈夫合葬在羅德島州普維敦斯（Providence）。

我最親愛的妻子

　　至為明確的跡象顯示，我軍將於近日動身，也許近在明日，我可能無法再寫信給妳，因此現在禁不住寫幾句，或許信到妳眼前時我已不在人間。我軍之前進可能數日不止，熱戰連連，場面可能慘烈，我亦可能殉難「上帝之意，非我」。如果有必要為國捐軀戰死沙場上，我已有心理準備。從軍的我對於此役使命之信心堅定，毫無疑慮，勇往直前不退卻。我知道美國文明之前途寄託於此役，也知道獨立戰爭時的先人拋頭顱灑熱血，今人對他們虧欠至深。我願意、全心願意拋棄今生的喜樂支持政府並報答先人。

　　但是，我親愛的妻，犧牲我一己之喜樂，必然連帶犧牲妳幾乎所有喜樂，必然帶給妳一世憂慮哀傷，我知道，因我個人長年嘗盡孤兒的辛酸，如今竟以此辛酸供養我親愛的幼子。在悠然隨風飄揚的軍旗下，我對妳情意無限濃，但愛國心勝過一切，愛妻與子女無力抗衡，我捨家為國是軟弱嗎？甚或可恥？

　　夏夜安詳，兩千弟兄沉睡我周遭，對許多人而言或許是長眠前的最後一夜，此時我無法對妳描述心境。我懷疑死神正潛伏我身後，毒鏢瞄準我，而我此刻與上帝共餐與國與您。我時常再三捫心自問，我是否錯抱動機，竟決定葬送親人所有幸福，但我苦思不出錯在哪裡。純正愛國心，加上我尊崇我鼓吹之原則，我對尊嚴的愛壓倒貪生怕死之心，促使我挺身而出，我奉行不悖。

　　莎拉，我對妳的愛至死不渝，愛直如粗纜繩捆綁我，唯有萬能上帝可解除。然而我對國家的愛如疾風席捲我，以鐵鏈束縛我，牽我上戰場，我無力抗拒。與妳同在時的極樂時光如今蜂擁而來，我深深感激上帝與妳賦予我如此綿長之回憶。要我捨棄這些回憶何其困難。若上帝恩准，妳我或許能相愛再相愛，看著兒子茁壯成受人尊敬的青年，如今要我將這些希望燒成灰，何其困難。我知道我何德何能，不敢奢望聖恩，但我隱約耳聞微微細語，或許是我兒艾格的祈禱傳至天庭，我可望毫髮無傷回到親人身邊。若我遭不測，我親愛的莎拉，千萬勿忘我對妳的愛之深，

勿忘我在戰場最後一口氣將用來輕喚妳名

原諒我諸多缺點，原諒我對妳造成諸多心痛。這些年，我是多麼不體貼，多麼愚昧！我多麼樂意以淚清洗妳歡樂日子上的小污斑，多麼欣然對抗今生的厄運，以免妳與兒子受傷，可惜我無能為力，我必須從靈界守護妳，盤旋妳左右，看妳在人間以嬌嫩身軀抵擋狂風暴雨，黯然耐著性子等候我倆復合不再分離之日。

可是啊莎拉！如果人死能復生，能在親人身邊無形無影來去，我將永遠伴隨妳左右，無論是在最亮麗的白晝或是在最黝暗的黑夜，在妳最快樂的時刻，或在妳最陰霾的時辰，生生世世。每當微風輕拂芳頰，它將是我的氣息。每當涼風舒緩妳隱隱痛的太陽穴，它將是我路過的靈魂。莎拉，勿為我死而哀悼。就當我走了一樣，等我等到重逢的那天。

至於我的兒子，他們將和我一樣，成長過程體會不到父親的愛與關懷。

威利還太小，不久將忘我，但藍眼艾格必能記住父子嬉鬧情景，深藏在最模糊的童年記憶中

莎拉我對妳有無限信心，妳必定能以母愛灌溉他們，栽培出健全人格。請轉告我母親與岳母，我請眾神祝福她們

喔！莎拉我屆時將等妳帶我走向吾兒

蘇利文

Copy of a letter from Sullivan Ballou to
his wife before the battle of Bull Run

Headquarters
Camp Clark
Washington D. C.

July 14th 1861

My Very dear Wife

The indications are very strong that we
shall move in a few days perhaps tomorrow And lest I should
not be able to write you again I feel impelled to write you
a few lines that may fall under your eye when I am am no
more. Our movement may be one of a few days duration and
be full of pleasure. And it may be one of severe conflict and death
to me "Not my will but thine O God be done" if it is neces
-sary that I should fall on the battle field for my Country I
am ready. I have no misgivings about or lack of confidence
in the Cause in which I am engaged, and my courage does
not halt or falter. I know how American Civilization now
leans upon the triumph of the Government and how great
a debt we owe to those who went before us through the blood
and suffering of the Revolution; and I am willing perfectly
willing to lay down life all my joys in this life to help
maintain this Government and to pay that debt.
But my dear wife, when I know that with my own joys I lay
down nearly all of yours, — and replace them in this life with care

and sorrow when after having eaten for long years the bitter fruit of orphenage myself, I must offer it as their onely sustenance to my dear little children. is it weak or dishonourable that while the banner of purpose flotes calmly and proudly in the breeze. underneath my unbounded love for you my dear wife and children should struggle in fierce though useless contest with my love of Country

I cannot discribe to you my feelings on this calm sum mer night when two thousand men are sleeping around me. many of them enjoying the last perhaps before that of Death. And I suspicious that Death is creeping behi nd me with his fatal dart am communeing with God my Couⁿtroy and thee. I have sought most closely and dilegently and often in my brest for a wrong motive in thus hazerding the happiness of all that I love and I could not find one. A pure love of my Country and of the princefels I have advocated before the people and the name of honour that I love more than I fear death. have called upon me and I have obeyed.

Sarah my love for you is deathless it seemes to bind me with Mighty Cables that nothing but Omnepotence can break And yet my love of Country comes over me like a strong wind and bears me irresistably with all those chains to the battle field the memories of all the blissful moments I have enjoyed with you come crowding over me. and I feel most deeply grateful to God and you that I have enjoyed them so long. And how hard it is for me to give them up! and burn to ashes the the hopes of future years when God willing we might still have loved and loved together and see our boys grow up to honourable manhood around us. I know I have but few claims upon Divine Providence but something whispers to me perhaps it is the wafted prayer of my little Edgar that I shall return to my loved ones unharmed. If I do not my dear Sarah never forget how much I loved you nor that when my last breath escapes me on the battlefield it will whisper your name

Forgive my many faults and the many pains I have caused you How thoughtless how foolish I have sometimes been! How gladly would I wash out with my tears every little spot upon your happiness and struggle with all the misfortunes of this world to shield you and my children from harm but I cannot I must watch you from the spirit world and hover near you while you buffet the storms with your precious little freight - and wait with sad paitience till we meet to part no more

But Oh Sarah! if the dead can come back to this earth and flit unseen around those they love I shall be always with you in the brightest day and the darkest night amidst your happiest sceans and gloomiest hours always always and when the soft breeze fans your cheek it shall be my breath or the cool air your throbbing temple it shall be my spirit passing by. Sarah. do not mourn me dead think I am gone and wait for me for we shall meet again.

As for my little boys they will grow up as I have done and

never know a fathers love and care

Little Willie is to young to remember me long but my blue-eyed Edgar will keep my frolics with him among the dimmest memories of his child hood

Sarah I have unlimited confidence in your maternal care and your developement of their characters. Tell my two Mothers I call Gods blessings upon them

Oh! Sarah I wait for you then come to me and lead thither my children

Sullivan

信之 *076*

家犬尚在

林恩舅舅致外甥

日期不詳

已逝動畫家查克・瓊斯（Chuck Jones）在動畫界是傳奇人物，成就輝煌，創造的經典角色包括嗶嗶鳥和大野狼，也導演過至今公認少有人能出其右的經典卡通《歌劇是啥？》（*What's Opera, Doc?*）。

在他精彩的繪本《恰克狂想曲》（*Chuck Reducks*）中，他推崇敬愛的「林恩舅舅」在童年教導他「動畫卡通創作的所有要領」，將舅舅描繪成影響一生各層面至深的人，稱讚他是「理想舅舅」，令他「崇拜」。舅舅的文筆也不錯。有一天，瓊斯家的愛犬泰迪不幸死了，舅舅馬上寫這封溫馨信給小查克和他的姐弟。

親愛的佩吉、朵樂絲、查克和迪克，

我昨晚接到一通電話，對方問，「你是林恩舅舅嗎？」

我說，「是啊。我的姓名叫林恩・馬丁。你是沒報戶口的外甥嗎？」

他回答說，「我是泰迪。」聽他口氣，他好像有點不耐煩。「我是泰迪・瓊斯，就是住在加州海洋公園市瓦茲沃斯街一一五號的家犬泰迪・瓊斯。這通是長途。」

「抱歉，」我說。「我不太想惹你不高興，不過呢，我以前沒聽過你講人話，只聽過你汪汪叫或哼哼哎，或對月亮亂吼一通。」

「罵人罵到自己了，」泰迪吸氣表示不屑，聽得出他真的很不耐煩。「告訴你吧，佩吉、朵樂絲、查克和迪克好像很難過，因為他們以為我死了。」遲疑一下。「呃，我應該算是死了吧。」

我承認，聽見狗承認自己死了，對我來說是全新的體驗，而且不盡然出自意料之中。「如果你死了，」不太確定該怎麼對死狗講話的我說，「你怎麼能打電話給我？」他又停頓一下，態度煩躁。顯然他愈來愈對我覺得不耐煩了。

「因為，」他以我聽過最懂得節制的狗嗓說，「因為狗活著的時候，即使小孩不清楚狗跑去哪裡了，他們知道狗還在。所以，我想讓他們知道，我就算沒命了，其實還在某個地方。」

「不如這樣吧，泰迪，我告訴他們說，你跑去狗天堂了，也許他們心裡會比較——」

「唉，別傻了。」泰迪清一清狗嗓。「咦，你住哪裡？」

「喂，不會吧？我們正在討論你去哪裡，」我對他吠。

「哇，你會吠耶，我怎麼不曉得。」聽他口氣，他很佩服我的狗語造詣。

「別把話題扯遠了，」我說。「你一定知道我住哪裡，不然怎麼有辦法打電話到我家？」

「天啊，你沒見過世面啦，」泰迪說。「我只說我打長途給

你，又沒說打電話。他們問我曉不曉得你住哪裡，我說你住在瓦茲沃斯街一一五號以外的地方，所以他們改撥別的號碼，就把我和你接在一起了。」

「我可以回撥給你嗎？」我迷糊地問。「也許這樣我能猜猜看。」

「理性一點啦，」泰迪說。「你我都不曉得我在哪裡了，你又怎麼能回撥給我？」

「得了吧，透露一點線索給我嘛，」我拚命乞求。「例如說，你身邊有沒有其他狗？我面對外甥，總不能講不出東西嘛。」

「你等一下，」泰迪說，想必正在左看右看。「我剛看見一隻巴哥犬和雪納瑞的混血狗，他有翅膀，飛起來的時候，雪納瑞的那半能離地，巴哥犬的那半被拖著跑，撞到草地上的火星塞。」

「火星塞？」

「好幾果園的火星塞，到處都是，有黃色的，紅色的，白色的，還有條紋的。可惜呢，我現在好像不必尿尿了，用力只撒出空氣。香香的空氣，」他驕傲地補充說明。

「聽來像狗天堂嘛，」我說。「有滿樹的羊排之類的東西嗎？」

「哼，」泰迪嘆氣道，「你雖然是中產到上中產階級的舅舅，思想卻怪得可以。不過，我打給你是因為佩吉、朵樂絲、查克和迪克信任你，對你講的話照單全收，我私下認為這種個性，再怎麼扯，都是『容易上當』。不管他們好騙不好騙，他們信任你，所以我想託你告訴他們，我仍然是他們家忠實高尚的老狗——講「高尚」是臭美啦——我身在一個他們看不見的地方，但我看得見他們，我會一直守在他們身邊，用眼睛、耳朵、鼻子守衛。告訴他們說，看不見我並不代表我不在。你可以比喻說，白天雖然看不見經度，也看不太清楚星星，其實兩種東西都在。你就發揮一點詩心啦，叫他們懷念我是一條『好狗』、老忠狗泰迪、來自馬緯度的狗星星。叫他們別擔心，如果有人或任何東西敢惹他們，我會吠叫到對方嚇掉褲襠。就算我翹辮子，我照樣能咬到惡魔叫媽媽。」

他告訴我以上的話。我沒問出他究竟在哪裡，不過我倒發現他不在哪裡——距離佩吉、朵樂絲、查克、迪克·瓊斯不太遠的地方。

無住所舅舅林恩·馬丁　敬上

信之 077

英國營火夜之淵源

不明人士致英國男爵

一六〇五年十月二十六日

在一六〇五年十月二十六日，蒙提葛（Monteagle）男爵四世威廉·帕克（William Parker）收到一封匿名信，寄件人勸他下週勿進國會，因為在場所有人將遇到「重大打擊」。匿名信上指的是英國史上的「火藥陰謀案」，意在摧毀上下院，策劃者是包括蓋伊·福克斯（Guy Fawkes）在內的一群人。男爵閱信後不但沒有依言燒掉信，反而把信交給薩里斯貝利（Salisbury）伯爵，消息最後傳到詹姆士國王。因此在十一月五日凌晨，福克斯在國會地下被揪出，三十六桶火藥也被破獲，陰謀無法得逞。

英國為慶祝這樁陰謀案失敗，多數民眾以營火焚燒福克斯的假人像。隨後兩百五十四年，每逢十一月五日營火夜，英國人仍以煙火和營火慶祝。

吾爵，基於我對您部分友人之敬愛，不願見您損傷，因此忠告您找遁辭避進國會以自保，因為天人共謀嚴懲今世邪心，勿輕忽此忠言，必退居鄉野以策安全，因為儘管表面平靜無波紋，國會即將遭受天大打擊卻不知凶手為何人。勿漠視此忠言，因為姑且一聽有益無害，閱後焚此信趨吉避凶，願上帝降臨恩典于你，善用聖福。

my Lord out of the loue i beare to some of youere frends
i haue a caer of youre preseruacion therfor i would
aduyse yowe as yowe tender youer lyf to deuyse some
eskeuse to shift of youer attendance at this parleament
for god and man hathe concurred to punishe the wikednes
of this tyme and thinke not slightlye of this advertisment
but retyere youre self into youre contri wheare yowe
maye expect the euent in safti for thowghe theare be no
apparance of anni stir yet i saye they shall receyue a terrible
blowe this parleament and yet they shall not seie who
hurts them this cowncel is not to be contemned because
it maye do yowe good and can do yowe no harme for the
dangere is passed as soon as yowe haue burnt the letter
and i hope god will giue yowe the grace to mak good
use of it to whose holy proteccion i comend yowe

信之 078

看妳怎麼回應囉

貝蒂・戴維斯（Bette Davis）致
女兒
一九八七

貝蒂・戴維斯的精湛演技十度獲金
像獎提名，兩次捧回大獎，為人津
津樂道。演藝生涯近尾聲時，在一
九八三年，她罹患乳癌，手術之後
接連幾度中風，因而半身不遂。後
來在一九八五年，女兒芭芭拉・戴
維斯・海曼（Barbara Davis Hyman）
發表備受爭議的回憶錄《家母的珍
寶》（My Mother's Keeper），揭露母
女心結，全書將母親描寫得不堪入
目。事隔兩年，貝蒂出版個人回憶
錄，結尾附上這封致女兒的公開
信。

親愛的海曼，

妳在回憶錄最後寫公開信給我，我決定如法炮製。

妳無疑具有寫小說的高深造詣。妳從小就很會講故事。這麼
多年來，我常告訴你，「BD，事情不是妳講的那樣。妳想像力太
豐富了。」

妳寫進回憶錄裡的許多場景，其實我都在大銀幕上演過。有
可能是妳把電影裡的「我」誤認是真實生活裡的母親。

妳說我愛批評與我共事過的演員，而且引述我的話，我對此
有強烈反感。妳多數地方引述錯誤，居心殘酷。我和烏斯蒂諾夫
合作愉快，對他的為人、演技都極為敬重。至於我對費・唐娜薇
的感想，妳寫的倒是沒錯，和她合作，確實讓人氣得七竅生煙。
不過，妳誣賴我說勞倫斯・奧利佛爵士演技不佳，這絕對是妳的
想像力在作祟。演技登峰造極如他的演員在影壇少見。

妳常告訴大家，出書的目的是幫助我深入瞭解妳，瞭解妳的
生活方式。抱歉，妳沒有達成目標。我被妳徹底搞糊塗了，現在
認不清妳是誰，更不明白妳的生活方式。

妳出書的出發點總歸一句話，就是妳缺乏忠誠心，枉費我以
優渥的環境栽培妳之恩。

妳在宣傳期接受許多專訪，有一次表示，如果回憶錄改編為
電視劇，妳指定葛蘭黛・傑克遜飾演我。妳如果懂一點禮貌，應
該請我飾演自己才對。

回憶錄裡值得我爭辯的東西很多，大多數我選擇視而不見，
但我無法漠視妳指責我因沒爭取到《亂世佳人》女主角而發飆。
該片女主角本來指定我，被我推掉了，原因是薩茲尼克先生本想
徵求我上司傑克・華納的同意，借用艾洛・弗林和貝蒂・戴維斯
飾演男女主角，被我回絕了，因為我覺得艾洛・弗林不適合演男
主角瑞特・巴特勒。在那時候，只有克拉克・蓋博才合適。因
此，親愛的海曼，別把我送回給塔拉，應該讓我回歸巫婆巷，回
到我們在優美緬因州海邊的老家，那裡以前住著一位心地善良的

女孩，名叫BD，不叫海曼。

　　妳在回憶錄最後那封信的結尾寫道：看妳怎麼回應囉，盧絲·伊麗莎白，我也以同樣的方式收尾：看妳怎麼回應囉，海曼。

盧絲·伊麗莎白

P.S.希望我總有一天能瞭解《家母的珍寶》書名是什麼意思。如果指的是錢，如果我沒記錯，這麼多年來，我是妳的珍寶才對。我至今一直在做同樣的事，因為妳以我為題出書能熱賣，沾盡了我的光。

忘卻你個人煩憂

海明威（Ernest Hemingway）致
費茲傑羅（F. Scott Fitzgerald）
一九三四年五月二十八日

費茲傑羅發表曠世鉅作《大亨小傳》後，在一九二五年著手籌備第四部小說《夜未央》（*Tender Is the Night*），故事圍繞著戴沃（Diver）夫婦迪克和妮可之間的風風雨雨，靈感大致來自墨菲夫婦傑洛德和莎拉。生活富裕的墨菲夫婦人緣好，和費茲傑羅夫婦（妻名賽爾妲〔Zelda〕）的社交圈重疊。第四本小說醞釀九年總算出版。一個月後，在一九三四年五月十日，費茲傑羅寫信給同是小說家的朋友海明威，請他坦白惠賜高見。這是費茲傑羅發表的最後一本書。
海明威的批評毫不留情，刀刀見骨，建議至今仍被全球文人視為無價之寶。
（海明威信裡提及的人與事包括：約翰‧斗司‧帕索斯〔John Dos Passos〕最近造訪佛羅里達州西嶼；海明威當時的妻子寶琳‧菲佛〔Pauline Pfeiffer〕以及第一任妻子哈德莉‧理察遜〔Hadley Richardson〕；文評人吉柏特‧歇爾茲〔Gilbert Seldes〕；費茲傑羅女兒絲高蒂；海明威分別與第一、二任生的邦比和派崔克；最後在信封上追加一句提到的短篇小說集是海明威在三三年秋發表的《勝者一無所獲》〔*Winner Take Nothing*〕。）

西嶼
一九三四年五月二十八日

親愛的史考特：

我喜歡也不喜歡。你的故事開頭把莎拉和傑洛德描寫得精彩（可惡，書被斗司拿走了，害我無法邊寫邊查書，指涉有錯之處請包容）。然後，你開始瞎扯，為他們的背景加油添醋，把他們寫成別人。不能這樣寫吧，史考特。如果你以真人為範本，就不能亂塞別人的父母給他們（畢竟他們是受自己的父母養育，被自己的遭遇型塑而成），不能逼他們做不願做的事。你可以寫你、寫我、寫賽爾妲、寫寶琳、寫哈德莉、寫莎拉、寫傑洛德，但你一寫就應貫徹到底，只能叫他們做他們肯做的事，不能叫他們做別人做的事。發明是天下最巧妙的事，但你不能捏造實際上不會發生的東西。

捏造是你我在文思泉湧時應當做的事，但是，捏造也應該據實捏造，以後演進才不顯得牽強。

可惡，你擅自挪移人物的過去未來，製造出來的不是人物，而是虛假得美侖美奐的個案史，該死。你的文筆不輸任何人，擺著才華不用，居然——算了，不罵也罷。史考特，看在眾神的份上，寫作應該據實寫，別擔心事實會傷害到誰或什麼，不要做這種沒大腦的折衷。你可以寫一本好書，可以拿真人當範本，例如傑洛德和莎拉，條件是你對他們瞭解要透徹，而就算你寫的是事實，他們讀到也無感或只有一絲絲感受。

裡面有些地方寫得不錯。小子們一個也不會寫，其他人的文筆更比不上你的一半，但你這本便宜行事太嚴重了，其實沒必要。

首先，我一向聲稱你欠缺思考能力。好吧，姑且承認你有思考能力。不過，在此假設你缺乏思考能力，你應該照你所知去寫，去發明，照實把人物的身世寫對。其次，從很久以前開始，你不再聽勸，只自問自答。你也加進一些不必硬加的好東西。忠言聽不進去，文人才會文思枯竭（我們都有枯竭的一天，不是針對你個人的侮辱）。多看，多聽，文思才源源不絕。你的眼力夠好，但你停止聆聽。

書寫得比我的批評好太多了，卻比不上你的潛力。

你可以上戰場研究克勞塞維茨將軍，可以鑽研經濟學和心理學，其他東西懂再多，對寫作中的你一點屁用也沒有。波，我們像蹩腳的特技人，但我們有幾招跳法還不錯，而連跳都跳不起來的特技人多的是。

看在基督的份上，儘管寫，別擔心小子們怎麼批評，也別管這一本會不會成為鉅作。我寫了九十頁的屎，才寫得出一頁傑作。我盡量把屎丟進廢紙簍。你覺得你被生活和環境所逼，不得不為錢發表作品。對是對啦，不過如果你搖筆桿夠勤，盡能力發揮，成為傑作的素材一樣多（套一句我們在耶魯的說法）。有心坐下來寫傑作的人反而寫不出傑作。歐爾茲那一票人差點毀了你，如果你能排除他們，儘可能別理他們，任憑觀眾在精彩的橋段叫好，冷場時倒開汽水，你就不會出事。

忘卻你個人煩憂吧。從一開始，我們全愛發牢騷，尤其是你，非得痛得呼天搶地才有辦法認真創作。但是，有痛的時候，你應該善用──不要用來便宜行事。要效法科學界，誠懇面對它，不要因為它發生在你或親友身上就認為意義不凡。

行筆至此，假如你對我開炮，我也不怪你。天啊，教別人怎麼寫作、怎麼生死等等，棒透了。

我想在你不沾酒時見面聊聊。那天在紐約，你醉醺醺的，根本聊不出東西。其實啊，波，你不是悲劇人物。我也不是。我們只不過是文人，應該做的事是寫作。全世界最需要工作紀律的人是你，而你卻娶了一個跟你的工作爭風吃醋的人，她只想跟你爭，毀了你。事實沒有如此單純。我認識賽爾姐的那天就以為她是瘋子，你居然愛上她，把情況搞得更複雜，更別忘了你是個酒鬼。但你喝酒不比喬埃斯兇，何況多數優秀作家是酒鬼。不過，史考特，好作家總能東山再起。一定能。和你自認棒透了的那段時期相比，現在的你更優秀一倍。你知道嗎，當時我覺得大亨小傳沒啥了不起。現在的你寫得出比你以前更好一倍的東西，只要你據實寫作，不要為作品未來的命運窮擔心。

繼續前進，寫作。

總而言之，我對你欣賞得不得了，希望有空聚一聚。我們有幾次聊得很暢快。記得巴黎訥伊的那傢伙嗎？他那時只剩半條命，我們去探望他。他今年冬天南下這裡。好傢伙一個，坎比‧錢伯斯。我常看到斗司。去年這段時間，他病得嚴重，現在健康了。絲高蒂和賽爾姐最近好嗎？寶琳要我向你問安。我們全家都還可以。她想帶派崔克北上匹葛特住兩三個禮拜。然後帶邦比回來。我們有一艘不錯的小船。我忙著一篇很長的故事，寫得很順。這篇難寫啊。

永遠的朋友

厄尼斯特

（寫在信封上：《太陽依舊升起》和電影如何？有機會嗎？我這信上沒提到你寫得好的部分。寫得多好，你心裡有數。你對短篇選集的見解很正確。我本想延後出版，想再添一則，可惜上次在《柯夢波丹》的那則沒趕上。）

信之 *080*

我註定成為作曲家

塞繆爾・巴伯（Samuel Barber）
致母親
一九一九年

塞繆爾・巴伯至今在作曲界依然是重量級人物。在一九三六年，才二十六歲的他譜出《弦樂慢板》（*Adagio for Strings*），躍居二十世紀人氣最旺的古典樂曲之林。一九五八年，巴伯以《凡妮莎》（*Vanessa*）榮獲普立茲音樂獎。才過五年，他以鋼琴協奏曲再奪普立茲獎。據說巴伯從小立志作曲：一九一九年，才九歲大的他寫了一封告白信，緊張兮兮地留在書桌上，希望被母親看到。母親果然看到了。一年後，巴伯開始創作第一部歌劇《玫瑰樹》。

限母親閱讀

親愛的母親：我寫這封信是想透露一個令我心煩的祕密，請妳讀了不要哭，因為這不是妳或我的錯。我想我最好趁早說，以免惹出風波。是這樣的，我不是運動員的料子。我註定成為作曲家，我自信總有一天會的。我想再要求妳一件事。——不要叫我忘掉這件不愉快的事，叫我趕快出去打球。——求求妳——有時候，我為這事好擔心，差點發瘋（不是太瘋），

愛妳的

山姆・巴伯二世

准許迫降

南越少校致美國中途號軍艦
一九七五年四月三十日

在一九七五年四月三十日，南越首府西貢被北越攻陷，為越戰正式劃下句點。在戰爭結束前幾天，美國發動「常風行動」，以直升機盡量撤美僑，在忙亂之中，中途號軍艦赫見一架 Cessna 兩人座 O-1 觀測機接近，然後在上空盤旋，飛行員是南越空軍少校黎邦，帶著妻子和五名子女，剛逃離崑山（Con Son）島。由於燃油見底，少校寫字條，朝著航空母艦甲板拋投，連續幾次失敗後，他把這封信綁在沉甸甸的手槍上，信總算沒被強風吹跑，墜落在擁擠的甲板上，信上請求迫降該艦。

艦長賴瑞·錢伯斯閱信後，立即調派所有可供支配的士兵，視需要騰出空位讓少校一家七口降落，盡可能把甲板上的 UH-1 休伊直升機推進海裡，而非只把艦上直升機挪到一旁。在缺乏尾鉤連接的情況下，少校平安降落，現場掌聲如雷。

請你們把直升機移到一邊，讓我能降落在跑道，我能再飛一小時，我們有足夠時間移動，請救我。

邦少校妻五子

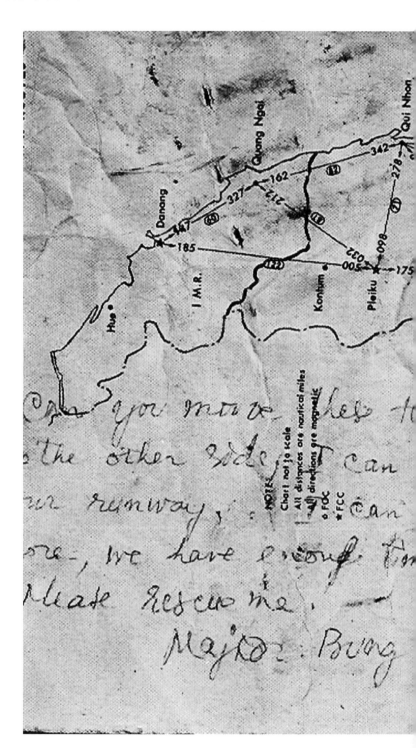

SOUTH VIETNAM—AREA OF COVERAGE

說，是的，
我想應徵工作

電玩設計師致主管
一九八九年

在一九八九年，應徵電玩設計工作的提姆・雪佛（Tim Schafer）接受電話口試，自曝玩該公司的盜版遊戲。口試結束時，考官請他寄履歷和簡介信至盧卡斯藝術公司（LucasArts）應徵助理程式師／設計員一職。這家電玩公司始於一九八二年，創辦人是喬治・盧卡斯（George Lucas）。由於口試時留下不良的第一印象，雪佛決定不寫簡介信，改以文字冒險遊戲的形式呈現志願。幾星期後，他接到錄取通知，隨後創作了冒險遊戲史少見的兩大作品：《猴島小英雄》（The Secret of Monkey Island）以及續集《勒恰克的復仇》（Monkey Island 2: LeChuck's Revenge）。

理想就業中心

IDEAL CAREER CENTER

Your quest for the ideal career begins, logically enough, at the Ideal Career Center. Upon entering, you see a helpful looking woman sitting behind a desk. She smiles and says, "May I help you?"

>SAY YES I NEED A JOB

"Ah," she replies, "and where would you like to work, Los Angeles, Silicon Valley, or San Rafael?"

>SAY SAN RAFAEL

"Good choice," she says, "Here are some jobs you might be interested in," and gives you three brochures.

>EXAMINE BROCHURES

The titles of the three brochures are as follows: "HAL Computers: We've Got a Number For You," "Yoyodine Defense Technologies: Help Us Reach Our Destructive Potential," and "Lucasfilm, Ltd: Games, Games, Games!"

>OPEN LUCASFILM BROCHURE

追求理想職業，理所當然該從理想就業中心起跑。一進中心，你見到一位看起來熱心的櫃檯小姐。她微笑說，「我能為您服務嗎？」

>說，是的，我想應徵工作

「啊，」她回應，「您想在哪裡就業？洛杉磯、矽谷或聖拉菲爾？」

>說聖拉菲爾

「選得好，」她說，「這裡有幾份您可能感興趣的工作，」說著遞給你三份簡介。

>細看簡介

三份簡介的標題分別是：「HAL電腦公司，號碼任君選」；「友友定國防科技，幫助我們發揮摧毀潛力」；「盧卡斯電影公司，遊戲、遊戲、遊戲！」

>打開盧卡斯電影公司簡介

The brochure says that Lucasfilm is looking for an imaginative, good-humored team player who has excellent communication skills, programming experience, and loves games. Under that description, oddly enough, is a picture of you.

>SEND RESUME

You get the job! Congratulations! You start right away!

>GO TO WORK

You drive the short commute to the Lucasfilm building and find it full of friendly people who show you the way to your desk.

>EXAMINE DESK

Your desk has on it a powerful computer, a telephone, some personal nicknacks, and some work to do.

>EXAMINE WORK

It is challenging and personally fulfilling to perform.

>DO WORK

As you become personally fulfilled, your score reaches 100, and this quest comes to an end. The adventure, however, is just beginning and so are your days at Lucasfilm.

THE END

簡介寫著，盧卡斯電影公司徵求一名富想像力、脾氣溫和、合群、溝通技巧絕佳、具程式設計經驗、熱愛遊戲的員工。奇怪的是，應徵條件下面居然有你的相片。

>寄履歷

你錄取了！恭喜！你立刻開始上班！

>去上班

你從家開車一小段路，來到盧卡斯電影大樓，發現裡面滿是友善的人，熱心帶你去找你的辦公桌。

>檢視辦公桌

辦公桌上有一臺夠力的電腦、一臺電話、幾項個人雜物、一些待辦的工作。

>檢視工作

工作富挑戰性，成就感也高。

>動手工作

獲得成就感時，績效衝上一百分，遊戲結束，但冒險旅程才剛開始，你在盧卡斯電影公司的日子也是。

結束

我們不再有權保持緘默

三十六位美國作家致小羅斯福總統
一九三八年十一月十六日

在一九三八年十一月九、十日，奧地利和捷克斯拉夫某些區域以及德國各地的猶太人成為標靶，商店、教堂、住家和人身頻遭惡意攻擊。儘管納粹黨擺出事不干己的姿態，其實暴動的源頭來自納粹宣傳部長戈培爾（Joseph Goebbels）的一席演說——政府將不阻撓自發性的示威。暴民騷擾毒打猶太人，放火搗毀打劫猶太建築，納粹爪牙也湊熱鬧。這次暴動因碎玻璃遍地，史稱「水晶夜」，直接導致九十人喪生，三萬餘猶太人被捕，多數被押進集中營。水晶夜也導致德國境內公開踐踏猶太人與特定團體，強化了納粹黨羽翼，推進亞利安民族的野心。

水晶夜引發國際同表震怒，其中有三十六名美國作家聯署，發電報給小羅斯福總統。儘管美國駐德大使被召回，德美兩國的外交和經濟關係互動如常。

致羅斯福總統

　　三十六名美國文人在此聯署發聲，我們不再有權保持緘默，一致認為美國人民與政府無權保持緘默，不能坐視德國政府繼續提高違反人性的舉動，繼續迫害無辜百姓，不能讓德國政府在屢次震驚國際之餘連番歡慶。

　　三十五年前，面對沙皇時代俄國的反猶太暴行，震驚的美國民眾群起抗議。如今面對納粹德國，若我們冷漠到無視他人苦難，若無法群起抗議反猶太暴動，那麼唯有上帝能保祐我們。我們不應讓外界認為美國人已麻木不仁。我們認為，納粹德國誓言藉大屠殺來解決經濟問題，美國人民若與德國政府維持經濟關係是極為不道德的舉動。我們要求總統斷絕我國與納粹德國之貿易關係，宣佈禁運所有納粹德國商品。

　　聯署人

　　NEWTON ARVIN PEARL BUCK S N BEHRMAN NORAH BENJAMIN VAN WYCK BROOKS JOHN CHAMBERLIN ALAN CAMPBELL MARC CONNELLY ROBERT CANTWELL PAUL DE KRUIF MAJOY GEORGE FIELDING ELIOT EDNA FERBER MARJORIE FISHCER JOHN GUNTHER DASHIELL HAMMETT SIDNEY HOWARD LILLIAN HELLMAN ROBINSON JEFFERS GEORGE S KAUFMAN LOUIS KRONENBERGER PARE LORENZ OLIVER LA FARGE EUGENE O'NEILL CLIFFORD ODETS DOROTHY PARKER MURDOCK PEMBERTON GEORGE SELDES ISIDOR SCHNEIDER JOHN STEINBECK ROBERT SHERWOOD DOROTHY THOMPSON THORNTON WILDER FRANCES WINWAR W S WOODWARD HELEN WOODWARD LESNE ZUGSMITH.

Postal Telegraph

THE INTERNATIONAL SYSTEM

RECEIVED AT

STANDARD TIME
INDICATED ON THIS MESSAGE

Commercial
Cables

All America
Cables

Mackay   Radio

This is a full rate Telegram, Cablegram or Radiogram unless otherwise indicated by signal in the check or in the address.

DL	DAY LETTER
NL	NIGHT LETTER
NM	NIGHT MESSAGE
LCO	DEFERRED CABLE
NLT	NIGHT CABLE LETTER
	RADIOGRAM

1938 NOV 16 PM 5 00

NB248 264 DL 78 EXTRA

AZ NEWYORK NY 16 425P

DIVISION OF
EUROPEAN AFFAIRS
NOV 18 1938
DEPARTMENT OF STATE

PRESIDENT ROOSEVELT

WASHN DC

THIS APPEAL COMES TO YOU FROM THIRTY SIX AMERICAN WRITERS. WE FEEL

WE NO LONGER HAVE ANY RIGHT TO REMAIN SILENT, WE FEEL THAT THE

AMERICAN PEOPLE AND THE AMERICAN GOVERNMENT HAVE NO RIGHT TO

REMAIN SILENT, WHILE A GERMAN GOVERNMENT CELEBRATES EACH OF ITS

SHOCKING VICTORIES IN THE INTERNATIONAL FIELD BY THE INCREASINGLY

INHUMAN OPPRESSION OF THOSE WHOSE ONLY CRIME IS THAT THEY ARE AT

THAT GOVERNMENT'S MERCY.

Postal Telegraph
THE INTERNATIONAL SYSTEM

Commercial Cables   All America Cables

Mackay   Radio

This is a full rate Telegram, Cablegram or Radiogram unless otherwise indicated by signal in the check or in the address.

DL	DAY LETTER
NL	NIGHT LETTER
NM	NIGHT MESSAGE
LCO	DEFERRED CABLE
NLT	NIGHT CABLE LETTER
	RADIOGRAM

RECEIVED AT

STANDARD TIME INDICATED ON THIS MESSAGE

1938 NOV 16 PM 5 00

NB248 2 NYC ROOSEVELT WASHN DC

THIRTY FIVE YEARS AGO A HORRIFIED AMERICA ROSE TO ITS FEET TO
PROTEST AGAINST THE KISHINEV POGROMS IN TSARIST RUSSIA. GOD
HELP US IF WE HAVE GROWN SO INDIFFIERENT TO HUMAN SUFFERING THAT
WE CANNOT RISE NOW IN PROTEST AGAINST THE POGROMS IN NAZI GERMANY.
WE DO NOT BELIEVE WE HAVE GROWN SO INDIFFERENT AND WE DO NOT
THINK THE WORLD SHOULD BE ALLOWED TO THINK WE HAVE. WE FEEL
THAT IT IS DEEPLY IMMORAL FOR THE AMERICAN PEOPLE TO CONTINUE
HAVING ECONOMIC RELATIONS WITH A GOVERNMENT THAT AVOWEDLY USES MASS
MURDER TO SOLVE ITS ECONOMIC PROBLEMS. WE ASK YOU TO SEVER
TRADE RELATIONS WITH NAZI GERMANY, TO DECLARE

Postal Telegraph

THE INTERNATIONAL SYSTEM

Commercial
Cables

All America
Cables

Mackay   Radio

RECEIVED AT

STANDARD TIME
INDICATED ON THIS MESSAGE

This is a full rate Telegram, Cablegram or
Radiogram unless otherwise indicated by
signal in the check or in the address.

DL	DAY LETTER
NL	NIGHT LETTER
NM	NIGHT MESSAGE
LCO	DEFERRED CABLE
NLT	NIGHT CABLE LETTER
	RADIOGRAM

1938 NOV 16 PM 5 00

NB248 3 NYC ROOSEVELT WASHN DC

AN EMBARGO ON ALL NAZI GERMAN GOODS, SIGNED

NEWTON ARVIN PEARL BUCK S N BEHRMAN NORAH BENJAMIN VAN WYCK BROOKS
JOHN CHAMBERLIN ALAN CAMPBELL MARC CONNELLY ROBERT CANTWELL PAUL DE
KRUIF MAJOR GEORGE FIELDING ELIOT EDNA FERBER MARJORIE FISHCER
JOHN GUNTHER DASHIELL HAMMETT SIDNEY HOWARD LILLIAN HELLMAN
ROBINSON JEFFERS GEORGE S KAUFMAN LOUIS KRONENBERGER PARE LORENZ
OLIVER LA FARGE EUGENE O'NEILL CLIFFORD ODETS DOROTHY PARKER
MURDOCK PEMBERTON GEORGE SELDES ISIDOR SCHNEIDER JOHN STEINBECK
ROBERT SHERWOOD DOROTHY THOMPSON THORNTON WILDER FRANCES WINWAR
W S WOODWARD HELEN WOODWARD LESNE ZUGSMITH.

信之 *084*

吉卜林傳授學童禮儀

吉卜林致校刊編輯
一八九八年復活節週一

英國肯特有一所男校荷斯蒙登
（Horsmonden），每月兩次發行校
刊《荷斯蒙登學校書信報》（*School
Budget*），號稱「男生編寫，男生
閱讀」，發行量小，編輯想吸引才
子，異想天開寄一份校刊給《叢林
之書》（*The Jungle Book*）知名作家
吉卜林，為下一期校刊向他邀稿，
大作家居然回信了，編輯群必定驚
喜異常。吉卜林列舉六項「學童禮
儀提示」，並索取稿費。在下一期
校刊裡，編輯果然全篇登載吉六
條，也寄支票給作家，但作家始終
未拿去兌現，目前陳列於英國波瓦
許的家庭故居展出。

開普敦
一八九八年復活節週一

致學校書信報編輯群。

紳士們——我收到未註明日期的來信，連同一份二月十四日出刊
的《學校書信報》。你們似乎狂妄自大到對你們今生或來世皆無
益處的程度。猶有甚者，你們疏漏了貴期刊印行的地點，也未說
明荷斯蒙登位於英格蘭哪一郡。

然而，儘管如此，我非常贊同貴刊的「學童禮儀提示」，擅作主
張再添幾項如下：

一、如果回答數字時不太有把握，邊咳邊答。如此一咳，可避免
　　對方要求「再說一遍」，五次當中有三次靈驗。

二、同年級的男同學裡最有用的兩種人是：a）老師的當紅炸子
　　雞，b）老師最忌諱的學生。稍微使點小聰明的話，a能讓校
　　長講完上半節，b能接棒撐完下半節。注意：其他同學應群
　　策群力，代b做罰寫的作業，以示報答。

三、星期一上午上課被老師問時，猜對答案的人身價相當於與體
　　重相等的黃金。

四、千萬不要遠遠迴避老師，應以心不在焉的神態擦身而過，同
　　時取出一封信，故作認真詳讀。老師或許會以為你正忙著其
　　他課程的作業。

五、被農夫追趕時，務必衝向最近的耕地，男童可奔越犁溝，大
　　人則陷泥濘無法自拔。

六、如果有必要取他人之蘋果，宜於週日取之，藏進帽子裡，總
　　比塞進上衣、釦成「緊身伊頓裝」來得好。

你們將發現這份建議值千金，但我——倘使此篇投稿能排版超過
一頁——願接受六便士的支票或郵政匯票，請儘早寄出。——

吉卜林　敬上

信之 085

性愛不會在單調的環境滋長

阿娜依絲 · 寧（Anais Nin）致
收集者（The Collector）

一九四〇年前後

已婚小說家亨利 · 米勒和已婚日記作家阿娜依絲 · 寧在巴黎認識，幾個月後在一九三二年，兩人開始熱戀，延續數年。在一九四〇年代，寧、米勒以及一群文人以一頁一美元的酬勞，為綽號「收集者」的隱名客戶撰寫情色小說，供他個人閱讀。「收集者」屢次堅持這些文人「少一點詩心」，盡量「著重於性愛」，寧於是寫了一封振振有詞的信給這位神祕人士，表達她的不滿。

親愛的收集者：

我們恨你。性愛變得露骨、制式、誇張時，成為一種機械式的沉迷時，其魔力盡失。性愛變得索然無味。在我認識的人當中，你最能啟發我們的是，大錯特錯的做法是讓性愛摒除以下元素：情感、飢渴、欲望、肉慾、遐思、異想、私交，以及能改變性愛色、香、韻、熱的深層關係。

在你的顯微鏡檢視下，性行為排除了助燃因子，錯過了什麼好東西你無法自知。智識、想像力、浪漫、情緒。這些東西能為性愛增添出奇的質感、微妙的形變、催情的元件。你在感官世界的門口畏縮不前。你讓感官世界凋零、失血、挨餓。

愛能為感官注入源源不絕的亢奮與新奇，如果你能以愛灌溉性生活，你勢必成為舉世無雙的男性。性力源自好奇心、熱情，如今你眼睜睜看著性的小火苗缺氧而死。性愛不會在單調的環境裡滋長。若無感覺、創意、心情，床第之間也無驚奇。性必須混之以淚水、歡笑、言語、承諾、情境、嫉妒、羨慕、五味雜陳的恐懼、海外旅遊、新臉孔、小說、故事、夢想、遐想、音樂、舞蹈、鴉片、葡萄酒。

你僅以潛望鏡窺視性愛一隅，漏看何其多的風光，享受不到各色各樣、永不重複的奇景。天下沒有兩根毛髮是一模一樣的，而你卻不准我們贅述一根毛髮。天下也無完全相同的氣味，但如果我們詳細描寫，會招你罵「寫什麼詩？省省吧。」天下沒有兩種肌膚具有相同的質感，也不會有一模一樣的光亮、溫度、陰影，不會有一模一樣的儀態。因為，受真愛蠱惑的有情人能道盡亙古的愛情傳說，範圍何其寬廣，年代演變何其劇烈，成熟與天真、變態與藝術、質樸動物與文雅動物之間的差異何其鮮明。

我們曾促膝暢談數小時，揣摩著你的觀點。如果你的感官已閉鎖，不再能感應絲綢、光線、色彩、氣味、品格、性情，現在的你必定乾癟到不成人形。人有許許多多的小感官，全如支流，匯入名為性愛的主流，滋潤著性愛。唯有性與心協同脈動，極樂方能產生。

阿娜依絲 · 寧

信之 *086*

親愛的「博士」

司法部長致三K黨
一九七六年二月二十日

一九六三年，阿拉巴馬州伯明罕驚傳爆炸案，造成第十六街教堂四名非裔少女喪生，據研判是針對黑人的恐怖攻擊行動。本案成為民權運動的轉捩點，多年懸宕未結。到了一九七○年，二十九歲的比爾・巴克斯里（Bill Baxley）當選阿拉巴馬州司法部長，新官上任宣佈重新偵辦本的決心，掀起撻伐的聲浪，敵意特別深的是當地的三K黨成員。一九七六年，白人至上份子艾德華・R・費爾茲（Edward R. Fields）博士致函部長，指控部長掀舊案有政治目的。費爾茲是全國州權促進黨（National States' Rights Party）的創辦人，也擔任三K黨新秩序團的「偉龍長」（Grand Dragon）。

部長的回信很精闢，言簡意賅。翌年，美國聯合三K黨成員羅伯特・錢布利斯（Robert Chambliss）因教堂爆炸案被判有罪發監執刑，於一九八五年死於獄中。

阿拉巴馬州司法部長
阿拉巴馬州蒙哥馬利市

一九七六年二月二十日

致艾德華・**R**・費爾茲「博士」
全國州權促進黨
喬治亞州馬里耶塔**30061**
郵政信箱一二一一號

親愛的費爾茲「博士」：
在此回覆你一九七六年二月十九日的信：你去吃屎吧。

司法部長比爾・巴克斯里　敬上

THE ATTORNEY GENERAL State of Alabama

MONTGOMERY, ALABAMA 36130

WILLIAM J. BAXLEY
ATTORNEY GENERAL

GEORGE L. BECK
DEPUTY ATTORNEY GENERAL

E. RAY ACTON
EXECUTIVE ASSISTANT

WALTER S. TURNER
CHIEF ASSISTANT ATTORNEY GENERAL

LUCY M. RICHARDS
CONFIDENTIAL ASSISTANT

JACK D. SHOWS
CHIEF INVESTIGATOR

February 20, 1976

"Dr." Edward R. Fields
National States Rights Party
P. O. Box 1211
Marietta, Georgia 30061

Dear "Dr." Fields:

My response to your letter of February 19, 1976,
is – kiss my ass.

Sincerely,

BILL BAXLEY
Attorney General

海里根遺書
（**Heiligenstadt**）

貝多芬致胞弟
一八〇二年十月六日

貝多芬近三十歲起，耳朵開始不靈光，竟然仍能譜出曠世佳作，難怪史稱音樂奇才。重聽的困擾引發連連抑鬱，令他幾度興起輕生的念頭，也因此避不見親友。三十二歲那年，他寫下這則盪氣迴腸的遺言，指示兩名胞弟在他死後拆封閱讀。在遺書裡，他解釋避世的舉止和緣由。儘管貝多芬耳聾了，他仍持續作曲長達二十五年，直到去世為止。

致弟卡爾與（友翰）貝多芬

　　唉，認為或說我心懷惡意、冥頑不化、不合群的你們，對我的誤解何其大。對我有此誤解的原因不足為外人道，你們有所不知。自幼我心靈充滿善意柔情，甚至立志成就大事業。然而，礙於六年來我深受惡疾之苦，無藥可醫，更遇上庸醫年復一年欺瞞我可望改善病情，最後我被迫面對事實，接受惡疾長年纏身之命運（治療需耗時數年，甚至康復無望）。

　　雖然我生性熱情活躍，甚至常被俗事分心，如今好景不長，我被迫孤立自我而獨居。有時我想忘掉這一切，唉，卻遭重聽的雙重打擊無情甩回原地。但我實在無法對人說，「講大聲一點，用喊的，因為我是聾子」。唉，我怎能坦言聽覺有病？聽覺曾經是我最完美無瑕疵的感官，理應比常人更完美，作曲界古今少有人能及。——唉我無法承認；因此，雖然我樂意與你們共處，但你們如果見我退縮，一定要見諒。

　　這份不幸遭遇對我而言是加倍痛苦，因為旁人必然對我產生誤解。與人相處時，我無法鬆懈，言談無深度，思想無以交流。我必須過著近乎獨居的日子，宛如被放逐。唯有在絕對必要時，我始能交際。每當我接近他人，一陣火熱的恐懼劈頭而來，唯恐洩露病情，因此近半年來，我幽居於鄉野。聰明醫師叮囑我，儘可能避用聽覺，以免進一步耗損，其指示幾乎與我目前心態一致，但有時我違背囑咐，屈從於呼朋引伴之欲望。

　　每當旁人聞遠處笛聲，我卻聽不見，每當旁人聞牧羊人歌聲，我卻又聽不見，簡直是奇恥大辱，迫使我走向絕望深淵邊。再多受一點辱，我必定就此結束一生。阻止我輕生的唯有我個人的才華。唉，在譜盡心曲之前，我似乎不可能撒手離世。於是，我忍受著這具臭皮囊，揹著這身不堪一擊的軀殼，一個能從最佳狀況倏然急轉直下的肉身。有人勸我，現在的我宜以耐心為嚮導，我耐著性子——我希望意志能堅定下去，直到冷酷的命運女神欣然干預。也許，我將有好轉的一天，也許不然；我已有心理

準備。——年方二十八，我便被迫高談哲理，唉，不容易啊，身為藝術工作者比常人更是難上加難。神啊，明察我最深的性靈，洞悉我內心深處有著一份對世人的愛，一份行善的渴望。唉，弟弟們，有朝一日你們閱讀此信之際，宜反省你們對我的誤解。有相同難言之隱的人見我病例，定能無懼肉身的局限，盡其所能，以獲得才子與世人的接受。

　　吾弟卡爾、友翰，我死後，如果施米德醫師仍在世，儘速代我請他描述病情，附上此遺言，尚祈世人在我死後能諒解我。在此，我指定你們兩位繼承我微薄的財富（富字或許言過其實），公平對分，彼此應忍讓互助。無論你倆對我造成何種傷害，我早已寬恕。卡爾吾弟，我特別感謝你近日對我表現的關愛，祝你日子過得比我更順利更自由。對子女灌輸美德教育，因為唯有美德能為他們帶來快樂，金錢不能。這是經驗談，是我在苦難中的寄託。多虧美德，多虧才華，我才不至於走上絕路——再會了，要相親相愛。

　　我感謝所有朋友，特別是李奇諾斯基親王與施米德教授。希望你們其中一人能代我保存親王提供的樂器，但切勿因此兄弟鬩牆。倘使變賣樂器的益處更高，那就賣吧。我死後若仍能幫助你們，我在墳裡也將含笑。帶著喜悅，我急奔黃泉。如果死神在我才華發揮至極致之前降臨，也不算來得太早。我但願能晚一點死——即使如此，我也應慶幸脫離苦海，不是嗎？死神啊，儘管來，我將勇敢面對。再會了，勿在我死後忘得我一乾二淨，這是我應得的報答，因我終生常惦記你倆，常思考討你們歡心之道，請永保歡心——

路德維格・貝多芬
於海里根
一八〇二年十月六日

Für meine Brüder Carl und   Beethoven

O ihr Menschen die ihr mich für feindseelig störrisch oder
Misantropisch haltet oder erkläret, wie unrecht thut ihr mir,
ihr wißt nicht die geheime ursache von dem was euch so
scheinet, mein Herz und mein Sinn waren von Kindheit
an für das zarte gefühl des Wohlwollens, selbst große
Handlungen zu verrichten dazu war ich immer aufgelegt,
aber bedenket nur daß seit 6 Jahren ein heilloser
Zustand mich befallen, durch unvernünftige Aerzte verschlimmert,
von Jahr zu Jahr in der Hofnung gebeßert zu werden,
betrogen, endlich zu dem überblick eines daurenden
übels (dessen Heilung vieleicht Jahre dauern oder gar
gar unmöglich ist) gezwungen, mit einem feurigen
lebhaften Temperamente sogar empfänglich für die
Zerstreuungen der Gesellschaft, mußte ich früh
mich absondern, einsam mein leben zubringen, wollte
ich auch zuweilen mich einmal über alles das hinaussezen,
o wie hart wurde ich durch die verdoppelte traurige
Erfahrung meines schlechten Gehörs. Denn zu ein D-
gehörten, und doch war es mir noch nicht möglich den
Menschen zu sagen: Sprecht lauter geschreyt, denn
ich bin taub, ach wie wär es möglich daß ich die
Schwäche eines Sinnes angeben sollte, der bey mir in
einem Vollkommenern grade als bey andern sein sollte
einen Sinn den ich einst in der größten Vollkommenheit
besaß, in einer Vollkommenheit, wie ihn wenige von
meinem Fache gewiß haben noch gehabt haben — o ich
kann es nicht, drum verzeihet, wenn ihr mich da zurück
weichen sehet, wo ich mich gerne unter euch mischte,
doppelt wehe thut mir mein Unglück, indem ich dabey verkannt
werden muß, für mich darf Erholung in menschlicher Gesellschaft, feinere unterredungen, wechselseitige ergießun-
gen nicht statt haben, ganz allein fast nur so viel,
als es die höchste Nothwendigkeit fodert, darf ich mich in gesellschaft einlassen, wie ein verbannter muß ich leben, nahe ich mich
einer gesellschaft, so überfällt mich eine heiße Aengstlich-
keit, indem ich befürchte in gefahr gesezt zu werden, meinen
Zustand merken zu lassen — so war es auch in diesen
halben Jahre, das ich auf dem Lande zubrachte,
von meinem vernünftigen arzte aufgefodert, so viel
als möglich meine gehör zu schonen, kam er meiner
jezigen natürlichen Disposition entgegen, ob ich gleich mancher
Gesellschaftlichen neigung hingerissen manchmal mich verleiten
ließ, aber welch eine demüthigung wenn jemand neben
mir stund und von weitem eine Flöte hörte und ich nichts hörte,
oder jemand den Hirten singen hörte, und ich auch nichts hörte,

Ludwig van Beethowen

善心接力

富蘭克林致班哲明‧韋伯
（**Benjamin Webb**）
一七八四年四月二十二日

美國國父富蘭克林比多數人多才多藝，頭銜依字母順序包括：社運分子、作者、商人、外交官、幽默作家、發明者、音樂家、政治人物、印刷商、科學家。他在一七八四年寫這封信給班哲明‧韋伯，由此信研判，他是近代最早倡議「善心接力」（pay it forward）運動的人之一。善心接力的概念是鼓勵借方與其還錢或人情債給債權人，不如轉而濟助有相同難題的對象，附帶相同的條件，請他們把錢傳遞給其他急難人士，以此恩恩相報下去，傳遍整個社會。富蘭克林寫這封信時，這種哲理尚未出現定稱，現在普遍稱為「善心接力」。

親愛的先生，

　　我收到你十五日速件，讀完信內之請願。你的狀況經描述令我悲痛。我在此寄上十法國金路易之票據，並非**贈予**，僅止于**借貸**。待你回祖國，保持良好品行，從商有所收穫，定能賦予你償債之能力。屆時若遇另一誠實人士陷入同樣困境，你報答我的方式是借這筆錢予他，吩咐他能力可及的時候，遇到相同機會，也以同等方式償債。我希望此錢以此方式輾轉多手，最後落入無賴漢的掌握而停止。這是我以小錢行善的伎倆。我不夠富裕，無法行大善，因此略施小技，讓小錢發揮最大功效。誠摯敬祝你請願成功，未來鴻圖大展。

　　　　　　　　　　　　　　你最忠實的僕人
　　　　　　　　　　　　　　富蘭克林

一九五六年六月十九日

艾迪的狗屋

男童致名建築師
一九五六年六月十九日

法蘭克・洛伊德・萊特（Frank Lloyd Wright）縱橫建築界七十年，設計了一千餘建築物，成品有五百三十二座。萊特於一九五九年去世，後獲美國建築師學會推舉為「美國史上最傑出建築師」。他最小的作品——也許是最不尋常的作品——創作於一九五六年。萊特曾為柏格家設計過房子，事後十二歲的兒子寫信，要求很簡單：想聘請萊特為家犬艾迪設計一座狗屋，附在家的旁邊。萊特翌年為狗屋設計了全套藍圖。建築史上的這一小件作品由男童父親施工，最後在一九六三年落成。

親愛的萊特先生

我是一個十二歲的男孩。我的姓名是吉姆・柏格，父親是鮑伯・柏格，你為他設計過一棟房屋。我有一份送報的工作，賺小錢花用並儲蓄。

我想請你為我設計一個狗屋，希望你能答應。這狗屋很容易建造，但必須附著在我們家。我的狗名叫艾德華，小名艾迪，今年四歲，換算狗年是二十八歲。他是一隻拉布拉多犬，身高兩呎半，身長三呎。我想蓋狗屋的主要原因是怕冬天。我爸說，如果你能設計狗屋，他願意幫我建造。如果你願意設計，我願意以送報薪水報答你的藍圖和材料。

吉姆・柏格　敬上

June 19, 19

Dear Mr. Wright

I am a boy of twelve years. My name
Jim Berger. You designed a house for
father whose name is Bob Berger. I
have a paper route which I make a
little bit of money for the bank, and
expenses.

I would appreciate it if you wou
design me a dog house, which wou
be easy to build, but would go with
our house. My dog's name i Edward,
we call him Eddie. He is four years
old'or in dog life 88 years. He is a
Labraidor retriever. He is two an
half feet high and three feet long.
reasons I would like this dog hous
is for the winters mainly. My dad
said if you would help me build it, but
will pay you for the plans and mat
out of the money I get from my ro

                    Respectfully yours,
                    Jim Berger

My dad said if you design the dog house he w
help me build it

But if your design the dog house I will
your for the plans and materels

```
Jim Berger
Box 437
San Anselmo
California

Dear Jim:     A house for Eddie is an opportunity.     Someday
I shall design one but just now I am too busy to concentrate
on it.     You write me next November to Phoenix, Arizona and
I may have something then.
```

TALIESIN

```
                         Truly yours,
                         Frank Lloyd Wright
```

June 28th, 1956

親愛的吉姆：

為艾迪造屋是個機會，哪天我有空一定會設計一間給牠，但目前我實在太忙了。你等到十一月再寫信去亞歷桑納州鳳凰城，也許到時我能專心為你設計。

法蘭克・洛伊德・萊特　敬上
一九五六年六月二十八日

親愛的萊特先生

我在一九五六年六月十九日寫信給你，請為我的狗艾迪設計一間狗屋以搭配你為我爸設計的房屋。你叫我十一月再寫信給你，所以我又來問你可不可以為我設計一間狗屋。

吉姆・柏格　敬上

Box 937
San Anselmos Calf
November 1, 1956
Calif

Dear Mr Wright

I wrote you June 19, 1956 about designin
my dog Eddie a dog house. *to go with the house you designed for my dad* You told me
to write you again *in November.* So I ask you again
Kould you design me a dog house.
            Respectfully yours;
            Jim Berger

信之 *090*

羞愧到準備沉入地洞

中國古信範本
西元八五六年

一千多年前的古人和現在差不多，有些人常在晚宴喝得醉醺醺，醜態百出，隔天醒來悔恨不已。在中國某一地區，這種情形似乎是稀鬆平常，該地「敦煌禮儀局」居然擬好這份道歉信，作為範本，供隔天宿醉半醒的地方官抄用，寄給晚宴主人，為昨夜醜態致歉。這版本的年代是西元八五六年。

（譯註：以下照英文直譯為白話文，以映照英文讀者的認知。）

昨天我喝了太多酒，醉茫茫，逾越了所有限制，期間使用的惡言粗語，全非出自本人的意識。翌晨，我聽聞此事，得知事情經過，頓時困惑不解，羞愧到想沉入地洞。酒後失禮是由於酒量甚小的我灌了太多。我謙卑相信，睿智仁慈的您不因我失禮而譴責我。近日我將親自登門道歉，目前僅以書信求您過目。別不多說，謹此。

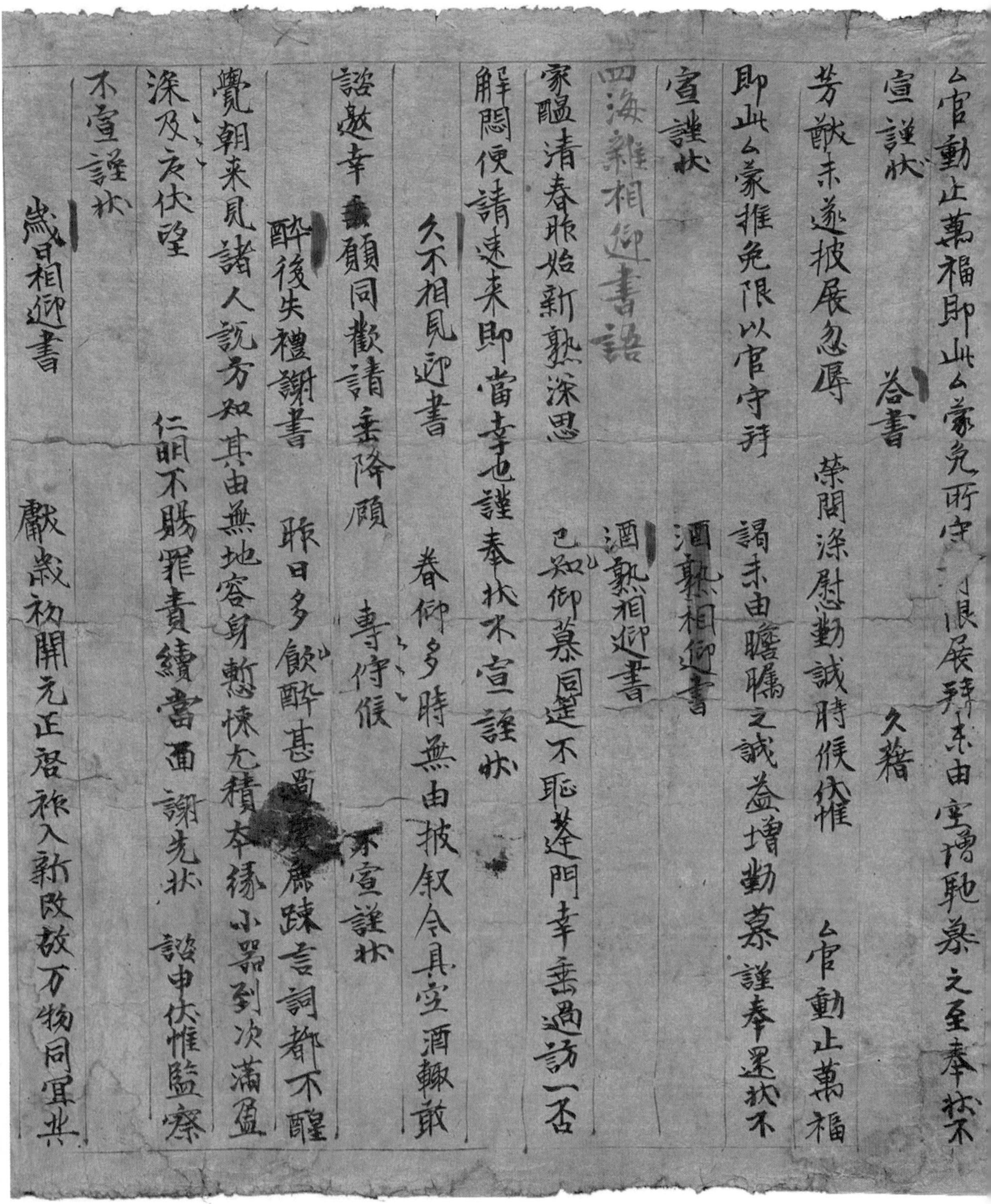

公官動止萬福即此公蒙免所守　恨展拜未由　室憧馳慕　之至奉狀不

宣謹狀　　　答書　　　久藉

芳猷未遂披展忽辱　榮問渌慰勤誠時候惟

即此公蒙推免限以官守拜　謁未由瞻賜之誠益增勤慕　謹奉還狀不

宣謹狀　　　　酒熱相迎書　　官動止萬福

四海雜相迎書語　　酒熱相迎書

解悶便請速來即當幸也謹奉狀不宣謹狀

家隅清春睰始新熟深思　已知御慕同逹不恥逢門幸垂過訪一否

謾邀幸垂顏同歡請垂降顧　春仰多時無由披敘今具空酒輙敢

久不相見迎書

醉後失禮謝書　　聝日多飲醉甚　　廉踈言詞都不醒

覺朝來見諸人說方知其由無地容身慚慄尤積本緣小器到次滿盈

仁明不賜罪責續當面謝先狀　諮申伏惟監察

深及冗伏望　　　　　　　　　寿侍候　　不宣謹狀

不宣謹狀　　　　　　歲旦相迎書

歲旦相迎書　　戱歲初開元正啟祇入新歐故万物同寅共

愁雲過，你我留

亨利・詹姆斯（Henry James）
致葛雷絲・諾頓（Grace Norton）
一八八三年七月二十八日

小說家亨利・詹姆斯在一八八三年接到老友葛雷絲・諾頓來信，字裡行間透露著令人憂心的情緒。葛雷絲是成功的散文作家，親人剛去世，情緒似乎陷入低潮，人生迷惘。詹姆斯本身也嘗過憂鬱症，回信時儘管以「我幾乎不知從何說起」開頭，其實言辭便給，內容溫情滿溢。寫這封信的前幾月，詹姆斯的父母雙亡。

我親愛的葛雷絲，

面對他人的苦難，我總覺得通體乏力。妳來信表白的苦難如此之深，我幾乎不知從何說起。我當然不會以這句話結尾——但我必須以這句話起始。在此種心境，妳並非孤立無援，真的。妳似乎將天下人的悲苦攬在自己身上。我能痛苦意識到，妳奉獻全部卻一無所獲，換言之，妳同情他人卻得不到回報——妳受盡了所有傷痛卻不得善果。然而——我決心僅以高度自制的語氣向妳訴求。

我不懂人**為何**降生在世——生命之禮不知來自何方，目的不明；但我相信，我們能繼續過日子，理由是（當然就某一限度而言）生命是我們所知最寶貴的東西，因此，在生命猶存時放棄生命，毋寧是大錯一樁。換言之，意識是一種無限大的力量，儘管有時意識似乎全被悲慘盤踞，但其實意識是一波接一波來，我們才不至於停止感受。只不過有時我們似乎有感，盡量去感受，祈望能感受，總有某種事物將我們固定住，在宇宙裡形成一立足點，妳我不宜輕言放棄。妳的意識沒錯，我們全是**一模一樣的**回音和震動。當妳對周遭萬物的興趣與憐憫形成一股永續而和諧的力量時，妳的情操才高尚。但我懇求妳，切勿濫施同情與溫情——謹記，每一生命皆有專屬之疑難，是別人的疑難，與妳無關，妳應滿足於自己的代數難題。不要太融入宇宙，應儘可能維持固態、高密度、恆常。世人同居一世上，有愛有知的我們最能不枉今生。我們互相扶持——縱使在不知不覺之間，人人各盡其力，為他人分擔負重，為集體的成就貢獻心血，讓他人有存活的希望。哀傷以巨浪的形式湧現，後浪推前浪——無人比妳更清楚——哀傷能淹沒我們。儘管哀傷或許能掐得我們差點窒息，哀傷走時卻能把我們留在原位，讓我們明白，哀浪強，我們更強，因為哀浪走了，我們猶在。哀傷能侵蝕我們，指使我們，但我們能反過來咬它一口，好好利用它。它是盲目的，我們卻多多少少看得清楚。我親愛的葛雷絲，妳正歷經黑暗期，無知的我雖完全看不見，但妳已被整得身心交瘁。幸好這只是一段黑暗期，不是終

站，更不是落幕。勿胡思亂想，勿鑽牛角尖，勿妄下結論，勿妄自決定——以**等**應萬變。風雨終將過去，終將恢復寧靜，**世人接受的**奧祕與破滅希望仍在，少數好人的溫情也仍在，全新的機會以及豐富的人生仍等著妳。各式各樣的事等著妳去做，而我願意從旁協助。此時此刻的唯一要務是不能**軟化**。我堅持妳有必要自我機械式凝結成型，萬一妳騎的馬脫韁狂奔，等牠停下時，馬鞍上坐著的仍是同一葛雷絲，不同的僅是稍顯狂躁。盡量不要病倒，就如此簡單，因為有健康方有未來。妳註定出人頭地，一定不能失敗。我對妳懷抱最和煦的溫情，也對妳信心十足。

始終不二心的友人
亨利・詹姆斯

一九八一年十月十一日

定能所向披靡

傑夫‧渥克先生
拉多公司
加州 **91522**
柏班克市華納大道四〇〇〇號

《銀翼殺手》原作者致傑夫‧渥克
一九八一年十月十一日

親愛的傑夫：

　　我今晚湊巧看見電視第七頻道播出「好萊塢萬歲」節目，裡面報導了《銀翼殺手》。（好吧，老實說，一點也不湊巧，其實有人通知我，今晚節目會報導《銀翼殺手》的消息，叫我不能錯過。）傑夫，看完後，尤其是聽完哈里遜‧福特討論劇情後，我的結論是，這部電影的確不是科幻片，也不是奇幻電影，而是哈里遜所說的：未來片。《銀》片上映後絕對會轟動，能衝擊到社會大眾，能打動創意人，此外，我相信，更能影響科幻小說整個領域。由於我寫、賣科幻小說已長達三十年，此事對我意義重大。我不諱言，近幾年來，科幻小說界一年不如一年，作品無論個人或整體而言，均無法與《銀翼殺手》匹配。本片主題並非逃避現實，而是超寫實主義，露骨、詳盡、道地，而且逼真得要命，結果我看完報導後，居然覺得日常「現實」生活相形失色。我想說的是，你們全體開創出的作品可能是獨特而嶄新的體裁，在繪圖和藝術表達方面均展現前所未有的突破。我認為，《銀翼殺手》必將革新大家對科幻小說的觀念，更能讓大家認識科幻的潛能。

一九六八年，作家菲利普‧狄克（Philip K. Dick）發表科幻小說《生化人是否夢見電動羊？》，背景是世界末日之後的地球，主角是瑞克‧戴卡德（Rick Deckard），以獵捕為非作歹的生化人領賞為業，美其言是逼生化人「退休」。書一推出，立刻引起電影公司競逐。最初商量過幾次，腳本初稿也送到狄克眼前，狄克都看不上眼。後來在一九八一年，雷利‧史考特（Ridley Scott）坐上導演椅，劇本由大衛‧皮柏斯（David Peoples）改寫，狄克見到即將上映的電影片段，看法徹底改觀，同一晚提筆寫信給製片公司，分享心得與興奮感。寄信五個月後，狄克過世，無緣見到電影《銀翼殺手》的成品。該片被許多人推崇為最佳科幻電影之一。

　　我可以這樣總結：科幻小說已無可避免地緩緩踏上單調的死路，變成近親繁殖、交互仿傚、陳舊腐朽的沃土。未料，中途殺出你們這群電影人，具備當今少有人能及的才華，為科幻小說界注入新生命，讓科幻重新起步。至於我個人在《銀》片的角色，我只能說，我的拙作或淺見竟能被提升至如此高超驚人的境界，這是我始料未及的結果。我的人生和創意工作因《銀翼殺手》而圓滿，我心堪慰。感謝你……《銀》片上映後票房一定長紅。《銀翼殺手》定能所向披靡。

菲利普‧K‧狄克　敬上

October 11, 1981

Mr. Jeff Walker,
The Ladd Company,
4000 Warner Boulevard,
Burbank,
Calif. 91522.

Dear Jeff:

    I happened to see the Channel 7 TV program "Hooray For
Hollywood" tonight with the segment on BLADE RUNNER. (Well, to
be honest, I didn't happen to see it; someone tipped me off that
BLADE RUNNER was going to be a part of the show, and to be sure
to watch.) Jeff, after looking --and especially after listening
to Harrison Ford discuss the film-- I came to the conclusion that
this indeed is not science fiction; it is not fantasy; it is
exactly what Harrison said: futurism. The impact of BLADE
RUNNER is simply going to be overwhelming, both on the public
and on creative people -- and, I believe, on science fiction
as a field. Since I have been writing and selling science fiction
works for thirty years, this is a matter of some importance to me.
In all candor I must say that our field has gradually and steadily
been deteriorating for the last few years. Nothing that we have
done, individually or collectively, matches BLADE RUNNER. This
is not escapism; it is super realism, so gritty and detailed and
authentic and goddam convincing that, well, after the segment I
found my normal present-day "reality" pallid by comparison. What
I am saying is that all of you collectively may have created a
unique new form of graphic, artistic expression, never before
seen. And, I think, BLADE RUNNER is going to revolutionize our
conceptions of what science fiction is and, more, can be.

    Let me sum it up this way. Science fiction has slowly
and ineluctably settled into a monotonous death: it has become
inbred, derivative, stale. Suddenly you people have come in,
some of the greatest talents currently in existence, and now we
have a new life, a new start. As for my own role in the BLADE
RUNNER project, I can only say that I did not know that a work
of mine or a set of ideas of mine could be escalated into such
stunning dimensions. My life and creative work are justified
and completed by BLADE RUNNER. Thank you...and it is going to
be one hell of a commercial success. It will prove invincible.

Cordially,

Philip K. Dick

信之 *093*

七三年二月二十四日

感激你，鮑伯

戰俘致勞軍巨星
一九七三年二月二十四日

美國藝人鮑伯・霍普（Bob Hope）
長年熱心勞軍，為軍人爭權益，國
會因此在一九九七年簽署一項法
案，頒發榮譽頭銜給霍普：全球
首位美軍榮譽退伍軍人，僅此一
位」。霍普行善的效果可由此信為
例證。這封信的作者是美國飛官費
德瑞克・弗羅姆（Frederic Flom），
在一九七三年的當時，在越南戰俘
營蹲了六年半的他即將獲釋。他從
另一位飛官戰俘那裡得知霍普常為
戰俘打氣，感動之餘寫這封信向紅
星致謝。

親愛的霍普先生，

　　這不過是一封影迷信，來自不同的地址。我是 F-105 飛行
員，一九六六年八月八日在北越上空被擊落，被俘虜至今，幸好
三天後即將重獲自由。在戰俘營裡，我們和外界幾乎完全隔絕，
但根據七二年被擊落的戰俘所言，美國部分民眾很支持戰俘，尤
其是你更鼎力為我們加油，所以我才提筆寫這封信。

　　我想謝謝你為我們盡過的所有心力。你是真正的戰俘之友，
我們每人寄一封信感謝你也不夠聊表心意。在無盡的寂寞暗夜
裡，我們幾度覺得被世人遺忘了。如今得知美國民眾仍未忘記我
們，而且還有像你這樣的明星以行動表達關懷，我們不禁身心振
奮，驕傲光榮。我在此向你以及全美國致上肺腑謝意，所有戰俘
想必與我有同感。

　　我們的國家和人民有一種說不出來的好。名人如果站出來，
可大幅影響國民的思想和態度。這份影響可以是正面或負面，可
以是好或是壞。謝謝你，鮑伯，感激你為美國和美好的美國生活
奉獻這麼大的心力。

敬祝你萬事如意，
費德・弗羅姆

24 Feb,'73

Dear Mr. Hope,

    Just another fan letter from a different address. I am an F-105 pilot, shot down over North Viet Nam on 8 August, 1966. I have been held captive since that time, but will finally be released in three days. We have almost no contact with the outside world in here, however, some word has gotten in, via POWs shot down in '72, concerning some of the activities of the American people, & you in particular, on behalf of the POWs. That is what prompted this note.

    I want to thank you for all you have done or attempted to do on our behalf. You are truly a POW's friend, & are deserving of more than just a letter from each of us. There have been many a dark & lonesome night when we have felt all but forgotten. It thrills our hearts & makes us glow with pride to learn that the American people have not forgotten us, & that a celebrity such as yourself has active concern. I extend to you & all of America my deep appreciation & I know I speak for all of us.

    There is something great about our nation & its people. A celebrity can have a large effect in influencing its thinking & attitude. This effect can be positive or negative, good or bad. Thank you Bob, for being such a large part of America & our wonderful way of life.

Best of luck to you,

Fred Flom

新的狗屁臺詞

亞歷・堅尼斯（Alec Guinness）
致安・考夫曼（Anne Kaufman）
一九七六年四月十九日

亞歷・堅尼斯在一九七六年寫這封
信時，正積極和導演亞倫・史卓
善（Alan Strachan）合寫新的舞臺
劇《犽猢》（Yahoo），堅尼斯本人
即將飾演男主角綏夫特（Jonathan
Swift）。當時他較知名的角色出現
在大衛・林恩（David Lean）執導
的幾部電影裡，包括經典片《阿拉
伯勞倫斯》，以及為他贏得奧斯卡
獎的《桂河大橋》。在這封信裡，
他以好氣又好笑的語氣，簡短提到
即將扮演的一角，而這角色不久將
把他的名氣推向更高峰。安・考夫
曼是他的摯友，兩人通信頻繁。
（信裡提及安的「小媽」是她的繼
母——英國演員兼劇作家盧茵・
麥葛拉斯［Leueen MacGrath］。
繼母和英國作家蓋文・陽［Gavin
Young］是長年至交。）信裡提到的
角色是《星際大戰》裡的歐比王・
肯諾比（Obi-Wan Kenobi），日後
不僅為他的影迷群注入新血，也讓
入帳豐碩。

我親愛的安，

　　艷陽普照復活節，意味著戶外活動繁忙；蜜蜂在櫻花叢中嗡
嗡響；沃特護衛著在樹叢裡玩鬧的鳥兒；黃水仙凋零；美洲楊樹
香味隨風送；螞蟻寶寶行軍殺進髒亂的廚房；好酒等著被喝，萬
象詩情畫意，只可惜媳婦在家。她愛吵架、煩人、情緒不穩，幾
個小孩吵個不停。嚴格說來，小孩是還好啦，討厭的是他們不懂
規矩，腔調帶中下階級的鼻音。接下來十天，美魯拉會照顧他
們。我敢說，一旦他們的父母去（各別）渡假，小孩會乖得像天
使。以前常出現這種情況。我今晚已回倫敦拍片，這整個禮拜將
待在片廠。我喜歡這部片子嗎？我倒不覺得，——一捆又一捆的
粉紅紙上寫著新的狗屁臺詞，扔給我，沒有一句能明確界定我的
角色，甚至也沒辦法把我的角色搞得順眼一點。幸好麵包很可
口，就算《犽猢》上檔一禮拜就垮臺，也能幫我撐到四月。

　　謝謝妳寄的卡片。史卓善導演和我想研究劇本裡「慧點」的
地方？——我認定，若不是英語和美語對這單字的定義不同，不
然就是妳（可原諒）誤解其中一部分的語調——有點咄咄逼人、
嚴厲，一點也不含蓄。我真的認為，前半部分有點涼，而我不確
定該怎麼補救，只知道大概可以加幾句粗俗的話，再強調一下反
諷的東西。——總之，妳讀過就好，妳能認真看待它，證明妳有
善意。——我們決定採用一個有點年輕的設計師，名叫伯納・庫
蕭——我只見過他設計的一個景，差不多是六年前了，不過我認
為他的風格和理解無誤。艾琳・埃肯斯曾對它表達興趣，承諾飾
演凡妮莎（等等），前提是如果她爭取演出的一齣電影破局。過
兩個禮拜才知道。如果她進來，我會比較有自信，因為替代她的
人在電視上小有成就，不過在劇場是未知數。我朋友馬克・金斯
頓將飾演另一個男人。我們仍想不出適合扮演史黛拉的人選——
不過凡妮莎的角色非先搞定不可。

　　一個禮拜前，我和妳的小媽一起吃飯，她的氣色和精神比這
幾年任何一段時間都來得好。爽朗但不脆弱，而且好像生活順心

如意。蓋文也在（腳丫骨折），另外有個信伊斯蘭教的法國長舌婦。波斯之屎的朋友。

艾倫普萊斯的《綏夫特傳》一二集安然抵達，我正在看，相當枯燥，學術味太重，不過充滿實用的知識。妳對第三集怎麼說來著？我記不清楚了，一時也翻不出妳那封信。沒出版？絕版了？根本連寫都沒寫？話說回來，老子又欠妳什麼呢？拜託！──我在洛杉磯有不少美金正慢慢消失中──歡迎妳去用一些。誰曉得我下次會用來幹什麼呢？八成當衛生紙吧。

<u>週二</u>

一大早又晴空萬里。南喜·葛林來信了。──我邀請（名字不詳）（姻親）害我整晚惡夢做不完。討厭的想法很難甩掉，說來可悲，不是嗎？我被迫半夜兩點坐起來，閱讀半小時，才剷除腦子裡的妖魔。──賈森·坎寧吵著要我接《毛姆先生》（*Mr. Maugham*），幸好有《犴獝》當擋箭牌，就算演不出氣候，至少也有這點用處。

我該出門了，去片廠跟一個侏儒合作（人滿親切的，──而且上廁所必用坐浴盆）。和我合作的人還有妳的同胞馬克·哈密爾和丁尼生·福特（名字被我<u>搞錯</u>了吧？）或者是艾利森（？錯！*）──算了，總之是個手長腳長的懶散年輕人，大概學識豐富又風趣。可是啊，唉，天啊，天啊，他們讓我覺得我<u>九十</u>歲了──把我當成一百〇六歲看待。

愛妳的，

亞歷

*原信註：哈里遜·福特──聽過嗎？

18/9

Easter Monday '76

My dear Anne

The sun has shone all over Easter and that has meant out-of-door life; bees humming in the cherry blossom; Walter on guard against birds having it off in hedges; daffodils wilting; balsam poplars scenting the air; baby ants on the march into the grubby kitchen; good wine to drink, and all fairly idyllic except for the presence of my provoking, irritating and unbalanced daughter-in-law. And her squabbling children. The children are more or less alright, I suppose, except for their foul manners and nasal cockney accents. Merula has now got them for the next ten days and I bet that once their parents have gone on their (separate) holidays the children will prove angelic. That has been the pattern before. I have returned to London this evening for my stint at the studio for the rest of the week. Can't say I'm enjoying the film, — new rubbishy dialogue reaches me every other day ~~in~~ on wodges of pink paper — and <u>none</u> of it makes my character clear or even bearable. I just think, thankfully, of the lovely bread, which will help me ^{keep} going until next April even if 'Yahoo' collapses in a week.

Thank you for your card about that. Strachan and I have tried to prove where it is 'arch' — and I have decided either that Queen's English and U.S. usage of the word are at variance, or that you (forgivably) misread the tone of some of it — which is somewhat belligerent and harsh and far from coy. I <u>do</u> think the first half is a bit <u>cool</u>, and I'm not sure how to remedy that, except by possibly throwing in some coarse stuff and hotting up the ironies. — Anyway, it was nice of you to read it, and good of you to take it seriously. — We have settled on a youngish designer called Bernard Culshaw — I've only seen one set of his, and that about six years ago, but think he's got the right style and understanding. Eileen Atkins has expressed <u>enthusiasm</u> for it and promises to play Vanessa (et al) if a possible film she's keen on doesn't materialise. We shall know in two weeks. If she does it I'll feel more confident than with the alternative, who is good on T.V. but something of an unknown quantity in the theatre.

3

ALEC GUINNESS

My chum Mark Kingston will play the other man. Stella is still a blank in our minds — but the casting of Vanessa must be done first.

Dined a week ago with your little mum, who was looking better and in better spirits than I've known her in years. Bright but not brittle, and in full command — so it seemed — of her life. Gavin was present (with broken foot) and a garrulous French woman with Islamic leanings. A friend of the Shit of Persia.

The Ehrenpreis Swift volumes (1 & 2) arrived safely and I'm in to them. Rather dry and too academic but full of useful information. I can't remember what you said about Vol 3, and can't put my hand on your letter. It doesn't exist? Its out of print? It was never written? But what the Hell do I owe you anyway? Please! — I have a lot of dollars dwindling slowly in L.A. — you are welcome to some of them. And who knows what my next demand may be! Probably toilet paper.

<u>Tuesday</u>   4

Another bright day has dawned. A letter for
Harry Green in the post. — A nightmarish night
going round and round in my head my
irritation with Andrée (d — in — law). Isn't
it wretched how difficult unpleasant thoughts
are to shake off. I had to sit up and
read for ½ hour at 2. a.m. to exorcise
myself. — Garson Kanin plagues me about
'Mr. Maughams' but 'Yahoo', if it does
nothing else, has enabled me to side-step
that one.

    I went off to studio and work
with a dwarf (very sweet, — and he
has to wash in a bidet) and your
fellow countrymen Mark Hamill and
Tennyson (that can't be right) Ford —
Ellison (? — No!*) — well, a rangey,
languid young man who is probably
intelligent and amusing. But
Oh, God, God, they make me feel
<u>rusty</u> — and treat me as if I was
106.
        Love,
          Alec

* <u>Harrison</u> Ford — ever heard of him?

休想以詭計剝奪我臨終的大戲

麗蓓嘉・維斯特（Rebecca West）
致 H・G・威爾斯（H.G. Wells）
一九一三年三月

麗蓓嘉・維斯特是新聞工作者兼作者，在一九一二年狠批大作家 H・G・威爾斯的最新小說《婚姻》（*Marriage*），罵他是「小說界的老處女」。作家的反應是請她共進晚餐，她答應了，結果兩人墜入愛河，開始一段狂風暴雨不斷的婚外情，延續數月。在一九一三年三月，已婚而且比她大二十六歲的威爾斯和她分手。她傷心欲絕，以措辭激烈的這封信回應。但她並未落實她的威脅，兩人不久後不但復合了，還在一九一四年生了一個兒子，名叫安德魯。九年後，兩人才真正分手。

親愛的 H.G.，

接下來幾天，我不是一槍轟穿我的頭，就是對我自己做出比死更慘烈舉動。無論走上哪條路，我都將變成一個大不相同的人。我拒絕被人以詭計剝奪我臨終的大戲。

我不明白你為何三個月前追求我，現在卻不想要我。但願我知道原因就好了。我就是看不透這原因，痛恨這原因。最受不了的是，如果我痛恨你，我火冒三丈是因為你攔著不讓我心平氣和。當然，你相當有道理。我能給你的東西一項也沒有。你僅有追求刺激和慰藉的熱忱。刺激，你不再想要了，而我無法給人慰藉。唯有在人病重時，我才照顧他們。我把這一點發揮到破錶。自我反省時，我能想像，母親覺得和我住一起時，我的最大用處是在房子失火時救她逃生。

我一直知道，你總有一天會傷害我致死，但我希望時間地點由我自選。你總在不知不覺中兌我，而我也盡量斬我對你的情絲以寬容你，斬到僅剩你最想要的小東西。被人兌時，我總茫然無措，因為我能愛，簡直除了愛之外一無是處。我不是你願將就的那種人。你要的世界裡有一大堆像小狗狗的人，互相愛得死心塌地。你要的是能跟你吵架玩要的人，能發怒、能心痛的人，而非自焚的人。有人愛到觸礁受辱，自慚到兩度尋短，你猜不透這種人，覺得這種行為愚昧。有人喜歡到處點燃營火，卻又反過來培養對火的反感，我猜不透這種人，覺得這種行為愚昧。

你簡直是毀了我。我已經被燒到剩下地基了。我有可能自我再造，也可能不會。你說，迷戀是有藥可醫的。確實有。但像我這樣的人，拉著摯愛的事物當藤蔓，從一個摯愛盪向另一個，一閃神沒抓住，立刻墜落到一個毫無摯愛的地方，只見光禿禿的木板和鋸木屑。你徹底摧毀了我。你有自知之明。所以你才試著勸你自己相信，我是個未開化的匍匐無骨生物，因此無所謂了。當你說，「你在講未經大腦思考的話，麗蓓嘉，」講得多爽朗：你

自以為一句話講透我了。我不認為被你講對了。但我知道，你把我視為一個情緒不穩的年輕女子，莫名其妙心臟發作，在你大客廳裡東倒西歪，你從這種想法裡得到極大滿足。

這話隱然抬舉了你。但是，有些事我做得誠心誠意，做得乾淨俐落，卻被你奚落，令我恨你。有一次，你寫信給我，暗指我「自我感覺比實質價值更寶貴幾倍」，言下之意是我妄想陪名記者霍瑞修‧博頓利去布萊頓大都會飯店共度週末，而我在前一封信裡才說我愛你。星期五，你又再犯，說我追求的是正當的樂趣，說我的思想雖不算墮落，卻一聽到別人惡言提及真正美的事物就感到興奮。講這種話太惡毒了。曾經，你覺得我願意愛你是一件勇敢的美事。我仍如此認為。你的老處女觀念讓你覺得，無可救藥愛上一個男人的女人是不雅的畫面，是違反自然定律的現象。但你太文明了，不會有那種感覺。

若能換回你的懷抱，我犧牲性命在所不惜。

我但願你愛過我。我但願你喜歡我。

麗蓓嘉　敬上

P.S.不要拋下我讓我孤零零。如果我活下來了，偶爾寫信給我。你還算喜歡我，寫信總可以吧。至少我如此自欺。

信之 *096*

猥索而褻瀆聖明

電影公司董事長致主管
一九七八年二月二十日

在一九七八年二月,《萬世魔星》
(*Monty Python's Life of Brain*)即將
開拍前的幾星期,EMI電影公司董
事長伯納德・戴爾方特(Bernard
Delfont)爵士首度瀏覽腳本,見
到「猥索而褻瀆聖明」的字眼,因
此下令撤銷對該片的投資,令眾人
措手不及。驚惶的董事長寫這封信
給EMI主管麥克・狄立(Michael
Deeley)和貝瑞・史派金斯(Barry
Spikings),恐慌之情流露。幸虧
電影團隊找到新金主──披頭四
樂團吉他手喬治・哈里遜(George
Harrison)甚至抵押自己的房子下
注,事後證明是眼光獨具的投資。
董事長臨陣撤資的舉動被納入電影
裡,劇終前的最後一段臺詞如下:

「不然你以為,拍這爛片的錢是誰
出的?錢砸下去,休想回收了;你
知道嗎,我告訴他們,我對他們
說,伯納德,他們永遠休想撈回那
筆錢了。」

一九七八年二月二十日
致:麥克・狄立和貝瑞・史派金斯
EMI電影股份有限公司
加州比佛利山莊 **696231**

快速瀏覽一下蒙提・派森系列新片的腳本,我赫見這電影有違他
平常的電影風格,不是胡鬧片,內容竟然猥索而褻瀆聖明,EMI
投資這種電影絕對自毀形象。

每隔幾個字就出現刺耳髒話,也與蒙提・派森的形象背道而馳。

此事非常嚴重,我至感痛心,在查明白究竟之前,我無法批准此
片開拍。

我知道鮑伯・韋伯斯特和吉米・卡列拉斯絕對支持我意見,約
翰・瑞德的感想如何,我連想也不願想。

願聞高見的

伯納德・戴爾方特

倫敦時間十六時三十七分

EMI電影

28213 EMICIN G

20TH FEB 1978

ATTENTION MICHAEL DEELEY AND BARRY SPIKINGS
EMI FILMS INC
BEVERLY HILLS. CALIF.
696231

HAVE LOOKED RATHER QUICKLY THROUGH THE SCRIPT OF
THE NEW MONTY PYTHON FILM AND AM AMAZED TO FIND THAT
IT IS NOT THE ZANY COMEDY USUALLY ASSOCIATED WITH HIS
FILMS. BUT IS OBSCENE AND SACRILEGIOUS, AND WOULD
CERTAINLY NOT BE IN THE INTEREST OF EMI'S IMAGE TO MAKE
THIS SORT OF FILM.

EVERY FEW WORDS THERE ARE OUTRAGEOUS SWEAR WORDS
WHICH IS NOT IN KEEPING WITH MONTY PYTHON'S IMAGE.

THIS IS VERY DISTRESSING TO ME AND IS A VERY SERIOUS
SITUATION AND I CANNOT, UNTIL WE KNOW EXACTLY WHAT WE
ARE DOING, ALLOW THIS FILM TO BE MADE.

I UNDERSTAND THIS VIEW IS ABSOLUTELY SUPPORTED BY BOB WEBSTER
AND JIMMY CARRERAS AND I HATE TO THINK WHAT JOHN READ'S VIEW
WOULD BE.

PLEASE ADVISE

BERNARD DELFONT

TIMED IN LONDON AT   16.37.

+

EMI FILMS BVHL

28213 EMICIN G''

悲哀的女人！

重獲自由的黑奴致奴主
一八六〇年三月二十八日

在一八三四年，二十一歲黑奴賈姆·洛格（Jarm Logue）騎走主人的馬，逃至加拿大，獲得自由。他和弟妹出生就是奴隸，母親和弟妹仍在田納西州大衛森（Davidson）郡，遺憾未能逃脫。二十六年後，他在紐約州成家立業，姓名改成傑緬·洛根（Jermain Loguen），為黑人小孩創辦幾所學校，成為牧師，是知名的推動廢奴人士，發表過一本自傳，不料竟收到老奴主之妻寄來的一封恬不知恥的信，信中要求他為他騎走的馬賠償一千美元。洛根按捺怒火，以動人心弦的文字回信，蔚為傳世傑作。

田納西州莫瑞郡
一八六〇年二月二十日

致賈姆：——我現在提筆寫給你幾句，讓你知道我們所有人日子過得多好。我成了瘸子，但我仍能走動。其他家人一切安好。茹莉安好如常人。我寫信是想讓你知道我們的處境——原因之一是你騎走我家上等母馬「老岩」。母馬後來雖然回家了，身體卻大不如前。由於我目前手頭甚緊，因此決定賣掉你。已有人出價買你，但我認為不宜答應。如果你願寄給我一千美元，為老母馬賠償，我願放棄我對你的所有主權。你接到信之後儘快回信，讓我知道你是否接受我的提議。由於你逃走，我們被迫賣掉艾柏和安和十二畝地，所以我要求你寄錢回來，好讓我能贖回因你而賣的那塊地。我一收到上述款項，將寄收據給你。如果你不肯順從我的請求，我將把你賣給別人，保證你的日子不久後改觀。你一接到此信，儘快回覆。信寄到田納西州莫瑞郡畢格比村。你最好順從我的請求。

據我瞭解，你現在是牧師。南方人很惡劣，你最好回來對你的老朋友宣教。我想知道，你讀不讀《聖經》呢？如果讀，你告訴我，竊賊若不悔改、盲人引導盲人，後果會怎樣呢？我認為此時多言無益，明智言語點到為止。騙徒有何下場，你是知道的。你應曉得，我們把你當親骨肉拉拔長大，從不虐待你，何況在你逃走前不久，你主人問你願不願被賣，你還說你不願棄主跟別人走。

莎拉·洛格

一八六〇年三月二十八日
紐約州雪城

莎拉‧洛格夫人：——二月二十日的信收到了，感謝妳來信。許久未聞可憐老母的消息了，我很高興得知她仍健在，而且如妳所言「安好如常人」。我不清楚此言何意。只盼妳能細說她的近況。

　　妳是婦人，但侮辱人至此，妳的女人心何在？妳怎能狠心告訴我，妳賣掉我僅存的一弟一妹，只因我逃脫妳掌握、讓妳無法變賣我換取金錢。

　　妳賣掉我弟艾柏和我妹安，賣掉十二畝地，妳說是因為我逃走。如今妳竟以小至難以言喻的小心眼要求我回去，繼續當妳卑賤的動產，否則寄一千美元讓妳能贖回**土地**，卻不贖回我弟妹！假若我寄錢給妳，錢是用來贖回我弟妹，而非讓妳贖地。妳說妳是**瘸子**，居心無疑是想誘我憐憫，因為妳知道我素有同情心。我確實是打從心底可憐妳。儘管如此，我氣憤到言語難以表達的是，妳淪喪至此，殘酷至此，竟將我至親的心剁成千萬塊，竟不惜刺穿我們、押我們上十字架，以換取我們對妳的爛**腳**同情。悲哀的女人啊！在此鄭重告訴妳，我珍視自由，珍視我老母與所有手足，遠勝過妳的全身，絕對也勝過我個人生命，勝過天下奴主和暴君加起來的所有生命。

　　妳說有人出價買我，妳說如果我不寄一千美元回去，妳將賣掉我。幾乎就在同一句裡，妳不必換氣就說，「你知道我們把你當成親骨肉拉拔長大」。女人啊，妳會撫養親骨肉去市場賣嗎？妳拉拔他們長大，會把他們綁在木樁上毒打嗎？妳會拿鏈子把親骨肉綁成一串鞭策嗎？我流血流汗的手足們哪裡去了，妳能告訴我嗎？是誰逼他們下田種甘蔗和棉花，踹他們，銬住他們，鞭打他們，讓他們哀嚎至死，無親人聽得見他們慘叫，垂死時床邊無親人照料同情，下葬時無親人送行？悲哀的女人啊！妳會推說，做那些事的人不是我。那我如此回應，是妳丈夫沒錯，而妳在一旁默許惡行——從妳的來信可知，**妳**在心中默許一切。妳太可恥了。

　　咦，妳丈夫哪裡去了？妳信中未提，想必是死了，頂著殘害我家人的所有罪孽，去接受蒼天審判了。可憐的男人！我在陰間有一群被謀害的同胞，怒火滿腔，正等著見他呢。在那裡，自由和公理才是**主人**。

　　妳說我是竊賊，因為我騎走了老母馬。難道妳仍未體認到，我對老母馬的主權，凌駕**曼納西斯‧洛格**對我的主權？我偷走他的馬，他從我母親的搖籃偷走我，兩罪何者孰輕孰重？如果妳和他的推論是，我對妳

放棄所有權利，難道我不能依同理推論說，妳對我放棄所有權利？妳難道沒有學到，人權是相互的，互惠的，如果妳奪走我的自由和生命，妳也放棄自己的自由和生命？在上帝面前，在天堂之下，難道有哪條天法只針對一人而不適用於普世？

如果妳或他人覬覦我的人身權利，想知道我如何看待自己的權利，你們只需前來，動手奴役我。我不願寄錢，不願屈從于奴役，另一條路是什麼，妳認為我怕走嗎？且讓我告訴妳，妳儘管放話，我以無可言喻的鄙視與輕蔑面對。妳的脅迫不僅損人，也令人震怒。我將絲毫不為所動。縱使眨眼能免除我受妳迫害，我也不眨一眼。我與自由人種同在，感謝上帝他們同情我的權利，認同人類的權利。如果妳的特使和販夫敢來這裡二度奴役我，若妳有幸閃躲過我肆無忌憚的右臂，我相信我在本州本市之勇士力士朋友將群起營救我，為我復仇。

特此
J・W・洛根

信之 098

這不是演習

太平洋總司令致全軍艦艇
一九四一年十二月七日

一九四一年十二月七日上午七時五十八分在福特島，海軍少校羅根·C·拉姆希（Logan C. Ramsey）衝進海軍航空站（Air Station）指揮中心無線電室，下令儘速發佈這份公報給夏威夷區的所有艦艇，原因是他和一名同僚剛發現一架敵機從島上空俯衝而來，隨後是戰機俯衝前投彈傳來的爆炸聲——這是日軍集體突襲美國珍珠港的先發點。根據美國國家公園處，接下來兩小時，多達三百二十三架美國戰機以及二十一艘艦艇全毀或半毀，死亡人數共兩千三百八十八人，另有一千一百七十八人受傷。隔天，美國對日本宣戰，加入第二次世界大戰。

發自：太平洋總司令
致：夏威夷區目前全體艦艇
訊息：緊急

珍珠港發生空襲。這不是演習。

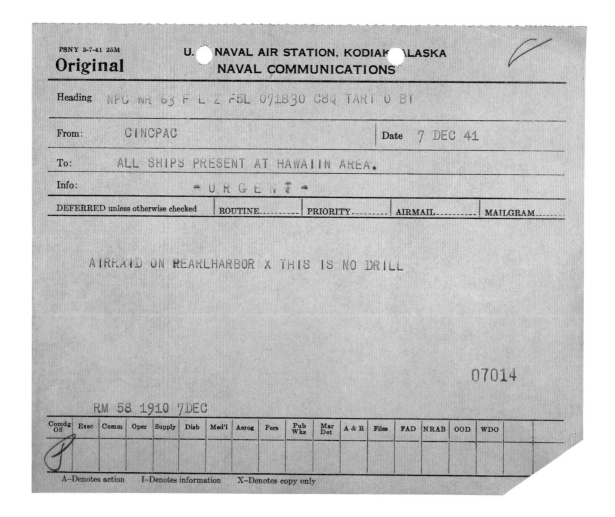

信之 *099*

親愛的八歲粉絲

**威爾 · 惠頓（Wil Wheaton）致
女影迷**
二〇〇九年

在一九八八年，十五歲的威爾
惠頓因參與《站在我這邊》（*Stand
By Me*）的演出，也在《星際爭霸
戰：銀河飛龍》裡有重複露臉的機
會，才八歲大的泰瑞莎 · 賈辛諾
（Teresa Jusino）就已經對他崇拜不
已，因此省下十二美元，申請加入
名為「意志威力」（WilPower）的
官方影迷社，等著會員獨享包寄
來，卻苦等不到，久而久之就忘了
這件失望的事。

到了二〇〇九年，泰瑞莎二十九歲
了，以寫作為業，有天竟然收到包
裹，裡面是她耐心等待了二十一年
的東西，附帶一封道歉函，信上歡
迎她加入如今已解散的粉絲社，執
筆人正是得知她遭遇的惠頓。

接到信後不久，泰瑞莎說，「二十
九歲的我對他獻上莫大的謝意。別
誤解喔，八歲的我還是非常非常高
興，不過二十九歲的我更能體會善
意的舉動，也希望感激之情的斤兩
比言語更重。」

親愛的八歲泰瑞莎，

讓妳等這麼久才收到意志威力影迷社的會員獨享包，本人在此向
妳致歉。是這樣的，十五歲的我在工作和課業之間忙得不可開
交，而負責寄獨享包給妳的人一定寄錯了，所以妳才沒收到。

影迷社已經好久沒辦活動了，但我還是附上一張會員卡給妳，加
上一張適合放進皮夾的小相片，再加上一張相片以顯示我有多麼
喜歡蝙蝠俠（暗示：超喜歡。）

影迷社運作期間，會員每年收到幾次關於我和我的工作的最新消
息，可惜好久以前就停止了。不過，我的最新消息是：我結婚
了，而且有兩個兒子——我愛他們勝過全世界任何東西。而且我
現在也以寫作為業了，和妳一樣！

在我收筆之前，八歲的泰瑞莎，我想告訴妳一件非常重要的事，
妳要仔細聽喔：等妳長大以後，妳會成為優秀的作家。我怎能預
知未來呢？不告訴妳。但我希望妳相信我；我是真的知道。所
以，要乖乖上學，凡事盡力而為，以妳希望別人對待妳的態度去
對待別人。

謝謝妳加入我的影迷社，

（簽名）

威爾 · 惠頓

信之 *100*

你生產的車子帶勁

末路狂徒致福特汽車創辦人

一九三四年四月十日

從一九三二年起，到一九三四年五月的浴血槍戰之間，駕鴛狂徒邦妮・帕克（Bonnie Parker）和科萊德・巴洛（Clyde Barrow）在美國中部一路殺人不眨眼，共犯一個換一個，令人聞風色變。這一組犯罪集團的知名度高，靠著馬力十足的交通工具躲避警網。從巴洛歷年來盜用的車子看來，他特別偏愛具備 V8 動力的福特 B 型車。在一九三四年，這對駕鴛檔逃不出警力包圍，被子彈打成蜂窩，一同葬身在愛車上，車子正是福特車。在駕鴛檔死前一個月，福特汽車創辦人收到一封車迷信，據說來自巴洛本人。這封信目前列入福特博物館的館藏，但是否為真跡，多年來仍無定論。

奧克拉荷馬州塔爾薩
四月十日
亨利・福特先生
密西根州底特律

親愛的福特先生：——

　　趁我仍能以肺呼吸的這時候，我想對你說，你生產的車子有多麼帶勁。我弄得到車子的時候，只開福特車，別的不屑一顧。福特車的速度穩定，從不故障，別家的車子全部沒的比。即使我做的事業不盡然合法，我不防告訴你，你的 V8 車棒的沒話說──

　　　　科萊德・強畢翁・巴洛　敬上

Tulsa Okla
10th April

Mr. Henry Ford
Detroit Mich.

Dear Sir:—
    While I still have got
breath in my lungs I
will tell you what a dandy
car you make. I have drove
Fords exclusivly when I could
get away with one. For sustained
speed and freedom from
trouble the Ford has got every
other car skinned, and even if
my business hasent been
strickly legal it don't hurt eny
thing to tell you what a fine
car you got in the V8—
        Yours truly
        Clyde Champion Barrow

Henry Ford
RECEIVED
APR 13 1934
Secretary's Office

愛你的老爸

雷根致兒子
一九七一年六月

在一九七一年六月，二十六歲的麥可‧雷根（Michael Reagan）在夏威夷迎娶十八歲女友，儀式莊重美麗。他的父親是未來的美國總統隆諾德‧雷根（Ronald Reagan），無法出席，但在典禮前幾天，麥可收到雷根的一封信，令他珍藏數年不忘。父親的信以愛與婚姻為題，充滿父愛與賢明的建議。

「這封信是老爸的肺腑之言，」麥可在二〇〇四年的回憶錄《演繹雷根》（*In the Words of Ronald Reagan*）裡寫道。「誠懇、念舊、充滿智慧。我第一次閱信時哭了。後來幾年，我重複讀了好多次。」

親愛的麥可：

我在信裡附上我提過的東西（一張撕毀的借據）。我可以就此停筆但我不想。

世上有許多「婚姻不幸福」的人，有許多喜歡諷刺婚姻的人，他們對婚姻的揶揄譏諷，你應該聽過不少。假如沒有人向你呈現過另一種觀點，我不妨向你提一提。人間意義最重大的關係莫過於婚姻，你已走進去了，而這段婚姻的好壞端賴你的決定。

有些男人認為，能證明男子漢氣概的方式只有一個，就是把更衣室裡講的所有笑話付諸實行，還自信滿滿以為老婆不知道就沒事。事實是，儘管老婆沒逮到衣領上的口紅印，沒戳破丈夫凌晨三點才回家的薄弱託詞，老婆確實心裡有數。在這種情況下，這段情的妙蘊失散了一部分。自毀婚姻而愛拿婚姻發牢騷的男人比較多，錯在妻子身上的例子太少了。物理學一條古老的定律是，獲得只能和付出相等，不會比付出多得到什麼。只肯為婚姻付出半份心力的男人只能獲得半套幸福。當然，將來你會有機會見到別人，遙想當年自由身，不禁想自我挑戰，看看現在的自己能否擄獲野花心。但是，讓我告訴你，想證明男子漢氣概和魅力，真正難的挑戰其實是和同一女人白頭偕老。願意外遇的蠢男人滿街都是，哪能證明男子氣概？女人聽過你打鼾，見過你鬍碴滿臉，照顧過生病的你，洗過你的髒內褲，如果你還能持續贏得芳心，那才是男子漢。如果你能贏得芳心，繼續讓她內心溫馨滿盈，你將能聽見天籟。你愛的女人見到你和祕書打招呼，或見到你問候你倆都認識的女孩，如果她心底產生問號，懷疑這女人是不是你半夜回家的原因，心裡必感羞辱，如果你真的愛她，一定不希望她猜忌，也不應讓任何野花見家花時睜眼暗笑，不應讓野花回想起你愛的家花曾被你短暫拒絕、轉投野花懷抱。

麥可，家庭破碎是什麼滋味，對人有何影響，你比很多人更能體會。現在你有機會把一個家安頓得幸福美滿。世上最大的幸福是下班後走向家門，心知門內有人正期待聽見門外的腳步聲。

愛你的老爸

P.S. 一天至少講一次「我愛妳」，永遠不會起風波。

我們迅速沉沒中

鐵達尼號致畢爾瑪號輪船（SS Birma）

一九一二年四月十五日

鐵達尼號是當年世上最大的一艘客輪，首航四天後在一九一二年四月十四日接近午夜之際，撞上冰山，開始進水，幾小時後沉進大西洋底。船難期間，有幾封電報傳遞消息，本書在此收錄其中兩則。第一則由畢爾瑪輪船在四月十五日大約凌晨一點四十收到，是鐵達尼無線電收發室傳出的最後一通完整求救訊號。第二則在兩三小時後發送，發自白星輪船公司，對象是倫敦郵政總局（鐵達尼號上有郵局員工），內文錯報乘客命運——後來喪生的乘客多達一千五百一十七人。

C/O SOS SOS cqd cqd – MGY（鐵達尼代號）

我們迅速沉沒中乘客正轉乘救生艇
MGY

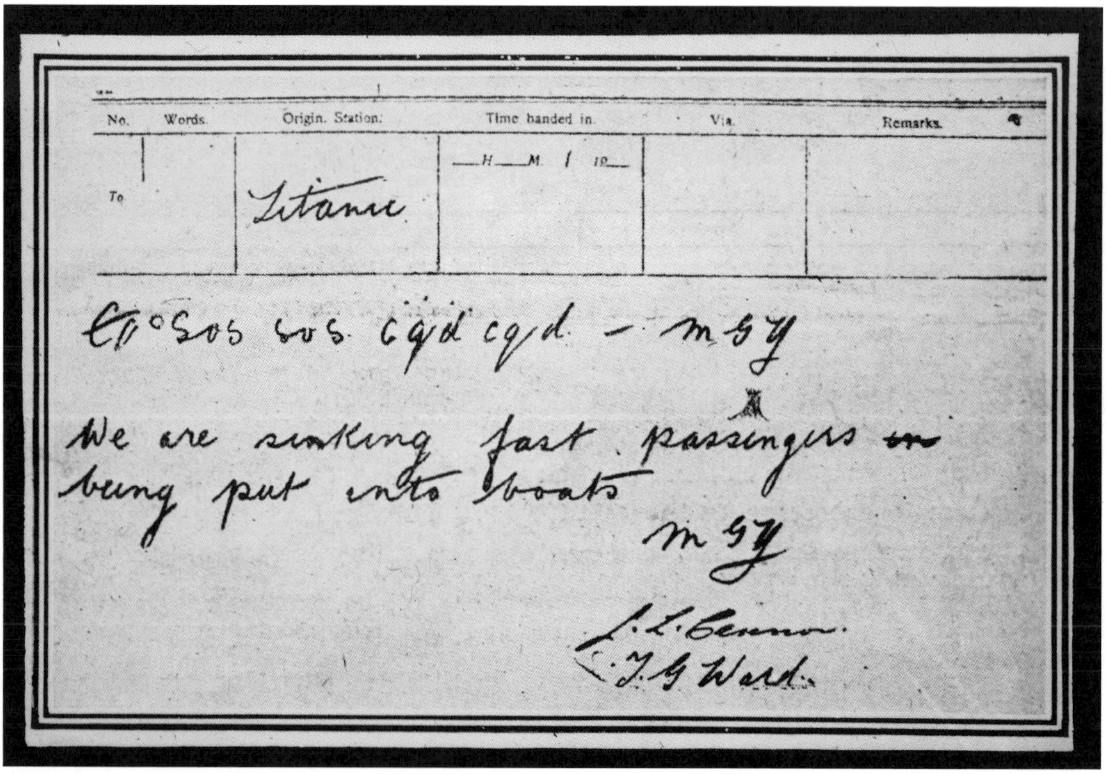

倫敦郵政總局長

承保人得自紐約的訊息指出維吉尼亞輪正在鐵達尼號旁待命無人
有生命危險

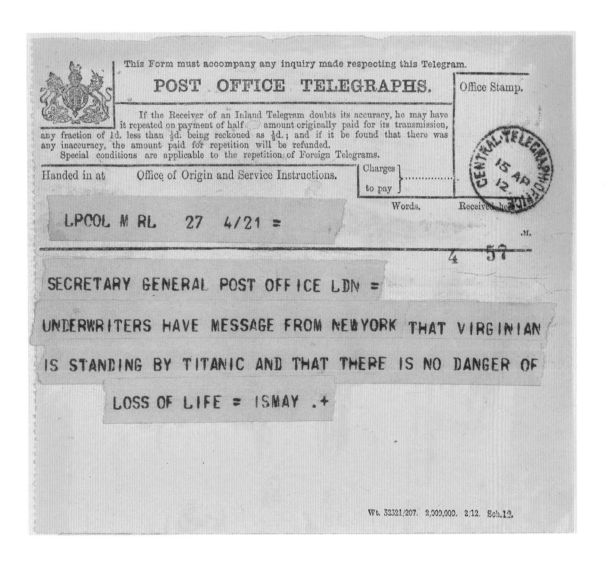

信之 *103*

芝加哥普爾曼大廈

一九〇九年二月六日

不可思議的巧合

林肯之子致雜誌主編
一九〇九年二月六日

一八六五年四月十四日晚間，美國
總統林肯在福特劇場看戲，遭二
十六歲的刺客約翰·威克斯·布
司（Wilkes Booth）從背後開槍，
翌晨喪生。四十四年後，林肯的兒
子羅伯特寫這封信給《世紀雜誌》
（*Century Magazine*）的主編理察·
季爾德（Richard Gilder），描述多
年前一件鮮為人知的不可思議巧
合。事情發生在總統遇刺前不久，
羅伯特的生死落在約翰·布司之兄
艾德溫（Edwin）手裡。艾德溫·
布司是知名演員。

我親愛的季爾德先生：

　　二月四日的來信收到了，但你在後記提及的幾首詩仍未寄
抵，我收到後將告知。我願藉此信回覆你信中提及的其他幾件
事。

　　關於希理繪製的林肯像，我已與漢斯岱德·瓦敘朋相商，得
知他本人不知父親 E·B·瓦敘朋先生是否曾擁有這幅目前由瓦
敘朋參議員收藏的林肯畫像。但他確實有一幅他父親的畫像，也
有幾幅歐洲政要的畫像，全出自希理之手，在我父親出任巴黎公
使期間為我父親完成。我亦得知，我父親的畫像由希理先生在一
八六〇年前後繪製，原版目前收藏於芝加哥紐貝利圖書館，並不
在我先前告知的芝加哥歷史學會裡。因此我針對此事在你的副本
裡稍事修改多處。

　　我曾告知艾德溫·布司救我一命，文中的敘述大抵正確，但
細節不盡完善。我不清楚是否值得修正——由你裁決。

　　事件發生在深夜，車掌站在月臺上，在臥鋪車廂門外售票給
一群乘客。月臺與車廂地板高度差不多，而車身與月臺之間當然
有空隙。在人群簇擁之際，排隊中的我被擠向車身，此時火車開
始移動，緊貼車身的我因而扭身，一時站不穩，兩腳踩進空隙，
頓時無助，幸好有人使勁揪住我外套領子，及時向上拉我一把，
我才在月臺上站穩。我轉身向救星道謝時，赫然發現其長相竟是
我熟知的艾德溫·布司，因此直呼其名向他表達感激之意。

（簽名）敬上

理察·華森·季爾德紳士
　　世紀公司
　　　　紐約市東十七街三十三號

February 6th, 1909.

My dear Mr. Gilder:

I have your letter of February 4th, but the poems you mention in your postscript have not yet come. I will acknowledge them when they do. In the meantime I think it well to write you about the other matters mentioned in your letter.

In regard to the Lincoln portrait by Healy; I have conferred with Mr. Hempstead Washburne, and find that he has himself no knowledge of his father, Mr. E. B. Washburne, having ever owned the portrait of my father which is now in the possession of Senator Washburn. But he has a portrait of his father, and of several European Statesmen, which were painted by Mr. Healy for his father while he was our Minister at Paris. I find also that Mr. Healy's original portrait of my father made about 1860 is in the Newberry Library, in Chicago, and not in the Chicago Historical Society, as I wrote you before. I have accordingly made some slight changes in your copy on this subject.

The account of my rescue by Mr. Edwin Booth, which I return to you, is essentially correct, but it is not accurate in its details. I do not know that it is worth changing - you can judge for yourself.

The incident occurred while a group of passengers were late at night purchasing their sleeping car places from the conductor who stood on the station plat- form at the entrance of the car. The platform was about the height of the car floor, and there was of course a narrow space between the platform and the car body There was some crowding, and I happened to be pressed by it against the car body while waiting my turn.   In this situation the train began to move, and by the

motion I was twisted off my feet, and had dropped somewhat, with feet downward,

into the open space, and was personally helpless, when my coat collar was vigor-

ously seized and I was quickly pulled up and out to a secure footing on the plat-

form.   Upon turning to thank my rescuer I saw it was Edwin Booth, whose face was

of course well known to me, and I expressed my gratitude to him, and in doing so,

called him by name.

Very sincerely yours,

Robert T. Lincoln

Richard Watson Gilder, Esq.,
    The Century Company,
        33 East 17th Street,
            New York City.

皮克斯電影沒有完成
之日

動畫大師致影迷
二〇〇八年十月十七日

彼得・達克特爾（Pete Docter）
是皮克斯電影《怪獸電力公司》
（*Monsters Inc.*）的導演，劇本曾獲
獎。在二〇〇八年中，年輕影迷亞
當寫信給他，他當時正忙著導演新
片《天外奇蹟》（*Up*）。亞當是皮
克斯電影的死忠影迷，也是業餘的
電影人，在信中對他表達仰慕之
情，並說他立志進入皮克斯工作。
亞當以為自己頂多接到偶像簽名
照，沒想到幾個月後，他驚喜收到
這封絢麗的插畫親筆信。

嗨亞當！

收到你親切來信已久，容我道歉現在才回信。最近工作忙得半
死。你來信想索取簽名照，但因為我本人不紅，所以手邊沒這類
東西。不過，我在信上畫了自畫像送你。

我相信你看得出畫中人和我長相神似。

電影裡講得故事好不好很重要，你說得很有道理。可惜的是，說
起來簡單，做起來可不容易。好的故事需要費很多心思（改寫、
改寫再改寫），才能到位。即使是到位了，通常我們還是沒辦法
百分之百滿意。

如同約翰・萊瑟特（John Lasseter）的口頭禪，我們家電影沒有
完成的一天，只有上映日。

希望你喜歡明年的《天外奇蹟》！

彼得・達克特爾

10·17·08

Hey Adam!

First off, let me apologize for taking so long to respond to your very kind letter. Things are pretty nuts around here.

You had asked for an autographed photo of me; I don't really have anything like that, not being famous. But here is a drawing of me for you

↑ I'm sure you can see the resemblance →

2

You are sure right about the importance of a good story in movies. Unfortunately, It's not as easy as it sounds. It takes a lot of work (and rework, and rework and rework) to get it right. And even then quite often we're not 100% pleased. As John Lasseter likes to say, our films don't get finished, they just get released.

Hope you enjoy "UP" next year!

Pete Docter

Boo!

願你我一同向上提升

禁書作家致荷蘭記者
一九八五年七月二十二日

作家查爾斯・布考斯基（Charles Bukowski）在一九八三年發表短篇小說選集《常態的瘋狂》（*Tales of Ordinary Madness*）。在一九八五年，荷蘭尼茲梅根（Nijmegen）市立圖書館接到當地讀者反應，宣佈該書「性虐待味極重，穿插法西斯意味的歧視語句，侮辱到同性戀等族群，」因而下架。並非所有人認同此決定。書下架幾星期後，地方新聞工作者漢斯・范登布羅克（Hans van den Broek）致函布考斯基，詢問他對書被查禁的感想。作者立即回信。

作者以強硬的論點為作品辯護，全信目前掛在流動書局 Open Dicht Bus 裡光榮展示。

親愛的漢斯・范登布羅克：

　　謝謝你來信告知我的作品之一被尼茲梅根圖書館下架，被禁原因是內容歧視黑人、同性戀和女性，為了性虐待而性虐待。

　　我擔心，遭歧視的其實是幽默感和事實。

　　如果我把黑人、同性戀、女人寫成壞人，那是因為我遇見的這些人確實惡質。「惡質」的事物很多——惡犬、惡檢，甚至也不乏「惡質」白種男人。差別在於，書寫「惡質」白種男人時，不會有人跳出來抱怨。天下多的是「好」黑人、「好」同性戀、「好」女人，我不必多說吧？

　　身為文人，我的工作是以文字拍照，我手寫我見聞。如果我描寫「性虐待」，那是因為世上存在性虐待，不是我憑空捏造的。如果我作品出現可怕的言行，那是因為這種言行在你我生活中確實存在。若說邪心在人間暢行無阻，我和它不屬於同一國。我未必認同我作品裡發生的事，也不會為了渲染黑暗面而大作文章。此外，匪夷所思的是，批判我作品的人似乎略過部分段落不讀，無視裡面的喜、愛、望。我過的日子，我經歷過的年份，我的一生，起起伏伏，有光明也有黑暗。假使我僅挑「光明」寫個不停，從不提黑暗，那我這文人未免太虛偽。

　　有必要逃避現實、自欺欺人的那種民眾，才會使出檢查制度這種工具。說穿了，他們的恐懼來自無能面對真相，而我無法對這種人發洩怒火。對他們，我只有一種惶恐沉痛。在他們成長的某階段，大人一定對他們遮遮掩掩，不讓他們認清世事的全貌。人間的觀點豈止千萬種，他們只學到以單一觀點看世界。

　　書被地方圖書館查禁下架，我並不失望。畢竟，我的作品竟能喚醒這些膚淺之流，我臉上有光。但如果今天被禁的書是別人的作品，我會傷心，因為禁書通常是坊間少見的佳作。縱觀古今，禁書常演進為經典，史上被視為驚世悖德的作品如今卻成為無數大學指定讀物。

　　我並不是說我的書是必讀經典。我的意思是，在我們這時代，在此時，在許多人可能正嚥下最後一口氣的此刻，世上居然

仍有滿腔怨的小心眼族，仍有人在獵巫婆，仍有人否認現實，多麼令人氣結，令人悲哀到無以復加。是的，這些人有權活在你我之間，這些人是人類的一份子。如果我尚未書寫到他們，也許我應藉此信著墨發揮，這樣就夠了。

　　願你我一同向上提升

（簽名）　敬上

查爾斯・布考斯基

信之 *106*

必定有個啥？

怪咖大使致外交部長
一九四三年四月六日

第二次世界大戰方酣時，英國駐俄
大使是以作風怪誕聞名的亞契柏·
克拉克·克爾（Archibald Clark
Kerr）爵士。他在一九四三年四月
六日致函外交部長瑞吉諾·潘布洛
克（Reginald Pembroke），成為傳
世經典。事由是他遇見一位姓名諧
音太不湊巧的土耳其外交官。此信
足以證明——如果還有證明的必要
——早在網際網路盛行之前，惡搞
姓名諧音和輕微的仇外意識等等惡
狀已大行其道。

英國大使館，倫敦

潘布洛克部長
外交部
倫敦

一九四三年四月六日

我親愛的老瑞，

在這些個黑暗的日子裡，人往往會尋找從天而降的微光。我
的日子大概比你更陰暗，因此，天啊，再微弱的光芒，我也求之
不得。但我是個正直之士，偶有微光落在我身上，我不願卑鄙自
私，所以我在此與你分享一小片照亮我晦暗日子的光輝，告訴
你，上帝賜予我一位土耳其同事，他的名片說，他名叫穆斯塔
法·康特（譯註：Mustapha Kunt，發音近似「必定有個逼」。）

老瑞，你我偶爾難免覺得春風臨身，但絕少有人會把這種事
印在名片上。唯有土耳其人會。

（簽名）
亞契柏·克拉克·克爾爵士
英國大使

送五兒進海軍是一件苦事

母親致美國海軍
一九四三年一月

一九四二年十一月，所羅門群島爆發為期三天的瓜達爾卡納島（Guadalcanal）海戰，美國軍艦朱諾號（Juneau）遭兩枚日軍魚雷擊沉，造成六百八十七名士官兵喪生，其中五人是亞莉塔·蘇利文（Alleta Sullivan）的兒子。在十個月之前，五兄弟才結伴同時入伍，盼能並肩作戰。兒子為國捐軀兩個月後，母親聽見凶多吉少的謠傳，寫了一封感人的信，寄給海軍人事局，請求告知真相。未久，她接到回信，寄件人並非人事局，而是美國總統羅斯福。

蘇利文家兄弟五人陣亡的消息曝光後，美軍開始實施免役政策——如果一家有任何人服役期間喪生，其餘兄弟可免服兵役。

愛荷華州滑鐵盧市
一九四三年一月

海軍人事局

親愛的長官：

我寫這封信的原因是，有謠言指出，我的五個兒子在去年十一月作戰時喪生。告訴我的人是這裡的一位母親，她收到兒子來信，她兒子聽說我的五個兒子全死了。

這消息傳遍了全市，我聽了好擔心。我的五個兒子一年一同加入海軍，日期是一九四二年一月三日。他們在朱諾號巡洋艦上服役。我最後一次接到他們的消息是在十一月八日。信上的日期是十一月八日，海軍。

五人的首名和次名分別是：喬治·T、法蘭西斯·亨利、喬瑟夫·E、麥迪森·A、亞柏特·L。若謠傳屬實，請據實通知我。塔瓦薩軍艦即將在二月十二日啟用，我將去參加典禮。如果我五兒遭不測，我仍將出席典禮，因為這是他們的心願。我不願打擾你們，但我實在好擔心，好想弄清楚是不是事實，所以請告訴我。一口氣送五兒進海軍是一件苦事，但我為我兒子感到光榮，高興他們能服役捍衛國家。喬治和法蘭西斯在荷威艦上服役過四年，我曾有幸在一九三七年登艦參觀。

我很高興海軍賜予我參與塔瓦薩艦啟用典禮的榮幸。我丈夫和女兒將與我同行至波特蘭。

敬上

亞莉塔·蘇利文夫人
愛荷華州滑鐵盧市
亞當斯街九十八號

我親愛的蘇利文先生夫人：

我得知兩位的英勇兒子作戰時失蹤，因此親自動筆寫信給兩位。我完全明瞭，盡再大的力也難以解消兩位的哀慟。

身為海陸軍總司令，我想讓兩位知道，全國同心為你家致哀。我在此為全國致哀並表達謝意。持續奮戰的我們必須維護士氣，以免士官兵白白犧牲性命。

經海軍部告知，我瞭解喬治・湯瑪斯、法蘭西斯・亨利、喬瑟夫・尤金、麥迪森・埃柏、艾柏特・里歐曾表示服役於同一艘艦艇的意願。我相信，他們並肩作戰的景象必能使大家動容。其中一兒子寫道，「我們將共組一支無敵隊伍。」我軍凱歸的關鍵正是這股凜然的正氣。

去年三月，本部為表揚蘇利文夫人您與兒子的愛國心，指定您參加軍艦啟用典禮。據我瞭解，現在您出席典禮的決心更加堅定。您的無私精神與勇氣對我有莫大的啟示作用，相信對全美國人民亦然。面對悲劇的您仍能不屈不撓、信念堅定，令我深信國民具有大無畏、意志堅強的精神。

在兩位苦難時刻，我致上萬分同情，祈禱兩位能找到唯有萬能上帝可賜予的慰藉與協助。

（簽名） 謹此敬告

富蘭克林・D・羅斯福

好東西跑不掉

作家約翰・史坦貝克（John Steinbeck）致長子

一九五八年十一月十日

作家約翰・史坦貝克出生於一九〇二年，著有《憤怒的葡萄》（*The Grapes of Wrath*）、《伊甸園東》（*East of Eden*）、《人鼠之間》（*Of Mice and Men*）等經典，全球各地書迷不下千萬人，是當代最富盛名的作家之一，並於一九六二年榮獲諾貝爾文學獎，聲望抵達巔峰。在他獲獎前四年，史坦貝克肩負著文學以外的任務。那年，他的長子湯瑪斯（Thomas）十四歲，情竇初開，從寄宿學校寫信向父親和繼母報告說，他愛上名為蘇珊的妙齡女子。史坦貝克在同一天回信，以愛為主題，向兒子提出曠世建議。

親愛的小湯：

我們今早收到你來信。我在此以我個人觀點回覆，繼母依蓮當然會以她的觀點回覆。

首先——如果你墜入愛河了，那是好事一樁，差不多是天下人能遇到最棒的一件事。你可別讓人輕視或小看這件事。

其次——這世上的愛有幾種。一種是自私、小心眼、黏人、自我中心的愛，會使人以愛來自捧。這種愛既醜陋又蹩腳。另一種愛能讓你發揮全心全意的善，讓你懂得體貼、待人親切，更懂得尊重——不僅是人與人之間的相互尊重，更涵蓋一種更高深的尊重，懂得視對方為獨特而珍貴的個體。第一種能把你變得噁心、卑微、衰弱，第二種卻能釋放出你心中的力量、勇氣、良善，甚至能發揚你有卻不自知的智慧。

你說這份情不是少年亂愛。如果你感覺如此深刻，那當然不是亂愛。

但我不認為你問的是我的感想。你比任何人更清楚。你找我是希望想想辦法，這我倒能幫忙。

辦法之一是沉浸在愛的光輝裡，為愛而慶幸感恩。

心中有愛是最棒最美的好事，你應盡情享受。

如果你愛上一個人，說出來也無傷大雅，但你必須記住，有些人個性非常害羞，因此有些時候，說與不說，必須將對方害羞列入考量。

女孩有辦法感應到你的心意，但她們通常也喜歡聽你親口說。

有時候，基於某種因素，你有心卻無人領，這並不表示你的心意比較不寶貴或不太好。

最後，我懂你的感覺，因為這種感覺也在我心中，而我很高興你終於有這種感覺。

我們很樂意認識蘇珊，非常歡迎你帶她回來。但這事應由依蓮安排，因為這是她的專長，她會非常樂意幫忙。她也懂得愛，也許她能幫你的地方比我更多。

另外，別為了失落而擔心。如果愛對了，愛就會發生——重點是不要太急。好東西是跑不掉的。

愛你的

爸

十七世紀倫敦大火

郵政局長致各地局長
一六六六年九月四日

在一六六六年九月二日凌晨，倫敦普丁（Pudding）巷一家麵包店失火，火勢迅速蔓延，最後焚燬全市，造成七萬多民眾流離失所，據信全毀的住家大約一萬三千戶，史稱倫敦大火。最早淪陷的郵局位於克羅克（Cloak）巷，局長詹姆士·希克斯（James Hicks）使出渾身解數，急忙盡量搶救郵件，然後帶家人逃命至巴內特（Barnet）鎮，驚魂未定的他才寄這封信給各地郵政局長，通告這件仍未結束的災難。

紳士們，

　　萬能上帝引領烈焰親臨聞名大城倫敦，火勢於週日凌晨約二時在普丁巷麵包店始燃，該店位於新費許街王首酒館後方。儘管用盡所有辦法，火勢仍不可擋，入夜前已燒燬倫敦泰半區域、聖馬格納斯教堂。通往席斯之橋半毀。大火延燒至水濱、坎農街、道蓋特，週一更引燃葛瑞休斯街、朗巴德街、孔希爾、坡特里、巴索羅謬巷、瑟羅格摩頓街、洛斯貝里。昨夜與今日，大火肆虐全市各區，遠至檀普巴爾、霍朋橋、史密斯菲爾。各界咸信，大火勢不可擋，唯有上帝發揮無限智慧，方能阻撓祝融前進。我攜家人來至巴內特暫居赤里翁客棧，並無大礙，感謝上帝恩典，卻因敝局之嚴重損失與災情而甚感焦慮，但我奉命通知各位，碩果僅存之部會首長信件必定儘速寄抵各位手中，若我接獲廷等地指示亦傳達之，亦通知何信來自廷，亦將之儘速安然送抵諸君，謹願上帝施恩終結烈焰我將重啟普通郵件遞送如常願上帝賜福謹此

　　　　　　　　　　　　　　哀痛之友
　　　　　　　　　　　　　　詹姆士·希克斯。

九月四日晚間十一時於巴內特

To my good ffriends ye Postmasters betwixt London
& Chester & so to Holly head.

Gentlemen
    it hath pleased Al: God to visit this famous city of L: with most
raging fire wch began on Sunday morning last about 2 a clock in Pudding lane,
in a bakers house behind the Kgs head taverne in new ffish strtt & though all
the meanes possible was vsed yet it could not bee obstructed but before night
it had burnt most part of ye City wth S^t magnus church & part of ye Bridge
to L: Hith to the water side, Canon strtt, Dowgate, & vpon munday struck
vp to Gratious strtt, Lumbard street, Cornhill, Poultry Bartholomew
lane, ffrogmorton strtt, Coathbury & the last night & this day raged
through all parts of the city as far as Temple Barr, Holburne bridge
Smithfild, & by all conjecture is not by any meanes to bee stopped
frō a further ruine except god in his infinite wisdome prevent it
& I am at ye Red Lyon in Barnett wth my family & blisse god in reason
able good health, notwithstanding great losse & sufferings by this
distractions of o^r office yet I am Comanded to let you know y^t what
Letters Come to yor hands frō any ministers of state y^t giue giue y^m
all quick & speedy dispatch to mee hi[?]r y^t I may Convey y^m hence
to Court or such places as I may receiue direction for, & I am also
to intimate to you y^t if w^t Letters are sent to you frō Court I shall haue
them sent forwards frō hence to you with speedy Care & conveyance
& so soone as pleasith god to put an end to ye violence of this fire
some place will bee pitch on for ye ginerall Correspondence as
formerly of wch you shall God willing haue advice at p^rsent this
is all

                                        yor sorrowfull friend
Barnet sep. 4. 11 at night   James Hicks.

猶如殺人後自白

達爾文致植物學家
一八四四年一月十一日

在一八五九年，達爾文發表《物種
起源》（*On the Origin of Species*）一
書，驚動社會，從此改變人類對世
界的見解。書一出版，立即引發各
界議論，也讓民眾大開眼界。達爾
文的進化論一言以蔽之，就是物種
並非亙古不變，而是慢慢演進以順
應周遭環境，最具優勢、最能調
適的物種因而繁衍不息。在本書
問世前十五年，達爾文初探「物
競天擇論」，曾寫信給植物學家朋
友喬瑟夫・D・胡克爾（Joseph D.
Hooker），提及這條震撼全球的理
論，並將此舉譬喻為「殺人後自
白」。

致吾摯友，

　　我必須寫信感激你上一封來信，以告知我對你所有觀點與事
實甚感興趣。——你自稱「不擅整理延伸觀點」，請容我對此擅
作詮釋——意即，見識淺薄者與漫遊收集者常恣意胡亂臆測，你
並不會忘情其中。——我認為，動不動籠統歸納的傾向可惡透頂
——

　　你認為巴塔哥尼亞高原的邊線應劃在哪裡？——道比尼出書
可界定過？我相信他在黑河採集頗豐，巴塔哥尼亞高原在該地保
留固有的荒涼景象；在布蘭卡港乃至於以北地區，巴塔哥尼亞的
特徵漸漸融入拉普拉塔的沙草原。——南巴塔哥尼亞植物生態
（我在該地時採集了所有開花中的植物）如果用以對照道比尼在
北巴塔哥尼亞採集到的植物，應有所穫。——我對金恩的植物一
無所知，但他的鳥類棲地謬誤甚多，他聲稱來自聖麥哲倫島的種
類，我在巴西、火地島以及佛德角島都見過。——你所言的布朗
先生一事很丟臉，我曾懷疑過，但無法容許自己相信此類謠傳。
——費茲洛伊在自序裡苛責我，令我憤慨異常，但倘若其言辭更
苛刻也不至於白寫。我採集的隱花植物已送至伯克萊，數量不
多。我不信他已發表，但他幾年前寫信給我，說他已全盤描述但
不知遺忘在何方，麻煩你主動與他聯繫，否則為同一件事再付出
心血並不值得。——採集隱花植物方面，我的最佳（仍屬貧乏）
成果來自喬諾斯群島。——

　　有勞你代我觀察一小件事，亦即帶鉤的種籽。無論是任何植
物，只要是無大型四足動物的島上特有植物，例如葛拉帕戈斯群
島、聖赫勒拿、紐西蘭。種籽生鉤，若在此地有，理所當然會被
視為用來鉤住動物皮毛。——

再佔用你一些時間，請你告訴我，在聖赫勒拿、葛拉帕戈斯群島與紐西蘭等島上，屬種的數量是否多於珊瑚礁島，是否如我所信多於極地？（這些無疑將列入你的《南極植物誌》（*Antarctic Flora*）中吧？）以極地海域海貝的種類而言，確實如此。——相較之下，珊瑚礁島物種較多，你認為原因是種籽自各地漂流而來嗎？這也是我的假設。——

　　你在克爾格倫群島是否曾採集海貝？願聞其特徵。？你的來信引發我濃厚興趣，令我厚顏屢問不休，請你勿為此操煩，因為我知你工作繁忙，時間寶貴。

　　除了對南半球陸地的興趣之外，自從我返國以來，我一直從事一件非常放肆的工作，我自知無人不斥之為蠢到極點。——我對葛拉帕戈斯群島物種的分佈與美洲化石哺乳動物之特徵甚感詫異，決心盲目採集各項事實，或能一探物種之奧祕。——我廣閱農業與園藝書籍，從不停止收集知識——最後，靈光乍現，我幾乎能確信（有違我先前之見）的是，（猶如殺人後自白）物種並非恆久無變異。拉馬克胡言亂語「前進傾向」、「意志遲緩動物的調適」等等，上帝禁止我苟同，但我導出的結論與拉馬克理論不無近似之處——但變異定律的構想是全然相同——我認為我發現了（放肆！）物種巧妙適應各種挑戰的簡易法。——想必你閱讀至此開始嘟噥，心想「我竟與此輩通信，浪費光陰。」——若時光倒流五年，我必有同感。——我擔心你對此信之冗長嘖有煩言，請見諒，我起筆時並未懷惡意。

相信我，摯友
Ｃ・達爾文　敬上

Jay 1844.

Down. Bromley Kent

My dear Sir

Wednesday Thursday

I must write to thank you for your last letter; I to tell you how much all your views & facts interest me. — I must be allowed to put my own interpretation on what you say of "not being a good arranger of extended views" — what is, that you do not indulge in the loose speculations so easily started by every smatterer & wandering collector, — I look at a "strong tendency to generalize" as an entail evil —

What limit shall you take on the Patagonian side — has d'Orbigny published, I believe he made a large collection at the R. Negro, where Patagonia retains its usual forlorn appearance; at Bahia Blanca & northward the features of Patagonia insensibly blend into the savannahs of La Plata. The Botany of S. Patagonia (& I collected every plant — flowers at the season when there) would be worth comparison with the N. Patagonian collection of d'Orbigny. — I do not know anything about Kings' plants, but his birds were so inaccurately habitated, that I have seen specimen from Brazil, Tierra del & the _Cape de Verde Id_ all said to come from the S. Magellan. — What you say of M.r Rome is humiliating; I had suspected it, but would not allow myself to believe in such losses. — FitzRoy gave him a ~~puff~~ ^{vol} in his Preface, & made me very indignant, but it seems much harder one had not have been wasted. My cryptogamic collection was sent to ~~Hooker~~ Berkeley; it was not large; I do not believe he has yet published an account, but he wrote to me some years ago that he had described & mislaid all his descriptions. W.ld it not be well for you to put yourself in communication with him; as otherwise some things _(these two)_ will perhaps be twice laboured over. — My best collection of the cryptogamic. was from the Chonos Islands. —

Would you kindly observe one little fact for me, whether any species of plant, _peculiar_ to any isl.d as Galapagos,

St. Helena & New Zealand, where there are no large Quadrupeds, have hooked seeds; — such hook, as if observed here would be thought with justness to be adapted to catch into wool of animals,

Would you further oblige me some time by informing me (though I forget this will certainly appear in your Antarctic Flora) whether the in isl like St. Helena, Galapagos, & New Zealand, the number of families & genera are large compared with the number of species, as happens in coral-isl, & as I believe? in the extreme Arctic land. Certainly this is case with marine shells in extreme Arctic seas. — Do you suppose the number of species in proportion to large groups, in owing to the chance of seeds from all orders, getting drifted to such new spots? as I have supposed. —

Did you collect sea-shells in Kerguelen land, I sd like to know their character..?

Your interesting letters tempt me to be very unreasonable in asking you questions; but you must not give yourself any trouble about them, for I know you fully & worthily are employed.

Besides a general interest about the Southern lands, I have been now ever since my return engaged in a very presumptuous work & which I know no one individual who w[oul]d not say a very foolish one. — I was so struck with distribution of Galapagos organisms &c &c & with the character of the American fossil mammifers, &c &c that I determined to collect blindly every sort of fact, which c[oul]d bear any way on what are species. — I have read heaps of agricultural & horticultural books, & have never ceased collecting facts — At last gleams of light have come, & I am almost convinced (quite contrary to opinion I started with) that species are not (it is like confessing a murder) immutable. Heaven forefend me from Lamarck nonsense of a "tendency to progression" "adaptations from the slow willing of animals" &c — but the conclusions I am led to are not widely different from his — though the means of change are wholly so — I think I have found out (here's presumption!) the simple way by which species become

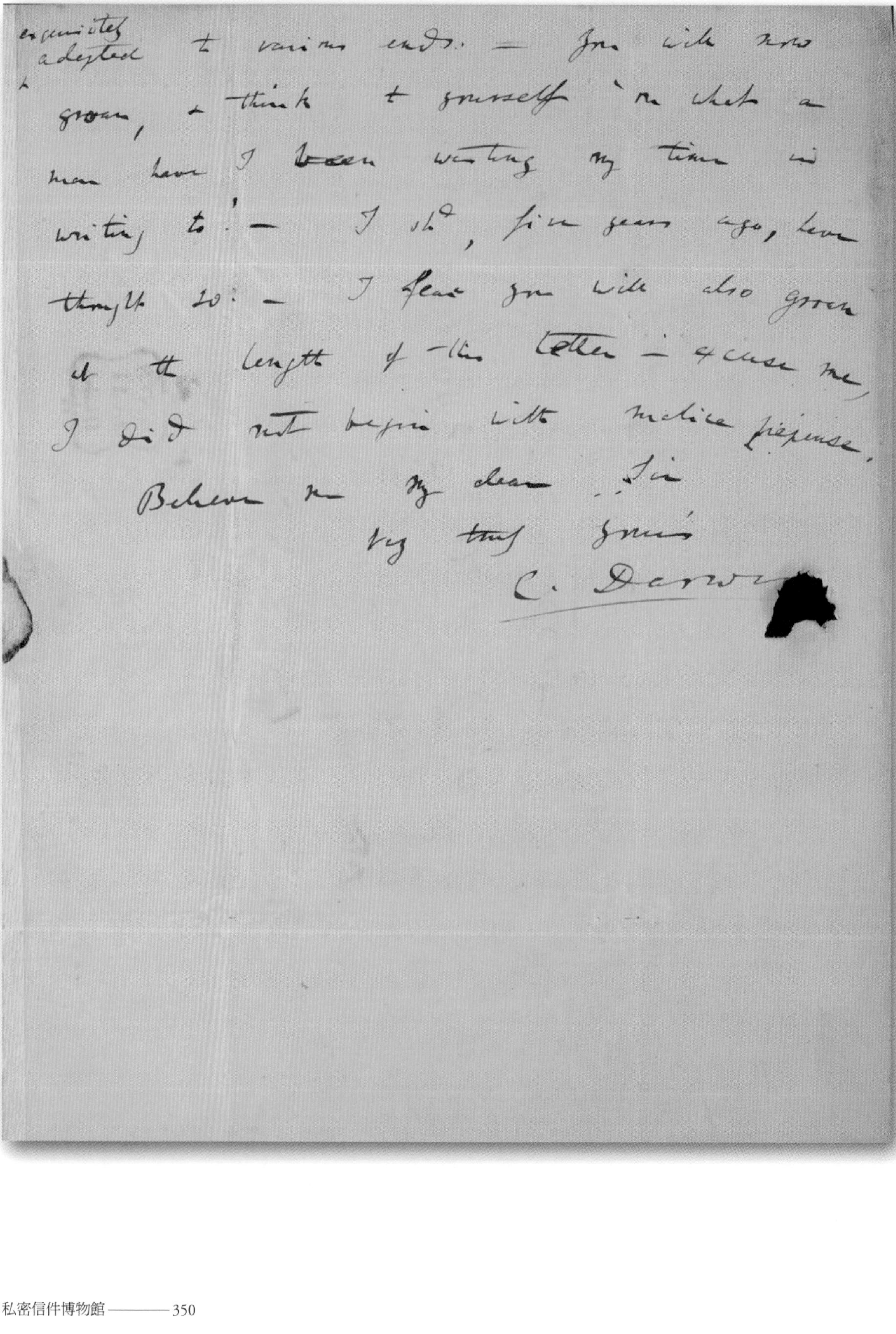

exquisitely
adapted to various ends. — You will now
groan, & think to yourself 'on what a
man have I been wasting my time in
writing to.' — I shd, five years ago, have
thought so: — I fear you will also groan
at the length of this letter — excuse me,
I did not begin with malice prepense.

Believe me my dear Sir
very truly yours
C. Darwin

幾乎。幾乎。

出版社致葛楚・史坦因
（**Gertrude Stein**）
一九一二年四月十九日

讀者對詩人作家葛楚・史坦因的寫作方式有兩極化的反應。不喜歡的讀者認為，帶有節奏的重複語句加上意識流風格，簡直無法理解，讀不出道理。喜歡她作品的讀者卻認為，這種風格清新。在一九一二年，出版人亞瑟・C・菲費爾德（Arthur C. Fifield）讀了她反覆語較多的一份手稿《美國人面面觀》（*The Making of Americans*），決定退稿，附上這封寫法仿傚她特色的詼諧信。

親愛的女士，

　　我唯獨一人，唯獨一人，唯獨一人。唯獨一人存在，一次只唯獨一人。不是兩人，不是三人，而是唯獨一人。唯獨一條命可活，一小時唯獨六十分鐘。唯獨一雙眼。由於唯獨一人，由於唯獨一雙眼，由於唯獨一次，由於唯獨一條命，我無法閱讀妳的手稿三四次。連一次也讀不下去。唯獨看一眼，唯獨看一眼就足夠了。在此地幾乎連一本也賣不出去。幾乎。幾乎。

　　萬分感謝。我將以掛號信退還手稿。唯獨一手稿，唯獨一掛號信。

　　　　　　　　　　　　　　　（簽名）　敬上

致葛楚・史坦因小姐，
法國巴黎花街二十七號

FROM ARTHUR C. FIFIELD, PUBLISHER,
13, CLIFFORD'S INN, LONDON, E.C.

TELEPHONE 14430 CENTRAL.

April 19 1912.

Dear Madam,

I am only one, only one, only one.
Only one being, one at the same time.
Not two, not three, only one. Only one
life to live, only sixty minutes in one
hour. Only one pair of eyes. Only one
brain. Only one being. Being only one,
having only one pair of eyes, having
only one time, having only one life, I
cannot read your M.S. three or four
times. Not even one time. Only one look,
only one look is enough. Hardly one
copy would sell here. Hardly one. Hardly
one.

Many thanks. I am returning the
M.S. by registered post. Only one M.S.
by one post.

Sincerely yours,

Miss Gertrude Stein,
27 Rue de Fleurus,
Paris,
France.

約翰・藍儂簽了我買的專輯

藍儂殺手致紀念品專家
一九八六年四月十日

在一九八〇年十二月八日，全球知名度最高的明星之一約翰・藍儂走出紐約公寓，被一位收集簽名的歌迷攔住。歌迷默默遞給他一張藍儂專輯《雙重幻想曲》（*Double Fantasy*），索取簽名。藍儂簽了。幾小時之後，在大約相同地點，同一歌迷馬克・查普曼朝藍儂背部開四槍，藍儂傷重不治，凶手則等候警察趕到。六年後，凶手在紐約阿提卡（Attica）監獄服刑期間，寫信給紀念品專家詢問藍儂簽名的專輯。

一九八六年四月十日
星期四

親愛的（刪）

首先，我希望這封信的內容只有你知我知，請保密，謝謝。

今天你上安迪・湯瑪士在WWKB電臺主持的「水牛城脫口秀」，我聽到了，從你的嗓音，我認為我能信任你，所以寫信請教一件非常隱私的問題，另外也有幾個不相干的問題想請教。

在一九八〇年十二月八日，我槍殺了約翰・藍儂。稍早，在那天的下午，我請他在《雙重幻想曲》專輯上簽名，他簽了，也註明年份一九八〇。我把專輯放進警衛櫃檯裡面，警方逮捕我之後，在櫃檯找到專輯。這些年來，我多次嘗試取回這張專輯（也請了兩個律師），一直沒結果。我想把專輯拍賣掉，捐錢給兒童慈善單位。我覺得這是我所能盡的一點心意。我想請教你的是，像這樣的東西價值多少，怎麼估算呢？我常想寫信給買賣商（例如查爾斯・漢米爾頓[Charles Hamilton]），問他這件事，但一直沒寫。我猜，聽你上節目讓我對你產生信任感——我有點算是一個隱士。像這樣的東西，價值到底多少呢？只能在拍賣的時候才可決定嗎？我願聽聽你的意見。

我有一本《蘇菲・塔克自傳》（*Autobiography of Sophie Tucker*），裡面有她的簽名題贈。我想知道這東西是否值錢。這本｛無｝封皮，書況不是很好。

另外，你手邊有沒有史蒂芬・金的親筆信呢？這類東西價值多少？或者有沒有J・D・沙林傑的信呢？任何他的親筆信都好。

如果你認識的商人手邊有以上任何一項，可以請你寄他們的地址給我嗎？

親切感謝你，

（簽名）

M・查普曼

81 A 3860

紐約州阿提卡14011

阿提卡監獄一四九號信箱

April 10, 1986
Thursday

Dear

First, I'd like you to keep this letter confidential—between us only. Thank you.

I heard you today on Andy Thomas's Buffalo Talks (WKBW) and felt at last you were sincere. I could write you concerning a very personal matter. I do have some random emotions which will follow).

On December 8, 1980 I shot and killed John Lennon. Before this, earlier in the afternoon, I had asked him to sign his Double Fantasy album. He did this also signing the date: 1980. I then placed this album inside the security guard's booth where it sin front of the my arrest. I have tried unsuccessfully for years (and 2 attorneys) to get this item back. I believe it was auctioned and lost; the rumor to a children's charity. I feel it was the least I could do. Now, is there any way to assess the value to an item such as this? I have often wanted to write a dealer (Charles Hamilton comes to mind) concerning this but haven't. I guess listing, to you convinced me I could trust you—I'm somewhat of a recluse.

Is there a value that could be assigned to an item like this? Is this something that could only be determined at auction? Please let me know your feelings on this.

I have an autographed photograph of Sophie Tucker (He inscribed) and was wondering if this is worth anything. There is no dustwrapper and the condition isn't that great.

Also, do you have any Sophie Kirk holograph material available? What is the worth of such items?

On J.D. Salinger letters available? I would like my holograph letters.

Could you send me any address of other dealers who might have any of the same items?

Thank you kindly,
Mark David Chapman

M. CHAPMAN
81 A 3860
Box 149
ATTICA CORRECTIONAL FACILITY
ATTICA, NY 14011

值得擔心的事

費茲傑羅致女兒

一九三三年八月八日

作家費茲傑羅的作品名列二十世紀最廣獲好評、歷久不衰的小說之林。他在創作空檔寫給名人的書信也膾炙人心，例如好友海明威、傑出編輯麥克斯威爾‧普金斯（Maxwell Perkins）、作家妻子賽爾妲，不勝枚舉。然而，他寫的信當中，給女兒絲高蒂的信份外真情流露，至為親暱。在給女兒的信中，他以獨門方法傳授人生道理給女兒，此信即為一例。女兒當時十一歲，正在外地參加夏令營。

馬里蘭州托森鎮羅傑佛吉區和平軒
一九三三年八月八日。

親愛的派：

我非常堅持要妳盡本份。可以多寄一些資料說明妳讀的法文書嗎？妳的日子過得快樂，我很高興──但我對快樂的信心向來不高。我也從來不信悲哀。這些東西常出現在舞臺上、影視裡、印刷品，從來不太會真的發生在生活裡。

人生最受我重視的是美德的回報（依各人造詣而定），我同樣重視不盡本份所應受的懲罰──比回報重一倍。莎士比亞有一首十四行詩，妳去請泰森老師在夏令營圖書室找找看，裡面有一句是：「凋腐百合花比雜草更惡臭百倍。」

今天腦袋空空，人生似乎圍繞著寫一篇《週六晚郵報》新聞報導。我思念妳，總往歡樂的一面去想；但如果妳再喊我「阿爸」，別怪我把白貓抱到外面，每次妳頂撞，我就痛打他屁股六下。妳會動容嗎？

我將安排夏令營帳單。

蠢材，我將收尾。值得擔心的事：

去擔心勇氣

去擔心清潔

去擔心效率

去擔心馬術

去擔心……

不值得擔心的事：

不必擔心一般人的意見

不必擔心洋娃娃

不必擔心過去

不必擔心未來

不必擔心成長過程

不必擔心被人超前

不必擔心戰勝

不必擔心失敗，除非是個人過失導致

不必擔心蚊子

不必擔心蒼蠅

不必擔心所有昆蟲

不必擔心父母

不必擔心男生

不必擔心失望

不必擔心喜樂

不必擔心滿足

值得思考的事：

我的真正目標是什麼？

和同年紀的人比較之下，以下三項我到底有多好：

(a) 學業

(b) 我真懂人心嗎？我能否跟他們和樂相處？

(c) 我是否盡力讓自己成為有用的人，是否怠忽不用？

最親的愛，

爹地

P.S. 被妳喊阿爸，我治妳的辦法是改妳名為「蛋」，意味著妳停留在生命起始階段，可以讓我隨興拿起來敲碎打開。假如我向妳同年的人透露這名字，我認為大家會喊成習慣。「蛋‧費茲傑羅」。一生被人東喊「蛋‧費茲傑羅」，西罵「臭蛋‧費茲傑羅」，或被心存惡念的歹人亂取其他綽號，妳願意嗎？妳敢再試一次，我對天發誓，這名字跟定妳了，甩不甩得掉，要看妳造化如何。何苦自尋煩惱呢？

總之還是愛妳。

一八二四年一月九日

我芯裡有賊

査爾斯・藍姆（Charles Lamb）
致伯納・巴屯（Bernard Barton）
一八二四年一月九日

詩人散文作家査爾斯・藍姆生病數
星期，寫不出具有建設性的東西，
於是寫信向同為詩人的好友伯納・
巴屯訴苦——事後藍姆坦承只是
「重感冒」而已。這封信對感冒的
描述可謂史上最一哭二鬧三上吊的
一則。藍姆誇大其詞自憐，自我揶
揄，巴屯未能讀出詼諧的意涵，立
刻回信，真心為好友的健康擔憂。

親愛的 B.B.——

　　被無堅不摧的白日夢魔擊垮的滋味如何，你可明瞭？法爾斯塔夫稱之為「私生子疲乏」——凡事提不起興致、坐臥都不對勁，——全然無生息，全然無味覺，——活力暫停，——對周遭渾然無感，——成了一團麻木、嗜睡、一無是處的東西，——上下裡外徹底僵化，——對過往事物渾然不覺，猶如牡蠣，——腦筋混沌，——鼓起肌肉對抗如千針猛刺的意識。你可曾罹患非常嚴重的感冒，全然下不了決心，臣服於熬成粥的過程？我苦命至此長達數星期，成了我的藉口。我的手指在信紙上沉甸甸拖行，依我所見，從這裡爬完半張紙的距離長達二十三弗隆（譯註：共四點六公里）。我無言可寫，苦思不出要事。我比拒否更斷然，比煎餅更平坦；比帕克法官戴假髮時的假髮底下更空虛；比演員下臺後的鄉村舞臺更無趣；一團謎，一顆○！我的生命跡象僅剩偶然一激咳，胸中積痰悶痛不消。我對人世感到厭煩，人世對我亦有同感。白晝化成了昏暮，而我認為不值得燃燭。我芯裡有賊，但我鼓不起勇氣吹熄。我吸入窒息；我無法辨別小牛肉與羊肉；凡事提不起我興致。現時十二點，索臺爾（譯註：當時人人喊打的殺人犯）正步上新絞場，劊子手傑克・凱屈精神飽滿，捲起油污的袖，主宰生死大權，而我卻無法發牢騷，無法反思道德意義。如果你告訴我，世界末日在明天，我會只說，「是嗎？」我尚存的意志力不夠，寫下 i，省略了頭上那點，更無力梳眉毛。我的眼睛陷入頭顱裡，頭腦告假，去沼澤鄉見窮親戚，也不說何時回來。我的腦殼是窮文人街上的一間出租閣樓，裡面甚至找不到一張凳子或有裂痕的夜壺。雞頭被斬後，雞身仍能跑動幾步，同理我手也能依慣性寫字，寫的人不是我。痛風、膽炎、牙疼的一陣激痛，——聽覺器官裡有一隻螻蛄，視覺器官裡有一隻蒼蠅。痛苦即人生——愈激烈愈能證明人生存在。奈何，這份冷淡，這份死氣沉沉！你可曾被頑強的感冒纏身，——六七星期持續不消的寒意，希望、恐懼、意識、一切停擺？然而，我竭盡所能對抗，試過葡萄酒、烈酒、香菸、鼻菸，份量不計，但似乎每試非但未見好

轉，反而加重病情。我改睡濕氣重的房間，對我無益；我深夜返家，仍不見明顯改善！我被鎖進這具無生命的軀殼，有誰能救我？

　　時間是十二時十五分，索臺爾此時已踏上歸路，也許在天蠍座垂釣，凱屈正為他的裝束討價還價，起價三枚半克朗銀幣，猶太人猶豫一陣後，念在購得裝束後能帶上街展示討賞，終於首肯。

C.L.（藍姆）

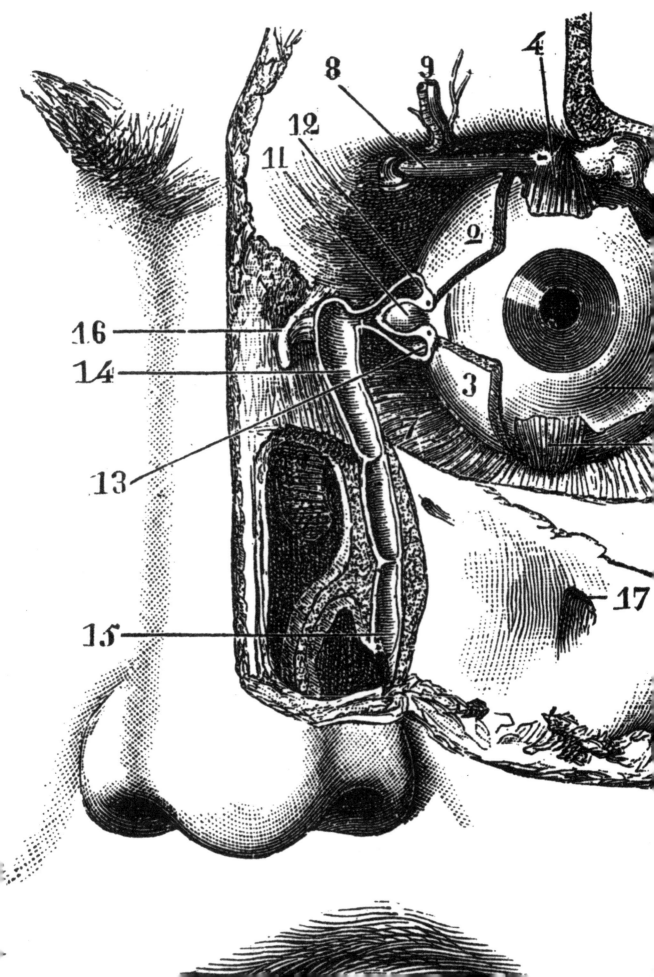

信之 *115*

投我一票我將助你

盲童致艾森豪總統

一九五六年

麻州普金斯（Perkins）啟明學校是
全球首創的視障教育機構，一九
五六年，該校十三歲學生以布萊葉
（Braille）點字法，寫信給美國總統
艾森豪獻計。這封信以厚紙和鐵
筆寫成，由老師在點字上方翻譯，
內容是短篇演講稿，提供給競選連
任的艾森豪發表。艾森豪雖然未採
用，但在十月二十四日，盲童竟接
到艾森豪來函致謝。

普金斯啟明學校
麻州水鎮七十二號

親愛的艾克，

　　我決定寫一小段演講稿送你，希望有助你打贏選戰。

　　投我一票我將助你。我將降價也降稅。我也將幫助黑人，讓
他們可以上學。

　　祝你十一月好運。

約翰・柏琉
十三歲小六

一九五六年十月二十四日

親愛的約翰：

最近收到你的點字信，我有多麼欣喜，說出來你一定不相信。這
一門學問很深奧，你想必練就了一身技巧，令我萬分欽佩。

感謝你寄給我一小篇講稿幫助我打贏選戰。你預祝我十一月勝
選，對我的意義也很重大，令我感激不已。但願我也能點字回信
就好了，不過我相信老師一定很樂意讀信給你聽。

我希望你求學愉快，善用你在水鎮享受到的良機。再次感謝你的
用心。

獻上最高的祝福，

（簽名）　敬上
艾森豪

約翰・柏琉
麻州水鎮普金斯學校
牟頓宿舍

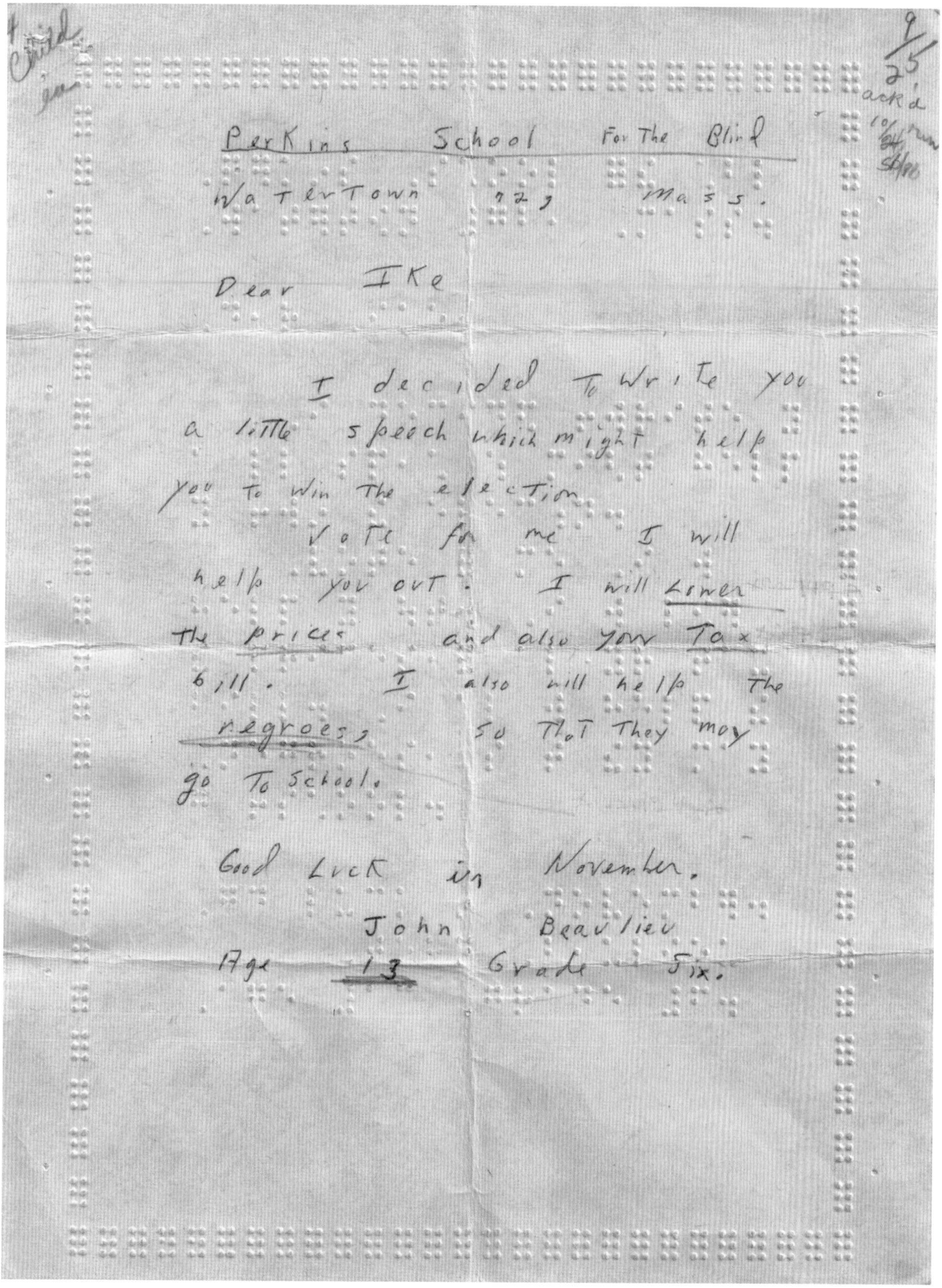

9/25
ack'd
10/8/52 per
st/do

Perkins School For The Blind

WaTerTown 72, Mass.

Dear Ike

I decided To Write you
a little speech which might help
you to win the election
Vote for me. I will
help you out. I will Lower
the prices and also your Tax
bill. I also will help The
negroess so ThaT They may
go To School.

Good Luck in November.

John Beaulieu
Age 13 Grade Six.

October 24, 1956

Dear John:

I can't tell you how pleased I was to receive the letter you wrote me recently in Braille. I certainly admire the skill that you must have had to master such a difficult art.

It was nice of you to send me a little speech to help win the election. Your good luck wishes for November mean a lot to me too, and I am very grateful to you for them. I wish I were able to write back to you in Braille also, but I am sure that one of your teachers will be happy to read this to you.

I hope you're enjoying your schoolwork and are taking advantage of the fine opportunity that you must have in Watertown. Many thanks again for being so thoughtful.

With best wishes,

Sincerely,

(Sgd.) DWIGHT D. EISENHOWER

John Beaulieu
Mouton Cottage
Perkins School
Watertown, Massachusetts

sb/cdj

CROSS CARD FOR STAFF SECRETARY.

科學家會祈禱嗎？

愛因斯坦致主日學小女生
一九三六年一月二十四日

愛因斯坦是全球頂尖知識分子，名氣更可能凌駕科學界之上，時常被人問及宗教觀。在一九五四年，他讀到哲學家葛金（Eric Gutkind）的書，不久後寫信和作者討論宗教，內容至今仍引發辯論，以下是經常被人引述的一段：

「對我而言，『上帝』一詞只彰顯人性弱點，是人性弱點的產物，而《聖經》收錄的種種故事固然莊重，卻仍屬遠古傳奇，相當幼稚。（以我個人而言）再精闢的詮釋也無法改變這觀點。」

在愛因斯坦如此表態之前十八年，也就是一九三六年一月，名叫菲莉絲（Phyllis）的女童代表主日學全班同學，寫信給愛因斯坦，問法稍有不同。她只問，「科學家會祈禱嗎？」愛因斯坦不久後回覆。

我親愛的愛因斯坦博士，

　　我正在上主日學，班上討論到這問題：科學家會祈禱嗎？我們首先探討的是，人能不能同時信教信科學。我們正寫信給幾位科學家和大人物，希望能問出一個答案。

　　誠心盼望您能回答我們的問題：科學家會祈禱嗎？他們祈禱什麼？

　　我們就讀小學六年紀，老師是艾莉絲小姐。

尊此，
菲莉絲

───────────

一九三六年一月二十四日
親愛的菲莉絲，

　　我會盡量以最淺顯的方式回應妳。我的回答如下：

　　科學人相信，世界上所有事物，包括人類所做所為，全有自然定律可循。因此，科學人無法傾向於相信事物的因果能被祈禱影響——祈禱是一種藉超自然力實踐的心願。

　　然而，我們不得不承認，我們對這些作用力的知識不盡完善，因此到頭來，信不信世上有個至高無上的鬼神，全看個人信念而定。即使當前科學日新月異，這種信念仍普遍。

　　但反過來說，潛心奉獻科學界的人無不深信，某種鬼神確實會在宇宙定律裡顯靈，它確實比人類高高在上。因此，鑽研科學的行為能衍生一種特殊的宗教感受，而和較天真的人對照之下，這份感受絕對大異其趣。

誠摯祝福妳的
A．愛因斯坦

於印度 C.P. 沃答哈
三九年七月二十三

看在全人類份上

印度聖雄甘地致希特勒
一九三九年七月二十三日

一九三九年，德軍侵佔捷克斯拉
夫，歐洲緊張情勢升高。主張非暴
力的印度獨立運動領袖甘地在同年
七月二十三日致函納粹德國領袖希
特勒。甘地的信寫得簡明扼要，懇
求希特勒「看在全人類份上」避
戰，可惜遭英國政府干預而無法寄
達。一個多月後，德軍侵犯波蘭，
就此展開人類史上最血腥、範圍最
大的二次世界大戰。

親愛的朋友，

　　吾友近日屢屢請求我看在全人類份上寫信給你，但被我回
絕，因為我的信總給人一種狂妄的觀感。我隱隱明白，我不宜過
慮，應向你提出我不值一文的訴求。

　　當前大戰一觸即發，恐將迫使人類退回蠻荒時代，而眾所週
知的是，全球能避免這場戰爭之人非你莫屬。你追求的目標究竟
何等重要，為何非得付出如此高的代價不可？鄙人曾刻意迴避戰
爭，成效不容小覷，你可願聞鄙見？斗膽寫信給你，若有冒失之
處請見諒。

　　依然是你真誠的朋友

　　　　　　　　　　　　　　　　　　　　　　　　（簽名）
　　　　　　　　　　　　　　　　　　　　　　　　甘地

　　　　　　　　　　　　　　　　　　　　　　致希特勒君
　　　　　　　　　　　　　　　　　　　　　　德國柏林

As at Wardha
C.P.
India.
23.7.'39.

Dear friend,

Friends have been urging me to write to you for the sake of humanity. But I have resisted their request, because of the feeling that any letter from me would be an impertinence. Something tells me that I must not calculate and that I must make my appeal for whatever it may be worth.

It is quite clear that you are today the one person in the world who can prevent a war which may reduce humanity to the savage state. Must you pay that price for an object however worthy it may appear to you to be ? Will you listen to the appeal of one who has seliberately shunned the method of war not without considerable success? Any way I anticipate your forgiveneas, if I have erred in writing to you.

Herr Hitler
Berlin
Germany.

I remain,

Your sincere friend

M.K.Gandhi.

我尚未槍斃她

詩人致出版社友人
一九二七年五月五日

長老教會醫院
紐約市內
東七十街四十一號
五月吧，我想

作家桃樂西·派克（Dorothy Parker）是阿爾岡昆圓桌文人會（Algonquin Round Table）的創始成員，以諷刺文學著稱，也是知名文評。她在一九二六年發表首部詩集《麻繩夠長》（*Enough Rope*），佳評如潮，翌年卻因身心交瘁而住院，病因之一是和美國出版商司沃·科林斯（Seward Collins）偷情，過程風風雨雨，期間兩人遠遊歐洲，與海明威、費茲傑羅等人面晤。她養了一條蘇格蘭梗犬，名叫黛絲，住院後託姐海倫代為照顧，雖然無愛犬陪伴，她仍覺得遠離風雨住院是求之不得的喘息空檔，但她也嫌日子平淡得令人心煩。在五月五日，她寫信給科林斯，以趣事傳達住院近況。

親愛的司沃，老實說，從小學音樂，得過四次痲疹，花了大筆鈔票矯正牙齒，照理說我的教養很好，不應該拿鉛筆寫信才對。但我請護士拿墨水給我——低聲下氣請求喔——護士走後，我至今見不到人影。所以，我親愛的，我就這樣認識了（後來當上將軍的）葛蘭特少校。

也許，唯有可靠的人允許我玩墨水。

我現在簡直健康到快爆炸了，而迄今一直蒙著白面紗的醫藥世界，現在懷抱著高遠的希望——我喜歡這話的風格——你應能想見高遠的希望盛裝打扮，被帶去競技場，然後被帶去梅樂氏喝茶。也許你無法想像——可惡，算了。

這間醫院是我最喜愛的一型，大家的動作非常明快，消毒得徹底，親切，溫馨。但他們老是拿體溫計戳人，或開燈照人，或教人進行職業療法（製毯——培養這種興趣多麼心曠神怡！），讓人沒機會蒐集新聞用來寫信。

當然，倘使我認為你願意聽，我可以告訴你，這裡原本有個狡猾的四歲小毛頭，成天在走廊來回跑，而且從聲音判斷，他穿著小號的馬蹄鐵——某人送他一串鑰匙玩，祝他早日康復，結果鑰匙在他奔跑時鏗鏘響，跑到我門口時，這個像大男人的小傢伙會扔下鑰匙，等我聽慣了鑰匙墜地的聲音後，他會唬我，連續兩三次過門不停，也不扔鑰匙。現在呢，他被帶到樓上動手術治療肩膀，醫生認為他再也沒辦法動右臂了。也好，讓他沒辦法再胡搞。

另外有位護士，她對我說，她很慚愧自己是個無可救藥的騷包，但她自稱就是把持不住。她也喜歡把「美麗如畫」（picturesque）這字發音成「皮克丘瑞斯鳩」，把「獨特」（unique）唸成「友膩鳩」，而且常常沒事把這些字硬塞進日常對話裡，自己帶頭笑。此外，她離開病房時常說，「後會有期。」我尚未槍斃她。禮拜一再說吧。

最重要的一個是走廊對面的一位紳士。他心地善良，可惜做事無效益。他生了一堆膽結石，躺在床上，送一隻烏龜來陪我

玩。不騙你。送一隻烏龜來陪我玩。我正在教牠玩雙手橋牌。等我長大，氣力也夠強，我打算跟牠賽跑，從病房頭跑到病房尾再折返。

若能見到黛絲該多好啊，可惜有些人心胸太狹隘，不准病人帶狗進醫院。就算能帶狗來，我也信不過這些狗屁醫生。她如果能活著走出去，甲狀腺八成會被換成天竺鼠的甲狀腺。海倫說她很乖——被拔毛了，少女般的腰身再現。我本以為，那隻忠心小野獸會趁我不在家大吃特吃，而你知道她不應該吃肉。但她像幼犬一樣愛玩，現在有了九個新玩具——三顆球，六種絨毛動物。她堅持把全套玩具咬上床，和海倫一起睡，結果把海倫整得最近有點憔悴。

應我淚眼要求，海倫對她說，「桃樂西向妳問好。」

她說，「誰？」

我附上不知名友人寄來的一個小東西。唉，算了。這裡有一首文學性質的詩，名叫《在切爾西氣喪》（*Despair in Chelsea*）。

> 歐斯伯·西特韋爾
> 無法稱心排泄。
> 其弟沙切維瑞爾，
> 認為他永遠無解。

自喬治·摩爾的《埃瑟·瓦特斯》（*Esther Waters*）以來，這鐵定是最無趣的一封信。但是，一有最新消息，我必定好好寫幾封給你。在我死後，康克萊特—史瑞納先生可以寫成書——那個正經八百的傢伙。

但此時，我寧可得知你近況。你在遠行時，若遇到哪家好人想讀《幸運先生的空想》（*Mr. Fortune's Maggot*），我這裡有六本。

愛

桃樂西——

母親臨終前，我曾許諾她，這輩子拒寫後記，可惜我非把大驚奇留到最後寫不可。我體重掉了二十二磅。

信之 *119*

致青年詩人之信

芮諾·瑪麗亞·里爾克（Rainer Maria Rilke）致法蘭茲·卡普斯（Franz Kappus）
一九〇三年二月十七日

在一九〇二年奧地利維也納，十九歲的軍校生法蘭茲·卡普斯有心成為詩人，所以寄幾則作品給深具影響力的波希米亞—奧地利籍詩人里爾克，懇請她惠賜高見。幾個月後，里爾克果然回信了，本書收錄如下。基本上，里爾克建議卡普斯多多內省，不必尋求他人的建言。兩人的交流並未到此為止。小詩人再度去信請教大詩人，雙方魚雁往返延續五年，里爾克不斷回信，建議的種類很多，寫詩只是其中一項。青年詩人的偶像去世後三年，他在一九二九年將里爾克的回信集結成書發表，成為經典書《致青年詩人之信》（*Letters to a Young Poet*）。

巴黎，
一九〇三年二月十七日

惠鑑，

　　我幾天前才收到你的來信。你的信寄得自信飽滿而懇切，我想謝謝你。除此之外，我幾乎幫不上忙。我無法細究你的詩句，因為我實無批判心。文藝評論者無以為據，所寫的評語薄弱，若言之有理，多少是僥倖的誤解。評論者多半希望我們相信，人間事皆可理解，皆可表達，其實不然。多數事件發生在文字穿不透的領域，無從表達起，而最難表達的莫過於文藝作品。文藝是奧祕的東西，人生人死，文藝不逝。

　　以此開場後，恕我僅進一步告訴你，你的這幾首詩缺乏個人風格，但它們確實初顯個人沉潛風格。最顯著的例子是最後一首《我的靈魂》。在這一首，藉由文字與韻律，你的心呼之欲出。《致里奧帕第》寫得美，的確與那位孤獨偉人培養出一份親屬感。儘管如此，這幾首仍未寫出主題性，無法獨立，甚至最後一首和《致里奧帕第》亦然。伴詩而來的信寫得親切，主動向我表白諸多短處，但我讀詩後卻無法明瞭你所指為何物。

　　你問我，你的詩寫得好不好。你問我。你也問過其他人。你向幾家雜誌社投稿。你找他人的詩來比較，被主編退稿時，你心情波動。好，（既然你允我建議）我求你戒除以上的行為。你現在的做法是向外看，而這正是你現階段萬萬不應做的事。無人能輔導協助你，無人。捫心自問你搖筆桿的初衷是什麼，探究它是否紮根深植你心田最深處；問你自己，假使你被迫封筆，你是否非死不可。最要緊的是——在夜闌人靜時分自問：我非寫不可嗎？追問出一個有深度的答案。若答案是肯定的，若你以堅決而簡明的「我非寫不可」回答此一認真問題，那就根據這份需求來構築人生；縱使在人生最淡漠淒冷的時刻，你的人生必須是這份心向的寫照與證言。接著，接近大自然。接著，揣摩開天闢地第一人，試著說出所見、所感、所愛、所失。勿寫情詩；起先避走太平易或太尋常的形式：這方向太難走，因為若想寫得出色，文筆必須過人，羽翼必須豐滿，方能在眾多經典傑作之中獨樹一

幟。因此，暫且不要涉足這類常見主題，宜從日常生活尋找素材。描述你的哀愁欲望、稍縱即逝的念頭、對某種美的崇尚——以友愛謙沖的誠懇言語描述這些，並在表達自我時引用周遭事物、夢境、往昔光景。若你自覺日常生活貧乏，切勿怪罪生活，應責怪你自己，應告訴自己，你的詩心不足，無法召喚人生豐富的內涵，因為對創作者而言，天下無貧乏之地，無平淡之邦。假若你置身監牢，高牆擋住外界聲響，你難道無法重溫童年？往事如金銀屋，珍貴如王公寶庫。將你的注意力轉向那方。盡量喚醒沉睡的感官，接觸豐盈的往事。你的個性將更為堅實，孤寂將延展，四壁將擴充為居家，遠方雜人雜音過門而不入。——自我反思後，忘情於內心世界後，若詩心油然而生，落實為文字，你將不會再考慮請他人評斷優劣。你也不會再以詩投探雜誌社的興趣：因為你將從詩裡見令私心歡愉的個人事物，悟人生片段，聞人生之天籟。情勢塑造出的藝術品有好無壞，僅能藉其源頭論其良莠，無人能置喙。因此，摯友，我對你的建議僅止於此：步入你內心，在生命源頭探底。你在泉源處將尋獲「為何需要創作」的解答。默然接受心聲，不需質疑。也許，事後將證明，文創是你的職志。果真如此，你應接受命運安排，肩挑重任，承受其浩瀚宏偉，不再奢求外界賞賜酬報。因為，創作者必須自成一天地，與大自然交融，自給自足。

話說回來，倘使你反躬自省、退居孤寂內心世界，也許你不得不放棄成為詩人的志向；（如我所言，不寫作也能生存的人就不應企圖靠寫作維生。）但縱使詩途無望，我請你做的內省也不至於白費。你的人生將因而找到方向，我祝福你走得平順、豐碩、寬廣，美好到我無以列舉。

我還能再對你多說什麼？我覺得，世間萬物皆有其應有的比重；更何況，我僅盼能建議你在發育全程繼續默默成長，認真成長，不宜冒然侵擾，萬萬不宜向外觀望，期待外界回答一些唯有你、唯有在最靜謐時分、唯有內心最深處可能回答的問題。

你信中提及荷洛塞克教授之名，令我欣喜。教授和藹可親，知識淵博，我對他尊敬而感激，延續多年至今，有勞你代我傳達這份心意。他仍把我放在心上是好事，而我也懂得珍惜。

你慨然寄託於我的詩在此寄回，我再次感謝你展現莫大而真誠的自信，我竭盡所能，盡力真心為你解惑，讓身為陌生人、價值微薄的我多一點價值。

誠摯感念你的：
芮諾・瑪麗亞・里爾克

你見證的新生何其偉大！

馬克・吐溫致詩人惠特曼
一八八九年五月二十四日

惠特曼有「自由詩體之父」之稱，是美國詩壇一大文豪，在一八五五年自費出版畢生詩選《草葉集》（*Leaves of Grass*），由於筆法有違常態，用語「猥褻」，被眾多文評嗤之以鼻，但後來慢慢吸引讀者，佳評逐年高漲，對後世的影響無可度量。在一八八九年五月，惠特曼七十大壽將至，大文豪馬克・吐溫致函恭賀他，細數惠特曼一生見證到的所有新發明，以整整四頁向當代豐功偉業致敬。

致沃特・惠特曼：

　　你走過的這七十年，湊巧正是世界史上最偉大、造福人類最鉅、進步最長足的時代。這七十年間的成就拉大動物與人類之間的差距，功勳遠勝先前任何五世紀的總和。

　　你見證的新生何其偉大！蒸壓器、蒸汽輪船、鋼鐵輪船、鐵路、改良至完美的軋棉機、電報、電話、留聲機、攝影機、凹版印刷、電鑄版、煤氣燈、電燈、縫紉機，以及奇妙、種類歧異的無數煤焦油產品，為神奇時代增添最新最稀罕古怪的奇蹟。而你見證過更偉大的新生事物；你見到了應用麻醉劑的手術——苦痛乃千古不變的常理，自分娩起片刻不離人生，如今終於將從地球上消蹤滅跡。你見到了奴隸獲釋，你見到了法國推翻君主制，英國皇室被降級為一部外觀威武的機器，表面上關注國家大事，其實卻與政府搭不上關係。是的，你的確見證了許多——但請再逗留一會兒，因為最偉大的新生事物仍未到。再等卅載，然後俯瞰地球！見證過種種奇蹟的你將再見到層出不窮的奇蹟。你亦將見到最驚人的成績——人類終於長高到近乎極限！——仍持續長高，你觀察可見其茁壯。到了那一天，端坐寶座之人，或坐擁鄰人可望而不可及之富貴之人，必定急忙穿上拖鞋，準備熱舞，因為音符即將飄送。靜待見證這時刻吧！敬愛你的三十人在此貢獻年歲——我們在壽命銀行總共結餘安康六百歲，你儘管提領三十——堪稱全世界詩人收到最貴重的壽禮——坐下靜候。等到你見到長人出現，瞥見其旗幟上映照的遠陽光輝，你方能心滿意足西歸，因為開天闢地所為何人你已見到，因為你知道，他將宣佈，人類合作之效益應勝過你爭我奪，普世價值觀也應據此原則排序。

馬克・吐溫

Hartford, May 24/89.

To Walt Whitman:

You have lived just the seventy years which are greatest in the world's history & richest in benefit & advancement to its peoples. These seventy years have done much more to widen the interval between man & the other animals than was accomplished by any five centuries which preceded them.

What great births you have witnessed! The steam press, the steamship, the steel ship, the railroad, the perfected cotton-gin, the telegraph, the telephone, the phonograph, the photograph, photo-gravure, the electrotype, the gaslight, the electric light, the sewing machine, & the amazing, infinitely varied & innumerable products of coal tar, those latest & strangest marvels of a marvelous age. And You have seen even greater births than these; for you have seen the application of anæsthesia to surgery-practice, whereby the ancient dominion of pain, which began with the first created life, came to an end in this earth forever; You have seen the slave set free, You have seen monarchy banished from France, & reduced in England to a machine which makes an imposing show of diligence & attention to business, ~~but~~ but isn't connected with the works. Yes, you have indeed seen much — but tarry yet a while, for the greatest is yet to come. Wait Thirty years, & _then_ look out over the earth! You shall, marvels

upon marvels added to these
whose nativity you have witnessed;
& conspicuous above them you
shall see their formidable Result
— Man at almost his full stature
at last! — & still growing, visibly
growing while you look. In that
day, who that hath a throne, or
a gilded privilege not attainable
by his neighbor, let him procure
him slippers & get ready to
dance, for there is going to be
music. Abide, & see these things!
Thirty of us who honor & love
you, offer the opportunity. We
have among us 600 years, good
& sound, left in the bank of life.
Take 30 of them — the richest
birth-day gift ever offered to

poet in this world — & sit down
& wait. Wait till you see that
great figure appear, & catch
the far glint of the sun upon
his banner; then you may depart
satisfied, as knowing you
have seen him for whom the
earth was made, & that he
will proclaim that human
wheat is worth more than
human tares, & proceed to
reorganize human values
on that basis.

Mark Twain

信之 *121*

愛因斯坦的一大失算

愛因斯坦致羅斯福總統
一九三九年八月二日

一九三九年，物理學家愛因斯坦向同領域的專家利奧‧西拉德（Leo Szilard）和尤金‧維格納（Eugene Wigner）請教後，於同年八月二日，致函當時美國總統羅斯福，警告以鈾製造原子彈的確可行，建議美國政府可採取何種措施。羅斯福總統閱信後指示成立布里格斯鈾顧問委員會（Briggs Advisory Committee on Uranium），這單位慢慢演化為龐大的曼哈頓計劃，隨後開發出「小男孩」和「大胖子」兩顆原子彈，在一九四五年被用來轟炸廣島和長崎，造成二十餘萬人死亡。

愛因斯坦日後表示，簽署這封信是「我一生中的一大失算。」

致美國總統
F‧D‧羅斯福
華盛頓特區白宮

總統先生：

E‧費米與 L‧西拉德最近以手稿和我聯絡，兩人新近的研究令我預期鈾元素可望在不久的未來轉化為重要的新能源。根據種種跡象顯示，政府當局宜密切關注之，必要時更應儘速採取行動。我因而相信，我的任務是提出以下事實與建議，供總統參考：

過去四個月來，約里奧在法國與費米、西拉德在美國研究有成，認為未來可望集合大批鈾元素以產生核子連鎖反應，進而觸發巨大動能，也生成巨量類似鐳的新元素。這份潛力幾乎確定能在不久的將來實現。

此種新現象亦能藉以活用，以製造炸彈，可想而知但並未有十足把握的是，或許能因而研發出威力大無比的新型炸彈。此型炸彈只需由船載運一枚，在港口引爆，即可能摧毀全港，並殃及周遭地域。然而，此種炸彈極可能太重，無法空運。

美國現有的鈾礦質差量寡，加拿大與前捷克斯拉夫境內的鈾礦豐富，但目前最重要的鈾產地位於比利時屬剛果。

有鑑於此狀況，總統或許認為，我政府應與研究連鎖反應的物理學家建立常態合作關係，而常態合作的可行管道之一是由總統您任命值得信賴的人，或許由此人擔任非官方角色，任務可涵蓋以下事項：

a）接觸政府部會，知會進一步的研發成果，並建議政府如何採取行動，側重於解決美國鈾礦來源之問題。

b）當前實驗局限於大學，受制於大學實驗室預算，若政府能在經費不足時提供資助，定能加速實驗進度，總統任命之人可透過私交，和願意捐款推動此理念之民間人士合作，或者尋求備有合適實驗器材之產業實驗室配合。

據我所知，德國已接管捷克斯拉夫鈾礦，下令禁止出口，其行動如此明快之因，或許與主事者有關：柏林的威廉凱撒研究所

（Kaiser Wilhelm Institut）此刻正仿傚美國，有意在鈾研究方面跟進，而德國副國務卿之子馮衛沙克與該單位掛鉤。

（亞柏・愛因斯坦） 敬上

Albert Einstein
Old Grove Rd.
Nassau Point
Peconic, Long Island

August 2nd, 1939

F.D. Roosevelt,
President of the United States,
White House
Washington, D.C.

Sir:

Some recent work by E.Fermi and L. Szilard, which has been com-
municated to me in manuscript, leads me to expect that the element uranium may be turned into a new and important source of energy in the immediate future. Certain aspects of the situation which has arisen seem
to call for watchfulness and, if necessary, quick action on the part
of the Administration. I believe therefore that it is my duty to bring
to your attention the following facts and recommendations:

In the course of the last four months it has been made probable -
through the work of Joliot in France as well as Fermi and Szilard in
America - that it may become possible to set up a nuclear chain reaction
in a large mass of uranium,by which vast amounts of power and large quantities of new radium-like elements would be generated. Now it appears
almost certain that this could be achieved in the immediate future.

This new phenomenon would also lead to the construction of bombs,
and it is conceivable - though much less certain - that extremely powerful bombs of a new type may thus be constructed. A single bomb of this
type, carried by boat and exploded in a port, might very well destroy
the whole port together with some of the surrounding territory. However,
such bombs might very well prove to be too heavy for transportation by
air.

The United States has only very poor ores of uranium in moderate quantities. There is some good ore in Canada and the former Czechoslovakia, while the most important source of uranium is Belgian Congo.

In view of this situation you may think it desirable to have some permanent contact maintained between the Administration and the group of physicists working on chain reactions in America. One possible way of achieving this might be for you to entrust with this task a person who has your confidence and who could perhaps serve in an inofficial capacity. His task might comprise the following:

a) to approach Government Departments, keep them informed of the further development, and put forward recommendations for Government action, giving particular attention to the problem of securing a supply of uranium ore for the United States;

b) to speed up the experimental work,which is at present being carried on within the limits of the budgets of University laboratories, by providing funds, if such funds be required, through his contacts with private persons who are willing to make contributions for this cause, and perhaps also by obtaining the co-operation of industrial laboratories which have the necessary equipment.

I understand that Germany has actually stopped the sale of uranium from the Czechoslovakian mines which she has taken over. That she should have taken such early action might perhaps be understood on the ground that the son of the German Under-Secretary of State, von Weizsäcker, is attached to the Kaiser-Wilhelm-Institut in Berlin where some of the American work on uranium is now being repeated.

Yours very truly,

A. Einstein

(Albert Einstein)

信之 *122*

速來我身旁

賽爾妲致費茲傑羅
一九二〇年九月

一九一八年，十七歲的賽爾妲·莎
爾（Zelda Sayre）甫從高中畢業，
七月間出席一場鄉村俱樂部舞會，
結識二十二歲的法蘭西斯·史考
特·費茲傑羅。當時費茲傑羅是美
國陸軍少尉，立志在小說界揚名立
萬。費茲傑羅對賽爾妲一見傾心，
賽爾妲對他的好感略低，因為她對
費茲傑羅的前途存疑。兩年後，費
茲傑羅以小說《塵世樂園》（*This
Side of Paradise*）初試啼聲暴紅，不
久後她同意結婚，金童玉女瞬間
在「絢爛二〇年代」的紐約成為名
人，緊接著小夫妻貪杯成癮，時常
爭吵，成為文學史上婚姻路最顛簸
的冤家之一。

這封信寫於一九二〇年兩人大吵一
架之後，由賽爾妲執筆，時間在婚
禮之後半年。兩人在一九三四年勞
燕分飛。

我望向鐵軌遠方，見你前來——破霧靄匆匆來的是你那可愛
的皺長褲——沒有你，最親愛最親愛的你，我無法看、無法聽、
無法感受、無法思考——無法活——我好愛你，今生再也不願你
我分離一夜。這好比乞求暴風雨、致命美感、孤單至白頭饒我一
命似的。我好想吻你——好想吻吻頸背秀髮開始處，吻你胸膛
——我愛你——愛你多深，我有口難言——一想到我在你知我心
之前**死去**——谷佛，你非得試著體會我愛多深——你不在身旁，
我變得多麼動彈不得——我甚至無法恨這些可惡的人——除了我
們，無人有權活著——他們玷污了我們的世界，而我不恨他們，
因為我如此渴求你——快來吧——速來我身旁——縱使你恨我，
縱使你如癲瘋病患渾身膿瘡，沒有你，我也活不下去。縱使你帶
野花私奔，餓我打我——我仍渴求著你。我**知道**——

愛人、愛人、親愛的——
你的妻

文藝無用論

**奧斯卡‧王爾德（Oscar Wilde）
致讀者**
一八九一

年輕人柏努夫‧科雷格（Bernulf Clegg）讀完才子王爾德的小說《格雷的畫像》（The Picture of Dorian Gray）後感到困惑，不久，在一八九一年，寫信給作者，客氣地請他解釋前言裡的「天下文藝皆無啥用處」。未久，作者以這封信回覆。

親愛的讀者先生

文藝無用，因為其目的僅止於產生一種心境，意不在授業解惑，亦不在影響言行。文藝精純無雜質，其樂趣之暗示亦精純無雜質。倘使有人審思文藝作品之後起而行，無論言行屬於哪一類，該作品若非不入流，即是其人對整體文藝觀感產生誤解。

花朵無用，文藝亦無用。花之所以綻放，為的是自尋其樂。賞花的我們能獲得片刻樂趣，我們與花之關係僅止於此。人當然能賣花，從中得利，但此舉與花並無關聯，不涉及花之本質，僅有附帶性質，堪稱誤用。此題材三言兩語難盡，恕我愈描愈模糊。

奧斯卡‧王爾德　敬上

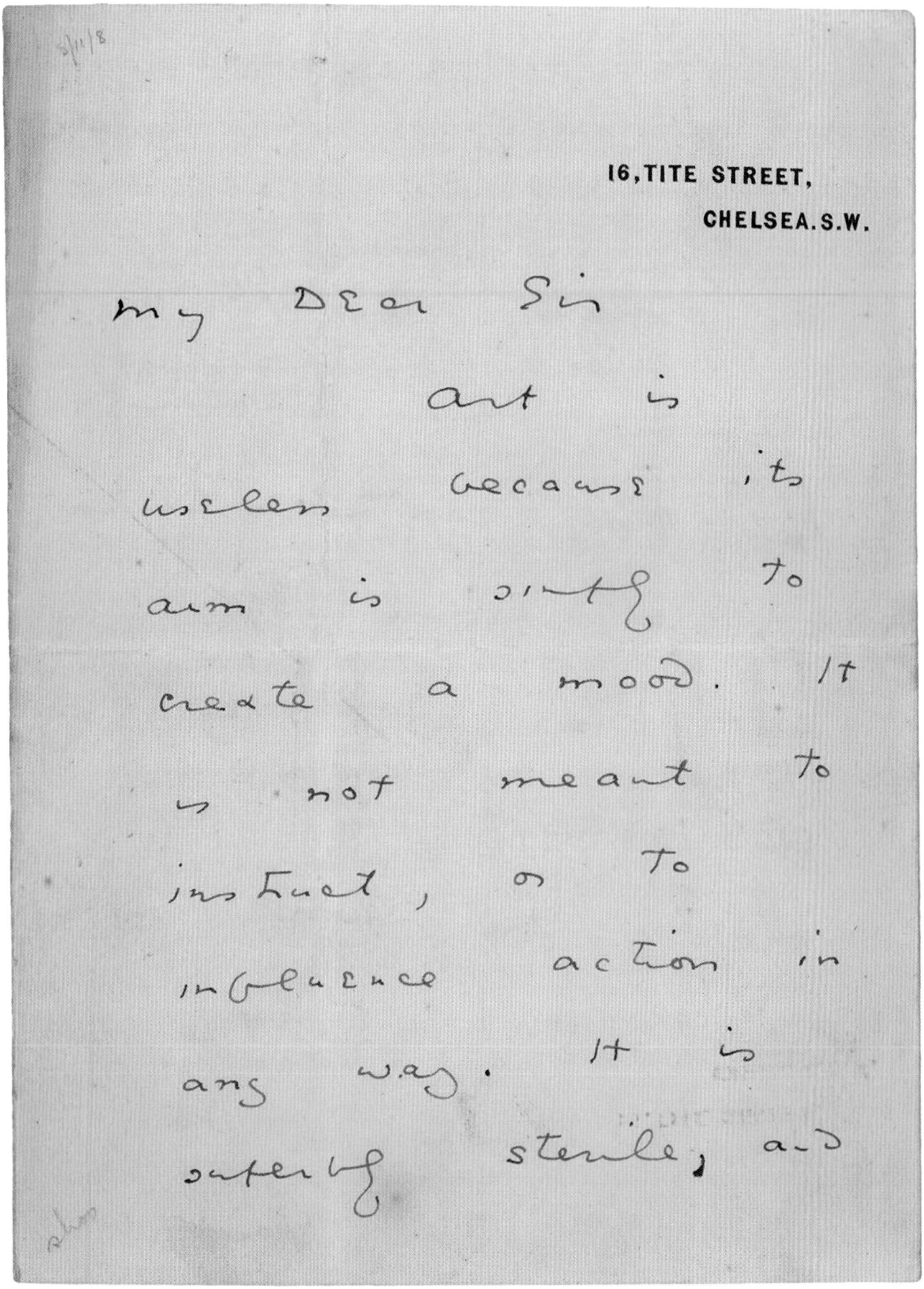

8/11/8

16, TITE STREET,
CHELSEA. S.W.

My Dear Sir

art is
useless because its
aim is simply to
create a mood. It
is not meant to
instruct, or to
influence action in
any way. It is
superbly sterile, and

the note & its
pleasure is sterility.
If the contemplation
of a work of
art is followed
by activity of any
kind, the work is
either of a very
second - rate order,

or the spectator
has failed to
realise the complete
artistic impression.

a work of
art is useless as
a flower is useless.
a flower blossoms
for its own joy.
we gain a moment
of joy by looking
at it. that is

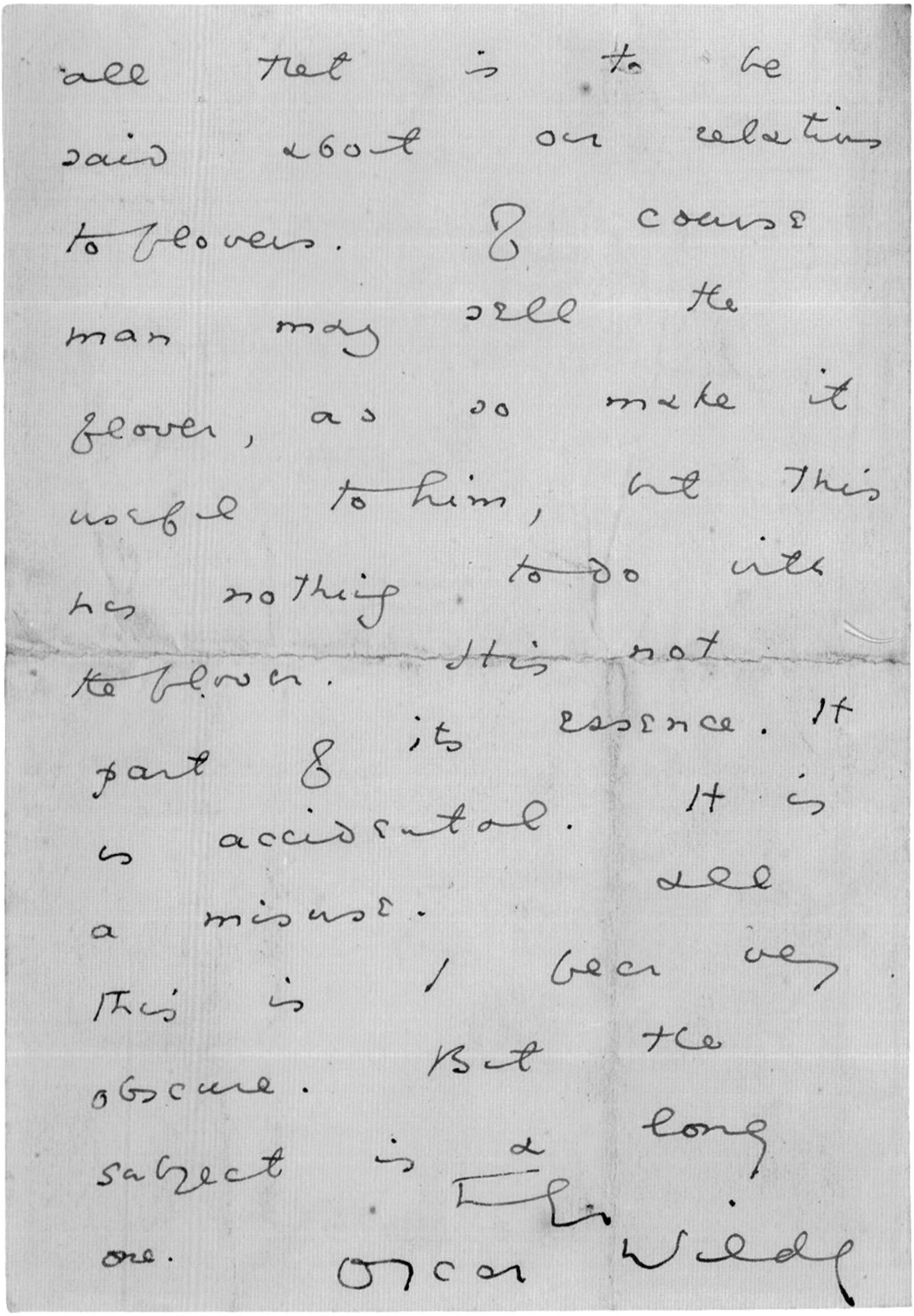

all that is to be
said about our relation
to flowers. Of course
man may sell the
flower, as so make it
useful to him, but this
has nothing to do with
the flower. It is not
part of its essence. It
is accidental. It is
a misuse. All
this is I fear very
obscure. But the
subject is a long
one. Oscar Wilde

託付給高手

米克・傑格致安迪・沃荷
一九六九年四月二十一日

在一九六九年，滾石樂團籌備第九
張錄音間專輯《順手牽羊》(*Sticky
Fingers*)時，找上風靡國際的畫家
安迪・沃荷，請他設計對摺型的封
套。沃荷首肯後，立刻收到主唱米
克・傑格的這封信。信的內容輕
鬆簡短，親切叮嚀沃荷，不要把封
面設計得太複雜，以免印製過程出
紕漏。沃荷非但不聽，更反其道
而行，設計出一份難忘的封面：
沃荷找旗下男模喬・達勒山卓 (Jo
Dallesandro)，拍攝牛仔褲襠的大
特寫，搬上唱片封套，並附上一道
能開能合的拉鏈，結果橫生無數枝
節，嚴重時更導致唱片本身磨損。

一九六九年四月二十一日

致安迪・沃荷，
紐約州紐約市 **10003**
聯合廣場三十三號

親愛的安迪，

我們新專輯能請到你來擔任美術設計，我實在太高興了，在此奉
上兩盒材料和唱片供你參考。

以我粗淺的歷練，我認為專輯封套設計得愈複雜——例如超出一
般獨立兩頁或單頁對摺的模式——製造就愈容易出包，愈容易拖
延到讓人著急跳腳。話雖這麼說，封套如何設計，全由高手您決
定，悉聽尊便……另外也煩請回信告知你想要多少錢。

若有進一步資訊，紐約有一位艾爾・史戴克勒必定會聯絡你，八
成會緊張兮兮叫你「快一點」，你不理他也行。

愛，
米克・傑格

21st April, 1969.

Andy Warhol,
33 Union Square,
W.N.Y.10003,
NEW YORK

Dear Andy,

I'm really pleased you can do the art-work for
our new hits album.   Here are 2 boxes of material
which you can use, and the record.

In my short sweet experience, the more complicated
the format of the album, e.g. more complex than just
pages or fold-out, the more fucked-up the reproduction
and agonising the delays.   But, having said that, I
leave it in your capable hands to do what ever you
want..........and please write back saying how much
money you would like.

Doubtless a Mr.Al Steckler will contact you in New
York, with any further information.   He will probably
look nervous and say "Hurry up" but take little notice.

Love,

MICK JAGGER

第五號屠宰場

大兵馮內果致父親

一九四五年五月二十九日

二次大戰萊茵戰役期間，在一九四四年十二月，二十二歲的美國兵馮內果陷入敵陣，被威瑪軍擒獲，成為戰俘。一個月後，馮內果和其他戰俘被押至德勒斯登（Dresden）勞動營，被幽禁在地下屠宰場，德軍稱之為「第五號屠宰場」。緊接著在二月，德勒斯登遭砲擊，死傷慘重，幸好戰俘被關在地下才逃過一劫。馮內果與倖存者協助清理善後。

同年五月，馮內果在戰亂失所營裡寫信向家人報平安，描述被俘虜與死裡逃生的經過，日後更將這段經歷改寫成小說《第五號屠宰場》，成為經典之作。

寄件人
一兵 K・馮內果二世，
12102964，美國陸軍。

致科特・馮內果，
印第安納州印第安納波里市威廉斯溪。

親愛的家人：

聽說上級大概只會以我「作戰失聯」為由通知家人。我從德國寫過幾封家書，你們八成也沒收到吧。所以，有待我解釋的東西很多，我概述如下：

希特勒想做最後一博，強渡比利時和盧森堡，我軍被打得七零八落——七個裝甲師瘋狗似地攻擊我軍，我的單位因而和荷吉斯的第一集團軍脫隊，在我單位左右側的美軍其他師設法撤退成功，我們奉命留在原地奮戰。以刺刀對付坦克，根本沒多大用處：我們的彈藥、糧食、醫藥品枯竭了，傷亡超過仍能作戰的兵員，我們只好投降。我因此在一九四四年十二月十九日淪為戰俘。我聽說，一〇六師因而獲頒總統勳章，也拿到蒙哥馬利將軍頒發的英國勳章。值得嗎？我呸。我是少數沒受傷的人，為此我感謝上帝。

被俘虜之後，我們不吃不喝不睡覺，被押著行軍到林堡，走了大約六十英哩吧，我猜，然後被趕上火車廂拘禁，每六十人擠一節車廂，裡面既小又不通風，而且沒有暖氣，更沒有衛生設備，地板滿是未乾的牛糞。車廂太小，大家只能輪流，一半人站著，讓另一半的人先睡。就在林堡的這條鐵路支線上，我們熬了幾天，渡過耶誕節。在耶誕節前夕，由於車廂外面沒有任何標誌，慘遭英國空軍低飛轟炸，誤殺了我們大約一百五十人。耶誕節那天，我們有一點水可喝，慢慢橫越德國，來到柏林南邊姆伯格的大戰俘營。我們在元旦那天獲釋，走出火車廂。德軍為了除虱，趕我們去沖澡，熱水燙得要命。由於十天來大家飢渴受凍，突然被熱水當頭一澆，很多弟兄承受不住而暴斃，幸好我挺過來了。

根據日內瓦公約，軍官和士官戰俘不必服勞役，可惜你們知道，我是區區一個兵。在一月十日，一百五十個小兵被運到德勒斯登服勞役。仗著我懂一點德文，我成為這群弟兄的連長。不幸的是，我們遇到的守衛是虐待狂，生病不給醫，衣物破了沒得換，長時間從事艱難到極點的苦勞。每人每天分到的糧食是兩百

五十公克的黑麵包和一品脫的無調味料馬鈴薯濃湯。我拚命爭取了兩個月，想改善我們受到的待遇，但守衛總以冷笑回應。最後我罵他們說，等俄軍來，看我怎麼收拾你們。結果我挨了一小頓揍，連長的頭銜被摘掉。挨打是小事——有個小弟兄活活被餓死，另有兩個因偷糧食而被黨衛軍槍斃。

在二月十四日前後，美軍來了，英國空軍跟進，雙方在二十四小時摧毀德勒斯登全城——可能是全球最美的城市——造成二十五萬人喪生。但我沒死。

之後，我們奉命從防空洞搬屍出來，裡面有女人、兒童、老男人，有的被震死，有的窒息，有的被燒死。我們把屍體搬到市區，點燃幾場大火燒掉，被老百姓咒罵丟石頭。

巴頓將軍攻下萊比錫後，我們徒步疏散到薩克森尼——捷克斯拉夫邊境的赫勒克希斯朵夫，逗留到大戰結束為止。有天，守衛棄我們而去，我們好高興，俄軍則一心一意想掃蕩我們這區零星的抗軍，P-39戰機低飛轟炸我們，死了十四個人，但我活過來了。

我們八人偷走一群牛和一臺牛車，穿越蘇臺德地區和薩克森尼，八天期間沿途打劫，吃喝豐盛如君王。俄軍很迷美國人，在德勒斯登接我們，然後租用福特卡車載我們去位於哈雷市的美軍防線，之後我們飛到巴黎外港。

我目前位於巴黎外港戰俘遣返營，在紅十字俱樂部裡寫信，吃喝飽足，也有餘興節目。想當然爾，返美的輪船班班客滿，我只能耐心等候，希望一個月後能回國。一到美國，我可以在亞特柏里放二十一天的休養假，補領大約六百美元的薪餉——更能放假六十天！

我想說的東西太多了，其餘的事以後再敘。我這裡無法收信，所以別寄信來。

一九四五年五月二十九日
愛，
科特二世

Pfc. K. Vonnegut, Jr.,
12102964 U. S. Army.

TO:

Kurt Vonnegut,
Williams Creek,
Indianapolis, Indiana.

Dear people:

I'm told that you were probably never informed that I was anything other than "missing in action." Chances are that you also
failed to receive any of the letters I wrote from Germany. That
leaves me a lot of explaining to do -- in precis:

I've been a prisoner of war since December 19th, 1944, when our
division was cut to ribbons by Hitler's last desperate thrust through
Luxemburg and Belgium. Seven Fanatical Panzer Divisions hit us and
cut us off from the rest of Hodges' First Army. The other American
Divisions on our flanks managed to pull out: We were obliged to
stay and fight. Bayonets aren't much good against tanks: Our
ammunition, food and medical supplies gave out and our casualties
out-numbered those who could still fight - so we gave up. The 106th
got a Presidential Citation and some British Decoration from Mont-
gomery for it, I'm told, but I'll be damned if it was worth it. I
was one of the few who weren't wounded. For that much thank God.

Well, the supermen marched us, without food, water or sleep to
Limberg, a distance of about sixty miles, I think, where we were
loaded and locked up, sixty men to each small, unventilated, un-
heated box car. There were no sanitary accommodations -- the floors
were covered with fresh cow dung. There wasn't room for all of us
to lie down. Half slept while the other half stood. We spent
several days, including Christmas, on that Limberg siding. On
Christmas eve the Royal Air Force bombed and strafed our unmarked
train. They killed about one-hundred-and-fifty of us. We got a

little water Christmas Day and moved slowly across Germany to a large
P.O.W. Camp in Muhlburg, South of Berlin. We were released from the
box cars on New Year's Day. The Germans herded us through scalding
delousing showers. Many men died from shock in the showers after ten
days of starvation, thirst and exposure. But I didn't.

Under the Geneva Convention, Officers and Non-commissioned
Officers are not obliged to work when taken prisoner. I am, as you
know, a Private. One-hundred-and-fifty such minor beings were
shipped to a Dresden work camp on January 10th. I was their leader
by virtue of the little German I spoke. It was our misfortune to
have sadistic and fanatical guards. We were refused medical attention and clothing: We were given long hours at extremely hard labor.
Our food ration was two-hundred-and-fifty grams of black bread and
one pint of unseasoned potato soup each day. After desperately trying
to improve our situation for two months and having been met with bland
smiles I told the guards just what I was going to do to them when the
Russians came. They beat me up a little. I was fired as group
leader. Beatings were very small time: -- one boy starved to death
and the SS Troops shot two for stealing food.

On about February 14th the Americans came over, followed by the
R.A.F. their combined labors killed 250,000 people in twenty-four
hours and destroyed all of Dresden -- possibly the world's most
beautiful city. But not me.

After that we were put to work carrying corpses from Air-Raid
shelters; women, children, old men; dead from concussion, fire or
suffocation. Civilians cursed us and threw rocks as we carried bodies
to huge funeral pyres in the city.

When General Patton took Leipzig we were evacuated on foot to
Hellexisdorf on the Saxony-Czechoslovakian border. There we remained

until the war ended. Our guards deserted us. On that happy day the Russians were intent on mopping up isolated outlaw resistance in our sector. Their planes (P-39's) strafed and bombed us, killing fourteen, but not me.

Eight of us stole a team and wagon. We traveled and looted our way through Sudetenland and Saxony for eight days, living like kings. The Russians are crazy about Americans. The Russians picked us up in Dresden. We rode from there to the American lines at Halle in Lend-Lease Ford trucks. We've since been flown to Le Havre.

I'm writing from a Red Cross Club in the Le Havre P.O.W. Repatriation Camp. I'm being wonderfully well feed and entertained. The state-bound ships are jammed, naturally, so I'll have to be patient. I hope to be home in a month. Once home I'll be given twenty-one days recuperation at Atterbury, about $600 back pay and -- get this -- sixty (60) days furlough!

I've too damned much to say, the rest will have to wait. I can't receive mail here so don't write.   May 29, 1945

                    Love,

                    Kurt - Jr.

敬謝

編纂這本書，撰寫說明文，期間我得助於無數好人，在此首先感謝頭號貴人：髮妻 Karina，感謝她永不休止的支持。我想感謝所有幫助我的人，但我特別感激妻子在為我憂心如焚時沒讓我識破。出書過程中，我基於不同因素，也對下列恩人有所虧欠，所有人值得我特別在此一提：部落格訂閱者、夠力的 Unbound 出版社的所有人，尤其是 John Mitchinson 和 Cathy Hurren、Frederick Courtright、Caz Hildebrand、Andrew Carroll、James Cameron、Sam Ward、Nick Hornby、Patrick Robbins、Robert Gibbons、Amir Avni、Frank Ciulla 和家人、Connell 夫婦 Margaret 和 Hugh、Bob Mortimer、Jim Temple、Moose Allain、Nigel Brachi、Bob Meade、Denis Cox、BBC 的 Lauren Laverne 以及所有人、Jason Kottke、Leslie Barany、Graham Linehan、Roger Launius、Henry McGroggan、John Johnson、TinyLetter、Anna Neville、Monica White、Stacey Chandler、Suzanne Aldridge-Peacock。最後，同樣要感激我的親朋好友。

PERMISSION CREDITS

on behalf of Mary Soames; p.125 Photograph of Virginia O'Hanlon kindly supplied by Jim Temple; p.126-127 Alfred Wintle's letter to The Times reproduced with kind permission of The Times / NI Syndication; p.128-129 Emma Hauck, Inv. No. 3622/5 "komm" (Letter to husband), 1909, pencil on document paper; Inv. No. 3621, untitled (Letter to husband), 1909, pencil on paper. © Prinzhorn Collection, University Hospital Heidelberg, Germany; p.130-131 Letter and translation courtesy of Bill Gordon/www.kamikazeimages.net; p.132-133 Letter from Linda Kelly, Sherry Bane, and Mickie Mattson to President Dwight D. Eisenhower Regarding Elvis Presley [Textual Records]; White House Central Files (Eisenhower Administration), 1953-1961, Item from Collection DDE-WHCF; Dwight D. Eisenhower Library, KS [online version available through the Archival Research Catalog (ARC identifier 594353) at www.archives.gov; May 1, 2013]; p.134-141 Robert Scott's last letter to his wife reproduced by kind permission of the University of Cambridge, Scott Polar Research Institute; p.142 Letter from Jack Kerouac to Marlon Brando reprinted by permission of SLL/Sterling Lord Literistic, Inc. Copyright by Jack Kerouac; p.142 Kerouac, Jean Louis Lebris de (Jack) (1922-69) Important letter from Jack Kerouac to Marlon Brando suggesting that Brando play the role of Dean in a proposed film of Kerouac's book 'On the Road', c.late 1957 (print & pen and ink on paper), Kerouac, Jean Louis Lebris de (Jack) (1922-69) / Private Collection / Photo © Christie's Images / The Bridgeman Art Library; p.146 Amelia Earhart, letter to George Palmer Putnam (February 7, 1931). Amelia Earhart ® is a trademark of Amy Kleppner, as heir to the Estate of Muriel Morrissey, www.AmeliaEarhart.com;p.146 Courtesy of Purdue University Libraries, Karnes Archives and Special Collections; p.147 Eddie Slovik letter from The Execution of Private Slovik (1970) by William Bradford Huie; p.149 © Bettmann/Corbis; p.150-151 Galileo Galilei letter to the Doge of Venice, August 1609, and Notes on the Moons of Jupiter, January 1610. Special Collections Library, University of Michigan (Ann Arbor);p.152 Birch bark letter courtesy of Gramoty.ru; p.153-155 Denis Cox to the RAAF, letter courtesy of Courtesy of Denis Cox. Reproduced with permission; p.156-160 Letter from Lucy Thurston to Mary Thurston reprinted from Life and times of Mrs. Lucy G. Thurston, wife of Rev. Asa Thurston, pioneer missionary to the Sandwich Islands (1882); p.161 Hawaiian Mission Children's Society; p.163 © Bettmann/Corbis; p.165 Emily Dickinson, letter to Susan Gilbert (June 11, 1852), Reprinted by permission of the publishers from The Letters of Emily Dickinson, Thomas H. Johnson, ed., Cambridge, Mass.L The Belknap Press of Harvard University Press, Copyright © 1958, 1986, The President and Fellows of Harvard College; 1914, 1924, 1932, 1942 by Martha Dickinson Bianchi; 1952 by Alfred Leete Hampson; 1960 by Mary L. Hampson; p.167-168 Image of anonymous letter to Martin Luther King, courtesy of P. Christie. Reproduced with permission; p.144-52 Francis Crick, letter ["A most important discovery"] to his son, Michael Crick (March 19, 1953). Reprinted by permission of the family of Francis H. C. Crick; p.169-178 Autograph letter outlining the discovery of the structure and function of DNA, Cambridge, 19th March 1953 (pen & ink on paper), Crick, Francis (1916-2004) / Private Collection / Photo © Christie's Images / The Bridgeman Art Library; p.179-181 Letter to Ludovico il Moro from Atlantic Codex (Codex Atlanticus) by Leonardo da Vinci, folio 1082 recto, Vinci, Leonardo da (1452-1519) / Biblioteca Ambrosiana, Milan, Italy / De Agostini Picture Library / Metis e Mida Informatica / Veneranda Biblioteca Ambrosiana / The Bridgeman Art Library; p.182 Flannery O'Connor, letter to her teacher (March 28, 1961) from The Habit of Being: Letters of Flannery O'Connor, edited by Sally Fitzgerald. Copyright © 1979 by Regina O'Connor. Reprinted by permission of Farrar, Straus & Giroux, LLC; p.183 Mondadori via Getty Images; p.184-189 Elvis Presley's Letter to President Richard Nixon, 12/21/1970; White House Central Files: Subject Files: EX HE 5-1; Nixon Presidential Materials Staff; National Archives and Records Administration [online version available at www.archives.gov; May 1, 2013]; p.190-193 Fyodor Dostoyevsky to his brother (December 22, 1849) from Dostoevsky: Letters and Reminiscences (1923); p.192 Popperfoto/Getty Images; p.195-196 Jackie Robinson, ["17 million Negroes..."] to Dwight D. Eisenhower (May 13, 1958). National Archives and Records Administration, Dwight D. Eisenhower Library, White House Central Files, Box 731, File OF-142-A-3. Jackie Robinson ™ is a trademark of Rachel Robinson by CMG Worldwide, www.JackieRobinson.com; p.197 Coconut shell paperweight on which JFK's SOS is carved, © The John F. Kennedy Presidential Library and Museum. Used with permission; p.198-200 Spike Milligan, ["Oh Christ, the cook is dead..."] to Stephen Gard (February 28, 1977) from The Spike Milligan Letters, edited by Norma Farnes (Michael Joseph, 1977). Reprinted by permission of Spike Milligan Productions Ltd; p.198-200 Letter courtesy of Stephen Gard; p.201-203 Memorandum from Speechwriter William Safire to President Nixon, 07/18/1969 [Textual Records]; White House Staff Member and Office Files (Nixon Administration), Item from Collection RN-SMOF; Richard Nixon Library, CA [online version available through the Archival Research Catalog (ARC identifier 6922351) at www.archives.gov; May 1, 2013]; p.204-219 Laura Huxley, letter to Julian Huxley (December 8, 1963), reprinted with permission of The Aldous and Laura Huxley Literary Trust; p.204-219 Image courtesy of Erowid Center's Stolaroff Collection. Used with permission; p.220-222 Letter from Stephen Tvedten reprinted by kind permission of Stephen Tvedten and his beavers; p.224-229 Letter from Dr. Ernst Stuhlinger to Sister Mary Jucunda, courtesy of NASA; p.197 NASA/SCIENCE PHOTO LIBRARY; p.230-231 Kurt Vonnegut, letter to Charles McCarthy (November 16, 1973) from Palm Sunday: An Autobiographical Collage. Copyright © 1981 by The Ramjac Corporation. Used by permission of Delacorte Press, an imprint of The Random House Publishing Group, a division of Random House, Inc. Any third party use of this material, outside of this publication, is prohibited. Interested parties must apply directly to Random House, Inc. for permission; p.232-234 Image of letter from Mark Twain to a salesman (1905), courtesy of Berryhill & Sturgeon; p.235-237 Letter reproduced by kind permission of Iggy Pop; p.235-237 Image courtesy of Laurence; p.238-239 Mario Puzo, letter to Marlon Brando (1970). Reprinted by permission of Donadio & Olson, Inc. © 1970 Mario Puzo; p.238-239 Autograph letter to Marlon Brando, c.1970 (pen on paper), Puzo, Mario (1920-99) / Private Collection / Photo © Christie's Images / The Bridgeman Art Library; p.241 Image of Roger Boisjoly memo courtesy of Joel Stevenson; p.242-246 Grace Bedell, letter to Abraham Lincoln, Courtesy of the Burton Historical Collection, Detroit Public Library; Abraham Lincoln, letter to Grace Bedell, courtesy of Library of Congress; p.247-249 James Cameron letter to Leslie Baranie reproduced by kind permission of James Cameron; p.247-249 Photo of James Cameron's letter © Leslie Barany. Used with permission; p.250-251 Letter to Eung-Tae Lee courtesy Andong National University; p.253 Photograph of Ayyab's letter to Amenhotep IV courtesy of Rama/Wikimedia; p.254-259 Sullivan Ballou letter © Abraham Lincoln Presidential Library & Museum (ALPLM). Used with permission; p.260-261 Lynn Martin (Uncle Lynn), ["I'm still someplace"] to Chuck Jones from Chuck Jones, Chuck Reducks: Drawings from the Fun Side of Life (Time Warner, 1996). Reprinted with the permission of Linda Jones Enterprises, Inc.; p.262-263 Anonymous letter to William Parker (October 26, 1605) courtesy of the National Archives. Used with permission; p.265 Bette Davis, ["It's up to you now"] to B.D. Hyman from This 'n That by Bette Davis, with Mickey Herskowitz(New York: G. P. Putnam's, 1987). Bette Davis ™ is a trademark of the Estate of Bette Davis, www.BetteDavis.com; p.266 Silver Screen Collection/Moviepix/Getty Imagesp.267-269 Ernest Hemingway, letter to F. Scott Fitzgerald (May 28, 1934) from Ernest Hemingway Selected Letters 1917-1961, edited by Carlos Baker. Copyright © 1981 by The Ernest Hemingway Foundation, Inc. Reprinted with the permission of Scribner, a Division of Simon & Schuster, Inc.; p.269 Mondadori via Getty Images; p.271 © Bettmann/

臉譜書房

私密信件博物館
Letters of Note

作　　者	史恩‧亞緒爾 Shaun Usher
譯　　者	子玉
裝幀設計	廖韡
總 經 理	陳逸瑛
總 編 輯	劉麗真
業　　務	陳玫潾
行銷企畫	陳彩玉、蔡宛玲
責任編輯	林欣璇
發 行 人	涂玉雲
出　　版	臉譜出版
	臺北市中山區民生東路二段141號5樓 02-25007696
發　　行	城邦文化事業股份有限公司
	英屬蓋曼群島商家庭傳媒股份有限公司城邦分公司
	臺北市民生東路二段141號11樓
	讀者服務專線：02-25007718；02-25007719
	服務時間：週一至週五9:30～12:00；13:30～17:30
	24小時傳真服務：02-25001990；02-25001991
	讀者服務信箱E-mail：service@readingclub.com.tw
	劃撥帳號：19863813 書虫股份有限公司
	城邦網址：http://www.cite.com.tw
	臉譜推理星空網址：http://www.faces.com.tw
香港發行	城邦（香港）出版集團
	香港灣仔駱克道193號東超商業中心1樓
	電話：852-28778606／傳真：852-25789337
	email：hkcite@biznetvigator.com
馬新發行	城邦（馬新）出版集團
	Cite (M) Sdn. Bhd. (458372 U)
	11, Jalan 30D/146, Desa Tasik, Sungai Besi,
	57000 Kuala Lumpur, Malaysia
	電話：603-90563833／傳真：603-90562833
	email：citekl@cite.com.tw
一版八刷	2021年4月
	版權所有，翻印必究（Printed in Taiwan）
I S B N	978-986-235-491-9
	定價750元
	（本書如有缺頁、破損、倒裝，請寄回本社更換）

國家圖書館出版品預行編目資料

私密信件博物館／史恩‧亞緒爾（Shaun Usher）
著；子玉譯. -- 初版. -- 臺北市：臉譜出版：
家庭傳媒城邦分公司發行, 2016.02
　　面；　公分. --（臉譜書房）
ISBN 978-986-235-491-9（平裝）
1.書信　2.世界傳記
781　　　　　　　　　　　　　105000475